MODERNITIES

ART-MATTERS IN THE PRESENT

MODERNITIES

ART-MATTERS IN THE PRESENT

Joseph Mascheck

THE PENNSYLVANIA STATE UNIVERSITY PRESS
UNIVERSITY PARK, PENNSYLVANIA

Library of Congress Cataloging-in-Publication Data

Masheck, Joseph.
    Modernities : art-matters in the present / Joseph Masheck.
        p.   cm.
    Includes bibliographical references.
    ISBN 0-271-00808-3
        1. Modernism (Art)   2. Postmodernism.   3. Art, Modern—20th
century.   I. Title.
    N6494.M64M37   1993
    720'.9'04—dc20   91–24286
                                                                  CIP

Published by The Pennsylvania State University Press,
Suite C, Barbara Building, University Park, PA 16802-1003

For M. W.

CONTENTS

LIST OF ILLUSTRATIONS

PREFACE

These are the essays of a generalist as well as a modernist, an unrepentantly historicizing art historian as well as a contemporary critic.

Just what art history and criticism *are* seems even less certain now than it did a decade ago. Today it is not uncommon for art historians effectively to renounce art, or to work in the field like registered aliens whose hearts are somewhere else. In critique, French-inspired delusions of revolutionary grandeur, elitist as ever, hold a tiresomely literary sense of theory contemptuously above the world of work and artworks, while in practice the same smugly antihumanist discourse, ironically or not, sustains the marketing of one or another line of suavely tailored anti-artists.

If we can all deride the vulgar "marketplace" of art, how many will risk a marginality fashionable only in theory to advance worthy unknown work? When I took up the case of Mike and Doug Starn they were still in art school. When, as editor of *Artforum* some years back, I decided to put works by Elizabeth Murray, Sean Scully, Martin Puryear, and others on the cover of the magazine, these were considered eccentric choices—didn't I know! Sometimes one's enthusiasm will have paled by the time intellectual fashion comes round: Robert Smithson seemed more imposing to me twenty years ago—only one other Columbia art historian, George Collins, seemed interested in him when he spoke *next door* in the school of architecture—or even ten years ago, than he does now, though I suppose I owe him something in even daring to say so. (Smithson is simply no Beuys, despite the fascination he enjoys among young American postmoderns as accessibly legendary.) Then again, even in classical philology "junk" texts can also be significant: at least treating the unknown triviality as a masterpiece is merely a venial sin, compared with ignoring the truly great.

I do hate reading about the same official artists, especially as purveyed over and over, to borrow Gertrude Stein's term, by "village explainers"; but of what use is grand theory, either, when it functions jargonesquely within "the social" as just so much software for a redundantly automatic critical "praxis"?

Well, where do I think I stand, ideologically? I have always approached art as a product of work in an at least relatively unalienated condition, with its material, technical, and conceptual aspects open to regard, and possibly guiltlessly pleasurable regard at that. This entails both objectification and a responsive, associative (re)contextualizing of the art object with ideas that it incarnates, resembles, or provokes, ideas being as historical as other cultural things. It is *just because* I never expect artworks or ideas to be "original"—except, say, in the essentially concocted sense of Poe's "Philosophy of Composition" (1846)—that I tend to be relentlessly historicizing; for just as art revises what was already there, the artwork will oblige the revision of what we thought we knew. In this sense, I do find myself especially interested in whatever significance carries over, or what new signification shows up, when works of art affiliate with objects or ideas out of their usual synchronic context.

Let me confess to a deep-seated skepticism toward narrative, especially in the ordinary literary sense that bored and frustrated me from an early age and helped drive me away from expository prose and fiction, toward lyric poetry, and on to architecture and all abstract art. If even *this* is a narrative, I'm sorry. What else can I do here? At least I can claim that it is no less provisional than the working narratives of many of the essays in this book. To be more affirmative: I tend to interrogate new art with respect to old, but from anywhere in the historical memory bank: one might think of the information stored on a computer disk nonhierarchically at random spots, with meaning accessible only through patterns of interrelating conditions. If that counts as narrative, so be it; but I would prefer to think of a kind of silent algebra of relations like that which prevails between the simultaneously coexistent elements of a painting.

In terms of the politics of modern art history, I am not such a relativist as to think that modernity collapsed, or should have, under the last straw of a simplistic, doctrinal "modernism" trademarked circa 1965. In one sense, any number of modernities is possible. Yet in another, all possible modernities (including the electronic) presuppose, or even reiterate, that very first, the great florescence of formal and structural consciousness in Neolithic, or Old Stone Age, art. Two generations ago, Max Raphael and

Herbert Read were not quite alone in understanding this, after Roger Fry's insight ("The Art of the Bushmen," 1910) petered out. Not that I understood *them* yet in 1965, either, obsessed as I was in my youth, even before I knew of the term, with "significant form." (I know why some of us do not want to talk about form in that way, but it still amazes me that so many, apparently, cannot even see it.)

I ask myself where modernity began within my own historical experience. Mondrian and Mies van der Rohe, but also Duchamp, were my first loves in art: absolute art, with a rather middle-class sense of the avant-garde on the flip side. But *my* first twentieth century was also, much like that of T. E. Hulme, whom I admired in my teens, out of the eighteenth, with the moral rigor of Constructivism as neo-Neoclassical. Indeed, for me, studying the eighteenth century, and Renaissance and Baroque architecture and thought behind it, was practically remedial—as to most of us Americans history generally is remedial, a constant backfilling. This seems worth mentioning as I introduce some of my work from the last decade because nothing in the perplexing postmodern situation has more fascinated me as a historian and critic than those moments when the definitively *moderne* has been shifted back in position as the latest *ancien*.

Today, for better or worse, there is nothing like a classical ideal of modernity. But what is difficult to explain now that "utopian" is such a bad word, is how in the 1960s there was nothing necessarily utopian, in itself, in holding onto an essentially idealist aesthetic. Any dashed utopian hopes I have harbored have not been hopes for art. Nobody ever led me to expect art to change the world, except insofar as it holds up the possibility of surmounting—not necessarily evading—alienation. No; the great false expectation of my generation, which must trace back to our parents' all-in-it-together morale during World War II, was not aesthetic at all but glaringly social, namely, that of an expanded gentility, an opening access to haute-bourgeois institutional culture (not patronizing "alternatives"), in which first the middle class and then others would be able to share. Once, at the turn of the sixties, the Swinging-London *International Times* managed to put it all quite simply and clearly: "We want an eighteenth century for everybody!"

By now I could hardly hope to acknowledge everybody who has in one way or another made this book possible, considering the truly various occasions of the original essays. Donald B. Kuspit was helpful in getting what was to prove an *ur*-project under way. Later, in changed circumstances, Arthur C. Danto and David Carrier were decisive in making it possible to realize the project in its present form. Not having had research assistance for the last ten years, I am all the more grateful to Philip Winsor, senior editor of the Penn State Press, for his patience as well as his enthusiasm, and to Cherene Holland, Peggy Hoover, Steven Kress, and Janet Dietz, also of the Penn State Press.

Because some of these essays were written under conditions of extreme professional insecurity, I can now also happily thank certain other colleagues and friends for their vital support, in one way or another, in those years: James S. Ackerman, Peter Bannan, Mike Bidlo, Myles M. Bourke, David Christman, Mark Denbaux, Risa Dickstein, David Jacobs, Thomas Nozkowski, Peter Plagens, Richard Pugliese, Joyce Robins, Meyer Schapiro, Eduard F. Sekler, Paul Zwietnig-Rotterdam and, especially, Marjorie Welish.

INTRODUCTION IN PRAXIS

In June 1990, when this book was nearing completion, I happened to discover, or rather, rediscover, two eighteenth-century paintings in the National Gallery of Ireland which I cannot have thought about for the last twenty years, which is to say, since I was still a student. Because I prefer considering actual works of art to discussing theory of theory, I can probably do no better in introducing the reader to this selection of my more recent writings than to treat these two paintings—both, tellingly, historicizing, but with contemporary implications—as they now confront me in my own problematic modernity.

It cannot surprise me that both works date from the eighteenth century, and are by Neoclassical artists at that; nor even that both derive in turn from Renaissance paintings, in both cases by Raphael, academic hero of the nineteenth-century reactionaries but genius of classical structure all the same. Winckelmann claims in the *Reflections on the Imitation of Greek Works in Painting and Sculpture* (1755) that a "noble simplicity and quiet grandeur (*edle Einfalt und stille Grösse*)" marks, alike, Greek art and Raphael's, the latter "attained through imitation of the ancients (*der Alten*)" (chap. 4).[1] Related claims in Reynolds's own *Discourses* form a contribution to theoretical criticism of some modern interest: Roger Fry, annotating the *Discourses* in the early twentieth century, would find them, in turn, a useful antidote to lingering nineteenth-century Romantic subjectivity.[2]

The first of the two paintings in Dublin, by the Englishman Sir Joshua Reynolds, toys with Gothicism as a childhood of art surpassed in a today all too suspicious self-confidence; the second, by the Bohemian-born Anton Raphael Mengs, is a full-scale recapitulation from the moment when art history began again, or began as modern, and the Renaissance became clear as the first *modern* "antiquity." In terms of present-day theory, the former work is essentially ironic while the latter far from ironically pushes analogy as far as identity (while typically, this question is more complex if we consider that the first depends internally on stylistic analogy, and the second has, externally as it were, some inevitably ironic effect). But even the essential historicity of these paintings would be merely curious if it didn't seem all the more timely with the possibility that a third great phase of art, that of the classically modern, with Neoclassical form as part of *its* antiquity, may or may not have ended.

Reynolds's *Parody of Raphael's "School of Athens,"* of 1751 (Fig. 1), is an oddity for him—or is it? This is a group portrait of eighteenth-century gentleman-dilletantes arranged in stagey parody of Raphael's noblest composition, *The School of Athens,* in the Vatican, itself a kind of conceptual mapping of the great schools of antique philosophic thought. Only here men in elegantly worldly eighteenth-century dress occupy a *Gothic,* or at least literarily "Gothick," interior rather than the grand new sacred space of the rising Saint Peter's. It could once have gone without saying that the philosophical *School of Athens* and the theological *Disputà,* of Raphael's great frescoes in the papal chambers, are among the most widely influential compositions in postmedieval art. (I myself have long remarked upon the chunky pier of Saint Peter's in an early stage of its construction at the right of the *Disputà* as an uncanny adumbration of Frank Lloyd Wright's Unity Temple, of 1904–6.)

---

1. Johann Joachim Winckelmann, *Reflections on the Imitation of Greek Works in Painting and Sculpture,* trans. Elfriede Heyer and Roger C. Norton (La Salle, Ill., 1987), 37, 39 (English, here altered), with 36, 38 (German).

2. *Discourses Delivered to the Students of the Royal Academy by Sir Joshua Reynolds, Kt.,* ed. Roger Fry (London and New York, 1905), passim.

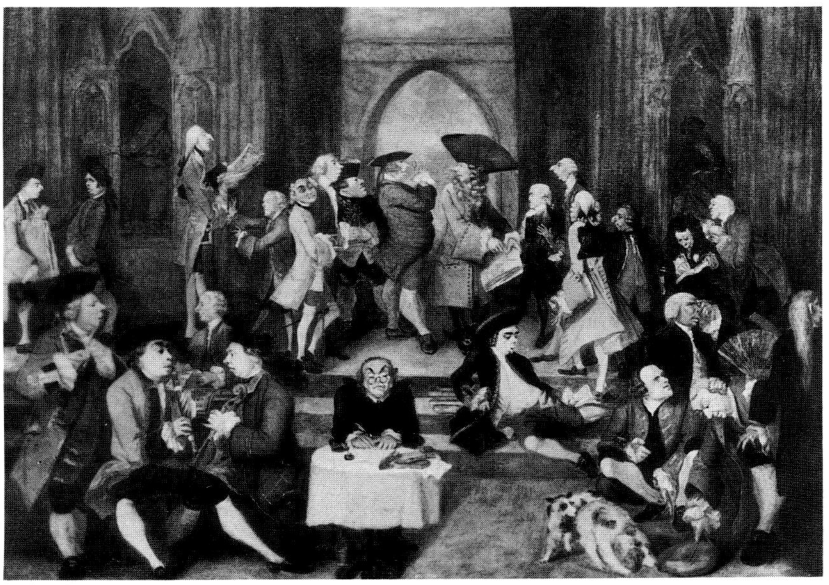

Fig. 1   Joshua Reynolds, *A Parody of Raphael's "School of Athens,"* 1751, oil on canvas, 97 x 135 cm.

As a kind of men's-club artistic, and anti-Roman artistic blasphemy, Reynolds's picture (and I use the word with its bourgeois sense of the auction house in mind) is, at least today, something rather more esoteric than, for instance, Mozart's "Musical Joke" with obviously wrong notes. For in modern times, at least since about World War I, it has to be remedially explained that Gothic architecture was seen as hilarious if not monstrous from the classical standpoint that Reynolds himself epitomized. This thoroughly Protestant picture, hopelessly commonsensical in its middlebrow whimsicality and a tad complacent in its own tasteful and witty didacticism, is interesting as an image *of* artistic style essentialized in caricature—two styles, in fact, to the extent that Reynolds's own also participates in the joke—as well as of stylishly artistic bourgeois life-style.

It is more than a joke, however; or the joke has more to it. In the *Essay on Criticism* (1711) Alexander Pope had struck a precociously modern note with the thought that even the most apparently rigorous classicizing forms might be fated to a relatively medieval, ruinously Gothic crudity, with time: "Our sons their fathers' failing language see / And such as Chaucer is, shall

Dryden be" (II.482–83). In actual fact, Reynolds himself went on to design a *Nativity* in stained glass for a Gothic window of the chapel of New College, Oxford, three years after painting this stylistic *Caricatura,* as it has sometimes been titled. Soon Richard Hurd, an Anglican bishop, would suggest, in *Letters on Chivalry and Romance* (1762), that the Gothic had its own quite serious beauty: "If you judge Gothic architecture by Grecian rules, you find nothing but deformity, but when you examine it by its own the result is quite different."[3] Another antiquity! Still, until Pugin, in architecture, "Gothick"—as in the "Gothic" novel of William Beckford, who like Reynolds took early interest in the "Italian primitives"—was pretty much only historical kitsch, as Reynolds plays with it here.

It is of course thanks to prints as a middle-class medium that Reynolds can take the visual composition of *The School of Athens* sufficiently for granted to send it up. In his Discourse VI at the Royal Academy, in 1774, this ultraclassicist will say that borrowing from the classics is fine and dandy, the works of the ancients being "a magazine of common property, always open to the publick," all the more handily with the modern increase of "an art scarce known in . . . [Raphael's] time; I mean that of engraving; by which, at an easy rate, every man may now avail himself of the inventions of antiquity."[4] In the 1769 First Discourse, in which a print by the Comte de Caylus of Raphael's *Disputà* is said to be "in every hand," Reynolds claims that it was under the stimulus of Michelangelo's Sistine ceiling that Raphael assumed his "grand style," leaving behind "a dry, [N.B.] Gothick, and even insipid manner."[5] He means picky-particular, but there is the word—the word for an idea, a nonclassical style-essence, as if that seemed paintable, that then already counted as content in his Dublin *Parody.* In 1751 Reynolds was only twenty-eight years old and no doubt feeling his oats with this painting, an intimate cabinet picture for those in the know. The painting is sportive, even sportively theoretical—maybe even in Nietzsche's despised sense of the "theoretical man." Is it as a youthful indiscretion that in his penultimate Discourse XIV (1790) Reynolds himself will dismiss, along with Mengs, the Pompeo Batoni on whose portraits he relied for some of the English and Irish sitters in this witty little stylistic pastiche, as, both of them, learned but uninspired Romanists?[6]

---

3. Quoted in Peter Collins, *Changing Ideals in Modern Architecture 1750–1950* (London, 1965), 37.

4. Joshua Reynolds, *Discourses on Art* (New York, 1961), 97.

5. Ibid., 24, 20, respectively.

6. Ibid., 218.

A question that it is unnecessary to pursue in detail, because Reynolds sets up just enough of a *School of Athens* to make it anything but a *School of Athens* by Gothicizing Saint Peter's and presenting his contemporaries in not classical but classical–stand-in, eighteenth-century dress, is how Raphael was of absolutely central importance to Reynolds's theory of copying the masters to learn the timeless truth of form. After all, he himself is seen to have done just that, though if "Raphael's materials are generally borrowed, . . . the noble structure is his own."[7] In 1774, "it is from his having taken so many models, that he became himself a model for all succeeding painters; always imitating, and always original," while with an allusion to the ancient rhetorician Quintilian Reynolds now warns that although Raphael's own sense of form makes him such a great model himself for the aspiring artist, one should not imitate him or anyone else alone.[8] Along with this as commonplace advice comes the interesting observation, almost subversive of the theory in which it is embedded, that somehow "the works of the moderns are more the property of their authors."[9] Now if a premodern, Raphael, becomes the equal of the ancients, just where does that leave the early-modern Raphael *hommage?* Whether or not Reynolds would have been able to fathom the "appropriation art" of our time, he stood "against that false opinion, but too prevalent among artists, of the imaginary power of native genius, and its sufficiency in great works."[10]

Soon after Reynolds's parody, *School of Athens,* Anton Raphael Mengs produced as his first painting on arriving in Rome, in 1752, a serious copy of the *School of Athens* (1755; Victoria and Albert Museum). And copying Raphael Sanzio, word for word as it were, is just what Anton Raphael Mengs did more than once, including a *Sistine Madonna* (Bergen, Norway, Billedgalleri). Here there is obvious postmodern interest in wholesale recapitulation, as in the work of such contemporary "appropriation" artists as Mike Bidlo, trained in the Bauhaus tradition of objectified abstraction, and Sherrie Levine, who began as a kind of photo-conceptualist and prefers to sacrifice painting to idea and game move. The status of Raphael's art in

---

7. Ibid., 76 (Discourse V).

8. Ibid., 94–95 (Discourse VI).

9. Ibid., 97.

10. Ibid., 101. For a useful critical discussion of the continuing possibility of creativity after the demise of a (fundamentally Romantic) sense of originality, see Richard Schiff, "Making a Find: An Argument for Creativity, Not Originality," *Structuralist Review,* II (Spring 1984), 59–80.

the eighteenth century was tantamount to Greek and Roman art in the Renaissance, that is, as a second antiquity, which we can see all the more clearly now that Neoclassicism too is a closed case, itself susceptible (only) to revival.[11]

What purports to be Raphael Mengs's Dublin redo of Raphael Sanzio's *Transfiguration* (Fig. 2) is awesome only partly for its (own) physical immensity, standing, or hanging, nearly fourteen feet tall.[12] Now according to Reynolds's Fifth Discourse, pronounced in 1772 when Mengs was still living, the large fresco format had helped Raphael avoid a tendency to overdo detail that is evident in his oil paintings, "except perhaps the *Transfiguration.*"[13] Here, too, while Mengs takes up in restatement a very important subject for the theory of painting, the very limitations of his version make for a doubled experience, with the eighteenth century translucently overlaying, even as it unveils, the sixteenth: an exaggerated marmoreal sculpturesqueness, and slightly hysterical intensification of affect, as if supercharged in relay (in his article on "Painting," written for the first edition of the *Encyclopaedia Britannica,* Mengs says, "The expression . . . must be strong, so that the dumb shew may be perfectly and readily understood"[14]). Frankly, I positively like the way such a dutiful copy has so clearly, all the same and at the same time, the look of its own time.

On the first count, of theory: one cannot confront this image without acknowledging the scriptural Transfiguration itself a critical subject, comprising as it does Jesus, Moses, and Elijah as momentarily co-present in historical time (then this, *qua* "vision," made manifest for later times); no wonder this is a paramount subject in the antiliteral, strongly antipictorial, Orthodox *ikon* tradition. Raphael's vision an *ikon*-painter would find alarmingly naturalistic, poisoned as it were by assimilation to a tainted world (how unfortunate the choice, in the American philosopher Peirce's theory of language, of the term "icon" for a *depiction,* of all things). But had not the "original" *Transfiguration* been carried, one might say like a Western

---

11. On some contemporary artists who advance this sense of Neoclassicism come second time round, see Joseph Masheck, "Neo-Neo," *Artforum* (September 1979), repr. in his *Historical Present: Essays of the 1970s* (Ann Arbor, 1984), 231–48.

12. At 4.11 x 2.74 meters, the painting is just slightly taller and slightly narrower than Raphael's (4.05 x 2.78). According to Michael Wynne, *Later Italian Paintings in the National Gallery of Ireland: The Seventeenth, Eighteenth and Nineteenth Centuries* (Dublin, 1986), 75–76, cat. no. 120, it is "attributed" to Mengs.

13. Reynolds, *Discourses,* 75.

14. Anton Raphael Mengs, "Painting," in *Encyclopaedia Britannica: A Dictionary of Arts and Sciences Compiled upon a New Plan,* 3 vols. (Edinburgh, 1771), III, 449.

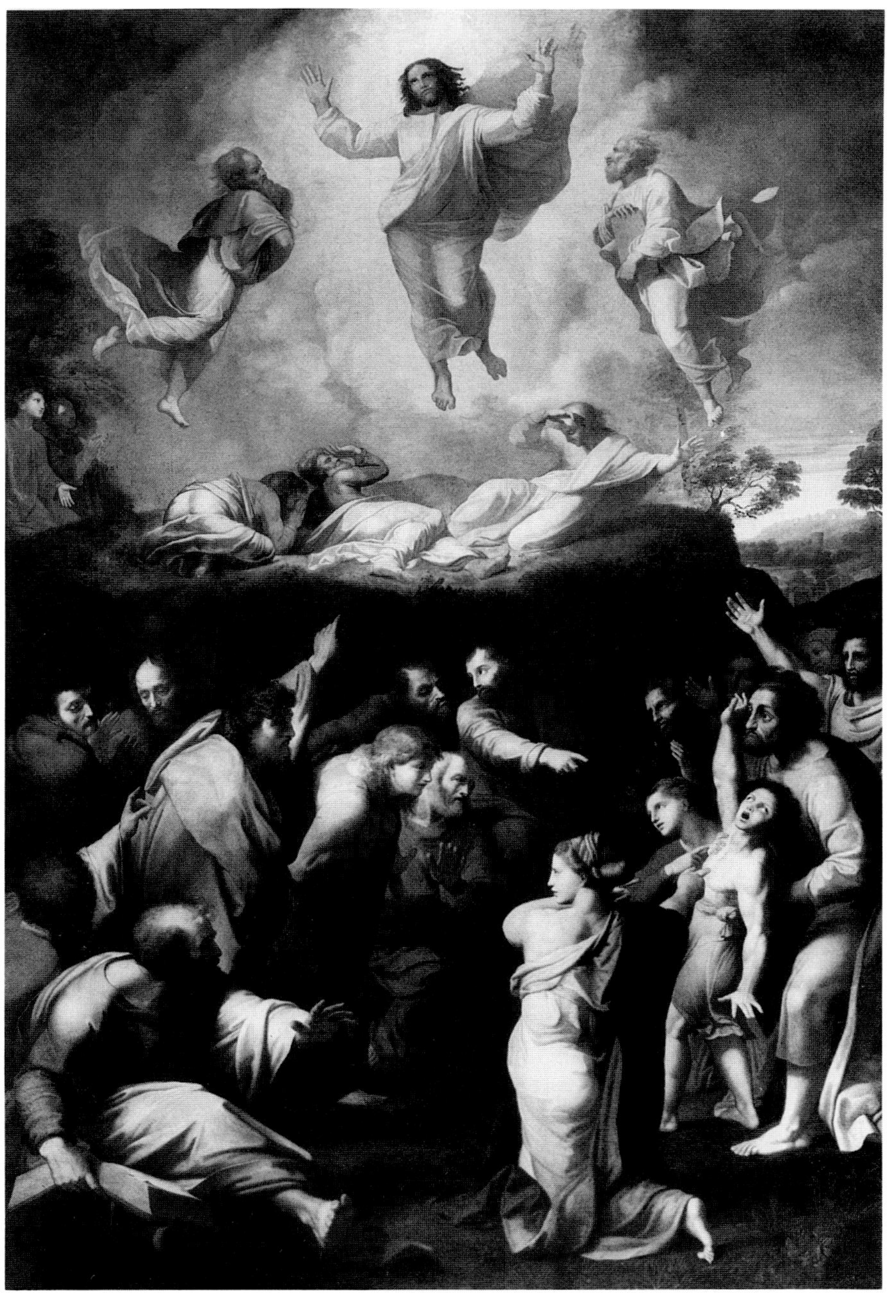

Fig. 2   Anton Raphael Mengs, *The Transfiguration*, c. 1760(?), oil on canvas, 411 x 274 cm.

equivalent of an *ikon,* in Raphael's own funeral procession? And then did not Mengs, peculiarly enough for a West European, defer quite respectfully to the model image of Raphael, rather like an *ikon*-painter, instead of "inventing" one out of typical occidental ego? Second, it—and why not call Mengs's painting *Transfiguration II,* like a sequel?—confronts me with a vivid actualization of the whole "neo" idea of recapitulation and the fresh or second start, and not only of Renaissance classic-revivalism as a new "old testament" to eighteenth-century Neoclassicism.

I take Mengs's restatement of the truth of Raphael as very much that of a *believer* in the truth of a certain kind of form as well as the religious content, all the more shadowed though at least one of these two beliefs may be by a need for re(in)statement under a secularization that cannot be simplistically blamed on the Renaissance. In this sense too, it seems possible to describe Mengs's *Transfiguration* as, if anything, all the more markedly religious in light of Lessing's Enlightenment demand, in the *Laocoön* (1766), that the artist be completely consumed by aesthetic considerations and ignore religious subject matter. Like a dogmatic modern formalist, Lessing rejects religious antiquities as having their aesthetic value spoiled by, as it were, ethnographic significance: "we should," he says, consider as works of art only productions "which are the handiwork of the artist, purely as artist, those where he has been able to make beauty his first and last object. All the rest, all that show an evident religious tendency, are unworthy to be called works of art."[15] Schlegel, however, for whom Raphael's *Transfiguration* "seems to form the last link between the genuine style of the old masters and the more artificial taste of modern schools," suggests that in art usually only such widely comprehended miracles as the Transfiguration will convincingly move the spectator to religious emotion.[16]

On the modern front, it should not be overlooked that in a vital passage early in *The Birth of Tragedy* Nietzsche finds in just this particular "symbolic

---

15. Gotthold Ephraim Lessing, *Laocoön: An Essay Upon the Limits of Painting and Poetry,* trans. Ellen Frothingham (New York, 1957), 63.

16. Friedrich von Schlegel, *Description of Paintings in Paris and the Netherlands in the Years 1802–1804,* in his *Aesthetic and Miscellaneous Works,* trans. E. J. Millington (London, 1881), Letter II (1803), 44; Schlegel speaks further of "this modern manner, richer indeed in art, but less imaginative and beautiful," and says that here "the subject altogether is treated with a superficial, lightly-kindled enthusiasm," unlike the earnest devotional attitude of earlier painters (45). Comment on the Transfiguration theme (with the Ascension likewise mentioned), from "Second Supplement of Old Paintings" (1804), excerpt translated by Peter Wortsman and Gert Schiff in Schiff, ed., *German Essays on Art History,* The German Library (New York, 1988), 67.

painting," or, more precisely, Raphael's original (or, again, a print of that), classic Apollonian *mere appearance* rendered as a sublimely pure tincture, above and almost literally beyond the suffering of the world. Here Nietzsche follows, only to exceed, Hegel, who in the *Aesthetics: Lectures on Fine Art* already suggests more prosaically that Raphael's *Transfiguration* "falls apart into two actions" unless, instead of regarding it only *"externally,"* one comprehends "the *spirit* of the composition" by which an invocation of Christ enables a miracle to take place on earth (Pt. III, III.i.2c).[17] But Nietzsche submits to the vision of a vision: "From . . . mere appearance arises, like ambrosial vapor, a new visionary world of mere appearances, invisible to those wrapped in the first appearance" (sect. 4).[18] It is this ultimate in Western religious representation, realized by Raphael and then reiterated by Mengs, that in his spiritual aestheticism, compared with which Lessing's aestheticism and Hegel's spirituality run thin, Nietzsche beholds. Now in terms of Danto's discussion of *The Birth of Tragedy,* Mengs's artful *Transfiguration,* as a "re-presentation," perhaps pushes Raphael's back into a position more analogous to that of the once divinely bestowed immediate "presentation," in just such a miraculously confrontational *Vorstellung* (literally, "fore-putting") as the biblical Transfiguration itself.[19]

Of course, what confronts us now is not Raphael's *Transfiguration,* not even at a photograph thereof; however, it would be going too far to say that this life-size replication is *anything but* Raphael's image because it does reiterate a certain configuration of forms first composed by him. I notice that the early translation of Wölfflin's *Die klassische Kunst* (1899), Englished anonymously in 1903, which is to say the version that the early twentieth-century British formalists would have read, carries a preface in which the then director of the Dublin National Gallery, Walter Armstrong, explains that Wölfflin concentrates "on composition, or design, to use that word in its widest sense, dealing chiefly with the character and action of figures, and the pattern made by them." "Speaking broadly," Armstrong says, Raphael's "reasoning is the unconscious reasoning of the painter put into

---

17. Georg Wilhelm Friedrich Hegel, *Aesthetics: Lectures on Fine Art,* trans. T. M. Knox, 2 vols. (Oxford, 1974), II, 860. In their *Journal,* Edmond and Jules Goncourt had already likened Raphael's *Transfiguration* to "wallpaper" and criticized the colors as crude (4 May 1867).

18. Friedrich Nietzsche, *The Birth of Tragedy and The Case of Wagner,* trans. Walter Kaufmann (New York, 1967), 45.

19. Arthur C. Danto, *The Transfiguration of the Commonplace: A Philosophy of Art* (Cambridge, Mass., 1981), 18–20.

words. . . . Anyone reading Herr Wölfflin carefully may fairly assume that he is following the workings of Raphael's mind as he builds up things like the *Disputà,* the *School of Athens* and the *Madonna di San Sisto.*"[20]

Now Wölfflin says that the *Sistine Madonna* had to be hung high if the important effect of the Madonna's descent from heaven toward the spectator were not to be lost, adding in a footnote that is dropped in the standard modern translation by Peter and Linda Murray, *Classic Art* (1952), that this may in fact be seen in the case of a (N.B.) *copy* in the Leipzig museum.[21] Next he mentions the frame of the original, in Dresden, as architecturally overbearing, and discusses in a long note (retained by the Murrays) the relative virtues of no less than six modern *reproduction prints* of the picture, published from 1815 onwards.[22] The more patient readers of Walter Benjamin may sense what I am driving at here: that Benjamin himself could have been, or might as well have been, stimulated by Wölfflin the formalist's initial sensitivity to the museological presentation as well as to the reproduction history of this painting of major importance to his argument. One of Benjamin's own long notes to "The Work of Art in the Age of Its Mechanical Reproducability" (1936) also concerns the exhibition history of the *Sistine Madonna,* in particular, how, thanks to the research of Hubert Grimme (1864–1942), we ought to understand the painting as not having been painted as an altarpiece at all but, quite otherwise, as part of the temporary decoration of Sixtus's casket as the pope lay in state immediately below it.[23]

A new generation would find its own dissatisfaction with Mengs, and J. A. D. Ingres's redo of Raphael's *Sistine Madonna* within the pictorial space of *The Vow of Louis XIII* (1824) shows classicism as anxiously polemical, if not antimodern. Yet Ingres's *Vow,* too, is very much a believer's painting, for art as well as faith. Today, a host of cynics would employ it to address a "loss of aura," either in the sense that by 1824 Raphael's image was in need of some artificial respiration, or in the sense that Ingres here begins an undermining of the original only accelerated by extremely popular photo-

---

20. Heinrich Wölfflin, *The Art of the Italian Renaissance: A Handbook for Students and Travellers* (London and New York, 1903), "Prefatory Note," viii.

21. Ibid., 137 n. 2.

22. Ibid., n. 3.

23. Walter Benjamin, "The Work of Art in the Age of Mechanical Reproduction," in his *Illuminations,* ed. Hannah Arendt, trans. Harry Zohn (New York, 1969), 217–51, here 244–46 n. 8. Following Andrew Arato and Eike Gebhardt, editors of *The Essential Frankfurt School Reader* (New York, 1978), 353 n. 93, and others, I have altered the translated title of Benjamin's essay.

reproduction of the *Sistine Madonna* over the remainder of the century—conveniently oblivious, however, to the fact that in the tradition in which Benjamin wrote, *Entzauberung* ("disenchantment") with good aura, was a sad thing for modern mankind.[24] On the other hand, it must be in the light of the appropriation art of the mid-1980s that one is even curious to see just what Mengs's *Transfiguration* specifically looks like: formidable as it is, who but a specialist would ever have even wanted to see it reproduced before, as something at all by Mengs, when he or she could have had a "reproduction" of Raphael's image instead!

My epigraph comes from half a century after *The Vow of Louis XIII,* when there was no turning back from modernity, namely, from Baudelaire's "The Painter of Modern Life" (1863), the greatest essay ever written on an artist of mere fashion, Constantin Guys. More famous in the same passage is a remark on "the transitory, the fugitive, the contingent" as specifically and manifestly modern—but only, Baudelaire says, as "the *half* of art,"[25] modern art still also relating to the classical at least by default, with the passing of whatever once made an antique work itself the latest thing. In one sense, Baudelaire seems to be giving simpleminded advice to dare to be of one's time; in another, he struggles to articulate a dialectic of continuity and change in which, if the present produces anything eventually to be seen worthy of standing beside the art of the past, it will have immortalized just something in the life of our time that seems throwaway now.

No later modern understood that better than the perhaps greater Guys of our time, Andy Warhol, who knew something about making visual commonplaces his own. Were we to go on from here, it might, for instance, be by turning to his late takeoffs on Raphael's *Sistine Madonna,* one at least of which, *Raphael I: $6.99,* of 1985, is almost as large as, and for its airy *disegno* more sheerly huge than, Mengs's *Transfiguration.*[26] Indeed, except for one patch of pink, one patch of blue, and a red price-tag, Warhol's image consists of a wiry web of hard lines as in commonplace reproduction—which once meant engraving, or now, as readily, a reproduction of a reproduction by rubber-stamp or Xerox, what with a sideways doubling of

---

24. See ibid., esp. 191, 209, linking Max Weber's concept *Entzauberung* with Benjamin. Some American "theoreticians" now write as if all aura was bad and we have only to dance on its grave, which grotesquely distorts Benjamin's position.

25. Charles Baudelaire, "Le Peintre de la vie moderne" (1983), in his *Critique d'art,* ed. Claude Pichois, 2 vols. (Paris, 1965), II, 439–85, here 452–53.

26. Illus. in the Museum of Modern Art catalogue, ed. Kynaston McShine, *Andy Warhol: A Retrospective* (New York, 1989), fig. 453 on p. 394.

the madonna and Child and the commonplace price of $6.99 on the tag only rubbing in the image's status as monumentalized repro.

Reconnaissance might continue, but the two eighteenth-century paintings in Dublin are enough to exemplify an interreferral not only of images but also of ideas. Ideas, too, have histories, all the more urgently in our age of historical amnesia calling for retrieval and review. We may be swimming in images, but our culture hardly swamps us under a depth of ideas.

Foundations

Whatever else modernity means for art, it implies self-conscious detachment and specialization in essentially cultural production. Not that humanity isn't part of nature; but unless we are prepared to move all our art into the natural history museum—where Western naturalistic representation would look far stranger than abstraction beside most tribal arts—we have to acknowledge that the modern art of a hundred years only magnifies the cultural and technical, linguistic and semiotic detachment of all art. Perhaps a dogmatic "modernism," still exorcistically invoked by some of a certain age, fixated on art-about-art because at least such art was guaranteed not to be naturalistic. Okay, okay!

To the confusion of modern viewers of the art of all periods, a nineteenth-century notion of naturalistic representation still holds popular sway. It is still commonly assumed that art is to reflect nature, product for product (rather than, as Aquinas says, nature's *mode of operation*), as though whatever is sought in art could already be found in nature, no doubt in a less compromised state at that. Because with painting the problem usually entails some presumption of perspective rendering—as if something so conventional could be natural—traditionally in the West, according to the system author-ized by Alberti in the Renaissance and long academically established, I open with an attack, not so much on Alberti as on those who in modern times have hidden behind him to oppose the insight of modernity.

Artistic objectification survives re-centered and intensified, its true destination being the bringing into being of an art object, which is something more than a material commodity even when it is ab-used as such. Modernists tend to believe that artists have always been conscious of this, whatever else they were doing. Not exactly always. There had initially to be the great Neolithic revolution against a still earlier naturalism in art—as was first understood in modern times.

ALBERTI'S "WINDOW": ART-HISTORIOGRAPHIC NOTES ON AN ANTIMODERNIST MISPRISION

And anon as he had unshut the window the enchantment was gone.
—*Morte d'Arthur*, XI.iii

To J. B., D. C., A. C. D. and L. S. for provocations

Clichés, like weeds, prove difficult to uproot. In a note to "Hard-Core Painting" (1978), in a 1985 lecture on "Materiality and Constructive Tradition" at the Museum of Modern Art, and elsewhere, I have considered how Leon Battista Alberti's all-too-famous Renaissance idea of a painted image as windowlike does not simply apply to the (overall) surface of a painting, assumedly framed.[1] Alberti's main statement is: "First of all, on the surface on which I am going to paint, I draw a rectangle of whatever size I want, which I regard as an open window through which the subject to be painted is seen [*quod quidem mihi pro aperta finestra est ex qua historia contueatur*]" (*De Pictura*, I.19).[2] Aware that whenever I state this I incur a

---

1. Joseph Masheck, "Hard-Core Painting," *Artforum*, April 1978, repr. in his *Historical Present: Essays of the 1970s* (Ann Arbor, 1984), 153–69, here 167 n. 15. A considerably briefer form of the present essay, delivered as a lecture in July of 1989 at the Emma Lake (Saskatchewan) Artists Workshop, where I had the pleasure to be critic-in-residence, has appeared in *Source: Notes in the History of Art,* VIII / 4–IX / 1 (Summer–Fall 1989), 13–17 (where, however, the name of Ad Reinhardt is confused with that of Barnett Newman: see note 7 below). For commenting on earlier drafts whose augmentation now exempts them from culpability, I am grateful to James S. Ackerman, Paul Oskar Kristeller, and Meyer Schapiro.

2. Leon Battista Alberti, *On Painting and On Sculpture: The Latin Texts of De Pictura and De*

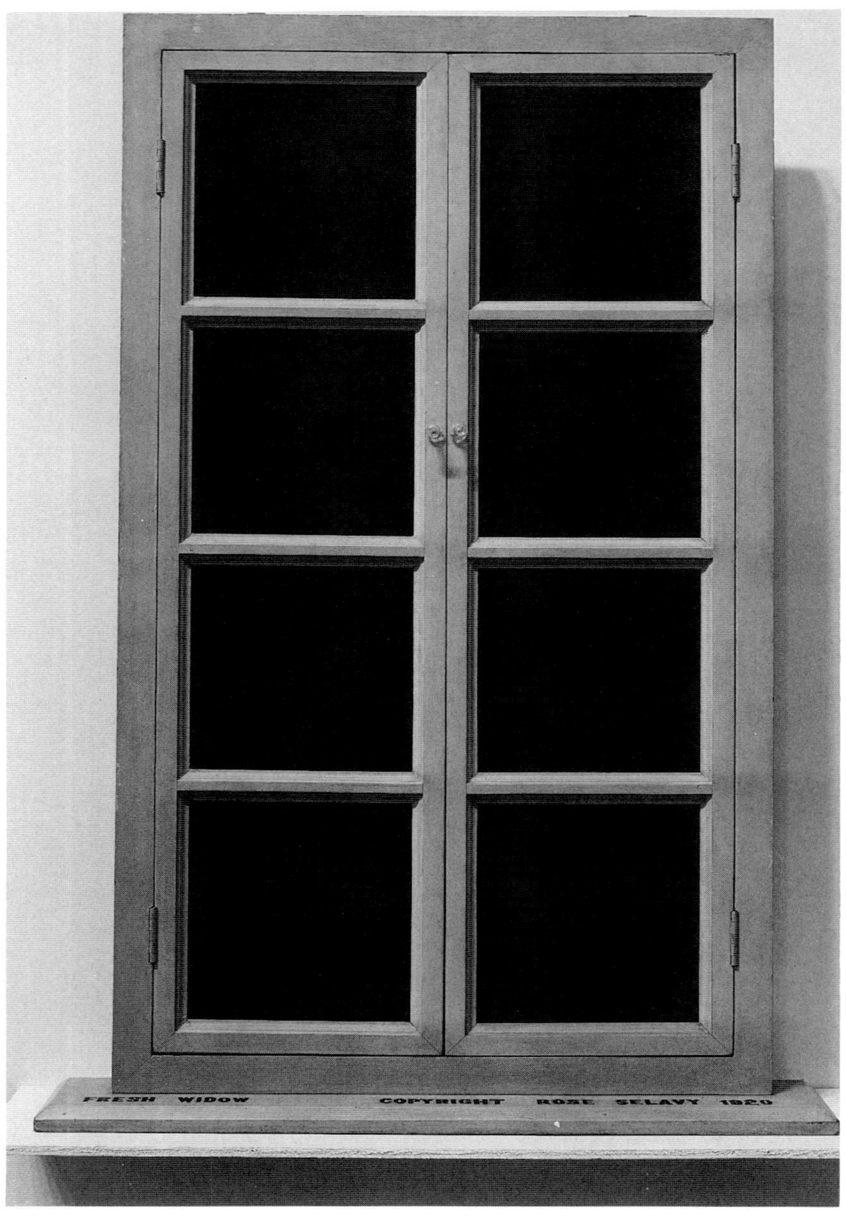

Fig. 3   Marcel Duchamp, *Fresh Widow,* 1920, miniature French window, painted wood frame and eight panes of glass covered with black leather, 30½ x 17⅝ inches, on wooden sill, ¾ x 21 x 4 inches.

heavy silence, I point out once more that what *De Pictura* I.19 maintains is that *if* you draw a rectangle then you *may* treat it—the drawn rectangle, that is, not the format-surface—as an open window. Of itself, the given conventionally flat format of painting, whether panel in the fifteenth century or stretched canvas since, neither entails nor implies Alberti's "window." The flat surface with edges precedes what Alberti calls a window, which is a construct, willfully imposed. The "window" idea, then, is a trope,[3] and a signal of the essentially fictive poetics of painting.

On this score Alberti is by no means as Albertian as is still often uncritically assumed, especially as the notion of the Albertian window has persisted beyond the long-since-repealed laws of perspectival rendering that for Alberti it had immediately served.[4] This would even have to include any moderns who, allegedly on Alberti's authority, presuppose the given format of painting to be windowlike for purpose of denial.[5]

As a specialized problem, Alberti's "window" shares in a larger problem of so-called postmodern culture that deserves to be faced: the failure of modernism to defend its claims to the culture of the past, resulting in its closure and containment as just another movement, almost just another chapter in Janson's *History of Art.* I am tempted to touch on related matters,

---

Statua, ed. and trans. Cecil Grayson (London, 1972), 55 (English), 54 (Latin); this edition presumed in citations below.

3. A painter, Marielle Tabart, calls my attention to the French expression *fenêtre ouverte sur le grand large,* a glimpse of, or insight into, the larger (or outside) world, or the future. See Paul Robert, *Le grand Robert: Dictionnaire alphabétique et analogique de la langue française,* 2d ed., ed. Alain Rey, 9 vols. (Paris, 1985), IV, 459, col. 2, with example from Baudelaire: "une apparence plus décidée de fenêtre ouverte sur l'infini."

4. Visual incidences of the window figure, even in classic perspective treatises, are probably rarer than one would assume: not one of the 160 plates in Pierre Descargues's *Perspective: History, Evolution, Technique* (1976; trans. I. Mark Paris, ed. Ellyn Childs Allison [New York, 1977]), illustrating treatises from the fifteenth into the nineteenth centuries, shows any image appearing through a window.

5. I.e., denial of the assumption that Albertian perspective was a modernizing, progressive gain for art. In the time of an earlier modernism W. Flemming, *Die Begründung der modernen Aesthetik und Kunstwissenschaft durch Leon-Battista Alberti* (Leipzig and Berlin, 1916), was responsible for an interesting error. Alberti says (II.26) he used to tell his friends "that the inventor of painting, according to the poets, was Narcissus," for "what is painting but the act of embracing by means of art the surface of the pool?" (*On Painting,* 61, 63 [English]). Already in 1924, Erwin Panofsky attacked Flemming, in *Idea: A Concept in Art Theory,* trans. Joseph J. S. Peake (New York, 1968), for taking this to derive from Plotinus, who invokes Narcissus "to warn against 'losing oneself' in mere visible beauty," whereas "Alberti (basing himself on Ovid . . .) used it to show that painting originated from love of the beautiful, and he compared painting with embracing an image (*not just a phantom!*)" (209 n. 32; emphasis added). The reality of the image, not illusion, would seem then to be the more truly Albertian point.

such as the function of traditional rendering in the education of abstract artists; or the long-standing resistance to all but stylistic revision in other departments of culture; or even the recent "postmodern" marketing of historical ignorance in art as a new sophistication whose superficiality counts as wised-up, while modernism is dismissed as uncool, if not (yet again) utopian.

Instead, by reviewing the more conspicuous and influential testimony of the last generation or two, I shall take up the more modestly scaled problem of the misconstrual of Alberti's central, utterly nuclear, remark in the theory of painting in our time. Here, by the way, the French and Italians are no doubt at a disadvantage for their having yet to establish a solid tradition of committedly abstract painting.[6] In America, however, by 1943 Mondrian, the author of "Plastic Art and Pure Plastic Art" (1936), was already established in New York, and Ad Reinhardt, decrying the "pathetic . . . artist . . . with his 'pictures in frames,' " could claim that "the distinction between a painting and a picture seems necessary."[7]

In a talk on "The Renaissance and Order" in New York, in 1950, de Kooning put up a charmingly brave struggle with received Albertian wisdom. The Renaissance painter, he begins by saying, "had this large marvelous floor that he worked on."[8] *He,* de Kooning, thinks first of the canvas, then accommodates the "floor": "The space . . . measured out on the original plane of the canvas surface became a 'place' somewhere on that floor. If he were a good painter, he did not make the center of the end of that floor—the vanishing point on the horizon—the 'content' (as the philosophers and educators of commercial art want to convince us nowadays that they [*sic*] did)."[9] De Kooning denies that "to a competent painter" perspective meant "an illusionary trick" for attaining depth, for "The world was deep already."[10] The Renaissance artist really "took it for granted that he could only measure things subjectively, and it was logical

---

6. Apologies to André Masson.

7. Ad Reinhardt, unpublished lecture (1943), in *Art-as-Art: The Selected Writings of Ad Reinhardt,* ed. Barbara Rose, The Documents of 20th-Century Art (New York, 1975), 47–49.

8. Willem de Kooning, "The Renaissance and Order" (given at "Studio 35"), repr. from *Trans/formation,* I/2 (1951), in *The Collected Writings of Willem de Kooning,* ed. George Scrivani (Madras and New York, 1988), 17–36, here 17. De Koonings's thinking of the floor as ground relates to Alberti's notion of dividing up a "pavement" receding squares (1.20–21; see *On Painting,* notes, 113–14, where also Grayson understands Alberti's assumed "drawing surface" (*areola*) as "quite separate from the painting surface and not necessarily of smaller dimensions" (113).

9. Ibid., 18.

10. Ibid., 19.

therefore that the best way was from the inside. It was the only way he could eventually project all the happenings on the front most plane."[11]

How, then, did the Albertian window-figure work come to be shorn of its metaphoric valence, especially in latter-day antimodernist discourse, even in America?

A distinguished colleague objects that it would be necessary to examine all extant versions of Alberti's statement to prove what I am saying, due (I agree) to likely discrepancies between his Latin version as a full-dress theoretical statement and the vernacular circulating among artists. That the present-day argument is theoretical can only underscore the importance of the Latin, which came to be dedicated humanistically "to Giovan Francesco [Gonzaga] Illustrious Prince of Mantua" ("You will see that they are such that their contents may prove worthy by their art of the ears of learned men, and may also easily please scholars").[12] Yet not only because Alberti took Italian seriously enough to write a grammar of Tuscan, but also because some of us see modernism itself in terms of shoptalk, the vernacular matters too.

Fortunately, Cecil Grayson has already performed a detailed collation of the surviving manuscripts, which all differ.[13] In Latin alone there are nineteen known mss. plus one printed text (1540). While no one version in either language is ultimate, it seems Alberti wrote *De Pictura* in Latin in 1435, then prepared an Italian version, which in some form was dedicated to Brunelleschi (1436?), and finally revised the Latin for its aristocratic presentation. As for the Italian, of only three mss., two are "very corrupt," with large chunks missing—though mostly after Book I, which contains the most problematic passage. For instance, one of these, from the late fifteenth century, was "edited and abbreviated by others than the author over a period of years during which the work was widely diffused and used by practising artists (though it is very difficult to see what profit these might have drawn from such a garbled version)."[14] In his own 1973 redaction of the Italian text Grayson gives the key passage thus: "*Principio, dove io debbo dipingere scrivo un quadrangolo di retti angoli quanto grande io voglio, el quale reputo essere una finestra aperta per donde io miri quello*

---

11. Ibid., 20.
12. Alberti, *On Painting*, 35.
13. Grayson, "The Text of Alberti's *De Pictura*," *Italian Studies*, XXIII (1968), 71–93.
14. Ibid., 75.

che quivi sarà dipinto."[15] Apparently none of the many detailed manuscript variants challenges this, which (as the blurring in the Italian version of the noble concept of *historia* need not detain us) is, on the crucial point, the same as the Latin in meaning.

Grayson himself is sufficiently bound by convention to underplay Alberti's open window as metaphoric in an introductory paraphrase: "Hence his famous visualization of painting as a window through which the observer, from a certain fixed viewpoint on this side, looks at the scene 'outside.' The painter's object is to represent on the surface corresponding to that window (the picture surface) the three-dimensional space 'beyond,' which is continuous with that in which he himself stands. The window is the intersection of the visual pyramid." Let me add that my teacher Rudolf Wittkower would here have recognized an Albertian phrase (III.52, *finis pictoris*) as also echoing in the title of Myfanwy Evans's still-interesting modernist anthology *The Painter's Object* (London, 1937)—of which Ad Reinhardt, for one, possessed a copy.[16]

Grayson is no more alone, however, in discounting theoretical and practical image-ination than he is in conflating two or more Albertian motifs. Alberti does earlier describe the painting surface as "like glass" (*admodum vitrea*; I.12),[17] i.e., as a translucent planar slice through the perspectival pyramid.[18] Caution, however: according to Fernand Braudel, fifteenth-century window glass was not very transparent and was anyway uncommon.[19] (An analogous "window" hypothesized by Leonardo da Vinci in his *Treatise on Painting* is described as being faced with oiled paper.[20])

---

15. Alberti, *Della Pittura,* in his *Opera volgari,* ed. Grayson (Scrittori d'Italia, no. 254), vol. III (Bari, 1973), 7–107, with notes on 299–340, here 36 (emphasis in original).

16. Rose, in Reinhardt, *Art-as-Art,* 45 (ed. note).

17. Alberti, *On Painting,* 49 (English), 48 (Latin).

18. For an emphasis on translucency over the, so to speak, hypothetically opaque material plane, see James S. Ackerman, "Alberti's Light," in *Studies in Late Medieval and Renaissance Painting in Honor of Millard Meiss,* 2 vols. (New York, 1977), I, 1–27, with II, pls. 1, 2.

19. Fernand Braudel, *Capitalism and Material Life, 1400–1800* (1967), trans. Miriam Kochan (New York, 1973), 121, 214.

20. Leonardo da Vinci, *The Art of Painting,* trans. and ed. John Francis Rigaud (1802; repr. New York, 1957), Article ccl, "Of the Painter's Window," 151 (the edition has some historiographic interest). M. H. Pirenne, *Optics, Painting and Photography* (Cambridge, 1970), 33–34, points to a passage where Leonardo does say, "Perspective is nothing else than seeing a place or objects behind a pane of glass, quite transparent, on the surface of which the objects that lie behind the glass are to be drawn" (*The Literary Works of Leonardo da Vinci,* ed. and trans. Jean Paul Richter and Irma A. Richter, 2d ed. [London, 1939; repr. 1970], no. 83). Especially as "quite transparent," this would still suggest a hyperbolic *concept* of a glass pane. Although there is *Hinterglasmalerei* ("painting on the back of glass"), as practiced by Constable and also the young

What glazed windows there were would hardly have revealed an undistorted, transparent view.[21]

It is also anachronistic to think of Alberti as assuming that a painting consists of oil paint on "canvas." Paint on cloth has a prehistory, but because Jacopo Bellini pretty much installed the new medium and format as we know it at just about the moment Alberti was writing, Alberti would practically have had to warn his readers not to think of (wooden) panel painting if the stretched canvas had had any significance to his theory. It is likewise anachronistic to think that, to Alberti or his early readers, "painting" connoted images of the unpoeticized terrain that one may see *out* a window, landscape having yet to emerge as a full-blown genre of painting in the Occident.

Although Alberti, as Robert Klein observed, was "not familiar with the studios" and wrote oblivious to certain fourteenth-century perspectival workmanly practices that more than survived him,[22] he nevertheless pronounces authoritatively: "on the surface on which I am going to paint, I draw (*inscribo*) a rectangle of whatever size I want, which I regard as an

---

Kandinsky as well as by folk artists, when Alberti speaks literally of *drawing* a rectangle on a real surface he obviously does not mean on glass. Elsewhere, Leonardo recommends that the actual windows of the painter's room be "made of linen, without crossbars," and blackened toward the edges: *Leonardo da Vinci on Painting: A Lost Book (Libro A) Reassembled from the Codex Vaticanus 1270 and from the Codex Leicester,* ed. Carlo Pedretti (Berkeley, 1964), 68–69, par. 79; for a swipe against Abstract Expressionism here, see Kenneth Clark's foreword, ix.

21. See Samuel Y. Edgerton, Jr.'s essay "The Renaissance Artist as Quantifier" (1978), in which a German woodcut from a century after Alberti is reproduced. The image shows an artist drawing on an angled table easel what he sees through an (N.B.) open window gridded with strings or wires, this from a treatise on perspective (Hieronymous Rodler and Johann II of Bavaria, *Ein Schön Büchlein und Unterweisung der Kunst des Messens,* 1531). Edgerton is reminded by it of "the fixed coordinates of a cartographic grid"; his essay is found in Margaret A. Hagen, ed., *The Perception of Pictures,* 2 vols., I, *Alberti's Window: The Projective Model of Pictorial Information* (New York, 1980), 179–212, here 182 with fig. 5.1 on 183. However, diagonally paned casements, like those of a transom still in place above this particular window, as well as of an adjacent window with a transom, have clearly been removed before the squaring of the view out the window began (this squaring-to-reduce, from nature to art, reverses traditional squaring of *studies* for enlargement, especially in mural painting). Svetlana Alpers, *The Art of Describing: Dutch Art in the Seventeenth Century* (Chicago, 1983), 138, warns that "cartographic grids, in general, must be distinguished from, not confused with, the perspective grid. The [cartographic] projection is, one might say, viewed from nowhere. Nor is it to be looked through. It assumes a flat working surface."

22. Robert Klein, "Pomponius Gauricus on Perspective" (1961), in his *Form and Meaning: Essays on the Renaissance and Modern Art,* ed. and trans. Madeline Jay, Leon Wieseltier and Henri Zerner (New York, 1979), 102–28; latter-day detections of Renaissance anti-Albertianism and "a more subtle type of 'non-Albertianism'" are noted in Klein's "Studies on Perspective in the Renaissance" (1963), op. cit., 129–40.

open window (*aperta finestra*)." This rectangle is willfully established by the artist somewhere—anywhere—within the limits of a surface having its own shape (in respect to whose edges Alberti already, in I.2, prefers "a metaphorical term from Latin . . . , the brim, or the fringe" to "horizon"[23]). Notice: if by a stretch of imagination he had actually been thinking of a glazed window, why would Alberti ever have specified it as open (*aperta finestra*; likewise in the Italian, *una finestra aperta*), for that matter, instead of *closed,* when what he was after was a figure implying a literally transparent plane? Finally, there is also the how-to-do-it apparatus of a thin "veil" (*velum*) of semitransparent cloth (II.31–32, 35; III.58) for translating, as with Dürer's famous gridded frame in the next century, three dimensions into two. True, a window concept might be said to return by implication where (II.49) Alberti allows, as an "ornament" distinctly "added to" the finished painting, for the possibility of an assumedly aedicular frame (with "sculpted columns, bases, and pediments")[24]—again, however, without implying glass. So, in any case, the "open window" motif occurs only once, in I.19, and there as a drawn, invented, imposed figure, by no means an implicit structure.

By now, of course, the tradition of taking painting's given format as a window, and of assuming that the conception was Alberti's, is a historical phenomenon in its own right, significant to modernists as a mistaken commonplace of the opposition. Although there is also a modernist of sorts in Ruskin, one can imagine the influence, direct or through teachers, on generations of English-language minds of his *Elements of Perspective,* which

---

23. Alberti, *On Painting,* 37.

24. Ibid., 93. But for the risk of adding to the long-standing confusion, there would be no reason not to allow that a picture *frame* is like a window (frame). Thus, for example: "the idea of a [N.B.] framed picture derives . . . from the fact of the usual framedness of the glimpse of nature we catch through the frame of the window or the door—or stage aperture . . ."; Sergei Eisenstein, "The Dynamic Square" (1930/31), in his *Film Essays and a Lecture,* ed. Jay Leyda (Princeton, 1982), 48–65, here 57. Meyer Schapiro oberves in his classic paper "On Some Problems in the Semiotics of Visual Art: Field and Vehicle in Image Signs," *Semiotica* I (1969), 223–42, that the framed image is a specific historical development that, belonging "to the space of the observer," proved dispensible with abstract or nonobjective art and now no longer serves "to accent the depth of a simulated space" (226–28). More generally: the boundary of a field "is like a window through which one glimpses only a part of the space behind it. In older art this allusion to an actual bounded field of a spectator was most often made by representing (N.B.) within the picture-field itself the stable enclosing parts of an architecture—doorways and window ledges—that defined a real and permanent frame of vision in the field of the signata" (241).

opens innocuously enough: "When you begin to read this book, sit down very near the window, and [N.B.] shut the window. I hope the view out of it is pretty; but, whatever the view may be, we shall find enough in it for an illustration of the first principles of perspective (or, literally, of 'looking through')." Furthermore: "Every pane of your window may be considered, if you choose, as a glass picture; and what you see through it, as painted on its surface."[25] The name of Alberti is not invoked, but for a good three pages an easy elision is sustained between the pane of window glass and the draftsman's sheet or painter's canvas.

What matters is not any innocent supposition that a window may happen to frame a stretch of the outside world picturesquely, but the polemical significance of insisting that a painting is supposed to be a window, onto or into any sort of "view," even once there was such a thing as abstract painting. Indeed, the conventional nineteenth-century conception long persisted, provoking in the New York School the distinction between a (false) *picture* and a (true) *painting* supposed to have eluded even the theoretical capability of André Breton, among the Surrealists.[26] My own need to split the Albertian textual hair must trace back to a sense, now unfashionable among self-advertised radicals but confirmed in the inspiring example of Wittkower, that the classics, *anciens* as well as *modernes,* actually do hold truth.

Without pretending to exhaust the evidence, one can say, in the first place, that around 1940 there was a responsible literature available in English. In *On the Rationalization of Sight* (1938) William M. Ivins, Jr., aware of a variety of sources, renders the vital passage safely, from Hubert Janitschek's (1877) edition of the Italian: "He says *I draw a rectangle* (which is to bound the picture he is going to draw . . .), *as big as I like, which for me*

<hr>

25. John Ruskin, *The Elements of Perspective; Arranged for the Use of Schools; and Intended to be Read in Connexion with the First Three Books of Euclid* (New York, 1885), 9.

26. In "The Photographic Conditions of Surrealism" (1981), in her *The Originality of the Avant-Garde and Other Modernist Myths* (Cambridge, Mass., 1986), 87–118, Rosalind E. Krauss sets up a supposedly "classical," though rather un-Artistotelian, notion of "representation" to show Breton as literarily prejudiced against the visual image; she observes him, in "Surrealism and Painting" (1925), "insisting on the impossibility of imagining a [N.B.] 'picture as being other than a window'" (94). Yes, there is a real problem with Breton. While in the original he does say the first thing he cares about with painting is that *"onto which,"* as a window, *"it gives,"* and whatever (in possible play on Alberti's *aperta finestra* as well as on *point de vue*) extends before him *"à perte de vue"* (blocking the view), these terms, themselves rather figured, concern a poetic transaction between what is "present" and what is "evoked." André Breton, "Le Surréalisme et la peinture" (here dated 1928), in his *Le Surréalisme et la peinture: suivi de Genèse et perspective artistiques du Surréalisme et de fragments inédits* (New York, 1945), 21–22; emphasis in original.

is like an open window through which I see whatever is to be painted."[27] Equally innocent, at least in this matter, is Anthony Blunt, whose treatment of Alberti in *Artistic Theory in Italy 1450–1600* (1940) mentions no window at all.

Erwin Panofsky may not be a hero of modernism, considering his notorious attack on Barnett Newman in the pages of *Art News,* but on the Albertian score he does not seem culpable either, at least not before the problematic moment. Showing how permeated by the thought of Ernst Cassirer is Panofsky's classic 1924–25 "Die Perspektive als 'symbolische Form,'" published in the Warburg Library *Vorträge* (1927), Michael Ann Holly has stressed that dazzling lecture as an argument, in effect on the modernist side, for the conventionality of perspective.[28] There Panofsky's phraseology does seem careful, as with "the 'correct' geometrical construction which was discovered in the Renaissance" and "most simply described . . . in accordance with its definition as a 'window' " and also with a more rigorous statement in which, significantly, his sense of the "picture plane" is itself much more virtual or hypothetical than many impatient moderns might, even today, expect: "We shall speak of a treatment of space as 'perspective' in the full sense when, and only when, there is not merely a foreshortening of single objects such as houses or pieces of furniture, but the entire picture—to use the expression of . . . [a] Renaissance theorist— is [N.B.] transformed into a window [N.B.] as it were, through which we look into the space beyond, when therefore the material surface of the painting or relief on which the forms of simple figures or things are drawn or modeled is *negated as such* and becomes simply a 'picture plane,' on which is projected the whole of that space seen beyond it and containing within itself all separate objects."[29]

---

27. William M. Ivins, Jr., in *On the Rationalization of Sight,* Metropolitan Museum Papers, no. 8 (New York, 1938), 22 (emphasis in original); contemporaneous in the field of modern art was Fritz Novotny's *Cézanne und das Ende der wissenschaftlichen Perspektive* (1938). Relying on Ivins, Miriam Bunim says carefully that in fifteenth-century Flanders as well as Italy "a generation of artists was prepared to undertake the solution of the problem of representation presented by the concept of the picture plane as a window through which the spectator views a realistic depiction of tridimensional space"; *Space in Medieval Painting and the Forerunners of Perspective* (New York, 1940), 174, also with reference to Panofsky's 1924–25 Warburg paper (see note 29 below).

28. Michael Ann Holly, *Panofsky and the Foundations of Art History* (Ithaca, N.Y., 1984), 130–57. In this, she calls on Ludwig Wittgenstein's "picture theory," without, however, considering his insight into mathematics itself as conventional rather than as founded on an objective logic. This is relevant because, as Wittkower used to emphasize, the fact that perspective rendering implied knowledge of *geometria* served newly in Alberti's time to qualify painting for the social dignity of the Liberal Arts.

29. Erwin Panofsky, "Perspective as Symbolic Form," anonymous translation from *Vorträge der*

In 1940, however, with *The Codex Huygens and Leonardo da Vinci's Art Theory*, Panofsky says rather summarily, "During the Middle Ages the picture was conceived as an opaque two-dimensional surface covered with lines and colours which were to be interpreted as tokens or symbols of three-dimensional objects. In the Renaissance, a picture was conceived as a 'window through which we look out into a section of the visible world,' to quote Leon Battista Alberti." Dürer, he does proceed fortuitously to add, "illustrates Alberti's metaphor."[30] Again, in one of the 1952 lectures constituting his *Renaissance and Renascences in Western Art* (1960), Panofsky says that "the objectively two-dimensional painting surface . . . has ceased to be an opaque and impervious working surface . . . and has become a window through which we look [N.B.] out." Here, however, he acknowledges "Alberti's window *simile*" (emphasis mine); and, repeating the opening thought of the "Symbolic Form" lecture, that according to Dürer "*Perspectiva* is a Latin word which means a view through something," he proceeds to say, *but in quotation marks,* that with the Renaissance "The picture is again a 'window,' " and "this 'window' is no longer what it had been before being 'closed.' "[31]

Of eventual transatlantic influence, even in "studio art," was Ernst

---

Bibliothek Warburg, 1924–25 (1927), photocopy in the Avery Library, Columbia University, New York, of typescript (presumably after that in the library of the Warburg Institute, London), 1 (emphasis mine). Inverted commas of the original German title allude to Cassirer's concept "symbolische Form." On the "picture plane": with Giotto and Duccio there is "*a resolution in the formal significance of the surface of representation.* There is no longer a wall or panel on which the forms of individual things are laid; it is once more a transparent plane through which we are to look into space . . .—we may already call it a 'picture plane' in the exact sense of the word," 11 (emphasis in original). By this sense at least, latter-day modernists who assume that the picture plane simply *is* the physical surface of the painting ground are wrong.

30. Panofsky, *The Codex Huygens and Leonardo da Vinci's Art Theory: The Pierpont Morgan Library Codex M. A. 1139,* Studies of the Warburg Institute, 13 (London, 1940), 92.

31. Panofsky, "*I Primi Lumi:* Italian Trecento Painting and Its Impact on the Rest of Europe," in his *Renaissance and Renascences in Western Art* (New York, 1969), 114–61, here 120, 124, 138, respectively. The developed window figure of the last passage reminds me, as a modernist, of a legendary set of three diagrams journalistically caricaturing important American abstract painting of the early 1960s. Under the heading "A Few Notes on Art," in the *New York Herald-Tribune,* 21 June 1963, p. 17, John Crosby showed three squares, the first horizontally bisected with its upper half darkened; the second bisected by a vertical line; the third completely darkened, each with a comment: "Mark Rothko, who painted [N.B.] pictures like this, drew the shade"; "And Barney Newman, who painted pictures like this, shut the door"; "And Ad Reinhardt, who painted pictures like this, turned out the lights." Unremarked, as far as I know, is the hypocrisy of the same paper, two pages away, decrying the censure of a Soviet critic and painter by the Central Committee of the Communist Party: "Shocking! Soviet Artist Owns an Abstract [N.B.] Statue" (15).

Gombrich's "Meditations on a Hobby Horse," originally contributed to a 1951 symposium at the Institute of Contemporary Arts, London. Despite a half-hearted qualification citing Panofsky on the *Codex Huygens* ("In theory, at least, painting becomes synonymous with geometrical projection"), Gombrich there describes "that 'rationalisation of space' we call scientific perspective by which the picture plane becomes a window pane."[32]

Rudolf Arnheim's *Art and Visual Perception* (1954) employs the window motif for a special purpose, in a risky manner: in the Renaissance "The [N.B.] frame was thought of as a window, through which the observer peeped into an outer world, confined by the opening of the peephole but unbounded in itself. In our . . . discussion this means that the frame was used as a figure, with the picture space supplying an underlying borderless ground."[33] Note that Arnheim's perhaps more *mat*like than *frame*like conception quite reverses what Alberti says insofar as the drawing of Alberti's initial quadrangle very much establishes a bordering "ground." Furthermore, it is countered by the claim of M. H. Pirenne: "In ordinary vision the spectator's awareness of the *surface pattern* pattern is obviously helped to a great extent by the frame or by the regular shape of the boundary of the picture."[34] According to Pirenne (speaking not of Alberti but of Leonardo), experimental evidence indicates that "the actual pattern *on the surface* of a representational picture must be perceived, as a surface pattern, even though the spectator may be dimly aware of this, *at the same time* as the objects represented are seen as a scene in depth."[35]

Two years after *Art and Visual Perception,* John Spencer's English Alberti appeared, in an American academic but widely accessible edition. It is, on our crucial point, safe and sound: "First of all about where I draw I inscribe a quadrangle of right angles, as large as I wish, which is considered to be

32. E. H. Gombrich, "Meditations on a Hobby Horse; or, The Roots of Artistic Form," in Lancelot Law Whyte, ed., *Aspects of Form: A Symposium on Form in Nature and Art* (London, 1951; repr. Bloomington, Ind., 1961), 209–28, here 221.

33. Rudolf Arnheim, *Art and Visual Perception: A Psychology of the Creative Eye,* rev. ed. (Berkeley, 1974), 239. Even given Arnheim's gestalt-psychological bias, "peephole" is a bad choice of word because it suggests something small enough to cast a camera obscura image (upside-down and *at* the observer).

34. Pirenne, *Optics,* 114 (emphasis added).

35. Ibid., 113-14 (emphasis in original). I intend to examine attempts, often desperate, to argue that the perception of surface pattern and a view in depth "at the same time" is impossible because one cannot "see two things at once," in a history of the idea of flatness in art theory. Although I have had to put this project aside for over a decade now, my article "The Carpet Paradigm: Critical Prolegomena to a Theory of Flatness," *Arts Magazine,* LI/1 (September 1976), 82–109, touches on the problem.

an open window through which I see what I want to paint" (elsewhere, "which to me is an open window from which the historia is seen").[36] Nevertheless, misconstrual would seem to have been on the increase.

Matters did not improve with the publication of John White's classic study *The Birth and Rebirth of Pictorial Space* a year later, in 1957. It was after two articles in the *Warburg Journal* (1949, 1951) and a London Ph.D. dissertation on perspective (1952) that White produced his still-popular *Birth and Rebirth,* which has had several British and American editions. White relied on Luigi Mallè's 1950 *Della Pittura.* However, the textual problem occurs not in the key quotation itself but at its splice with a defective paraphrase: "Alberti describes his actual method of perspective composition, *beginning with a suitably large square which* he says, 'I consider to be an open window through which I view that which will be painted there.' "[37]

More sweepingly problematic is White's reactionary delight in perspective and its seeming objectifications as downright reassuring, as he himself conveys in his introduction to the book: "The discussion of compositional problems is always liable to lead to the over-exercise of personal bias. . . . [But in perspective,] clarity and simplicity in shape and setting are characteristic of . . . [represented] objects. The distortion of all angles and surfaces can be measured exactly, and the accuracy of construction in relation to vanishing points and the like can be assessed in detail. . . . If enough care is taken, the visual facts to be discussed and interpreted can be very largely placed outside the sphere of argument."[38] Needless to say, what one is then left discussing in the representation is anything but its mimesis as art—hardly painting at all, merely, say, Spanish onions. Joan Gadol's book on Alberti (1969), otherwise not unique for its readiness to treat doorways (or intercolumniations) as tantamount to windows, has already specifically challenged White's sense of "practical," pretheoretical anticipations of the Albertian "window."[39]

---

36. Alberti, *On Painting,* trans. John R. Spencer (1956), rev. ed. (New Haven, 1966), 56, 109 n. 41, respectively.

37. John White, *The Birth and Rebirth of Pictorial Space* (London, 1957; also, New York, 1958), 122 (both), emphasis added; 2d ed. (London and Boston, 1967).

38. Ibid., 20–21 (same in all editions consulted).

39. Joan Gadol, *Leon Battista Alberti: Universal Man of the Early Renaissance* (Chicago, 1969). In stalking a metaphor, one had better avoid equating doors and windows. To Klein, who sees Alberti as less concerned with generating "probable" illusion than with serving "formal composition," he "treated painting as a 'false window' independent of the interior, rather than as a false door opening on the neighboring room" ("Pomponius Gauricus," 126).

Once Gombrich's *Art and Illusion* lectures were in wide circulation, White and Gombrich together would have been enough to encourage antimodernist misunderstanding of the Albertian "window." Modernists do have reason to be suspicious of Gombrich, whose insights seem to come as if with petitions attached, ready to sign, against anything radical. (By the way: now that the ideas in *Art and Illusion* are practically copyright "Gombrich," has no one yet noticed the clear adumbration of its main terminology by a "match[ing of] the data from the flux of visual experience with image-clichés," as already formulated in S. I. Hayakawa's "The Revision of Vision," for Gyorgy Kepes's *Language of Vision* [1944]?)[40]

Here is Gombrich on "the return to the classical ideal of the 'convincing' image in the Renaissance," in his 1956 Mellon lectures, published as *Art and Illusion* (1960), a book far too influential among those who know little else of art: "Alberti . . . described the [N.B.] frame as a window through which the beholder looks into the world of the picture." Only much later is one less recklessly told, "It was Alberti who first suggested the idea of *considering* a painting as a window through which we look at the visible world."[41] Despite Gombrich's later reliance, in *Means and Ends* (1976), on Grayson's new *De Pictura,* in 1976 he still speaks first of "the single frame which Alberti was to liken to a window," only stabilizing this further on by having Alberti "suggest that a painting . . . should be conceived as a window."[42]

Misconstrual of Alberti's definitive passage as enshrining illusionistic representation has proliferated. The wittiest critical response, for its clever comprehension of the kinship of frames of *mind* or outlook between the development of "scientific" perspective in Alberti's generation and the rise of Florentine capitalism (a theme also explored by Samuel Edgerton), is John Berger's 1972 remark that the concept of the Albertian window was

---

40. S. I. Hayakawa, "The Revision of Vision," in Gyorgy Kepes, *Language of Vision,* with introductory essays by S. Giedion and S. I. Hayakawa (Chicago, 1944), 8–11.

41. Gombrich, *Art and Illusion: A Study in the Psychology of Pictorial Representation,* The A. W. Mellon Lectures in the Fine Arts, 1956; Bollingen Series, xxxv/5 (New York, 1956), 152, 299 (emphasis added). Cf. now W.J.T. Mitchell, *Iconology: Image, Text, Ideology* (Chicago, 1986), 37: "Even Gombrich, who has done so much to reveal the historical and conventional character of this [Albertian] system, seems unable to break the spell of scientism which surrounds it, and frequently reverts to a view of pictorial illusionism as providing 'keys to the locks of our senses,' a phrase which ignores his own warning that 'our' senses are windows through which a purposive and acculturated imagination is looking, not a door that springs open to one master key."

42. Gombrich, *Means and Ends: Reflections on the History of Fresco Painting,* Walter Neurath Memorial Lecture (London, 1976), 39, 49.

really more like "a safe set into a wall, a safe in which the visible has been deposited."[43]

Samuel Edgerton is an established scientific authority, known for such works as *The Renaissance Discovery of Linear Perspective,* published in 1975. It is therefore interesting to see how close to trouble he comes in a 1978 lecture, where he gives a rather complicated description of an early Renaissance fresco. Of three adjacent images (described as "stories"!) in the Giottesque *Life of St. Francis* cycle, c. 1300, in the Upper Church at San Francesco, Assisi, Edgerton says, "the artist . . . has surely tried to create the illusion that one is looking at real-life scenes as if through a *window,*" while "all three scenes share a common painted frame." Only "as if" saves "this notion defined in the paintings at Assisi (i.e., that the picture be thought of as a window)," or that generally Western artists "were motivated by the picture-as-a-window concept."[44] Then again, a sufficiently subjunctive *as if*

---

43. John Berger, *Ways of Seeing* (London, 1972), 109.

44. Edgerton, "Renaissance Artist," 185. Edgerton also claims that Ambrogio Lorenzetti, in his *Good Government in the Country* fresco, c. 1335, arranged his elements, including a descriptive cartouche, "in his illusionary pictorial space 'behind' the [N.B.] fictional window" (187). But to say of the Giottesque fresco that "all three scenes share a common painted frame" might only be a careless way of saying that all three are similarly, even interdependently framed, albeit separately; but this one-for-three "frame," Edgerton says, "is an illusionary architectural opening [*an* opening, or three?] that the artist painted in the form of a surmounting cornice on modillions and supported by columns between each story." Now a "frame" cannot itself *be* an opening any more than a doughnut can *be* a hole; besides, the illusionistic vertical framing elements are not "columns," which being round would have much less to contribute perspectivally, but rather piers or pilasters. Individually, the same three images are said to "show only a naïve use of perspective (as was characteristic of medieval art generally)" (185), though "the painted frame clearly indicates that the artist intended the viewer to look at all three pictures together from a single viewpoint in the center." Edgerton should have noticed how little the discrete ambients of these three paintings entail a mundane consistency of earthly space: the image at the left, *The Sanctioning of the Rule,* shows a fourth-wall interior, securely centered; the central *Vision of the Chariot,* an outdoor scene with church building, also seen from without, cut away to reveal its interior; at the right, *The Vision of the Thrones* is an interior swamped by heavenly "outer" space. Cf. Alastair Smart on the same cycle of paintings: "whereas the scenes themselves are given their own independent perspective, the perspective of the entire frame*work* within each bay is related to the central point of that bay": *The Assisi Problem and the Art of Giotto: A Study of the Legend of St. Francis in the Upper Church of San Francesco, Assisi* (Oxford, 1971), 133 (emphasis in original). Smart also notices that, compared with Giotto at Padua, here "again and again we find that the orthogonals resulting from the rendering of a building from a particular angle are so contrived that they establish ascending or descending lines across the picture-plane, creating surface rhythms which are consistently employed to relate one fresco to another within each bay and to impose upon every group of scenes a harmonious *two-dimensional* pattern" (14–15, emphasis in original).

On supposedly "naive" medieval perspective, see Bunim, *Space in Medieval Painting.* With his earlier *Ten Books of Architecture,* Alberti himself is known to have suppressed his recourse to the is all one must finally demand. More safely, in the same collection in which Edgerton's lecture was published, H. A. Sedgwick says that "Alberti, in the earliest treatise on perspective construction, *compares* the picture frame *to* an open window through which the scene to be represented is viewed."[45]

In a paper delivered at a symposium on "Vision and Visuality" in 1988, Martin Jay, a historian, uses the phrase "contained . . . within the frame of the Albertian window"[46] safely enough, and takes "the transparent window that was the canvas, in Alberti's famous metaphor," as precisely that, metaphorical.[47] But he does not seem aware of how new the very sight of a canvas would have seemed to Alberti, perhaps assuming too literally that Alberti's *velum* connotes a support, or grid of *threads*.[48] Twice Jay refers to Rosalind Krauss's essay "Grids," saying that Krauss "has reminded us [that] Alberti's veil was assumed to correspond to external reality in a way that its modernist successor did not."[49] Krauss herself does not mention the name of Alberti in "Grids." Oddly, she does maintain that before a classic Mondrian diamond composition it is "as though we were looking at a landscape through a window, the frame of the window arbitrarily truncating our view but never shaking our certainty that the landscape [*sic*] continues beyond the limits of what we can, at the moment, see."[50]

---

works of medieval writers as well as ignoring medieval monuments, making it appear that he used fashionable, newly translated classical texts directly in order to " 'antiquiser' " his treatise: V. Zoubov, "Léon Battista Alberti et les auteurs du moyen âge," *Mediaeval and Renaissance Studies* (Warburg Institute), IV (1958), 245–66. On differences between Northern and Italian perspective systems in the fifteenth century, see Jacques Mesnil, *L'Art au nord et au sud des Alpes à l'époche de la Renaissance: Études comparatives* (Brussels and Paris, 1911); thanks to Meyer Schapiro for this latter reference.

45. H. A. Sedgwick, "The Geometry of Spatial Layout in Pictorial Representation" (1980), in Hagen, *Alberti's Window,* 33–90, here 40 (emphasis added).

46. Martin Jay, "Scopic Regimes of Modernity," in Hal Foster, ed., *Vision and Visuality,* Dia Art Foundation Discussions in Contemporary Culture, no. 2 (Seattle, 1988), 2–23, with discussion, 24–27; here 12.

47. Ibid., 6–7.

48. The Latin *"velum"* or Italian *"velo"* (Eng., "veil") is distinct in meaning from "vellum," for the writing and (medieval) painting surface; *velum* is also "sail," "piece of cloth," "awning," "curtain"; Ernest Klein, *A Comprehensive Etymological Dictionary of the English Language,* 2 vols. (Amsterdam, 1967), q.v.

49. Jay, "Scopic Regimes," 6 (quotation), 13.

50. Krauss, "Grids," in her *Originality,* 8–22, here 19, 21. This essay, reprinted from *October,* no. 9 (Summer 1979), is a revision of "Grids, You Say," in the catalogue *Grids: Format and Image in Twentieth-Century Art* (Pace Gallery, New York, 16 December 1978–20 January 1979; Akron [Ohio] Art Institute, 24 March–6 May 1979), unpaginated. Krauss discusses, and in the catalogue illustrates, a grid diagram from Goethe's 1810 text *Farbenlehre* that I had recently shown in my article "Hard-Core Painting," *Artforum,* April 1978 (repr. in *Historical Present,* unillus., discussion

Finally, I offer an instance from the recent writing of Arthur Danto, the philosopher and art critic. Speaking of the essential "metaphysical" distinction,[51] since the Renaissance, between a wall and any painting upon, or hanging upon, it, Danto has written: "We look through the surface at the scene situated in the illusory space, *as if* through a window. Indeed, the entire technology of painting was bent upon making the experience of seeing something through a window and seeing something in a painting perceptually indistinguishable."[52] Danto appears to be aware of the metaphorical standing of Alberti's figure. If anything slips in the latter sentence, which risks throwing away what has been contracted in the former, it would require another essay to consider what is truly encompassed by the "technology" of painting, and what, if any, are the merits of *in*distinguishability.[53]

Because Rudolf Wittkower and Ernst Gombrich were colleagues for years, I hope it is no more offensive to say this than to say that my dad can beat your dad, but Wittkower was not a reactionary. Neither, of course, is my other teacher, Meyer Schapiro, who, years ago, rose to Barnett Newman's defense against Panofsky's attacks. And it must be thanks to their care in putting such things that any too-plain talk of "Alberti's window" has never seemed quite right to me.

---

on 162). (Her confessing that she finds it "indescribably embarrassing to mention *art* and *spirit* in the same sentence" and her claim that God lost the Scopes trial [*Originality*, 10, 12] can be placed in light of "Hard-Core Painting" and the other essays in this "Iconicity" series; likewise, her attempt to suppress Ad Reinhardt's spirituality in a "Pandora's box" [ibid., 10] vis-à-vis documentation then being published by me ["Two Sorts of Monk: Reinhardt and Merton," *Artforum*, December 1978; repr. in *Historical Present*, 91–96]). A 1967 painting is illustrated in the *Grids* exhibition catalogue but not mentioned in her text no doubt as too mystical: Al Jensen's *The Reciprocal Relation of Unity 20–40–60–80 that Forms the Beginning of the Vigesimal System*, which is inscribed "The [N.B.] aperspective Structure of a Square." On the difference between a grid and a checkerboard pattern, and the development of the European chessboard in analogy with painting on a delimited rectangular field, see now Hubert Damisch, "L'Echiquier et la forme 'tableau,' " *Acts of the XXVI International Congress of the History of Art: World Art: Themes of Unity in Diversity*, ed. Irving Lavin, 3 vols. (University Park, Pa., 1989), I, 187–91.

51. It was in a book on the Realist Courbet that the modern Italian "Metaphysical" painter de Chirico wrote, "Who can deny the troubling connection which exists between perspective and metaphysics?"; Giorgio de Chirico, *Courbet* (Rome, 1925), quoted in James Thrall Soby, *The Early Chirico* (New York, 1941), repr. as *Giorgio de Chirico*, Arno Series of Contemporary Art, no. 33 (New York, 1969), 17–18. For my thoughts on de Chirico's pictorial conservatism, see Masheck, "The Pluperfection of de Chirico," in the Galerie Daniel Templon and Galerie Bruno Bischofberger catalogue *Bidlo (Not de Chirico)* (Paris, n.d. [1990]), 31–38.

52. Arthur C. Danto, "Art: Sienese Painting," *The Nation*, 6 March 1989, 317–20, here 317.

53. Dear Arthur: Let me simply say that, insofar as it ever fails to distinguish between any two things, perception is *at fault!*

As any stolid Neopalladian would, for his own "Brunelleschi and 'Proportion in Perspective,'" Wittkower worked from Giacomo Leoni's extravagantly handsome 1726 English version of Alberti, based on Cosimo Bartoli's sixteenth-century Italian edition.[54] Here the key sentence reads, perfectly safely, "First then upon the superficie whereon I am to work, I draw a square composed of right angles, as large as I think convenient; and this serves me as a window thro' which I am to view the story which is to be painted."[55] But allow me to range a little more widely, for I believe this great teacher encouraged a certain critical impatience with statements that are *merely* correct.

I like to think of the British Wittkower, who in one sense "found himself" in the (to me) rather Whiggish bubble of 1725, as very much one with the Berliner of 1925 whom I also knew. To think of him now as contemporary with the first Bauhaus *student* generation helps me to fathom his remarkably creative sense of classical orthodoxy. In the eight years I was privileged to be his student, I cannot quite remember our ever happening to talk about Kandinsky's 1926 "Bauhaus Book" *Point and Line to Plane*. But then why would we have had to, except to acknowledge that even there, in Kandinsky's carefully "schematic" sense of what he terms the painter's "Basic Plane,"[56] there can be detected still the timeless, classic truth of Alberti.

---

54. Rudolf Wittkower, "Brunelleschi and 'Proportion in Perspective,'" *Journal of the Warburg and Courtauld Institutes,* XVI (1953), repr. in his *Idea and Image: Studies in the Italian Renaissance,* ed. Margot Wittkower (London, 1978), 124–35. Leoni classily packaged Italian theory in appeal to new-moneyed British Neopalladians: see Wittkower, "Giacomo Leoni's Edition of Palladio's *Quattro Libri dell'architettura,*" *Arte Veneta,* VIII (1954), 310–16.

55. *The Painting of Leon Battista Alberti,* in *The Architecture of Leon Battista Alberti in Ten Books, of Painting in Three Books, and of Statuary in One Book* (London, 1726), fol. 8r.

56. Wassily Kandinsky, *Point and Line to Plane,* trans. Howard Dearstyne and Hilla Rebay, ed. Rebay (New York, 1947; repr. New York, 1979), 113–47. The very title of Kandinsky's book is tantamount to an allusion to *De Pictura,* I.2, on point, line, and plane.

2

ON CYCLADIC ULTRAMODERNITY

. . . assuming that art is not merely imitation of the reality of nature but rather a metaphysical supplement of the reality of nature, placed beside it for its overcoming.

—*The Birth of Tragedy,* xxiv

Such a big idea to throw out so hurriedly, like a mailbag from a moving train! Already in 1872 Nietzsche's not really so offhand crack announces the central doctrine of modernity as obvious except to those who have eyes yet will see not. Sometimes I wonder if Nietzsche might have known the work of John Lubbock, who in anthropology contemporaneously framed the, itself essentially modern, distinction between Paleo- and Neolithic culture. For to recognize in Neolithic art a willfully focused consciousness of form, this as a kind of dividend on specializing and intensifying refinement over generations, all in surmounting the givenness of nature, is to see something more deeply modern than just "streamlined," *moderne* shapes (perhaps now charmingly dated as such). Since "postmoderns" conveniently find history passé, I want to consider, before it is too late to tell, a specific enthusiasm for Cycladic and related Neolithic art, in a broad sense, among the classic moderns.

In the first place, such works are prehistoric but by no means primitive. Over and against Paleolithic naturalism, their intensified simplicities are accomplished with already supreme detachment. In them, it is sometimes as if the Greek archaic proper, that first dawn of classicism itself, were still just beneath the horizon. Some such pieces are absolutes beyond which no "progress" is possible, only development in perennial renewal.

A marked preference for "archaic" and geometric formal rigor first becomes evident not only in Neoclassical art but also in technical equipment from the Enlightenment and on into early modern industry. Thus the nineteenth-century American sculptor Horatio Greenough, seeking to cut through European cultural complexity with a pragmatic, all-American proto-Functionalism, praises a South Seas war club for its "Etruscan-like quaintness" as a lesson adaptable to industrial design.[1] Which, already, is not unlike a certain historically careless "functionalism" extended back to prehistoric art in the "Purist" polemics of the architect Le Corbusier and his circle in the 1920s.

Despite their attraction to the sleek shapes of Cycladic sculpture, the design-conscious Purists were too impatient to contribute to the French *rappel à l'ordre* after World War I an applied art of similarly sleek, efficient look, to acknowledge specifically Neolithic, vis-à-vis Paleolithic, form as more deeply, less superficially, analogous to the technical essentialization they themselves sought. A full-page plate in Amedée Ozenfant and Le Corbusier's *La Peinture moderne,* produced in 1927 from articles published in their periodical *L'Esprit Nouveau* (1919–25), displays one large and most elegant, plus two small, Cycladic figurines over the caption, believe it or not, "*Primitifs.*"[2] More subtly, the art historian Elie Faure, employing a juxtapository method also used by Corbusier to imply that works on facing pages show a comparably sophisticated development within different types[3] (and strongly influenced by Lamarckian evolutionism in biology), pairs a Cycladic figurine (dated seventh century B.C., however!) with a French Romanesque sculpture at the beginning of *L'Esprit des formes* (1927), the first volume of his general history of art; this is followed by a rather Egyptoid archaic Greek piece and another of the French Romanesque, leading into an extended series of pairings between classical Greek and classic French Gothic sculptures.[4] Nevertheless, Ozenfant's popular *Foundations of Modern*

---

1. Horatio Greenough, "American Architecture" (1843), in his *Form and Function: Remarks on Art, Design, and Architecture,* ed. Harold A. Small (Berkeley, 1958), 51–68, here 59.

2. [Amedée] Ozenfant and [Charles-Édouard] Jeanneret (called Le Corbusier), *La Peinture moderne* (Paris, n.d.), 30.

3. On the significance of this layout, see Reyner Banham, *Theory and Design in the First Machine Age* (London, 1960), 223–24.

4. Elie Faure, *Histoire de l'art,* I, *L'Esprit des formes* (Paris, 1927), figs. 4, 5 on pp. 2–3.

Art (1928) reproduces three Paleolithic figurines, one, the famous *Venus of Willendorf,* compared with a photograph of a fat woman in a one-piece bathing suit; only at the very end of his still-lively treatise does Ozenfant show what looks to be a Neolithic fishlike-Brancusian specimen, this not three times the same but once as-is—a "fairly 'good' form" that "can be improved"—then as if so improved by smoothing one juncture of tail and body, and finally as if "spoiled" by chipping a piece off and ruining the profile.[5]

Already quite early in the twentieth century, however, a certain *Urdummheit,* or "primal stupidity," in pre-Olympian Greek culture could strike even a classicist as rather more spiritually compelling. In the words of Gilbert Murray, "There is certainly some repulsiveness, but I confess that to me there is also an element of fascination in the study of these 'beastly devices of the heathen,' at any rate as they appear in early Greece, where each single 'beastly device' as it passes is somehow touched with beauty and transformed by some spirit of upward striving."[6]

It was above all Constantin Brancusi who in the classic phase of modernity carried over the spiritual intensity of the Neolithic into modern art, as Nietzsche would have understood. The actual influence of Cycladic sculpture on the master is complicated, apparently, by his having suffered from a textbook case of artist's influence-denial.[7] But Cycladicism patently constitutes a whole aspect of the work of this genius of modern sculpture. How obviously vital was his own profound Neolithicism is readily observed in the dissemination of Brancusi's work among the Constructivists. Thus the onyx *Torso of a Girl,* c. 1923 (Philadelphia Museum, Gallatin Collection), is illustrated in the British avant-garde publication *Circle: International Survey of Constructive Art* (1937) together with a *Bird in Space* and more or less Cycladicizing sculptures by Giacometti and Moore from 1936. Later, the resemblance of Brancusi's huge *Flying Turtle* of 1940–45 (Solomon R. Guggenheim Museum), to the highly abstract Cycladic and/or Anatolian figures (almost like chopping-knives) of "Kasura" type, is blatant. But that

---

5. Ozenfant, *Foundations of Modern Art,* trans. John Rodker (1931), augmented ed. (New York, 1952), illus. on p. 203 with comment on p. 199, and pp. 340–41, respectively.

6. Gilbert Murray, *Four Stages of Greek Religion: Studies Based on a Course of Lectures Delivered in April 1912 at Columbia University* (New York and Oxford, 1912), 16.

7. The question is surveyed in Angeliki Sachini, *Prehistoric Cycladic Figurines and Their Influence on Early Twentieth-Century Sculpture,* M.Litt. thesis, University of Edinburgh, 1984, pp. 85–96. Thanks to the author for kindly sending me a copy after the original version of the present essay appeared in the Ariadne Galleries catalogue *Idols: The Beginning of Abstract Form* (New York, 1989).

such are not merely formal likenesses may be appreciated with the help of Eliade, the historian of religion: "A half-literate person who revolutionized modern art! That seems unbelievable. And yet, if my point of view is accepted—namely, that Brancusi was a peasant who managed to *forget what he had learned in school* and thus rediscovered the spiritual universe of the Neolithic age—this exceptional creativity finds its explanation."[8]

The Surrealists deserve credit for retrieving Cycladic and related art from Puristic formalism and plumbing its spirit anew. Before a tall statuette of a helmeted bronze male nude, Levantine, from early in the second millenium B.C.,[9] it is natural to think of Giacometti. Even with Picasso, in whose paintings of around 1906–7 the influence of an "Iberian" art of about 700–200 B.C. is seen,[10] it now seems suggestive to look at the pliant, curvy little Iberian bronzes and to recall rubbery, attenuated figures in his Surrealistic paintings of the 1920s, while another larger Iberian figure of the sixth to fifth centuries B.C. even calls to mind otherwise supposedly "classical" figures by Picasso.[11] To speak more generally of Surrealist Cycladicism: that a Cycladic figure of "violin" type—or perhaps we should say "guitar," for reasons about to be seen—can readily be taken as a head, a torso, or both, no doubt owes something to a knowingly ambiguous superimposition of face upon torso in well-known examples of Surrealist art. That the first substantial publication of Cycladic sculptures in the Louvre, whose first piece was welcomed as early as 1872, and where Cycladic and also Anatolian "Kasura" pieces were on display since at least the turn of the century, occurred only in 1929 (a year after the publication of the British Museum collection, which also dates back to the mid-nineteenth century), also suggests the new contemporaneity in the later 1920s of such works.[12]

By the 1930s Cycladic and related sculpture was a handy exemplar of a certain timelessly "classic" but also availably *moderne,* lyrical-curvaceous

---

8. Mircea Eliade, *No Souvenirs: Journal, 1957–1969,* trans. Fred H. Johnson, Jr. (New York, 1977), 167, entry for 10 July 1962; emphasis in original.

9. In the Ariadne *Idols* catalogue, in which the other pieces mentioned here are also illustrated: cat. 104 on p. 101, with illus.

10. James Johnson Sweeney, "Picasso and Iberian Sculpture," *The Art Bulletin,* XXIII (1941), 191–98.

11. Ibid., cat. 140 on p. 119, with illus.; also, cat. 141, illus. on the same page (and in color on p. 48).

12. See, according to Sachini, *Prehistoric Figurines,* 68–69: Étienne Michon, "Idoles des Cyclades, Musée du Louvre," *Cahiers d'Art,* 1929, 251–57; F. N. Pryce, *Catalogue of the Sculpture at the British Museum,* Pt. I, vol. I, *Prehellenic and Early Greek* (London, 1928).

formal beauty. *Art Without Epoch,* subtitled *Works of Distant Times Which Still Appeal to Modern Taste,* a handsome album of black-and-white photographs of drawings, paintings, and sculptures to be savored, more than anything else, for self-evidently elegant form, opens with a plate of a third-millennium *Human Figure in Stone,* an "idol from the Greek Islands" in the collection of the Altes Museum, Berlin. Goldscheider, the compiler, comments: "Abstract forms, relying on the geometrical effect of light and shade; cubistic sculpture."[13] Significantly, the foreword to *Art Without Epoch* takes an ahistorical tack on behalf of a pure form "entirely bound up with our own time." Goldscheider doesn't actually use the term *form,* but does make clear that what is expected of the works shown is transhistorical with the initial announcement, "The history of religion has nothing to do with religious experience, and in the same way the history of art has no connection with artistic experience."[14]

But the finest modernist appreciation of Cycladic and similar art I know of is the passionate essay "About the Origins of the Doric Column and the Guitar-Woman," published by the Surrealist Wolfgang Paalen in the second number of his avant-garde periodical *Dyn,* in 1942.[15] First, considering that the Greek temples of classical times recapitulate an earlier wooden architecture, Paalen speculates on the origin of fluting with the use of the adze to dress logs for columns, stimulated in this by photographs taken by Eva Sulzer of timber buildings of the Northwest Coast Indians, photos that indeed convey a kinship of spirit as much as a formal resemblance. After pointedly contemning the "narrow utilitarian determinism" of "functionalistic" explanation, Paalen shifts to a row of five photos by Brassaï (and one drawing), a line-up of female statuettes as "very similar form-solutions" that are if anything all the more vivid thanks to differences of material and tools: two Alaskan "Punuk"-type figures, said themselves to resemble stone "idols" from Guerrero, Mexico (not shown), and then three Cycladic figures of the third millenium. Here the artist observes, "Among the prehistoric Greek statuettes from the Cyclades one sees a type so common and characteristic among the otherwise rare pieces of Cycladic origin that I feel justified in calling it the *guitar-type*"; also, "there exists a curious analogy to the stylization of Cycladic feminine idols into guitars: the Cubist

---

13. Ludwig Goldscheider, *Art Without Epoch: Works of Distant Times Which Still Appeal to Modern Taste* (1937), English ed. (London, n.d.), pl. 1, caption.

14. Ibid., foreword (unpaginated).

15. Wolfgang Paalen, "The Doric Column and the Guitar-Woman" as reprinted in his *Form and Sense,* Problems of Contemporary Art, 1 (New York, 1945), 50–53.

guitars becoming women." His point is not that either *derives from* the guitar: on the contrary, even the actual guitar is rooted in the very form of the female body we see so essentialized in the Cycladic figurines.

To Surrealism, too, one may trace at least some pseudo-Neolithicism encountered today in "postmodern" art. It seems barely a step from a bronze Arp *Idol,* of 1950, headless, with long swelling neck, shoulder blade–breasts, tapering waist, and punctuating navel,[16] to Joan Miró's bronze *Personnage* of 1973–81 (Fig. 4), cast from a plastic detergent bottle with added, tilted-square "head" and one extended arm. Of course there is also a "straight" modern sculptural tradition within which a preclassical, "Dorically" tough Neolithicism continues—as in a bronze asymmetrical brace of axelike forms whose title calls up the blacksmith of the Olympians, *Hephaestus III* (1971–72), by Dimitri Hadzi.[17] But now, with more pointed wit than revisionists usually summon, the postmodern sculptor Saint Clair Cemin has carved of mahogany an eight-foot-tall, mock-monumental *Sophie Sauvage*(!) (1989) in suavely pseudo-Neolithic—and also pseudo-Brancusian—style, whose head with protruding bangs(!) is itself like one of the inverted Anatolian head-torsos.[18]

No one who loves modernity, and more or less necessarily, with it, the Neolithic as mankind's true, initial modernity, can be pleased to see it handled as simplistically as Neolithic sculpture also was in the 1920s. It was a little too easy for Léger, another Purist, to have assumed that in aesthetically embracing an aircraft propeller as if it were Brancusi's utterly neo-Neolithic *Bird in Space,* people were necessarily surmounting the natural state in Nietzsche's sense: "You will find aeroplane propellers as wall ornaments in a popular dance-hall. Everybody admires them, and these propellers are very close to certain modern sculpture."[19] Yes; but what happens when it's a propeller instead of art—including his? Then it must be time to look again for general purposes of inspiration at genuine Neolithic art.

---

16. Illus., Michel Seuphor, *Arp,* Universe Sculpture Series (New York, 1961), pl. 10.

17. On whom, see my "Dimitri Hadzi's *Omphalos* for Harvard Square," *Arts Magazine,* LX/9 (May 1986), 62–64.

18. In the article by my former student Kirby Gookin, "Between States of Being: Saint Clair Cemin," *Tema Celeste* (Syracuse, Sicily), VII/3 (July–September 1989), 44–47, illus. on p. 46.

19. Fernand Léger, "Painting and Reality (Contribution to a Discussion Between Aragon, Léger and Le Corbusier)," in Myfanwy Evans, ed., *The Painter's Object* (London, 1937), 14–20, here 18. Cf. my essay "The Propeller and the *Bird in Space,*" below.

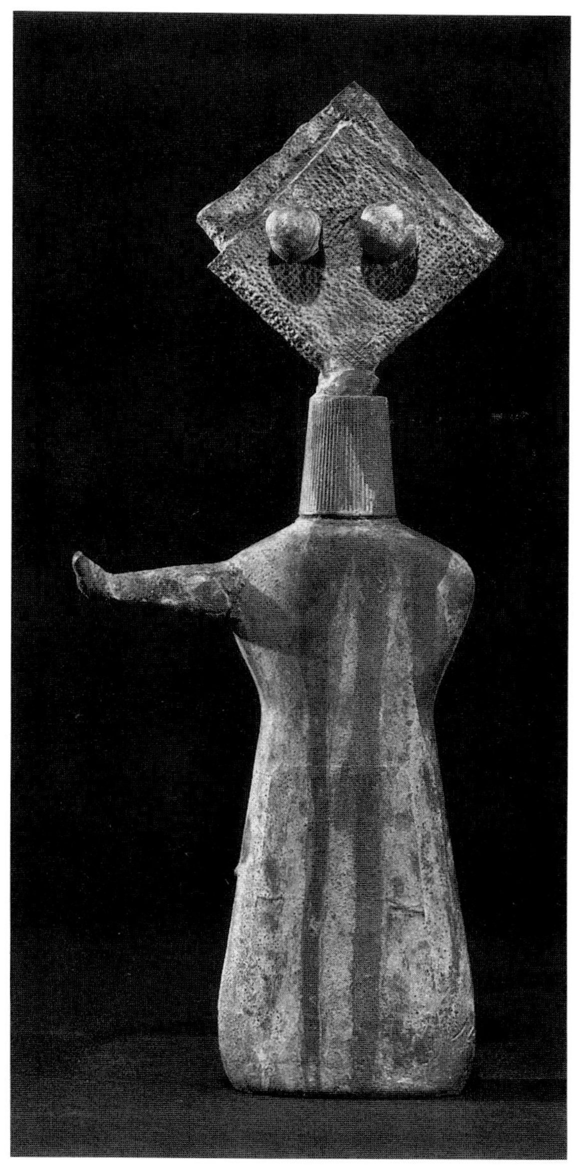

Fig. 4   Joan Miró, *Personnage*, 1973/81, bronze, 13¾ x
5½ x 2½ inches (edition of two).

3

NEOLITHIC-MODERN

There is hardly any time, never enough, not in this vulgar culture of the "bottom line." Is it any wonder people talk as if modernity were over with? But if Nietzsche is right the health of spirit cannot be so frail. No; purest thought and care persist, compounded on the triumph of the artful Neolithic makers. And in a catacomb culture, reverence for the past, devotion of memory, spending present time, may be radical.

A "small, heavy axe" one object is called by Max Loehr, a stone whose working dates perhaps from the Shang dynasty (Fig. 5). It looks heavy enough, though tightly, trimly so. Too beautiful to use, it seems, except in some sanctifying way. A joyful surety fills the transparent envelope of the thing's sheer form, as if the most artful turning of an edge could overrule entire wars. What a patiently powerful mass this is, sweeping and swelling like bold ridges in a peaking ocean. More than the mesmerizing pucker of Rilke's "Archic Torso" it calls to mind Winckelmann's barely contained passion for a single knee of one Greek statue, maybe even for one favored ripple in that knee. A hole, conically drilled with care against shocks to the stone's utter microstructure is off-centered so ultracarefully, placed by

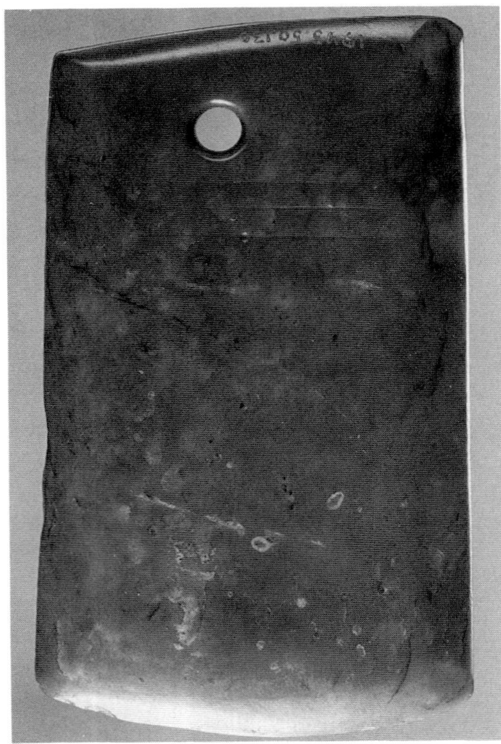

Fig. 5   Jade Axe, China,
probably Neolithic (c. twentieth century B.C.), fine-
grained, smoothly polished,
variegated light and dark
brown nephrite, 11 x 6.5 x
1.4 cm.

learned instinct right where it ought to have been until mountains
crumbled, had God drilled it into the exquisitely bowed flank of this sleek
mass.

Beauty this full almost has to be infertile for spending itself as if in a
single gasp, unlike the tedium of all mundane change and "progress." Only
what has blazed forth bravely out of barbarism into fineness can have had
the strength to come this beautifully to rest. Atomic missiles are a mere
spinoff of great work such as this, which shows all natural grossness
rendered up to mind.

What a perfect setup for the fresh reaffirmation of, as it were, neo-
Neolithic possibility in Malevich's *Suprematist Painting: Rectangle and Circle*
(Fig. 6) of probably about 1915 (though perhaps presenting itself as redone

Fig. 6 Kasimir Malevich, *Suprematist Painting: Rectangle and Circle,* 1915, oil on canvas, 43.1 x 30.7 cm.

later). In this consuming little painting a disc of black surmounts a vertical rectangle of sorts, both embedded in a field of white, although, as usual for this genius of articulated feeling, the quadrilateral is far too lively to pass for just another rectangle. Significantly, the brushwork varies: baldly flat in the disc, mossily pliant in the quadrilateral, lightly and leafily curling in the field. To my eye the black disc shows red (has it been altered?), while the so-called rectangle is a richly brooding blue, deeper and more thickly canvassy than even that of new dungarees. Both relate in an astute balance of attraction and repulsion, the one like some satellite that would fly off into the void but for the other's vigilant gravity. Off-center with respect to this blue zone, which itself stands slightly to the right within the all-enclosing white of the thing-at-large, the black disc hovers right above the quadrilateral's lefthand edge, which, now inescapably, is seen to tilt up leftward, rising to meet it. Thus suspended, midway between the painting's given upper rim and the defined upper edge of the zone of blue, the disc might seem to bob between the outside of the sprightly blue internal form and the interior limit of the concrete-objective canvas—were, that is, its placement not already optimal. Perhaps the tapering hold of the ancient axe shows up this palette-size painting as spreading the palette form out, inverted, with thumb-hole outside instead of within, since as a punctuation of the white field the black dot is also like a hole.

Now, please, another piece from China: a jade Shang dagger blade as distinctly directional in shape as some sharp tooth all set to gash, yet with formalities of restraint written all over it (Fig. 7). So finely adjusted, in fact, are its details that it seems designed more for intimate connoisseurship of eye and hand than for stabbing, displaying, that is, as much *lilt* as *lunge*. A vital asymmetry has top and bottom different, and most intensely toward the point, though how these edges kink in at the neck in different lengths also gives reason to understated parallel "collar" bands, transverse, one adjusted to the longer edge above and the other to the shorter one underneath. Similar bands, tighter for being more insistently incised, occur as ribbed horizontals on the flange of the hilt or *tang,* these intensely "expressed" in silhouette where they curve tautly around the edge. Consider, too, the punctures, major and minor: each falls along the axis of its respective part, their mutual disjunction conveying a shift, as from rest to action, in a sweep that begins all the way back where, of the three incisions of the end (where the hilt bands cut into the edge like bailing wire) the two that divide the half-widths of the hilt into halves again form

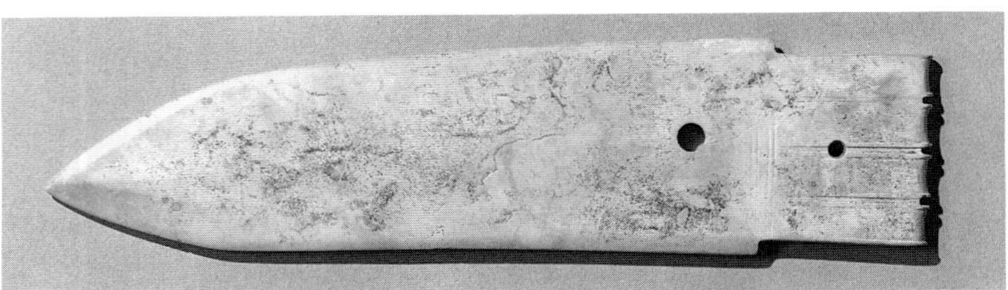

Fig. 7   Jade Dagger-Axe with Grooved Tang, China, Shang dynasty (second millennium B.C.), ivory-colored jade, Shang dynasty, 30 x 7.3 x .9 cm.

points of an equilateral triangle with the hilt's, or "lesser," puncture. This may be challenging to describe, but the real thing gathers all forces into the blade itself, shifting over the transverse collar as with the twist of a human wrist, into the dagger's business end. How instrumental this item ever was as a weapon is one question, how such beautiful thought in work implies enduring value in living, quite another.

Brancusi made a small yellowish-marble piece as elegant as this in Paris in 1920, a little arm (*not,* we are told, a child's hand, which would imply natural scale) (Fig. 8). Here, actually, is a special kind of distilled extrapolation from work already done by the same artist. For, as H. W. White observed, this is the same form as the lovely hand and arm, one of those folded so gracefully under the chin of Brancusi's totally streamlined head of *Mademoiselle Pogany,* made first of, also grainy, marble in 1912. If the entire Gothic was ever implicit in a pointed shoe, here in flagrant voluptuousness is all of bodily abstraction. Who knows what Duchamp might have thought of this anticipation of his later, pseudo-"abstract" pieces derived negatively as casts of female body parts (he might also have liked the fact that the arm was carved in France and yet is an English "foot" in length). Today there is something, too, of Bruce Nauman here, in the way, when set down, this lone and baseless arm presses down so transitively flat, practically a sculptural instance, impossibly enough, of "one hand clapping."

Now, uncannily, Joel Fisher, who for years has made tiny drawings by magnifying certain "imperfections" in his handmade papers, has on his own come across what might as well be the detached Pogany motif. It cropped up first in a paper piece of 1982 (Fig. 9), then developed into a

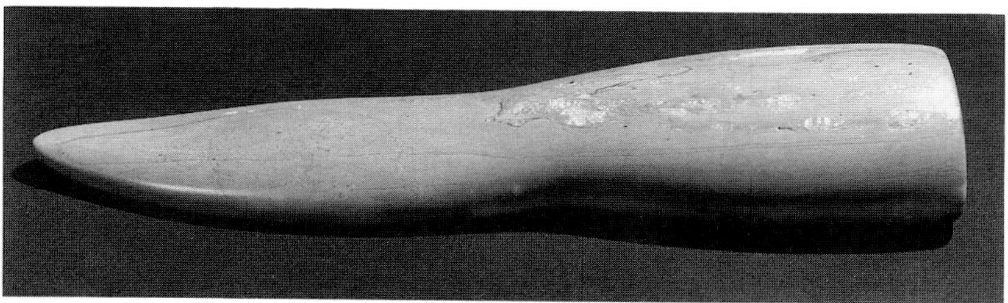

Fig. 8   Constantin Brancusi, *Hand of Mademoiselle Pogany*, 1920, yellow marble, length 30.35 cm.

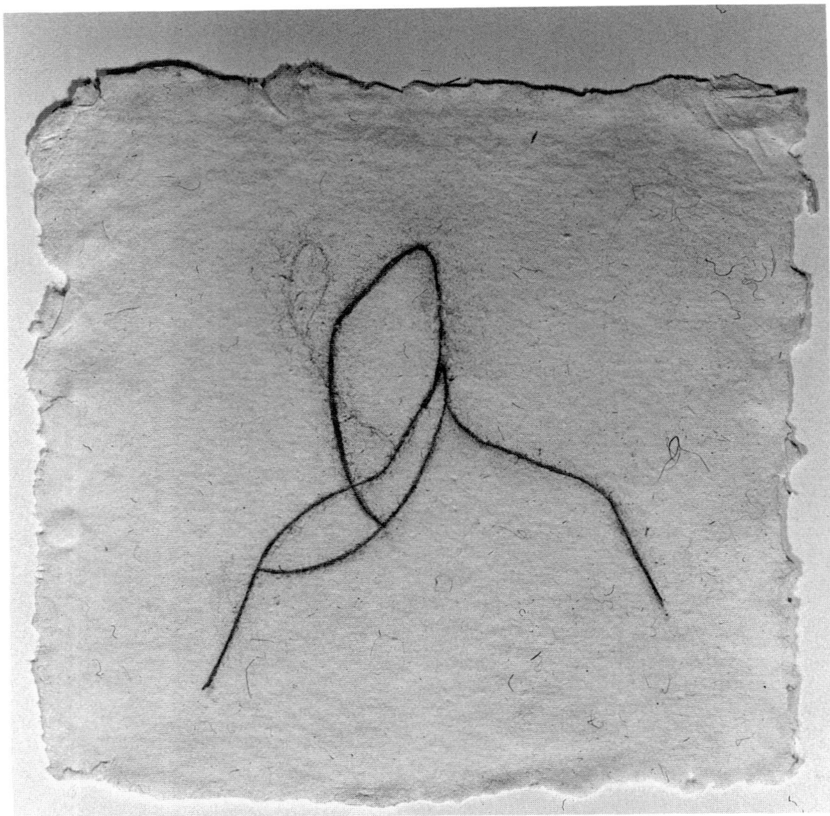

Fig. 9   Joel Fisher, *Drawing (for "Papabilus")*, 1982, conte crayon on handmade paper,
15 x 15 cm.

full-sized bronze bust called *Id* (1982–84), which thus became *Mademoiselle
Pogany*'s doppelgänger (little could Brancusi know), and finally became a
unique etching (1983) that thus puts the whole thing back onto paper, if
not the actual sheet from which it first was teased. So all the grand industry
of bronze, as the old Chinese would have understood, gets gathered back
into the fragility of the single leaf, as thin but as supple as culture itself.

ARCHITECTURE IN REVIEW

It was an interest in modern architecture, as I remember, that led me into the history of art. That at college I was also absorbed by literature, together with a third fruitless attempt to master the calculus, finally distracted me from an architectural career. But studying literature and art at once encouraged a sense of the culture-historical significance of forms. Any "formalism" with which I have ever been associated (to take advantage of the passive voice) derived more than anywhere else from the specially literary "New Criticism" that still throve in the early sixties, while a certain distaste for iconography only rendered all the more appealing the abstract forms of architecture.

Here I present three short pieces of general interest. The first of two book reviews, that on the letters exchanged among members of "The Crystal Chain," permitted me to extend an interest in German Expressionism to the speculative thought of Expressionist architects; it directs light into certain more introspective corners of Expressionism. By comparison, the review of Banham's study of American "daylight factories" and grain elevators, both types of great interest to European modernists early in this century, comes out into the sunlight.

Like an exhibition review, only of a building, the essay written on the opening of James Stirling's Sackler Museum at Harvard is a "take" more than a thoroughgoing white paper; yet it let me approach, in some small specific detail, the question of more or less purely modern survivals or continuities through the Postmodern architectural transformation. Besides, as a response to a Harvard building that I watched being built, this piece reminds me that it was while teaching on Quincy Street down from the Sackler, at the Carpenter Center for the Visual Arts, by Le Corbusier, that I conceived some of the rather more developed ideas in this book.

4

EXPRESSIONIST FANTASIAS: THE CRYSTAL CHAIN LETTERS

(Review of *The Crystal Chain Letters: Architectural Fantasies by Bruno Taut and His Circle,* edited and translated by Iain Boyd Whyte [Cambridge, Mass.: M.I.T. Press, 1985])

What on earth is this? Out of an Expressionist cabal, in the spiritual slump after World War I, comes a cache of architects' letters written in Germany from late 1919 through 1920 and exchanged privately in multiple copies. The "Gläserne Kette," or Crystal Chain, was a kind of club of avant-garde pen pals carrying on a speculative free-for-all that was at once schoolboyish and freemasonic (*we* know what building *really* means), yet also daring and very serious. The circle included Bruno Taut, Walter Gropius, the remarkable Hermann Finsterlin and others. Its thinking careens back and forth between inanity and brilliance, evidencing an almost "Beat" Expressionist integrity that now seems only more poignant by tinges, and some binges, of self-conscious mannerism.

Reading this collection of all the known correspondence is like eavesdropping; at first, one gets only drab stuff while straining to unscramble the more important, garbled things. The very setup can be trying: a circular game of catch in which one's mind will wander only to be called back by a medicine ball in the solar plexus. When the letters are about the correspondence itself, they are trivial: who has sent or gotten what, somebody's trouble with a Thermofax machine, why does *X* keep mum, etc. But it's worth persevering, for there's plenty in here if you work at it.

Like Expressionists at large, this baker's dozen of philo-architectural correspondents, who identified themselves by secret tags, was dissatisfied with the "Secession" mentality of the turn of the century and its acceptance of an incidental role for art in life. Bruno Taut, alias "Glas," got the circuit running, and his own Glashaus, that famous centralized, faceted, budlike building at the 1914 Deutscher Werkbund exhibition in Cologne, is the real seed for a number of designs by other members of the circle. Taut founded a Works Council for Art in the revolutionary circumstances of 1918; after the Nazis came to power, he was to spend three years in Japan, and his last three in Istanbul. In the group, Taut's letters are among the most significant, especially insofar as the Crystal Chain paralleled the early, Weimar, Bauhaus. The Chain gang pursued a kind of spiritual speculation that at the actual Bauhaus would become, whether by default or by design, the province of the pure painters Kandinsky and Klee, once they arrived (soon after this correspondence ends) in 1921. Hence painting is fairly unimportant in these letters. For an opposite reason, Dada obviously doesn't rate either: while indulging their own "crazy" smarts, the Dadaists just didn't give a damn about the spiritual condition of the cosmos. And that wouldn't do in the Crystal Chain.

As writing, the corpus of letters owes much flare, not to overlook some wearing mania, to contributions by (hysterical) Hermann Finsterlin, a.k.a. "Prometh," who appears surprisingly normal in a 1918 photograph in which he and his wife, profiled in twin, overlapping planes, à la Roman double portraiture and also Franz von Stuck, look with confident resolve leftward and upward into the future. Finsterlin's thought, most relentlessly Nietzschean in its aphoristic dazzle, is also precociously surreal, not to say proto-postmodern, in its narrative breakdown under imaginative overload.

As one might expect from these semiprofessional weirdos letting it all hang out, a rootedness in German Romanticism makes itself felt. Indeed, early on, Taut sounds a very German Romantic call in phraseology that recalls Carl Gustav Carus and others: "My sign language—to be the hieroglyph myself" (26 December 1919). A remark by the Czech designer Wenzel Hablik (and was his handle, "W.H.," meant to allude to the mysterious Shakespearean "Mr. W.H."?) is reminiscent of Blake on Joshua Reynolds: "And they smashed their slates into fragments and broke up ruler, triangle, and plumb-line. For the bird, the wasp, and the spider said that these were to blame for leading them into temptation in the first place" (28 July 1920). Enough, too, can be considered Whitmanesque, comparable to the way Whitman was welcomed in the *modernolatria,* as it has been called, of Italian Futurism.

The writers trade so freely in figurative language that their meanings are often lost, rather than fixed, in time. Much as common speech is loaded with so-called dead metaphors, this fascinatingly hermetic discourse contains figures that may or may not have transmitted what they seem to be saying. Take a remark in Finsterlin's "The Eighth Day" (i.e., of Creation): "Does not the dome of St. Peter's peer Lilliput-like from the depths of Messina like a giant sea urchin whose spines have been removed?" (undated). To this Hablik responds, "Should I therefore never build a dome because you compare Michelangelo's misfortune with the corpse of a cactus?" (28 July 1920). As is evident from the context, Finsterlin was defending himself against the accusation that his designs were imitative of natural form (what interested these artists was the *inorganic* naturalism that first becomes an issue in the *Goethezeit* and remains one down through the period of electron microphotography); Finsterlin's claim is that even Michelangelo's dome could be approached in the same way. So, then, is Hablik—evidently prepared to trash the dome, if only because it was uncool to use it to argue from authority—just giving the idea a little extra twist, or has he missed part of the point? The example is not momentous, but it says something about the way the reader has to do some demystifying hermeneutics.

The drawn projects by these adepts appeared in "public" publications as well as these private circulars. Some, particularly by Taut, are still impressive; others are interesting, though not necessarily intrinsically. True, it is easy to forget how new a design might have looked seventy-odd years ago; but there does hover an oddly 1950s-ish farfetchedness—something like the way the Sydney Opera House, say, looked forced even before it was finished. Even Erich Mendelsohn, after all, can remind us of Bendix washing machines and old Hoover vacuums. More affirmatively: examples of Hablik's calligraphic letters, also reproduced, are beautifully Massonesque. And something curiously akin to the entropic aesthetic of Robert Smithson appears, both in Finsterlin's writings and in certain of his drawings that are downright Smithsonesque—items such as a *Fantasy* by Wilhelm Brückman (code name, "Berxbach") and *Crystals,* by Paul Goesch (alias "Tancred"), both of 1920.

The issue of "paper architecture," with architecture on strike against the way things were in the world, was implicit in the very formation of the Crystal Chain as a means of sharing ideas and fantasies *instead of* building buildings. That, for a time, in the summer of 1920, some participants found an alternative outlet in film projects, is telling in light of the similarities between architecture and film as at once collective and auteuristic. Of course, the films didn't actually get made either, but theoretical aficionados of proletarian shoes in modern art and theory (I allude, of course, to van Gogh) will take interest in the wooden clogs of Bruno Taut's scenario after Hans Christian Andersen's "The Shoes of Fortune"—a script also notable for its Brechtian touches. As the exchange of communiqués draws to an end, the making of projects seems to have become unsatisfying, especially when the drawings wind up as simply another form of "studio art." While utopian thought was important for these artists' creativity and revolutionary spirit, it began to seem as if getting something done might be nice, and maybe even in one's own (life)time.

Now, however, this scrapbook, if not scrap heap, of ideas running wild offers much to consider on the subject of the spiritual claims of Expressionist art. Take the problem of an architectural transcendental that haunts the well-known opening sentence of Nikolaus Pevsner's *Outline of European Architecture* (1942), which maintains that a bicycle shed is a building but that Lincoln cathedral is a piece of architecture. It's easy enough to follow Hans Luckhardt (or "Angkor") when he says, "I am becoming more convinced that not only religious buildings represent the highest form of architecture, but that any building can reach this height if it embodies an intense and profoundly human 'Zeitgeist'" (31 May 1920). But then a passage in Taut's "My World-Picture," one that also invokes Meister Eckhart, might seem to open the possibility of a diffused and desacralized (yet perhaps transparently Protestant) religiosity: "The slope of the kennel roof, the cubic form of the most humble living-room, and every color too—all derive from the rays of the 'astral' crystal. In the final analysis nothing is formless—right to the limits of the Universal Nothingness" (19 October 1920). By the same token, might not the tone of the later Crystal Chain texts, characterized by Iain Boyd Whyte as "confessional," also be considered confessional in the Protestant denominational sense of the word, as in the standard rendering of Klee's contemporary *Schöpferische Konfession* (1920) as "Creative Credo"?

While we're at it: according to Whyte (any relation of Lancelot Law W., the naturalist of "form" so culturally influential a generation or so ago?), Taut's faith "was not specifically Christian." Yet this claim is made in a paragraph that details Taut's sense of the Kingdom, his involvement with the Apocalypse and his close reading of three mystics, not just the ever-trendy Eckhart. Somehow the claim seems square, much as ordinary television characters today never get to say or do anything religious unless it's their quirk. Nobody seems to have forced Taut to say that "architecture must become a gift of God, a heavenly blessing" (13 March 1920)—and how downright Lutheran, one might have thought, this notion of art as *grace*. Walter Benjamin's "Theologico-Political Fragment" (1955) may be of some help: "Nothing historical can relate itself on its own account to anything Messianic"; and yet, as at least those of the Crystal Chain who took up building could have understood, it is "through being profane," as Benjamin said, that "the profane assists . . . the coming of the Messianic Kingdom."[1]

---

1. Walter Benjamin, "Theologico-Political Fragment," in his *Reflections: Essays, Aphorisms, Autobiographical Writings,* ed. Peter Demetz, trans. Edmund Jephcott (New York, 1978), 312–13, here 312.

5

TEMPLES TO THE DYNAMO: THE "DAYLIGHT" FACTORY AND THE GRAIN ELEVATOR

For S. E. R.

(Review of *A Concrete Atlantis: U.S. Industrial Building and European Modern Architecture, 1900–1925,* by Reyner Banham [Cambridge, Mass.: M.I.T. Press, 1986])

So this is what the late Reyner Banham was up to in recent years. His classic *Theory and Design in the First Machine Age* (1960) is one of the few books on modern art I have ever enjoyed from cover to cover. *A Concrete Atlantis* is more specialized, but it too sustains intellectual excitement through patiently efficient analysis, research, and critique. Three long essays, two typological and one historiographic, together generate a convincing revisionist sense of the significance of engineered industrial building in America to European architects in the formative stage of modernism. Banham treats two building types, the reinforced concrete "daylight" factory and the classic grain elevator. Not vernacular and by no means anonymous, both were only recently established and, ironically, already obsolescent when for Europeans they became emblematic of with-it, truly twentieth-century design.

Interest in such material is not altogether new. For instance, Ada Louise Huxtable published articles on a couple of principal progenitors of the daylight factory in *Progressive Architecture* in 1957 (studies not noted in Banham's book). *A Concrete Atlantis,* however, takes on two entire building classes and brings their specifics into sharp focus. It is the result of much legwork as well as of important textual research. And I do mean legwork, such as climbing out of a motorboat in the Buffalo River and over a mountain of garbage to hold up a Xerox to see if something is just what Erich Mendelsohn once photographed. So Banham has surveyed, and in surveying illuminated, bodies of material that once looked specialist and exceptional and that now have their local and far-reaching art histories revealed.

Revisionism is never altogether easy to take, precisely because it's not simply a matter of proving the other guy wrong. One or another sacred cow does now have to move over a little.

Banham's treatment of Frank Lloyd Wright's demolished Larkin Building in Buffalo is a case in point. The loss of the 1904 office block (in 1950, after dereliction) is one we can all lament, even those for whom it was a favorite target for potshots against "Functionalism." Nor was Banham about to celebrate the building's disappearance. What he does show, however, is that the Larkin Building was only the centerpiece of a whole complex of non-Wright Larkin Company structures dating from slightly before and slightly after, much of which survives as a museum of exactly the kind of building the author is at pains to rescue from anonymity and premature generalization.

Closer to home: no longer, thanks to Banham, can one bomb through Bayonne, New Jersey, oblivious to Ernest L. Ransome's Pacific Coast Borax factory. On casual glance, it's a dog of a building, which, if not exactly lovable, does have redeeming features and historical importance. It was here, in 1902, that a serious fire stamped reinforced concrete construction as officially superior to bare steel.

Throughout his book, Banham is especially concerned with another of Ransome's buildings—the United Shoe Machinery Company, 1903–6, at Beverly, Massachusetts, which is related by more than international corporate patronage alone to none other than Walter Gropius and Adolf Meyer's classic textbook Faguswerk project, of 1911–14, in Germany. Later, in his more reflective third chapter, Banham's deliberately overcompensatory, nitpicking analysis of that monument exercises a refreshing but in no way philistine iconoclasm. Now maybe this is stretching things a bit, but under

the influence of Banham's stimulating thought it might even be possible to
see in Gropius and Meyer's famous model factory at the Cologne Werkbund
exhibition of 1914 not just the usually perceived Wrightean influence, but
also some echo of the final disposition of Albert Kahn and Edward Grey's
Ford Old Shop, 1908, near Detroit, as illustrated in the important Werkbund yearbook for 1913.

It must have been difficult for Banham to stick to the rigors at hand, for
the possibilities of tempting sidetracks occur at many points in his trimly
fluent narrative. For example, there is Banham's small point (in context)
that the daylight factory carries elements over from warehouse practice.
But isn't it important to acknowledge that the dynamic and irreducibly
human purposes of a factory absolutely contradict those of the properly
inert warehouse, with its thingly storage of materials and wares away from
harm of light? How much, then, would the first glass walls, despite
antimodernists, have looked distinctly *un*like warehouses—especially if one
recalls the typical *Warenhaus* of the old North German cities of the Hanseatic
League (a row of which was once sketched, nicely, in a letter by the young
Friedrich Engels).

A different issue suggests itself with Ransome's patented "Unit Construction System" for factories, a system that happened to precede by a
mile Le Corbusier's "Dom-ino" idea: to what extent was Ransome's system
prefabricational? Perhaps before a system can be considered prefab, enough
of its elements must be capable of serving in more than one way. Otherwise,
any building taken apart and put back together would have been "prefab-
ricated." Let's just call that food for further thought, though the question
does seem to hover over the figure of Henry Ford, his plants and their
products, if not over assembly-line production per se.

Do I find any of these objects of Banham's surprisingly winning
infatuation beautiful? Yes, but that's too easy an answer if it ignores
distinctions among the picturesque, the beautiful, and the sublime. Some
of these items are certainly *groovy,* regardless. The United Shoe Machinery
plant is an interesting case: it's so busy trying to be architectural in a
square way that you have to catch it unawares to see how good it actually
is—like, for comparison's sake, the surprisingly fine gymnasium of North-
eastern University in Boston, seen in just the right receptive mood. Banham
himself can get rather engagingly fussy in his connoisseurship of the various
works he discusses. For example, he seems hard on Albert Kahn's Packard
10 Building, Detroit, 1906, vis-à-vis Buffalo's Larkin C Building, erected
seven years later to company designs, but possibly this is because Kahn is

already known and, so, can "take it." A genuine stunner is the Larkin *R/S/T* Block, of 1911, by the prolific firm of Lockwood, Greene & Co. (originally of Boston, today New York), engineers—especially as seen in a pair of neo-1950s, rather Hedrich-Blessingesque photographs, one of a plunging, gleaming flank, the other a snappily squared-away end view, arranged as if in dress review for Ludwig Mies van der Rohe himself.

There is beauty indeed in the grain elevators (Fig. 10), something insistently unitary, segmental, repetitive, less "Gothic" than "Romanesque," whereas the factories keep offering unexpectedly self-conscious architectural detail. On the most elephantine scale the elevators offer a legible play

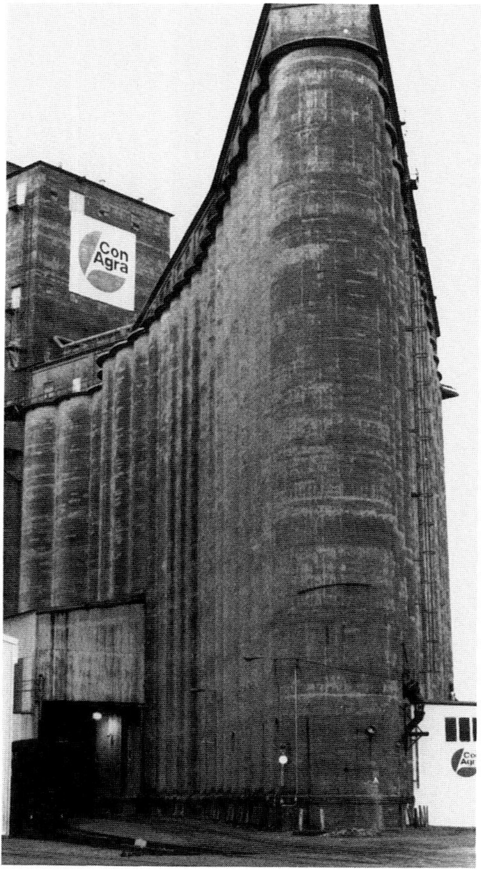

Fig. 10   Lake and Rail Grain Elevator, Buffalo, New York.

of units in regularly clustered, and also irregularly huddled, parts. Obviously, with these behemoths, sublimity is the dominant issue, but curiously enough I feel detained by the subtler question of their possible beauty, which may concern more than their regular, Constructivist (and proto-Minimal) aspect. A certain essential asymmetry and directionality of massing, whether accidental or determined, makes these structures seem arguably beautiful in a decidedly grandiose, Baroque way. What really must be sublime is the experience of viewing the largely disused but still almost intact array of huge cylindrical and prismatic elevators themselves massed along the winding banks of the Buffalo River. There, for one, the Washburn-Crosby (now General Mills) complex, ranging in date across the whole heyday of 1903–22, and though today past its glory days of World War I, is still majestic. And there, with A. E. Baxter's Standard Elevator of 1928, added onto during World War II, the whole type is clarified, fulfilled and consummated—and possibly confirmed, by then, by Corbusier's *Vers une Architecture* (1923; English translation as *Towards a New Architecture,* 1927) and the knowing modernism of the last generation.

Banham is a Constructivist at heart, but he is also a Constructivist with a heart. If by nature he likes structure that looks starched and pressed, the engineer in him is also interested in ad hoc, contraptional features. He proves capable, too, of appreciating Mendelsohn's Expressionist photographic take on the implicit moodiness—even before they assumed the easy melancholy of abandonment—of these spectacular, building-dominated sites. Unlike *Theory and Design, A Concrete Atlantis* is not concerned with painting in relation to the architecture at hand, although that architecture has the highest pertinence to a whole strain of Constructivistic architectural representation as abstract-concrete. Just that lineage ties O'Keeffe, Sheeler, and Niles Spencer not only to Ralston Crawford and ultimately Ellsworth Kelly, but to Christopher Wilmarth, William Tucker (in part), and others in latter-day sculpture as well.

After studying the factories and grain elevators, one is ready for the historical research and speculation of Banham's last chapter. Here, Walter Gropius—primed by that genius of engineered beauty, Peter Behrens, and the art theory of Wilhelm Worringer—appears as the figure most responsible for the reception of then recent American industrial building into the sphere of the new European *Baukunst,* where it actively displaced the fine-arts architectural tradition. Naturally, this version of the story tends to take some intellectual capital away from Le Corbusier, who might be said to have long ago won a MacArthur award for doing just that. Not that Banham has it in for Corbu, either; in fact, in this new book he takes the opportunity to extend the brilliant graphico-textual discussion of *Vers une Architecture* that was already a critical high point of *Theory and Design in the First Machine Age.*

At the end of *A Concrete Atlantis,* Banham sees the European cult of America as with-it condensed back into an Italian building of Futurist ilk—the famous Fiat-Lingotto automobile plant at Turin, by Giacomo Matté-Trucco and others, of 1914–26. Picking up in this section on a Corbusian trick of concluding a polemic with a turn of the page and a pictorial slap in the face, Banham attempts a verbal equivalent that does not quite work: his extended quotation from Edoardo Persico's wordy paean to the Fiat factory, though interesting as a moralized aestheticizing of Order, just can't function neutrally, given the political context from which it is drawn. I wish Banham had lived to have the chance, in a second edition, to write one more page and get the lid back on that can of worms. Unless, that is, he planned to look further still into the political problematic of "American Futurism" in Italy (as well as in the Russia of Lenin's New Economic Policy, where Albert Kahn was on direct lend-lease for factory design). In any case, the special scope of *A Concrete Atlantis* may be responsible for Banham's avoidance of European influences. After all, one can also see the Fiat plant, with its sheer on-rolling mileage of windows, as a descendant of Luigi Vanvitelli's early eighteenth-century Royal Palace at Caserta, which is likewise laterally sweeping and many-windowed, and which even has (Banham on Fiat-Lingotto) "cross blocks and light wells."

Though he is a transplanted European, Banham seems to have a provincialist axe to graind in *A Concrete Atlantis.* Despite New York's European image as capital of the twentieth century, he appears inclined to discount its importance. As for Buffalo, the state's second city, Banham likes it more for being where the Midwest begins. Yet so ready is he to share the Futurist desire for a Yankee-style pragmatic that he doesn't really bother with "local" American history. He doesn't consider, for example, the mentions of cement housing in Joseph Smith's *Book of Mormon* (1830), which surely reflect the discovery of natural cement in upstate New York, first at Syracuse in 1818, and then the important "Rosendale" cement, used in the construction of the Brooklyn Bridge, in 1825. And the Brooklyn Bridge itself (which was published as an engineering wonder in Europe even before its completion) may have yet further relevance: Banham refers to the reinforcing rods of "Ransome's unmistakable twisted square section (the subject of one of his earliest patents)." But is it mere coincidence that

Roebling's big breakthrough for the bridge specifically concerned the twisting of cable strands?

Furthermore, in pondering the legacy of the (brick) warehouse unto the reinforced concrete daylight factory, Banham might at least have mentioned James Bogardus's famous cast-iron facades on the downtown industrial lofts that now house so many of New York's young lawyers as well as the city's more prosperous artists. Reading *A Concrete Atlantis,* you would think we had to leave town for Bayonne just to find one daylight factory, whereas, according to the *A.I.A. Guide to New York,* we have William Higginson's Bush Terminal in Brooklyn, c. 1911, and the same designer's Sunshine Biscuit Company, 1913, in Queens—with the latter's facade having achieved typically New Yorkois universalizing diffusion thanks to the classic package design of Sunshine saltines. And, of course, nobody who has ever seen it will forget Cass—otherwise Mr. Woolworth Building—Gilbert's spellbindingly gigantic spaces in the Military Ocean (or Brooklyn Army) Terminal, of 1918.

Nevertheless, *A Concrete Atlantis* really does gain by its limits, and I hope my own thoughts here at least show how stimulating it is. *Daylight factory* can now become a common term.

6

LIVING MODERN:
JAMES STIRLING'S SACKLER
MUSEUM

The Arthur M. Sackler Museum at Harvard, by James Stirling Michael Wilford Associates (London), which opened in 1985, was initiated as a mere annex to take pressure off the neo-Georgian Fogg Art Museum (1927) across the street (Fig. 11). The project developed into a museum in its own right, modest in size but astutely thought through, for exhibiting, mainly, ancient and Oriental art. Curiosity about the building has stemmed from Stirling's reputation not only as a builder who formerly worked in extension of modern tradition, but also as an idea man with things to say about the relation of new architecture to old. His new museum must strike some as too allusively historicizing for "normal" modern, and others as too hopelessly modern to rate as "post-." I see the Sackler as steeped in speculation about what modernity might mean now that, say, a transparently "classical" sequence of rooms (galleries) that might have been laid out by Inigo Jones can present itself as timelessly abstract-geometric, whereas abstracted details from the classical vocabulary, especially *en collage,* already look like last year's trim from Detroit (Mies's revenge?).

A few weeks before the inauguration of the Sackler, and also in

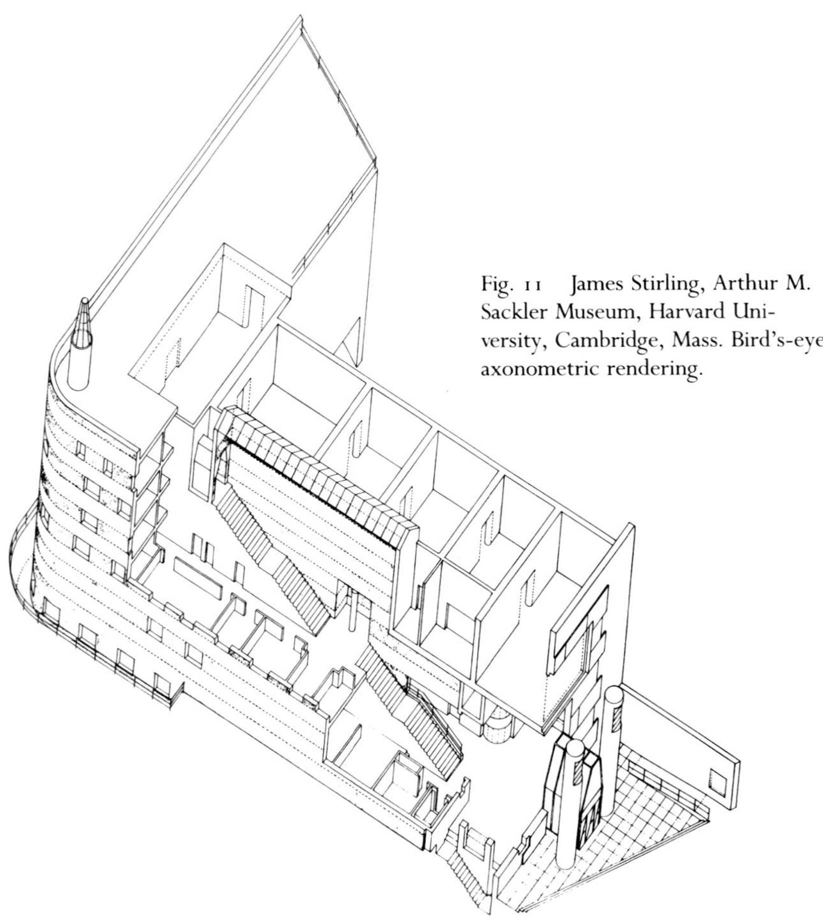

Fig. 11   James Stirling, Arthur M. Sackler Museum, Harvard University, Cambridge, Mass. Bird's-eye axonometric rendering.

Cambridge, M.I.T. opened its big new Jerome and Laya Wiesner Building, housing the M.I.T. Council on the Arts, a Media Laboratory and the List Visual Arts Center, the latter incorporating the Hayden Gallery together with the Baklar Sculpture Gallery and a "reference" gallery. The building, by—yes—I. M. Pei & Partners, hums with cybernetic efficiency. M.I.T.'s studio art program, the Center for Advanced Visual Studies, which one would have thought technically attuned enough, is not housed here; and, as to "media," apparently only things that can be plugged in or put onto a microchip need apply. The gallery spaces are serviceable but seem a bit like concessions to things left over from the world of those fragilely physical vacuum tubes of pretransistor times.

Otherwise, the only humane features of the M.I.T. project are, tellingly enough, three architectural collaborations by artists, who were brought in on the project at an early stage: Richard Fleischner provides a paved courtyard that locates the building, which looks less built than engendered by inorganic chemistry, in its surrounding visual space; Kenneth Noland's color bands in the chinks between panels of sheet-metal cladding add unabashed decorativeness to exterior and interior walls; a lobby bench and associated features by the late Scott Burton introduce a sculpturesqueness so winning that even Pei made an architectural response to it by altering certain structural curves. The collaborations themselves are fine; not so fine, the Reaganesque implication that (like cybernetic art?) big-deal architecture now has more important things to worry about than the art part, and can subcontract out the human touch. In a fast-lane way, Pei's Wiesner has to look "more modern" than Stirling's Sackler: amidst prevailing doubt, its fanatical, solid-state perfectionism seems, in the name of rationality, to ace out any deeper, pokily human consciousness.

In a season of museums "opening" like big shows (of themselves), Stirling's Sackler had an album of reviews: rather than rehearse all the stats on a house tour, I have preferred to use this occasion to comment broadly on this engaging building which I watched go up and have thought about a lot. Insofar as architects "solve problems," there is no doubt that the clever thing about the Sackler Museum is the way Stirling has packed together, almost puzzlelike, two narrow, tenementlike blocks—a six-story stack of offices and three double-height railroad flats of galleries—on either side of a single staircase that runs from bottom to top and practically from stem to stern. The staircase is in the tradition of rhetorically grand museum stairways; nevertheless, it is too, well, *housey*—narrow, tastefully makeshift, and serviceable—to be grand, even though tall and long. Eclectically enough, it puts me in mind of the nuttily tall and long domestic stairway of Fonthill Abbey, in the eighteenth century, though the generalized historical sophistication of Stirling's producerly "mix" seems more to the point than any specific sources, more or less remote. Especially in light of Stirling's contextualism of theory, the building's exterior deserves some critical priority anyway.

More thoroughly "designed," more densely worked, as architecture, than it might seem, the Sackler is surprisingly resistant to summary description. For instance, it has been said to rise from an "L"-shaped plan, which is true enough; but the "foot" of the "L" is the larger part, with the entrance in the "toe," opposite an end wall of the Fogg. Against a background of plain brick, the rather small facade is beefed up with a frontispiece of stone and glass, a pair of pylons like "Uni-Ball" pen caps, and a projecting glass vestibule (tip of "toe"). The stylish, upbeat complexity of the frontispiece Stirling has likened to a face, with perhaps significant casualness: he may mean either to outwit vulgar associationism, or to play on the sometimes preposterous literalism of architectural "semiotics," or *else* to imply, more consequentially for theory, that by now every hand one could deal has a full house of possible references. Actually, the whole entrance disposition (which may eventually have to change anyway with the addition of a bridge to the Fogg), while dapper, already hints at postmodern déjà vu—after all, the Sackler, raised between the new school of architecture (Gund Hall, 1972) and the Fogg Museum, was going to be *scrutinized*.

Truly more challenging, paradoxically or not, are the Sackler's radically plain side and rear walls, which wrap around a rounded corner with wide horizontal bands of alternating dark purple and sandy-toned brick. There are six whole bands of each, starting with dark at the bottom, plus another narrow dark strip up top and, finally, a little extra light brick connecting the flank with the light brick of the slightly higher and unstriped facade; more, shortly, on the little connection, which for now must seem like a fudge. Except for the first, street-level one, the dark strips are spliced, filmlike, here and there with just-plain windows that manage to look pointedly ordinary by a witty conflation of "cloth-coat" Yankee thrift and Venturian pro/antitastefulness. The architect is supposed to have pretty much just centered these windows in the rooms within, letting the chips fall where they might outside. If so, he was indeed lucky: they line up in rhythmic beats only to stretch nicely into unstressed syncopations further along. A maniacal positivist would have required complex mathematical determination to gainsay this serene an unfolding of simple form in variation. Well, this is cognitive too, boys!

For the opening, Stirling gave a genial and enlightening lecture at Harvard in which, however, homemade notions of "abstract" versus "representational" architecture became a nagging foible. His "abstraction" covers once standard functionalist nonobjectivity, while "representation" concerns adaptation to already built, and presumably not timelessly modern, surrounding styles. As long as Stirling is talking, the terms are serviceable; but on their own they are either mistaken (in prior, Venturian theory, the functionalist building is the *representational* "duck") or critically inadequate (as regards the "abstract" and naturalistically "empathetic" in Wilhelm Worringer's classic exposition). Stirling's twin terms are as undialectical as the Anglican "middle way" (you all argue first, then I can be liberal). Still, they do give access to his unusually penetrating working through of that most widespread cliché of popular architectural critique, the notion that a building ought to "fit in" or even "blend in" with its surroundings. Just to put it so points up problems: would the perfect building really dissolve completely into its context, without any but bit-part identity? And what about the next guy? Does he then have to characterize *this* building summarily, perhaps in caricature, before his own structure can be considered one of the array of different entities that must next be taken into account? And then, wouldn't all this guarantee eventual mediocrity?

What in theory is frustratingly hazy, however, can become interestingly complex in practice. With the Sackler, Stirling's eclecticism seems to involve whole past architectures—vernacular, historical, and modern. The artist seems to seek to make a new totality by evoking former totalities, not simply to make a new whole out of old spare parts. Here a vernacular aspect might obtain if the whole belted bulk of the Sackler is seen in terms of the "three-deckered" turn-of-the-century clapboard houses that abound in Cambridge, with their floors on a "side-hall" plan like that of the Sackler stairwell vis-à-vis the strings of offices (left) or galleries (right). Further, the odd little element mentioned above, which joins the facade and flank at the roof line with a couple of curious angles, can thus compare with the semihexagonal projecting bays typical of such originally working-class city houses, which sometimes, for that matter, have very irregular arrangements of windows on their flanks.

Everybody seems to notice that the alternating dark- and light-banded brickwork of the museum flank and rear wall echoes the longitudinally striped slate and terra-cotta tiling of the roof of nearby Memorial Hall (1878), by Ware and Van Brunt, a heroic crimson-brick pile that that the Michelin *Green Guide to New England* has the sheer French nerve to dismiss as "a bulky Victorian building." In this case, however, the visual parallel may only hint at a vital theoretical possibility that is not helped by Stirling's shallow *concept* of stylistic "representation." For if the Sackler really is tuned in on the wavelength of Memorial Hall, it should somehow be picking up on a Ruskinian ideal of the Gothic (including polychrome) that is not only one of the deep sources of modern theory but that was explicitly associated with programs for university museum buildings at Dublin and Oxford. Well, then, when one "represents" architecture architecturally, are generative ideas embodied in the "motive" building also necessarily carried over into its architectural "representation"?

Maybe the question is impertinently un-English in its sweep. The actual work of Stirling is sophisticated in the sense of architecturally knowing. It is no contradiction of this fact to notice in the Sackler a vague, pervasive, specifically British and unmetaphysical accent. Take, for instance, the earthbound entrance, including the slightly dotty climatological impracticality of its little step down; or the pudgy, semicolumnar wooden door jambs between the galleries, which manage to evoke what one might have thought the most unrevivably fugitive flavor of the British nineteenth century's own revivalism. In the close, almost maritime, quarters of the galleries most of the utilitarian hardware looks downright clunky, although the lintels of the same doorways make a formal virtue of necessity: in most, a centered hole (a few are blind) apparently serves some electronic security purpose, yet as dark circles these also line up smartly, marking as if for emphasis the formal idea of doorways in *enfilade*.

Also arguably British is the ocular central window, complete with optical trick, of Stirling's proposed bridge to connect the Sackler with the Fogg: by adjusting the penetration to the angle of the street below, this window manages to suggest Palladio's optical sense more than even Palladio's own or eighteenth-century English Neopalladian bridge designs, not to mention, for a more general classicism, Robert Adam. Typically for Stirling's contextualism, however, the bridge, once built, would also then "recall" the bridge punctured by classical windows (the center one round-headed) that already connects the Widener and Houghton libraries in Harvard Yard. (And since there is some local opposition to the Sackler bridge idea, let me say that I think it would look fine.)

However long the possible parade of local architectural kin, two proximate relations are of more than incidental relevance to this noted "later modern" British architect's signal American building. Inside the Sackler, in the stairwell—which is striped like the exterior but more gently, in painted plaster bands—the righthand, or gallery, wall is literally relieved by inset fragments of ancient Coptic architectural ornament. These small, venerable, abstract-ornamental fragments (collected, it happens, by none other than the distinguished aesthetician Nelson Goodman) are irregularly positioned over the vast expanse of wall (and can be studied from openings in the walls of the corridors on the office side). This kind of mural inlay finds adumbration in the entrance facade, likewise studded with ornamental reliefs of ancient and Renaissance style, of Robinson Hall, the old building still inscribed "ARCHITECTURE" diagonally across from the Sackler within Harvard Yard.

This "Architecture" connection is less than obvious only because Robinson Hall has its back to the Sackler. But if one walks down Quincy Street far enough to see its facade, what should turn up across the way, just beyond the Fogg, but the only American building of Le Corbusier, the 1963 Carpenter Center for the Visual Arts, housing Harvard's studio art program. For a long time I have mused over the idea that the Carpenter Center is a kind of *ars poetica,* a building about and in celebration of the building art. Suffice it to say, here and now, that this concerns the whole steamshiplike aspect of the building, as if in realization of the master's critical stimulation by modern ocean liner design 40 years before. Others have noted in Stirling's Sackler Museum occasional "portholes," shiplike railings and so on. Is it possible that, with so much more humility than I. M. Pei now occupying the site of Le Corbusier's catafalque at the Louvre, Stirling here quietly tips his architectural hat just over the head of the Fogg to Corbu, on the site where the old museum might once have been extended?

SCULPTURE AND THINGS

Compared with my devotion to painting, my concern with sculpture is less steady. Temperamentally, this may have to do with what seems like an off-duty, unredeemed materiality common in sculpture. Baudelaire felt similarly; and Gertrude Stein mobilized two premodern topoi in commenting that sculpture entails the bother of going all the way around it and that its material gives the impression of already having been formed beforehand. Of course, modern and contemporary sculpture does wrestle with just such issues.

The text on the "readymade" from my 1975 book on Duchamp was once unusual in insisting that Duchamp's found, manufactured *things* were indeed approachable as sculpture. Not unrelatedly, "The Propeller and the *Bird in Space*" is an attempt to come to terms with the problem of how even the modern art object must somehow be more than merely another object, even though popular familiarity with modern "styling," in relation to abstract sculpture, as with "design" in painting, once seemed to promise (all too) easy, demystified but also despiritualized, access to modernism.

Much contemporary sculpture has tended perhaps to outrun the limitations of substantial material presence rather than to transcend them; in painting, on the other hand, it is probably easier to get away with irony. Some of my most fruitful discussions of the question of *thingliness* in sculpture have been with Maureen Connor, whose work the next essay concerns; since I wrote it, Connor has significantly renegotiated Duchamp's ready-made bottle-rack form, specially refabricating it on large scale to a doubly ironical, quasi-naturalizing (!) purpose. Robert Gober's works play brainily against very commonplace forms, being anything but found things.

7

READYMADES: ART ACCOMPLI

The *Nude Descending a Staircase* may have announced Duchamp's modernity, but his most original contribution to the history of art was the readymade. A readymade is an ordinary manufactured object singled out and exhibited as art. The fundamental idea that value can be gleaned from unpromising sources was far from new (Shakespeare: "All places that the eye of heaven visits / Are to a wise man ports and happy havens," *Richard II,* I.iii.275–76). What was new was having nonaesthetic sources rise to the nobility of art with practically no artistic intervention. Duchamp's common objects selected from the real world vivified certain Cubist ideas about the concrete reality of the art object. The wit was in making a common object as remarkable as an art object at the same time.

Out of the plethora of origins for the readymade idea can be mentioned one peculiarly canny text from the Aesthetic Movement, a century ago. Its broader point is the relativity of beauty, against beauty of a conventional sort: "No object is so ugly that, under certain conditions of light and shade, or proximity to other things, it will not look beautiful; no object is so beautiful that, under certain conditions, it will not look ugly. I believe that in every twenty-four hours what is beautiful looks ugly, and what is ugly looks beautiful, once." These are the aestheticizing remarks of an admirer of Whistler's art of subjective sensibility; they come from a text known for its virtually Symbolist-Postimpressionist embrace of proto-abstract decorative significance, especially for the statement—"Primarily, a picture is a beautifully coloured surface, merely, with no more spiritual message or meaning . . . than an exquisite fragment of Venetian glass or a blue tile from the wall of Damascus."

In the same place this critic, by the name of Oscar Wilde, claims, "the commonplace character of so much of our English painting seems to me due to the fact that so many of our young artists look merely at what we may call [N.B.] 'ready-made beauty,' whereas you exist as artists not to copy beauty but to create it in your art, to wait and watch for it in nature." Needless to say, his terms now sound obsolete: not only the sense of the artist's outside world as basically "nature" but a sense of the unexpectedly art-worthy subject as specifically "picturesque," which comes right afterward. His spirit, however, is precocious enough: "of the young artist who paints nothing but beautiful things, I say he misses one half of the world. Do not wait for life to be picturesque, but try and see life under picturesque conditions. These conditions you can create in your studio, for they are merely conditions of light." Here again, sharing a Schopenhauerean detachment evident also in Whistler,[1] lingering Romanticism only disguises a fresh sense of that subject matter by which even a trivial piece of manufactured street hardware proves capable of fresh, unstereotyped artistic provocation: "In Gower Street at night you may see a letterbox that is picturesque."

Wilde's remarks derive from his lecture delivered at the Royal Academy Club, in London, in 1883.[2] Despite the possible "aesthetical" disqualifica-

---

1. Also of London: "And when the evening mist clothes the riverside with poetry, as with a veil, and the poor buildings lose themselves in the dim sky, and the tall chimneys become campanili, and the warehouses are palaces in the night. . . . Nature, who, for once, has sung in tune, sings her exquisite song for the artist alone"; James Abbott McNeill Whistler, "Ten O'Clock" (lecture, 1885; pub. 1888), in his *The Gentle Art of Making Enemies*, 2d ed. (London, 1892; repr. New York, 1967), 131–59, here 144; cf. the otherwise frightened Goncourts' aestheticizing description of the "picturesque" ruination of the Paris Hôtel de Ville during the Commune: *Pages from the Goncourt Journal*, ed. and trans. Robert Baldick (London, 1962), 193, entry for 28 May 1871. A sense of Schopenhauer's pertinence to the Anglo-American aesthetic of detachment may be gained from an utterly pessimistic short story written under the title "Schopenhauer in the Air" (1899) by the American critic who carried Whistlerianism into the Stieglitz avant-garde in the early twentieth century, Sadakichi Hartmann.

2. Oscar Wilde, "Lecture to Art Students," in *The Complete Works of Oscar Wilde*, XI, *De Profundis, Lectures and Essays*, ed. Michael Monahan and W. F. Morse (Garden City, N.Y., 1923),

tion, the vividness of the pointedly commonplace cast-iron mailbox as a kind of potential concrete correlative (admittedly for an embracingly "Impressionist" contextual experience of visuality that would have bored Duchamp) is uncompromised—even as followed by the less challenging suggestion that "on the Thames Embankment you may see picturesque policemen." Duchamp's hysterical anti-aestheticism is itself to a substantial degree an anti-*aestheticalist* response to the turn-of-the-century situation, pressed by one whose brothers were abler participants, in painting and sculpture, in the less evasionary, more revisionistically thoroughgoing, Cubist project of surmounting fin-de-siècle aestheticism.

The essential Cubist notion of the objective reality of a painting developed ultimately from Postimpressionism. Highly conceptual "Analytic" Cubism concentrated on this more urgently and, especially toward 1912, in a more critical way. Then in May 1912 Picasso made the first collage, the rope-framed *Still Life with Chair Caning,* attaching to the canvas a piece of real oilcloth, yet one which, by a nearly Duchampian irony, already actually *represented* chair caning. If Picasso, who had the benefit of Braque's moves in the direction of collage shortly before, had entitled the picture *Still Life with Oilcloth,* it could almost have been the first readymade as well as the first collage. Although Cubism had showed the capability of painting to *pres*ent reality as well as *rep*resent it, the concept of the readymade allowed Duchamp to introduce maximum *pres*entation and to reduce representation to the amusing redundancy of each object fully, accurately, and effortlessly representing itself both as a unique entity and as representative of some class of objects. This move involved an outwitting of Cubism in a chesslike way, where Duchamp had not done terribly well in the earlier stage of the painters' game. And it involved still more wit by overthrowing pictorial representation without resorting to abstraction, which in 1913 was coming into its own.

If a readymade is an amusingly self-representational sculpture, trivial in its motif, it is still sculpture nevertheless. Too much attention has been paid to the question of whether the readymade asserts or denies art, of whether it is in itself an art-object or an anti- or a counter–art-object. To deal with the readymade as sculpture is a subtler problem, even if its sculpturality seems absurd.

91–107, here 104–5. Another instance of the Wildean "Damascus tile" idea, from "Rose-Leaf and Apple-Leaf" (1882?; 1904), I have treated in Joseph Masheck, "The Carpet Paradigm: Critical Prolegomena to a Theory of Flatness," *Arts Magazine,* LI (September 1976), 82–109, esp. 95.

Once we admit Duchamp's readymades to the history of sculpture other insights emerge. It was Rodin who in the early years of modernism had developed the idea that practically every model is potentially beautiful as subject matter for sculpture. For Rodin beauty became virtually coextensive with the whole of life. Of course Rodin still assumed figuration, but his point was taken in opposition to the pseudoclassical tradition of a small number of subjects of implicit and guaranteed aesthetic value. His radically inclusive attitude toward the subject matter of sculpture opened the door through which the readymades eventually passed. As Rodin himself said, speaking of his deliberate violation of conventional beauty and pose in *The Walking Man* and/or *Saint John the Baptist,* "I only copied the model whom chance had sent me."[3]

In at least one case a readymade abstractly resembles a sculpture by Rodin himself. Duchamp's *With Hidden Noise* (1916)—in French, *A Bruit secret*—is an "assisted readymade" consisting of a ball of twine clamped by bolts between brass plates, with a mysterious object inserted by Walter Arensberg to rattle inside. As a cylindrical form tightly clasped by a pair of embracing elements it compares with Rodin's *The Secret,* of 1910, where a geometrical, pistonlike cylinder is firmly enclosed by a pair of (not un-Düreresque) hands. If Rodin's sculpture seems to differ too extremely in kind and form from Duchamp's, both are nevertheless very much involved with the sculptural idea of *clasping* a cylinder and with secrecy. Duchamp himself eventually produced an etching of Rodin's *The Kiss,* modified and entitled *Selected Details After Rodin* (1968).

There are also certain surprising affinities between Duchamp and Brancusi, the genius of modernist abstract sculptors. Both sent exhibits to the Armory Show in 1913. (Alfred Stieglitz would have a Brancusi show in his Photo-Secession Gallery in New York in the next year.) When the first sale of the John Quinn collection took place in Paris in 1926, Duchamp was invited to go to New York to arrange a Brancusi exhibition of works he had helped to purchase in Paris; he arranged another Brancusi show, again at the Brummer Gallery, in 1933.

Duchamp's difficulties with his *Fountain* (1917), the famous urinal readymade (signed "R. Mutt") that was rejected by the hanging committee of the New York Independents,[4] have a parallel in the rejection as obscene

---

3. Quoted, Albert Elsen, ed., *Auguste Rodin: Readings on His Life and Work* (Englewood Cliffs, N.J., 1965), 166.

4. Richard Hamilton pointed out that it was *present* at the exhibition, but behind a partition; see the Arts Council of Great Britain exhibition catalogue, *The Almost Complete Works of Marcel Duchamp,* 2d ed. (London, 1966), cat. no. 126.

of Brancusi's *Princess X* (1916)—abstract, but quite as genito-urinary in form—in Paris. When U.S. Customs maintained that Brancusi's works were not art but manufactured metal, Marcel Duchamp helped carry fifteen of the sculptor's works back on board ship to take them back to France and then on to an exhibition in Berlin. The *New York Times,* in its account of 27 February 1927, spoke of the sculptures Duchamp carried as being by "his friend Constantin Brancusi."

Brancusi's famous *The Kiss* (1908), in the Arensberg Collection, is one of the pieces whose acquisition at the Quinn sale Duchamp arranged. Thematically it relates to Duchamp's ink and charcoal *Study for Chess Players* (1911), which simultaneously represents two figures playing and two faces kissing, although the kiss motif was in wide currency from the turn of the century. In our own day, when Claes Oldenburg parodied Brancusi's *Kiss* in his print *Proposal for a Colossal Structure in the Form of a Clothespin—Compared to Brancusi's "Kiss,"* (1972) he used, in combination with a photograph of Brancusi's sculpture, a clothespin whose form is much like the figure identified by Duchamp as the "cuirassier" in his first *Cemetery of Uniforms and Liveries* (1913) study for *The Large Glass.*

Duchamp's readymades were an open-ended sequence of works begun after the *Nude Descending a Staircase* (1912), and concurrent with *The Bride Stripped Bare by Her Bachelors, Even* (1915–23; a.k.a. *The Large Glass*). They can be associated conceptually with the *Nude* and with such succeeding works as *The Passage from the Virgin to the Bride* (1912) and even *The Large Glass* itself. One connection is the theme of marriage and generalized female nudity, with a corollary involving the representative particularity of dressed males who are as identifiable by their work as the figures in Courbet's *Burial at Ornans* (1849–50)—the "malic molds" of *The Large Glass.* From this viewpoint, the readymade is an object *divorced* from utility, to play not only on the idea of divorce from a spouse but also on the idea of the unique but general bride as against the various but specific and typical potential husbands. Also, the readymades appeared as Duchamp the artist divorced himself from painting and began to present himself to his muse in various guises—thinker, worker in glass, chess player.

The "nine malic molds" of the *Large Glass* and the studies for them, beginning with the (eight) figures in uniform of *Cemetery of Uniforms and Liveries, No. 1* (1913), relate to the readymades because a man in uniform is a figure abstracted, an interchangeable representative of a type, a man with a ready-made identity. (The fundamental meaning of "ready-made" in English pertains to off-the-rack clothing.) In *Cemetery . . . No. 1* the uniforms are identified as those of a priest, a department-store delivery boy (the readymade *Bottle Rack* was to be selected the following year in a department store), a gendarme, a cuirassier, a policeman, an undertaker, a "flunkey," and a bellboy. Similarly, selection—*election?*—as a readymade implies an interchangeability with other, "peer" bottle racks, and at the same time raises that bottle rack to a different sort of peerage over and above all unennobled bottle racks (and other common or "commoner" objects), on the plane reserved for works of art. The ironic relation of "peer" in the sense of social superior to "peer" in the sense of social equal seems distinctly available in Duchamp's readymades, which really developed after his arrival in socially "leveling" America.

Duchamp began making readymades in Paris with the 1913 *Bicycle Wheel,* coined the term in New York in 1915—for *In Advance of the Broken Arm,* a snowshovel—and first exhibited the works as such at the Bourgeois Gallery (!) in New York in 1916, in a climate that for its own American reasons was already attuned to the idea of iconoclastic or anti-aesthetic subject matter in art. At the time of the Armory Show Robert Henri, for instance, had been advocating a radically inclusive attitude toward the subject matter admissible to painting. Stuart Davis noticed that for many painters of the time radicalism of subject matter actually became a distraction from abstract values, so that this otherwise progressive tendency had an ironic cut. Thus the readymades of Duchamp shared in a crucial dilemma of American art at the very time at which they joined it.

Actually, the readymades seem much more American than European, and Americans have probably had an easier time with them than Europeans. When Yeats saw the premiere of Alfred Jarry's proto-Dada play *Ubu Roi* in 1896 (for which Duchamp designed a bookbinding in 1935), he was bothered by the fact that the King's scepter was "a brush of the kind that we use to clean a closet."[5] As late as 1960, the director of the Kunstgewerbemuseum, Zurich—which normally exhibits applied art and design rather than art—could experience unaccustomed "laughs and smiles, little shocks and large wonders" on unpacking Duchamp's readymades. No doubt a people used to lawn planters made from tires, chandeliers from wagon wheels, and barstools from milk cans, is more predisposed to the readymade

---

5. Quoted in Edgar Wind, *Art and Anarchy,* rev. ed. (New York, 1969), 113 n. 16. Yeats's remark has a scatological implication if he meant a *water*-closet brush, which is possible because Jarry had been fascinated by such brushes on latrine duty in the French army; see Anthony Powell, "Proust as Soldier," in Peter Quennell, ed., *Marcel Proust 1871–1922: A Centennial Volume* (New York, 1971), 151.

idea than one dominated by canonical artistic taste: both approval and rejection can become wittily reversed and intensified. Duchamp's affection for America could sometimes seem patronizing, but it was real.

The essential commonness of the objects selected as readymades was also related to the everyday working aesthetics of the "Ash Can" School of painting in New York. Those painters of the grubby ordinariness of city life acquired their own collective tag in the very month in which Duchamp unveiled his readymade art in New York, April 1916. In the same year Hugo Münsterberg used the actual word "ready-made" in connection with the convincing representation of real life in the cinema. In his essay *The Photoplay; a Psychological Study* (1916) Münsterberg hailed the freedom from theatrical artificiality of the new art of film: if the producer "needs the fat bartender with his smug smile, or the humble Jewish peddler, or the Italian organ grinder, he does not rely on wigs and paint; he finds them all ready-made on the East Side."[6] It is not so far from the Ash Can attitude to the exhibition of a sanitary appliance as sculpture, especially when we note that—as with "dustbin" in Britain—"ash can" became a euphemism for a messier *garbage* can.

In one of his notes Duchamp proposes a "reciprocal ready-made": use a painting by Rembrandt as an ironing board. This unexecuted project has many implications. It obviously relates to the "corrected ready-made" *L.H.O.O.Q.* (1919), an ordinary photographic print of Leonardo's *Mona Lisa* with moustache and goatee added, whose title when pronounced in French means something like "She's a hot piece of tail" (also a late revision, without whiskers, *L.H.O.O.Q., Shaved* [1964]). There is a loss of confidence in the glory of painting, generating a hip iconoclasm in compensation for square idolatry. There is an assault on the detached, bourgeois sense of reality, of which the use of art as a pseudospiritual escape from the world of business and the abuse of the artist as an estranged oddball are merely aspects. A stretched, thickly coated canvas could certainly be used as an ironing board if anyone wanted to be utilitarian in the extreme. The only practical obstacles would be expense and the hilariously ironic fact that Rembrandt's *painterliness* (normally of such purely visual concern) would make it bumpy.

---

6. Hugo Münsterberg, *The Film; a Psychological Study; the Silent Photoplay in 1916* (New York, 1970), 50; the passage echoes certain texts of Hartmann. William James, also at Harvard, had used the adjective to describe spiritualistic believers: "They simply find various characters ready-made in the mental life, and these they clap into the Soul. . . . The soul invoked, far from making the phenomena more intelligible, can only be made intelligible itself by borrowing their form . . ."; *The Principles of Psychology,* I (1890; repr. New York, 1950), 347.

It is important that Duchamp mentioned Rembrandt in particular for this projected idea. Surely Rembrandt is the greatest exception to classical theories of selectivity and to modern theories of pure form. For instance, Sir Joshua Reynolds, in his sixth *Discourse* (1774), encouraged young art students by saying that it is sometimes possible to produce great work despite inadequacies in theory or method, using Rembrandt's very indiscriminateness of subject as an example: if one "makes no selection of objects, but takes individual nature as he finds it, he is like Rembrandt." The readymades are also about taking reality as one finds it, although the reality in question is the landscape/still life of manmade objects, from which some are borrowed like anonymous "portraits." In the time of Rembrandt, painting still had a preservative function, later subsumed by photography. The readymades show us that representation is normally a redundancy, and to that degree they share in more conventionally modernist trends in painting and sculpture. Where they differ from abstract art, however, is in their fully prosaic gratification of the desire for recognizable form at the very moment when it is finally abolished for aesthetic purposes.

With Duchamp the selection process was clearly not governed by an ostensibly "artistic" standard, but instead by a more practical sense of both typicality and careful randomness—like the accurate tables used in applied mathematics to ensure that one is working with truly random numbers. The readymades are philosophically *realistic:* they imply that objects like bottle racks or urinals are categorically interchangeable, and hence, that reality is connected and continuous. Yet they are also philosophically *nominalistic* because they undermine the possibility that any two objects might truly be identical. The paradox is not futile but fecund. It refuses to dissolve into absurdity because it sustains thought, common sense, and even a kind of *intellectual* good taste. Duchamp envisioned the range of the readymades as gradually expanding until coextensive with the whole galaxy of objects surrounding us. But the initial instances had to be chosen with consideration, and their number controlled, so that the wider implications would not be spent prematurely. The result was careful chance.

For more on the readymades, stay tuned . . .

8

THE PROPELLER
AND THE *BIRD IN SPACE*

How all too easy it has become to admire a ship or airplane propeller as a Brancusi *trouvé*. Much easier than before 1934, when the *Machine Art* exhibition at the Museum of Modern Art accomplished a definitive trade-off: simply suspend the Kandinsky–Rebay–Guggenheim ideal of spiritual value, and propellers and big electrical insulators will look just like abstract art that happens to be downright useful besides. Access to modernity instantly expands, but equally the likelihood of debasement. Witness the waxing and waning of "Functionalism" as mere style, in a vulgar material-ism inevitably demanding more in the way of charm and entertainment.

With the "object art" now around us—an après-Minimalism that gives up even Duchamp's poetry of the readymade in a coy clean-cutness of "pure" product and commodity—it becomes worthwhile again to see what else sculpture can offer in the way of objectification. Which is also to wonder what is still so unnervingly beautiful about a *Bird in Space* by Brancusi, above and beyond any sleek propeller with, when at rest, its own Hogarthian "Line of Beauty and Grace" (Fig. 12).

That modern industry is capable of generating newly beautiful and

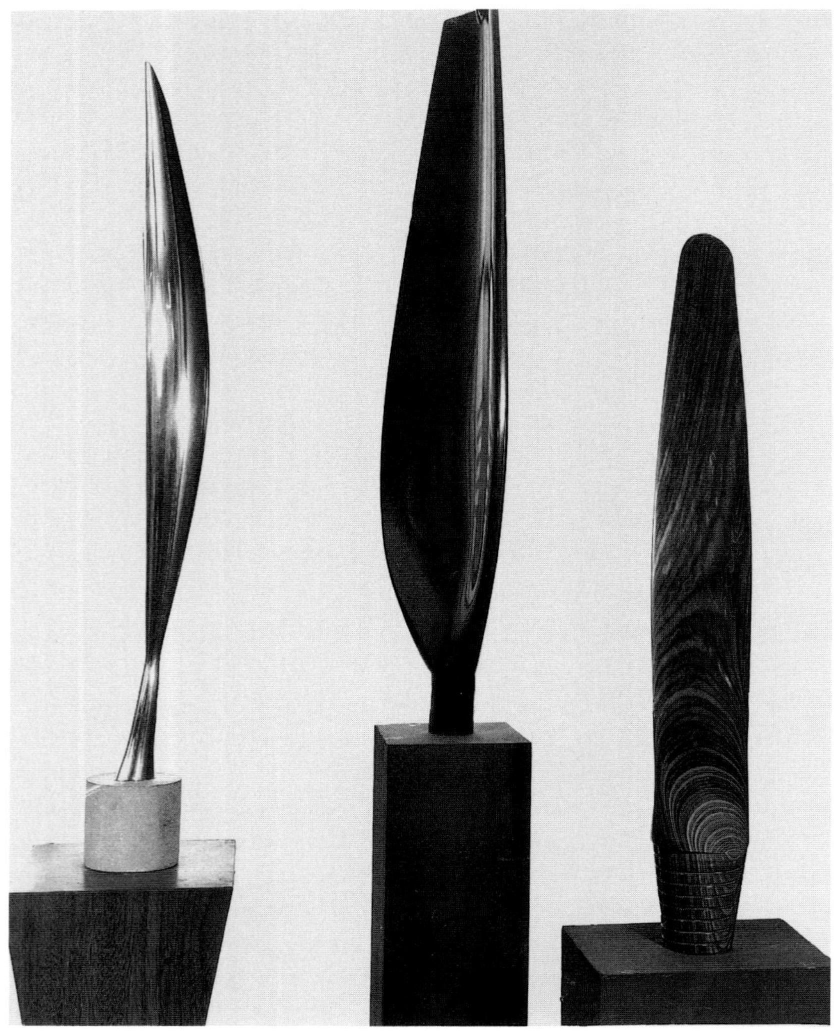

Fig. 12   Left to right: Constantin Brancusi, *Bird in Space*, 1928, bronze (unique cast), 58 x 8½ x 6½ inches; propeller blade, c. 1943, "Panelyte" (plastic and paper), height 62¼ inches, St. Regis Paper Co., U.S.A. (designer and manufacturer); propeller blade, c. 1943, wood, height 59⅞ inches, Regis Paper Co. (designer and manufacturer).

sublime forms was already apparent, proto-Futuristically, in the nineteenth century. From Turner's *Rain, Steam and Speed,* of 1844 (the same year as a Berlioz cantata for the opening of a railroad in France) and related literature of the locomotive, through the famous "Dynamo and the Virgin" chapter of *The Education of Henry Adams* (1907), a new aesthetic, inevitably threatening to convention, proved exciting to Italian Futurists (who likewise admired Whitman) and others. By the 1930s, however, the subtlety with which John Dewey manages to maintain some specifically humane instrumental possibility, in *Art as Experience* (1934), would have been lost on many, especially once *Machine Art* opened in the same year: "A work of fine art . . . is as much a part of the objective world as is a locomotive or a dynamo," indeed, but even the locomotive "operates in conditions where it produces consequences beyond its base physical being."[1] Of course, producing consequences beyond their bare physical being is just what artworks, all of Brancusi's *Birds in Space* included, have all along been doing.

Why, however, does the propeller, so readily welcome, maybe even primp for, modern aesthetic regard? As utilitarian as it is, the twin-bladed propeller, at least, betokens human approximation of natural, animal flight, with the complementary curves of a twin-bladed propeller like a sign of "infinity" realized (only in the nineteenth century was it established that birds in flight beat their wings in a figure-eight motion that opens into undulations in the linear path of flight[2]). Associated with the gratification of age-old and inveterate aspiration, it is no wonder that the propeller should also connote faith in technical progress; by the same token the "progressive" supersession of prop planes by jets tinges the propeller's *moderne* mystique with nostalgia.

In modest counterpart to the modern aircraft propeller is the electric

---

1. John Dewey, *Art as Experience* (New York, 1934), 146. Dewey's levelheadedness must have helped to overcome a dilettantish or even dandyish aestheticization of the machine that began quite early. One thinks of Brancusi's brassy Athena-like *Blond Negress,* of 1926, as well as *Bird in Space,* when reading the words of Huysmans's *A Rebours* (1884): "Does there exist, anywhere on this earth, a being conceived in the joys of fornication and born in the throes of motherhood who is more dazzlingly, more outstandingly beautiful than the two locomotives recently put into service on the Northern Railway? One of these, bearing the name of Crampton, is an adorable blonde with a shrill voice, a long slender body imprisoned in a shiny brass corset, and supple catlike movements; a smart golden blonde whose extraordinary grace can be quite terrifying when she stiffens her muscles of steel . . ." J.-K. Huysmans, *Against Nature: A New Translation of "A Rebours,"* trans. Robert Baldick, The Penguin Classics (Harmondsworth, 1966), 37.

2. James Bell Pettigrew et al., "Flight and Flying," *Encyclopaedia Britannica,* 11th ed., vol. X (Cambridge, 1910), 502–19, with diagrams.

table fan, grounded in the here-and-now by the ballast of its base. Perhaps it has in recent years become possible to think more concretely than ever of the forthrightly spartan fans designed from about 1908 onward for the A.E.G., or Allgemeine Elektricitäts-Gesellschaft (General Electric Company) in Berlin by the classic modern master of engineered beauty, Peter Behrens (Fig. 13)—including a true 1980s-style redo, a twin-bladed ceiling fan lovingly reconstructed by the present design department of AEG-Telefunken. Behrens's radical simplicity, still too transparent to stereotype, does more than negate ornamentation: by a kind of prose-poetry, it tightens bulk and condenses mass.[3] Interestingly, in relation to Brancusi, a critic in the Behrens orbit who was a disciple of Wölfflin wrote in 1909 of the

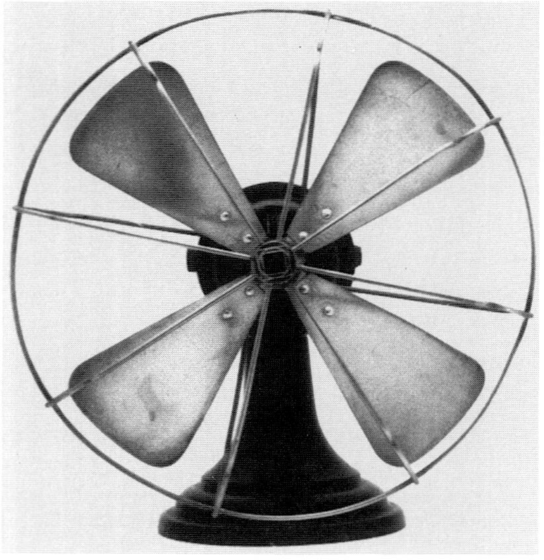

Fig. 13   Peter Behrens (designer), for A.E.G.,
Berlin, table fan, 1908. Photo © 1987 Wolfgang Volz,
with permission.

---

3. Stanford Anderson, "Modern Architecture and Industry: Peter Behrens, the A. E. G. and Industrial Design," *Oppositions*, no. 21 (Summer 1980), 79–97; on Behrens's early table and ceiling fans, see also Tilmann Buddensieg with Henning Rogge, *Industriekultur: Peter Behrens and the A. E. G. 1907–1914*, trans. Iain Boyd White (Cambridge, Mass., 1984), 396–405.

aesthetic impact of aviation: "The concept of top and base is losing its importance, which was derived from an earthbound viewpoint."[4]

Even as applied art, Behrens's fans imply something more than the point of origin of a high-tech look. It has become as challenging all over again to explain the conviction of this earliest phase of not simply decontaminated but positively rigorous design. Likewise the architecture of Ludwig Mies van der Rohe, who as a young man assisted, with Gropius and others, in Behrens's office, as spiritually gratifying, not just easy to keep clean. After an apprenticeship with the furniture designer Bruno Paul, Mies worked under Behrens from 1908 to 1911, right when the master was taking design responsibility for the A.E.G.

What now seem like exclusively technical, engineering pursuits in the early phase of modernity, when Cubism itself was emergent in painting, entailed a more searching penetration of the world by mind than the usual "utopian" characterization allows. Simultaneously with Mies's service under Behrens, the young Ludwig Wittgenstein was a research student in engineering at the University of Manchester. Wittgenstein was already keen on aeronautics, and he began to experiment with kites at the university's upper-atmosphere research station on his arrival in the spring of 1908. As if in a single extended train of thought, Wittgenstein's preoccupation with the design and testing of kites turned to concern for some self-sufficient means of propulsion, that is for some kind of propeller driven by an engine, and on from there to a desire to penetrate to the "foundations of mathematics," that led him to move to Cambridge, in the autumn of 1911, to study with Bertrand Russell.

Wittgenstein's early aeronautical enthusiasm would hardly have been eccentric at the time. In America, Orville and Wilbur Wright, after starting out with gliders in 1900 and progressing to teetering initial powered flights in 1903, had both negotiated full and proper airplane flights in 1908, in which year they also made a European tour. Louis Blériot first flew across the English Channel, from Calais to Dover, on 25 July 1909. The young Wittgenstein would surely have also been interested in Louis Paulhan's first flight from London to Manchester within twenty-four hours with only one stop, on 27–28 April 1910, winning a huge prize from the London *Daily Mail*.

In the mechanical engineering laboratory of Manchester, Wittgenstein produced his own experimental aircraft engine, a design for which has

---

4. Fritz Wichert, "Airship Travel and Architecture," in Buddensieg, *Industriekultur,* 231–32.

been published, though whether he ever designed an actual propeller is doubtful.[5] Wolfe Mays, who has looked into the matter, has found nothing.[6] G. E. M. Anscombe, literary executor of the philosopher, recalls no propeller design either.[7] The engine itself was a variable volume combustion chamber intended to power reaction jets at the tips of whatever propeller there was to have been (the basic idea, impractical for forward propulsion, was however employed on the vertical in Austrian-designed helicopters during World War II). Perhaps Wittgenstein's is a case of a propeller never substantially projected at all, thanks to his shift from engineering thought about the propeller as mathematically determinable in form, to the nature of mathematics itself as conventional rather than absolute.

Picasso and Braque apparently thought of their renegotiation of conventional artistic representation in analogy with the new aeronautics. Linda Nochlin reviews previous research in respect to a still life by Picasso wherein the cover of a patriotic pamphlet advocating aircraft development is prominent: *The Scallop Shell (Notre Avenir est dans l'air),* of 1912. It is said that for a while Picasso had on his studio door a sign reading "Defense de

---

5. W. Mays, "Wittgenstein's Manchester Period," *The Guardian* (Manchester), 24 March 1961, p. 10, with illus. In the clear reproduction now available in Michael Nedo and Michele Ranchetti, eds., *Ludwig Wittgenstein: Sein Leben in Bildern und Texten* (Frankfurt am Main, 1983), fig. 92 on 73, it is obvious that this variable-compression engine was intended to drive a twin-bladed propeller. In their caption Nedo and Ranchetti liken the design, based on Heron of Alexandria's principle of recoil or jet-propulsion, to a lawn sprinkler, and note (with other commentators) that during World War II the Austrian engineer Doploff used the same principle for a helicopter.

6. Mays, "Wittgenstein in Manchester," in Rudolf Haller and Wolfgang Grassl, eds., *Language, Logic and Philosophy: Proceedings of the IV International Wittgenstein Symposium,* 28 August–2 September 1979 (Vienna, 1980), 171–78. According to Wittgenstein's fellow engineering student Eccles, he sometimes discussed furniture and interior design—as if in anticipation of his work, notably regarding the underlying or "implicit" plumbing and heating systems, on the house he would one day so scrupulously design for his sister Margarethe Stonborough-Wittgenstein, in Vienna, itself preceding a (re)turn to philosophy at Cambridge.

7. G. E. M. Anscombe, in conversation, January 1987. According to Hermine Wittgenstein, "My Brother Ludwig," trans. Bernhard Leitner, in Rush Rhees, ed., *Ludwig Wittgenstein: Personal Recollections* (Oxford, 1981), 1–13, "He went on to the designing of a motor and the designing of an air screw" (12). Georg von Wright, *Wittgenstein* (Oxford, 1982), 17, reports, "It was the engine that absorbed his interest, but soon he concentrated on the design of the propeller, which was essentially a mathematical task"; after describing the reaction engine, von Wright adds, "I am told that Wittgenstein had patented some of his inventions in the field of aeronautics." Ray Monk, *Ludwig Wittgenstein: The Duty of Genius* (New York, 1990), 34, emphasizes that it was Wittgenstein's successful switch from the engine design to that of a propeller, in 1909–10, that earned him not only a fellowship for the next year but a patent, dated 17 August 1910, for "Improvements in Propellers Applicable for Aerial Machines"; Monk observes that Wittgenstein's dearest friend, David Pinsent, to whom the *Tractatus* would be dedicated in 1919, died in a plane crash while doing aerodynamic research, in May 1917 (154).

Parler au Pilote" (No Talking to the Pilot). He, at least, must have considered his partnership with Braque in pioneering Cubist painting to be analogous to that of the Wright brothers, having written a letter to his colleague with the opening "Mon cher Wilbur."[8]

In the larger party of Cubism, aviation was celebrated also in Robert Delaunay's telling conjunction of airplane and Eiffel Tower as kindred motifs from the realm of engineering pertaining respectively to the first, Postimpressionist, and the new, Cubist, generations. Witness *The Cardiff Team* (1912–13) and the blatantly enthusiastic *Homage to Blériot* (1913–14). Delaunay seems to muse on the propeller, in particular, not only as a "rationally" curvaceous form in its own right but also as generative, readily extrapolated by extension of the (twin-bladed) propeller's crossing arcs in alternating complementary relation, like intersecting sine curves, or reverberating into concentric circular, ovoid, and prolate forms. If the Eiffel Tower summarizes a good two centuries of French speculation on Gothic "engineering" construction, in rivalry with the academic tradition of classical, fine arts architecture, Delaunay's Cubist embrace of the airplane, preeminently the propeller as a brace of reverse curves, marks an absolute supersession of academic classicism on behalf of a truer *modern* rationality more worthy of classical dignity after all.

Even Marcel Duchamp's first readymade, the *Bicycle Wheel,* originally of 1913, has something to offer here, particularly in end view. Think of the slim, taut wire crossbracing of many experimental airplanes of the time, not to mention the literal borrowing for the construction of such aircraft of bicycle parts, such as wheels for landing gear. (The Wright brothers themselves had started out with a bicycle repair shop in Dayton, Ohio.) While Duchamp's *Bicycle Wheel* itself is normally described as mounted upside-down on its wooden stool, it is equally possible to describe it as very much "up in the air." By only a stretch, the rungs of its supporting stool might even be likened to the boxy wing structures of biplanes. Brancusi's first *Bird in Space* dates from a decade later. Without owing anything, by way of "source," to the *Bicycle Wheel* in its still flabbergasting objectivity, the developed *Bird in Space* form comes eventually to reflect sculpturesque interest back, most of all, onto the edgewise or end view of

---

8. Linda Nochlin, "Picasso's Color: Schemes and Gambits," *Art in America,* December 1980, 105–23, 177–81, 183, esp. 109 (Roland Penrose on letter opening) and 180 n. 20 (Pierre Cabanne on door sign; also, Robert Rosenblum on Picasso's interest in Cubist construction as like making airplanes).

Duchamp's joke that is more than a joke. Ironically, when the pure and lofty *Bird in Space* was denied duty-free entry by U.S. Customs and ordered subject to tax as metal in 1926, it was again his iconoclast friend who helped Brancusi carry the hefty transcendental thing back aboard ship.[9]

How to get from the materialist modernity of the Eiffel Tower and the utilitarian propeller, not to mention the gaga concreteness of the *Bicycle Wheel,* to the transcendent, aspirational splendor of *Bird in Space?* Perhaps by reference to a Cubist painting by Albert Gleizes, one of the three studies of the engineer John Roebling's Brooklyn Bridge, completed in 1883, a few years before Eiffel's tower. Modern artists, including many photographers as well as the poet Hart Crane, in *The Bridge,* have responded to the crisscrossing pattern of irregular lozenges generated by the intersection of the guys radiating—not unlike the spokes of the *Bicycle Wheel*—from the bridge's towers, with the vertical cables that support the roadway from the sweeping main cables above. Emil Otto Hoppé (who went on to take a daringly cropped close-up of a ship's rudder and propeller seen from below, the 1928 *Ship in Drydock*) was only the first to photograph what became a set motif of the oblique "harp strings" of the structure, with his *Brooklyn Bridge,* of 1919. In the 1915 *Brooklyn Bridge* (Guggenheim), however, Gleizes isolates a still more sculpturesquely beautiful feature of the bridge that goes surprisingly unremarked: namely, the way the major cables not only dip down below the roadway at the center but even more sweepingly dip under the roadway in an athletically attenuated follow-through at the anchorage (Fig. 14). The geometric "chord" thus described, where Roebling's principal cable veers down and up again against the roadway's edge, is precisely Gleizes's structurally concrete-"abstract" motif—most tellingly at the left, where a *vertical* line slices off a chord across an arc, much in the definitive manner of a *Bird in Space.*

The very conviction of Brancusi's device makes it possible to look back and acknowledge the highly significant structural detail that Gleizes synecdochically isolated in the bridge itself. Gleizes's painting, for its part, *abstracts* the engineering form as a new and independent armature for his Cubist landscape. So the cool grace of the engineering structure is assumed into the heaven of classic art, in the reflected glow of the *Bird in Space.* The

---

9. On Duchamp's readymades *qua* sculpture, see the essay "Readymades: Art Accompli," above; also, now, Edith Balas, "Brancusi, Duchamp and Dada," *Gazette des Beaux-Arts,* XCV (April 1980), 165–74. William A. Camfield, *Marcel Duchamp: Fountain* (Houston, 1989), 44, points out that in Duchamp's first known comment on them, in a letter to his sister Suzanne of 15 January 1916, the *Bicycle Wheel* and the *Bottle Rack* alike are referred to as "sculpture already made."

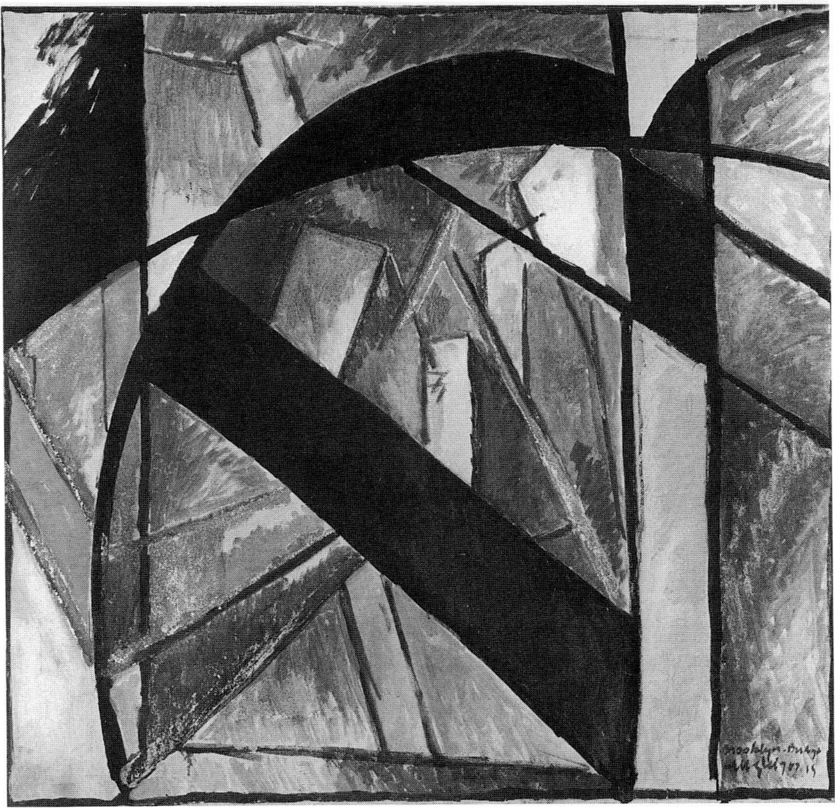

Fig. 14   Albert Gleizes, *Brooklyn Bridge*, 1915, oil and gouache on canvas, 40⅛ x 40⅛ inches.

Bird in Space, itself, will echo the *Venus de Milo,* whose figure, too, offers one plumb side versus the bowing curve of hip and thigh on the other: surely the feature that once prompted an earlier modern of classical inclination, Degas, to ask, "Have you seen . . . how she goes beyond the perpendicular?"[10]

Another bowed upright form, straight on one side and bulging into a

---

10. According to Charles W. Millard, *The Sculpture of Edgar Degas* (Princeton, 1976), 158, this comes from Georges Jeannoit, "Souvenirs sur Degas," *La Revue universelle,* 15 October 1933, pp. 152–74, and 1 November 1933, pp. 280–304. Rodin had published an essay on the sculpture in *L'Art et les Artistes* in 1910 and 1914, this later reissued as a luxury book, wherein, after speaking of "forms that suit (*conviennent*) . . . according to the irrefutable logic of harmonious necessity

sweeping curve on the other, is the centerpiece of Léger's 1918 *Propellers* (Museum of Modern Art). Léger would later reminisce about a visit, crucial for him and apparently for others, to the Salon of Aviation in 1911: "Before the World War I went with Marcel Duchamp and Brancusi to an airplane exhibition. Marcel . . . walked around the motors and propellers without saying a word. Suddenly he turned to Brancusi: 'Painting has come to an end. Who can do anything better than this propeller. Can you?' He was very strongly attracted to these precise objects; we were also, but not as overwhelmingly as he. I myself felt a preference for the motors, for things made out of metal, rather than the wooden blades. . . . But I still remember the bearing of those great propellers. Good God, what a miracle!"[11] Gleizes's reaction to the workings of the Brooklyn Bridge, in the Guggenheim painting, accomplishes more, in the way of architectural abstraction;

. . . in reciprocal dependence on life" (*À la Vénus de Milo* [Paris, 1945], 3–4), he addresses the statue: "Ô Vénus, arc de triomphe de la vie, pont de vérité, cercle de grâce!" (8). He praises the "generating profile" (*profil générateur*) of the torso (9), and remarks that in three-quarter view it is "streaming with clarity" (12). "O gloire totale de la grâce et du génie!" apostrophizes the modern sculptor (16). In the second, 1914, half of his study, Rodin bespeaks "this thigh, column of life" (17), and the way "A single curve, made by all those of the shoulders, limbs, thighs" describes the entire figure (18).

Aspects of the Greek *Nike* (or *Winged Victory*) *of Samothrace,* as well as the *Venus de Milo,* also in the Louvre, reverberate more vitally in the various versions of the *Bird in Space* than in, for instance, such diluted literalist, art-nouveau-into-*moderne* "Nike" applications as the Rolls Royce radiator ornament, entitled *The Spirit of Ecstasy* (c. 1911), by one Charles Sykes, a Royal Academician—which makes the Futurist rhetoric of Marinetti, in 1908, seem all the fresher: "A race-automobile adorned with great pipes like serpents with explosive breath . . . [*sic*] a race-automobile which seems to rush over exploding powder is more beautiful than the *Victory of Samothrace*"; F. T. Marinetti, "The Foundation and Manifesto of Futurism" (1909), trans. Joshua C. Taylor in Herschel B. Chipp, ed., *Theories of Modern Art: A Source Book by Artists and Critics* (Berkeley, 1970), 286. More metaphorically close to Brancusi, Le Corbusier, in his picture-book *Aircraft* (London, 1935; repr. New York, 1988), with several impressive close-ups of propellers, refers to the pioneers of aviation as visionaries "with their swallows crazily constructed of wood and canvas" (6), and remarks of another hood ornament: "I still constantly use a car which carries on its bonnet two unfolded winds and the words, paradoxical but full of hidden tenderness, 'Avion Voisin.' They cut Icarus' wings and put four wheels underneath him" (9).

A year earlier, a photograph of the *Nike* had appeared as the frontispiece to Dewey's *Art as Experience* (1934), where it emblematizes classic form carried progressively forward. Today, a bronze by the Danish sculptor Per Kirkeby, *Kopf ohne Arm II,* 1985, manages both to extend Degas's sense of the *Venus* and to enliven ours of the *Bird in Space* as a modern version of it, by evoking a looming vertical figure with one conspicuously flat side.

11. Quoted by K. G. Pontus Hulten, in the Museum of Modern Art exhibition catalogue *The Machine as Seen at the End of the Mechanical Age* (New York, 1968), 140, after the Haus der Kunst catalogue *Fernand Léger* (Munich, 1957), without reference; Dickran Tashjian, in the Brooklyn Museum catalogue *The Machine Age in America 1918–1941* (New York, 1986), 359 n. 68, has traced the source: Dora Vallier, "La Vie dans l'oeuvre de Fernand Léger" (interview), *Cahiers d'art,* XXIX/2 (1954), 133–77.

Léger, more disposed to embrace the propeller as is, nevertheless also digests it, here, as a lithely bowed shaped, flat along one side, in his abstract composition. Duchamp, meanwhile, already saw in the propeller all the pure form he could handle, as if "ready-made." If Wittgenstein's propeller project is our most important missing exhibit, a propeller *idea* was in a sense Duchamp's proto-readymade, only left "unexecuted" in 1911 (the pseudo-propelleresque *Rotary Glass Plate [Precision Optics],* made with Man Ray, dates from 1920).

Within the wider Purist movement, in which Léger played his real part, there developed the rather Platonizing concept of the *objet-type,* in a sense the opposite of a readymade. The *objet-type* was the ultrasimplified, typified form of an object that modern design was to realize, and Purist still-life painting to render, with its own new purity. Owing something to a theory of types developed by Hermann Muthesius, a founder of the Deutsche Werkbund, and emergent in Corbusier and Amedée Ozenfant's *Après le Cubisme* (1919), the *objet-type* is in one sense anything but a readymade: an idea, and ideal, of projective design in "applied art" for something subsequently to be mass-produced. Nevertheless, it *was* definitively to be mass-produced, and shows a tendency toward extreme generalization and formal self-evidence. The propeller as a type is a good example, all the more whenever it presents itself as a Brancusi *trouvé*. In *La Peinture moderne* (1927) Le Corbusier and Ozenfant praise the objects produced from an *objet-type* as subjects for painting, this for "a banality that makes them barely exist as subjects of interest in themselves, and hardly lend[ing] themselves to anecdote."[12]

Léger and the Delaunays were great enthusiasts of specifically aero-architectural abstraction, although Stanton Macdonald-Wright's 1920 *Aeroplane Synchromy in Yellow-Orange* (Metropolitan) can also be mentioned. Léger's own essay "L'Esthetique de la machine: l'objet fabrique" dates from 1923–24. There the artist remembers when once, the Salon d'Automne set up right by the Salon de la Locomotion Aérienne, he walked over and found aesthetic refreshment in the airplane exhibit. Especially memorable was a youngster visiting the art exhibition from the other side, his spiffy workman's garb more impressive to Léger than the paintings of nudes that

---

12. Reyner Banham, *Theory and Design in the First Machine Age* (London, 1960), 206–13; quotation on 211. On Purist taste for "readymades instead of applied art," see Stanislaus von Moos, "Le Corbusier und Loos," in his exhibition catalogue *L'Esprit nouveau: Le Corbusier und die Industrie 1920–1925* (Zurich: Museum für Gestaltung; Berlin: Bauhaus-Archiv and Museum für Gestaltung; Strasbourg: Musées de la Ville, 1987), 122–34, esp. 125–26.

drew his boyish interest. All the more after the aviation exhibit, seeing the colorful workman amidst the paintings only made the art look drabber still. Robert and Sonia Delaunay, altogether enthusiastic about aeronautical form, actively engaged in aviation exhibition design.

The first of Brancusi's *Birds in Space* date from this time, beginning with a marble of 1923, another dated 1923–24, and in 1924 the first bronze; the definitive form emerged in a marble of 1925 and carried through a dozen more versions, down to 1941.[13] The beauty of the classic *Bird in Space* owes much to its swelling upper mass as switching over into a reversed and partial swell below, with positive/negative, "Cubistic" continuity through the "switchover" along the single vertical axis. Just because the point of crossover is at once physically negligible and formally crucial—and considering Brancusi's own enthusiasm for aeronautical form, also conveyed in Léger—it is worthwhile wondering how a prior, minor series by the artist suggests likely reservations on Brancusi's part toward Puristic embrace of proto-functionalist enthusiasm in design.

The economical forms of Purism proved conveniently adaptable, as Kenneth Silver has stressed, in the nationalistic campaign for economic recovery in postwar France.[14] But already at the war's end, the English art critic Clive Bell was complaining, "People had grown so familiar with the idea of a cup, with that purely intellectual label 'cup,' that they never looked at a particular cup and felt its emotional significance."[15] The Purists would go after the simple "idea" of the cup, for easy industry replication and optimistic morale—and in his way Bell would as much as follow suit. But in 1917 or so Brancusi carved the first one or two of his archly unique wooden *Cup* sculptures, all completely solid and each with a different handle,[16] that by the time Bell's essay was collected in his *Since Cézanne*

---

13. Sidney Geist, *Brancusi: The Sculpture and Drawings* (New York, 1975), passim.

14. On the aesthetics of the "Call to Order," see Kenneth E. Silver, "Straightening Up After the Great War," *Artforum,* March 1977, 56–63, and subsequent writings. In the post–World War II period even Brancusi's art might be civilly accommodated for its simplicity of form by a Franco-American proselytizer for modern culture: "In sculpture, solid geometric subjects in one single mass-form naturally evokes [*sic*] the name of Brancusi," says Henri Martin Barzun in remarks on "Machine, Airship and Art: The 1913 'Cubist Revolution,' " in his *Orpheus: Modern Culture and the 1913 Renaissance: A Panoramic Survey 1900–1956* (N.p., 1960), 18.

15. Clive Bell, *Since Cézanne* (New York, 1928), 40.

16. One may think of the definitively humble wooden cup that Diogenes the Cynic wore hanging from his waist until throwing it away in anger on seeing a child drink water from cupped hands, realizing he could have done without even such a simple implement. Luther refers to this legend to condemn vaingloriously exaggerated humility, in a sermon of 7 November 1537, on Matthew 19:29.

(1928) had become a series, almost *rather than* a set, of four. Each *Cup* sculpture holds out firmly against being merely a cup: as otherwise cuplike as it might seem, it has no "inside" and hence could not even forcibly be used as a cup, as with a hypothetical "reciprocal readymade" (M.D.). Singly and together, the *Cups* of Brancusi are *noncups* indeed. That the series extended until "after 1925," thus overlapping with the early *Birds in Space,* helps to confirm the latter, as propellerlike as they may be seen, as *anything but* propellers. If anything, the *Bird in Space* is a metaphorical ramjet needing no power source, being always so stunningly *under way*—and was it not Bell who once said that assuming that artists do abstraction because they can't do representational art is like thinking that the R.A.F. flies because its men can't march? Eventually Bell's formalism proved conveniently amenable indeed to the connoisseurship of bourgeois "good design."

The poetically airborne, implicitly aeronautical *Bird in Space* made it possible to *trouver* the actual industrial aircraft propeller, but really the only worldly object deserving of close comparison with Brancusi's sleek bronze versions is the most famous object, itself so sculpturesque it is barely constrained as utilitarian, by that relentless perfectionist who trained under Behrens, Mies van der Rohe. In Mies's 1927 "Barcelona Chair," of chromium-plated steel, the single curves that sweep down on either side from a crossbar at the top of the back to form the front legs, intersect with the S-curves, this, again, suggestive of Hogarth's "Line of Grace,"[17] that extend from a crossbar at the front of the seat to become the rear legs. Brancusian too is the fastidiously handled point of intersection that, understatedly swollen by welds, is rather hublike, not unlike the hub of a propeller, at that. Seeing the "Barcelona Chair" as a would-be art object in miscellaneous contexts of bourgeois luxury is one thing; Mies's own deployments of it in his obsessively perfect spaces, where it is often more actively sculptural, is no doubt another.

Something else again is the simplistic argument for "good design" that presumes to take care of the spiritual *je ne sais quoi* of abstract (fine) art. It is in one sense shocking, if in another not at all, to find Clive Bell, the high priest of pure form, "getting down" to praise a modern picnic kit at the

---

17. Which, thanks to Giovanni Paolo Lomazzo's *Trattato dell'arte della pittura* (1584; trans. Richard Haydock, as *Treatise on the Art of Painting,* 1598), "Hogarth considered to be the fundamental line of Michelangelo's art"; Robert J. Clements, *Michelangelo's Theory of Art* (New York, 1961), 177. Plate 1 of Hogarth's *The Analysis of Beauty; Written with a View of Fixing the Fluctuating Ideas of Taste* (1753) instances the irregular, reverse-curving "Line of Grace" in faces, corsets, and cabriole chair legs as well as classical sculpture.

expense of a couple of admittedly clunky German Renaissance woodcarved boxes: this in, of all places, *Enjoying Pictures* (1934). Bell proceeds to generalize in terms that have pertinence today in respect to blunt "object art," terms that are good insofar as they show open-minded and flexible appreciation, bad insofar as they hint at an effete sort of slumming: "Who but prefers to an arty wardrobe handmade by a virtuous homespun craftsman somewhere in the Cotswolds and left unstained too, an elegant Rolls or a shapely, satisfying locomotive? Who does not like the photographs in *The Times* better than the paintings in the Royal Academy?"[18]

Between the World Wars, the modern movement would seem to have made hopeless concessions, in East and West almost alike, to hopelessly undialectical materialism. In exchange for the promise of an active role in social progress, Constructivism largely surrendered spirit, whether under the iron hand of Stalin or at the more willful and shameless service of West European and American notions of the unsentimentally up-to-date. Practically everywhere one finds the rich creativity of the prewar period trimmed back to a despiritualized "progressivism" all too readily broadcast, at small threat to prevailing systems. How readily a "bad" utopianism got retooled into a "good" (i.e., undialectically materialist) one. Here, then, comes the all too real propeller to bask in the aura of the *Bird in Space* (though there was less idolatry when the Symbol stood alone), and with it the whole hardware store of "modernist" applied art, plus eventually, the special boutique for painting and sculpture as no longer in need, thank you, of any spiritual justification whatever.[19]

There is no denying to some manifestations of Constructivism spiritual claims, although what besides an expedient illusion of political neutrality might be offered by an exclusively geometric idea of technological *flavor,* is still urgently at issue. Then too, some within the general trend were driven by a genuinely democratic artistic evangelism. Such enthusiasm on the part of Dewey, in America, was qualified by concern for individual and interior well-being and "growth." Still, the Lewis Mumford of *Technics and Civilization* (1934) is more problematic. Today *Technics and Civilization* can seem alarm-

---

18. Bell, *Enjoying Pictures* (New York, 1934), 102.

19. On the hardware problem: Joseph Masheck, "Embalmed Objects: Design at the Modern," *Artforum,* February 1975, 49–55. The design program of the (related) Institute of Contemporary Art, Boston, in the 1940s and 1950s has since been studied in terms of the ideology of consumerism by David Joselit: "The Postwar Product: The I.C.A.'s Department of Design in Industry" (1985), in Richard Hertz and Norman M. Klein, eds., *Twentieth-Century Art Theory* (Englewood Cliffs, N.J., 1990), 357–69.

ingly naive as an apology for the new order. In converting as much as possible into a new, as it were, "steel" standard of value, Mumford, however, does happen to show himself one of the few to have taken Duchamp's readymades with the modicum of immediate artistic seriousness that their very irony requires: one may find Mumford's coinage debased, but it proves good enough to cover, for Duchamp's "cheap, ready-made articles, produced by the machine," a certain "esthetic soundness and sufficiency." On the other hand, claiming in the same book that Brancusi offers "the most complete as well as the most brilliant interpretation of the capacities of the machine," Mumford says that, "looking at the bird, one thinks of the shell of a torpedo."[20]

The Wittgenstein who lost interest in the propeller his engine would have powered in favor of speculation on mathematics, might have approved some earlier remarks by Dewey, in *Reconstruction in Philosophy* (1920)— notwithstanding the fact that even today, ironically, an engineer I know can actually still insist that there is some one Platonically "real," ideal propeller that in sublunary conditions can only be approached. For Dewey, at pains to revise the polarity between the artistic-contemplative and the practical-scientific, claims there that the structure of mathematics has by no means "sprung all at once from the brain of a Zeus whose anatomy is that of pure logic": on the contrary, mathematical structure is experimental, with "a history in which matter and methods have been constantly selected and worked over on the basis of empirical success and failure."[21] "It is difficult," Dewey says, "to imagine any high development of the fine arts except where there is curious and loving interest in forms and motions of the world quite irrespective of any use to which they may be put." Without scientific practicality, "man will be the sport and victim of natural forces which he cannot use or control," while without aesthetic contemplative-ness, "mankind might become a race of economic monsters, relentlessly drawing hard bargains with nature and with one another, bored with

---

20. Lewis Mumford, *Technics and Civilization* (New York, 1963), 351, 356–57, respectively, as noted in the fine essay by von Moos, "The Visualized Machine Age; or, Mumford and the European Avant-Garde," in Thomas P. Hughes and Agatha C. Hughes, eds., *Lewis Mumford: Public Intellectual* (New York, 1990), 181–32 (notes, pp. 403–14), here 211–12. Soon after Mumford's text, Sheldon and Martha Candler Cheney, *Art and the Machine: An Account of Industrial Design in Twentieth-Century America* (New York and London, 1936), 31, remark more wildly, "Any well-informed art student will be able to point out certain common principles of form relationship and expressiveness of materials, in [George] Sakier's plumbing fixtures and Brancusi's sculptures . . ."

21. Dewey, *Reconstruction in Philosophy* (New York, 1920), 137.

leisure or capable of putting it to use only in ostentatious display and extravagant dissipation."[22]

It is easy enough to say that we need both mentalities, but Dewey conveys the conviction of his understanding with a remarkably vivid turn of phrase. The very process of abstracting that makes science possible has, in his example, a peculiarly Brancusian ring: "The trait of flying is detached from the concrete bird."[23] And art, after all, has what may be called its spiritual utility. At the same time, man cannot live by art alone, if only because "while saints are engaged in introspection, burly sinners run the world."[24]

Dewey himself played a part in the influential *Machine Art* exhibition in the spring of 1934 at the Museum of Modern Art, as Sidney Lawrence has discovered. The Modern held a contest for the "most beautiful" *thing,* and alongside balloting by the general public, Dewey, Amelia Earhart, and a science museum official got to choose their favorites. Dewey came in second, with, guess what, a boat propeller.[25]

If that sounds unwittingly Dada, consider a special problem with the readymade, its precociously direct succession to the status of fine art—ironic fine art perhaps, *but there we are*—well before the museum in effect posed the much squarer question, Did you know that propellers can be lovely, practically as lovely as what you already think of as art? No wonder why, after the fact, the defense of any sort of transcendent value in sculpture per se would become more problematic than ever. What, on one hand, is to distinguish from Picabia's *Ass,* a photograph of a triple-bladed marine propeller positioned with two fins up as would-be "ears," this having seventeen years earlier served for the cover of the August 1917 number of the New York Dada magazine *319,* from the Modern's outdoor

---

22. Ibid., 126–27.

23. Ibid., 151. Apropos of Duchamp: the word "ready-made" occurs some ten times in this book, always in line with what is certainly its original sense of off-the-rack clothing; e.g., "fixed, ready-made, static properties of things" (158). "Ready-made" seldom occurs in Dewey's much longer *Art as Experience,* of fourteen years later, where one instance concerns criticism that "reacts from the standardized 'objectivity' of ready-made rules and procedures" (304).

24. Ibid., 196.

25. Sidney Lawrence, "Clean Machines at the Modern," *Art in America,* February 1984, 127–41, 166–68, with illus.: "original," pre-1934 marine propeller, on p. 127; installation of "Machine Art" and street sign for the exhibition, this incorporating another *actual* marine propeller, on p. 129; photo by Paul Parker of Amelia Earhart holding first-prize spring, Dewey holding second-prize marine propeller, and Charles Richards holding third-prize ball-bearing unit, on p. 131 (on the surprisingly widespread ball-bearing motif in contemporary art, see von Moos, "Visualized Machine Age," 202–9).

sign for *Machine Art,* a shadow-box containing a rather similar (real) propeller "by" Sullivan Shipyards, Inc., mounted likewise in a "Y" position?

In 1944 the designer Serge Chermayeff and René D'Harnoncourt, then a vice president and later the director of the Museum of Modern Art, could write: "The approximation of the organic and continuous flowing surfaces of the new mold technology to the free forms of Miró and Arp, and the similarity between a propeller blade and a Brancusi sculpture indicate the basic affinity between the tasks of the artist and the engineer both of whom endeavor to find the most adequate formulation of specific human demands within universal principles of order."[26] So it's supposedly all formal problem-solving, more or less. On the other hand, when the museum later published a still-standard handbook to the design collection, in 1959, now seeking to comprehend electronic materials (and thus in some sense anticipating Pontus Hulten's *The Machine at the End of the Mechanical Age* show, of 1968), what had to be explained was "the dematerialization of finite shapes into diagrammatic relationships."[27] But then dematerialization without some form of spiritualization sounds very much like annihilation.

Mounted and on duty in the posture of an art object, the propeller does look like an elegant Brancusian . . . *thing.* Even when mounted under the rubric of *design,* which should hardly matter wherever abolition of distinction between fine and applied art is avowed, it has in a sense less specificity, and possibly more anonymity, than it might have in an aeronautical museum. As no more than a generic example, maybe with "nice legs," it yet has to bear whatever generalized meaning, as concerns technological culture, is loaded onto it. Besides, there may be implied patronization, as if the engineers and craftsmen responsible for the object most likely either overlooked or underestimated its beauty; or else a begging of the central

---

26. Under "Design for Use," in *Art in Progress,* "A Survey Prepared for the Fiftieth Anniversary of the Museum of Modern Art" (New York, 1944), 195. The literalization of Brancusi's airborne metaphor is also evident in a postwar tendency to give the very title of Brancusi's increasingly famous piece as "Bird in *Flight.*" No less an authority than Edgar Kaufmann, Jr., himself of the Modern, wrote in 1950, "The love of perfect shapes which Brancusi lavished on his *Bird in Flight* echoes softly but clearly in . . . [a] molded knife handle and in the knife's proportion"; Kaufmann's *What Is Modern Design?,* in the museum's Introductory Series of the Modern Arts (New York, 1950), 6, as quoted in Joselit, "Postwar Product," 360. At least in Gerald Fitzgerald's translation, Renato Poggioli makes the same mistake, and worse, in *The Theory of the Avant-Garde* (1962, trans., Cambridge, Mass., 1968, repr. New York, 1971), "Brancusi's [N.B.] functional Bird in Flight" (139).

27. Arthur Drexler and Greta Daniel, *Introduction to Twentieth-Century Design from the Collection of the Museum of Modern Art, New York* (New York, 1959), 94; also cited in Lawrence, "Clean Machines," 139.

question, since advocacy of pure form as consequence of unimpeded function depends on evidence selected principally for formal appeal.

To see a *mass-produced* industrial product in light of applied art perhaps is to begin to recognize applied art or industrial design as the only art most people will ever closely encounter in *mass culture* (then, mass culture itself begins inescapably to seem *social*-engineered). If not simply the design movement's "fault," this problem showed up within the sphere of design even before Walter Benjamin's "Mechanical Reproducability" essay, published in 1936. It was certainly apt of Catherine Bauer, two years earlier, in a review of "Machine Art," observing that "the machine implies . . . reproducability," to frame the question in terms of the garment industry, with the very term "ready-made" conspicuously concerning off-the-rack clothing: "Very few of us could afford the extravagance of real handicraftsmanship, or individual tailoring, whether in houses or garments, and we had to be satisfied with 'reproductions.' "[28]

If Bauer did not develop her art-critical remarks into social critique, in the chapter on "The Culture Industry" in their *Dialectic of Enlightenment* (1944), Horkheimer and Adorno would claim, "What connoisseurs discuss as good or bad points serve[s] only to perpetuate the semblance of competition and range of choice" between two products, one by Chrysler and the other by General Motors. That, however, glosses over the old art-theoretical problem of utility versus ostensible beauty—with *Consumer Reports,* for instance, providing a critique of utility and only incidental critique of a product's looks. True, on the fine-art side, "with the cheapness of mass-produced luxury goods and its complement, the universal swindle, . . . that art renounces its own autonomy and proudly takes its place among consumption goods constitutes the charm of novelty."[29] Some, after all, have accused Duchamp, and in his day, even Brancusi, of novelty; and the readymades are sometimes taken quite jealously by artists as works of an enterprising cleverness that only saw a loophole and first cheatingly exploited it, despite Duchamp's own attitude as at once more aristocratic—above such mercenary affairs—and more populistic—"giving it away." Even now, however, the issue is still skirted of how such high-technology "products" as an aircraft propeller are, for being scrupulously "tooled" by

---

28. Catherine Bauer, "Machine-Made," *The American Magazine of Art,* XXVII/5 (May 1934), 267–70, here 270, 267, respectively.

29. Max Horkheimer and Theodor W. Adorno, *Dialectic of Enlightenment* (1944), trans. John Cumming (New York, 1982), 123, 157.

proud if anonymous machinists,[30] rather less unlike traditional art objects than either more casually mass-produced objects or "novelty" fine-art-works: the propeller as fine-art production within the industrial-art category.

What some see as a general, international totalitarian style in the 1930s was in part an attempt (too) grandiloquently to project "machine aesthetics" onto society, especially in great public works, as if social were tantamount to heroic, scale—obviating need for any further, perhaps stick-in-the-mud, "aesthetic" sublimation. Not that the pseudoartistic bombast that issued from this was harmless, if not for serving fascist depersonalization directly, then by firing a cult of worldly "progress" on the social scale.

For something like a literal artistic embodiment of the latter one can now refer, thanks to the wealth of documentation in the catalog of the Brooklyn Museum exhibition *The Machine Age in America 1918–1941*, to Oscar J. W. Hansen's 30-foot bronze *Winged Figures of the Republic* (1935–38), twin ornamental sculptures for Hoover Dam, in Dewey and Mumford's own time.[31] Here an extruded, propellerlike sleekness, evocative of electrical power and propulsive force in a way that harks back rather pedantically to Henry Adams's first apprehension of the dynamo as challenging the spiritual power of the *Virgin of Chartres* meets up with the general idea of the *Nike* (or *Winged Victory of Samothrace*), in popularizingly "traditional" sculptural application of the notion of propeller-as-Brancusi. The unapologetic public-works ostentation of Hansen's figures may well bespeak the great dam as "driving a hard bargain with nature," though precisely, of course, as self-consciously industrial, "applied," or "ornamental art." Much more convincing now, as "applied Brancusi" sculptures, are certain snazzy assemblages of highly machined and finished parts, by Theodore Roszak, which manage at once to be Constructive and Surreal: in *Bi-polar in Red* (1938), of metal, plaster, and wood, two conical forms, one above the other, touch points at the center, like an inverted *Bird in Space* idea.

The swan song of the propeller as Brancusi *trouvé* must be the scene in Antonioni's *Blow-Up,* of 1966, in which the so with-it young London

---

30. An exception: "The fault of the Duchamp readymade is that it idealizes an industrial product by severing it from its origins in working class craft and claiming it as a trophy of capitalist cunning. . . . The readymades and multiples of Duchamp are denigrations of working class relations to production and idealizations of capitalist relations to production and consumption"; Carl Andre, "Against Duchamp" (1973), *Praxis: A Journal of Radical Perspectives on the Arts,* 1/1 (Spring 1975), 115.

31. Illus., *Machine Age,* fig. 4.23 on p. 115.

photographer (David Hemmings) buys one in an antiques shop and "grooves on it" on the studio floor where he also "shoots" fashion models.[32] Yet sometimes today actual or "found" industrial propellers still present themselves within abstract sculptures. Donald Lipski, who subsumes industrial hardware into "hard" Surreal sculptures, has made several pieces out of boat propellers. Otherwise, Wade Saunders, himself an abstract sculptor, has written of Mark di Suvero's attraction to heavily thingly, found matériel, "things whose identity can't be subverted—a giant propeller, for example," in the case of di Suvero's *Sunflowers for Vincent* (1978–83). Such an element may not be thoroughly subsumed into the new conception, finds Saunders, who then would "rather talk to the designer or maker of the propeller than to the sculptor."[33]

Postmodernistically, Joel Otterson makes reference to Brancusi in his work, particularly with two tall, slender, freestanding pieces made of end-to-end baseball bats plus other thingly equipage and entitled *Bat in Space.* Otterson's Brancusi-isms are obviously parodic, though probably not so much against the master as against the cult of culture and, even more, the indulgences of this culture and its artworld here and now. Like other works by Otterson, one bat piece from 1984 has a post-Pop, ironized "all-American," self-consciously fetishizingly *sportif* aspect that is totally trophy-like—comprehending, while it's at it, an actual athletic trophy as well as a bottle of soda pop of air-headedly technological blue hue. "Heavier" in their wit are two *Non-Found/Un-Found* sculptures of 1986, one having the title extruded to *Non-Found/Un-Found Attracting Configurations,* whose pair of—already absurdly "improved," industrially "perfected"—aluminum baseball bats fused tip-to-tip, is subsumed, as rather subversively "found," for a thing so common, under a more metaphysical look (Fig. 15).

Even quite different earlier works by Otterson, however, pertain to the line of thought being navigated here. Take his lumpy, somberly uningratiating conglomerates of little bits of junk and pseudoprecious stones, sometimes hanging free, like some desperately homemade cannonball, from the ceiling: these might as well be mockeries of Gabo's Constructivist idolatry of the plumb line as emblem of attainable perfection. Yet Otterson's

---

32. Thanks to Mary K. Weatherfield for reminding me of this.

33. Wade Saunders, "Risk and Balance," *Art in America,* December 1983, 128–35, here 134. Joseph Pennell, a Whistler disciple drawn to the "wonder of work," meaning heavy industry and construction, made at least one print of giant ship propellers in a defense plant; on him in light of Robert Smithson, see my "The Panama Canal and Some Other Works of Work" (1971), in Masheck, *Historical Present: Essays of the 1970s* (Ann Arbor, 1984), 117–25.

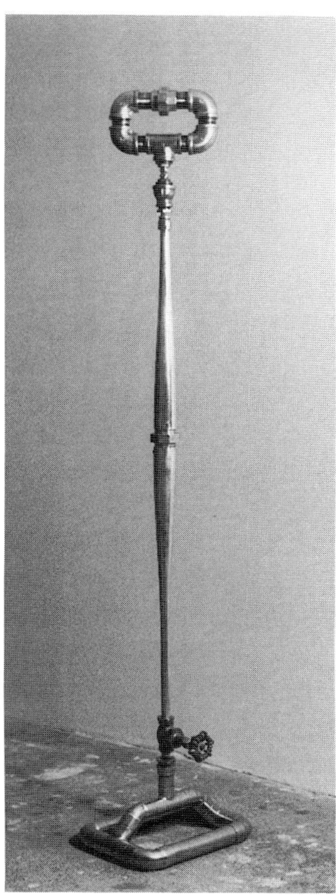

Fig. 15   Joel Otterson, *Non-Found/Un-Found,* 1986, copper, brass, steel, and aluminum, 80 x 17 x 13 inches.

sculptures are double-edged in that they pursue a perfectionism of their own without pretense. The evident pains this sculptor takes in his handling of pipes and plumbing fixtures may not equal those of Wittgenstein worrying for a good year about how to get two radiators and their necessary plumbing to fit together absolutely right in the corner of a room, but Otterson's elements are hardly aimless in formal effect. Almost like it or not, this artist shows modernity to be surprisingly elastic as he extends it one more time to a point where the next ordinary propeller might threaten to seem practically as good as (just) another *Bird in Space.*

Brancusi's by no means naturalistic *Bird* is not a bird but a "bird," and as such one of the most winning essentializations of natural into "pure" form in classic early modern art.

As I write this, Time-Life Books is engaged in a television and direct-mail promotion for a "Library of Curious & Unusual Facts." One of the volumes, apparently that entitled *Feats and Wisdom of the Ancients,* purports scientifically to present, from an Egyptian tomb, "a perfect, 7-inch scale model of a working glider—2,100 years old," this as evidence that the ancient Egyptians already knew glider flight! Can the history of science ever have heard a more preposterous claim than this, of finding a "scale model" of no definite prior object?

Apparently it does not sufficiently impress those who make this claim that the object in question is an actual-sized but "poetic," metaphorical (or even toy) "bird" rather than a wrong-sized aircraft, even if it can actually be made to sail through the air—as birds *as well as* airplanes do. The piece in question, 18 centimeters long and known as the "Saqqara Object," in the Egyptian Museum, Cairo (Inventory No. JE.33109; Exhibit 6347), "was discovered at Saqqara [in] 1898 among [N.B.] carved wooden representations of birds"; it is only because "no bird has a parallel wing and deep vertical tail fin" that "some aviation historians and engineers around the world have been tempted to compare this model to our modern plane."[34] Which is to say that even at the turn of the twentieth century some think the Saqqara Object is a model of a glider only because it isn't naturalistic enough to seem an image of a bird. For them, quite clearly, the propeller has utterly displaced the *Bird in Space.*

---

34. Letter from the general director's office of the Egyptian Museum, Cairo, 5 May 1991. Also helpful in the matter of the Saqqara Object were Florence Friedman, of the Museum of the Rhode Island School of Design; Mary Gow, of the Brooklyn Museum; and Susan Lukesh, of Hofstra University.

9

ATTAINING TO NATURE: MAUREEN CONNOR

In opposition to the prevailing culture and its favored forms of sublimated art, a notion of nature as a simple given, to which one might withdraw from cultural complexity, was manifest, often to markedly feminist purpose, in much sculpture of the 1970s. When early on, Maureen Connor began to disassemble clothing and to piece together the textile elements thus obtained into reliefs and then freestanding sculptures, her project was already more complex than most contemporary primitivizing reversals, with their tendency to offer anything fibrous or raggedy as approximating a look of myth or, by a favorite justification of the time, primeval "ritual." Differently, what Connor has been up to is sophisticatedly related to nature; it is, if anything, open and ceremonious rather than obsessively ritualistic, which may also be to say that it is rather Baroque.

In systematically disassembling clothing, specifically in undoing its once literally *con*structive seams, Connor was in one sense dismantling conventional, especially female, dress; at the same time she was returning her materials, those very stuffs, not simply back closer to the state of natural fibers and, by implication, to traditionally female processes of spinning and weaving, but most precisely to a calculated industrial neutrality where, as Marx was interested to consider, natural material is first regularized in preparation for subsequent production—the neutrality, that is, of standard art materials, including canvas and linen considered as yard goods. Note how literal Connor's "deconstruction" was: whereas Rodchenko's famous Constructivist clothing for workers is usually considered at the stage of patterns, as pieces cut out to shape and awaiting assembly into wearable garments, this artist arrived in reverse at cloth shapes of the kind only to rework them, in turn, into categorically "de-applied" art (sometimes, indeed, as mock paintings, as with her 1978 relief *Count Orgaz Comes Again*).

Most consistent in the development of Connor's sculpture over the last decade has been one or another way of fixing what is essentially draped cloth, as if in literal concretization of that most "abstract" feature of classical artistic practice, the drapery study as an exercise in sheer form and light-and-shade. An installation in the museum and cloister of Santa Maria de Castello, at Genoa, in the summer of 1986, is telling in this regard: Connor set white plaster drapings in a row of blind cloister windows, like "statues" in niches, and before an early Renaissance fresco of prophets, at one end of the row (itself *en grisaille*) she set on the floor what looks like a whole grouping of white-draped figures, minus bodies. Her new works, of wax and plaster, depend upon and extend such sculpturesque thinking; in them the provisional character of the drapery study is still felt in the working of voluptuous billows, rippling convolutions, and distinctly fleshly edges.

But precisely in having the only partial closure, or rather the open completeness, of shells, or even more, boat hulls, they assume a new self-definition and identity as wholes. Surely one can read the abalonelike gorgeousness, not to mention the inward-turning concavity, of Connor's new pieces (Fig. 16) as categorically female as well as related to an entire tradition of shell ornament at once bound to nature and abstractly vitalistic, extending from Mannerism through the Baroque to the fantastic extravagances of imaginative designs for objects by Juste Aurèle Meissonnier in the Rococo. As to boats, the very way they pertain to the working culture of men while being linguistically considered feminine, may be implicated. There is, too, the hanging of ship models like altar lamps in churches in maritime locales (even in New York), punning on the idea of the architectural "nave" as like a ship (Lat., *navis*). Before several of Connor's new sculptures one might well recall Bernini's ultimately Baroque fountain in the form of a ship, the *Barcaccia* (1627–29), itself a concretized metaphor

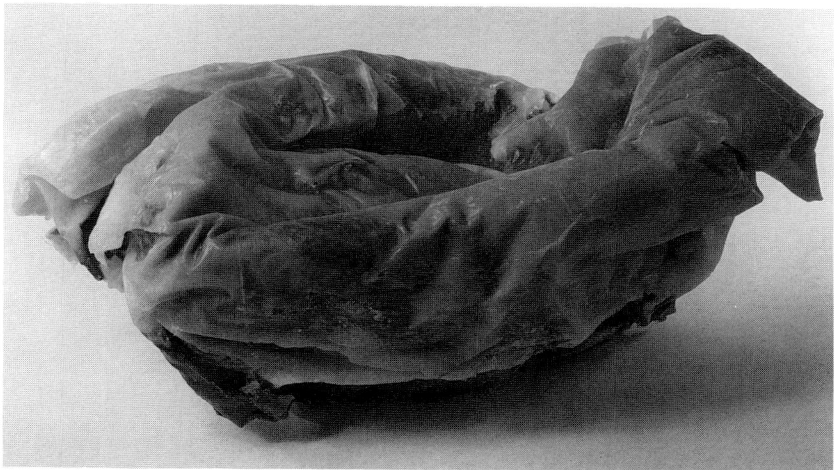

Fig. 16   Maureen Connor, *Fibrillation,* 1986, wax, plaster, and cloth, 25 x 11 x 11 inches.

for the Church in the sense of the "ship of state" and a sculpture that has been described as a "strange vessel, a kind of aquatic mutation, [which] combines the . . . mouldings of a ship, and fleshy edges, almost as if it were some sort of giant fish"; in a "prodigious fusion of vital forces," it is said, the *Barcaccia* "approaches" an organic state.[1]

Connor's *Floating Island* (1985) is unique among her boatlike new pieces in hanging free in midair, like one of the churchly ship models. In making this piece the artist was conscious of the fact that the, to them, massive sailing ship of Captain Cook struck the natives of Hawaii (who knows how metaphorically) as a "floating island," which, as a present-day recollection of a specific and historical early encounter with tribal culture necessarily entails a "primitivism" of a sophisticated order. One need not even notice *Floating Island* is modeled over one of those vacuum-formed, plastic topographical relief maps, to see as expressively considered the muddy, earthen brownness of its encaustically clotted, virtually barnacled, surfaces. As a matter of fact, thanks to the necessity of melting the wax, and to the piece's free suspension in the air, all the earthly elements of nature must be implied.

---

1. Howard Hibbard and Irma Jaffe, "Bernini's *Barcaccia,*" *The Burlington Magazine,* CVI (April 1964), 159–70, here 168.

That the much larger *Lifeboat* (1986), of an icy waxen whiteness, is too slim and lithe, like a canoe, simply to "represent" a lifeboat, at least one of familiar type, only heightens the purely sculptural aspect of a shape whose pointed "prow" drags on the floor while *her* blunt "stern" hangs from a single cord from the wall. In overtone, this work is at once local-primitive, resembling as it does the "dugout" canoes of Indians native to New York; American-mythic, what with the classic "Whiteness of the Whale" of Melville's *Moby Dick*; and modern-universalizing, at least in line with all the UFOs, those ultimate vessels of wonder, commonly reported as "cigar-shaped." These are, of course, free associations; but Connor's work at large welcomes associations that concern not nature merely, but human consciousness rooted in nature.

With the floor-bound *Swell* (1986), Connor has directly determined a sculptural metaphor, in an aim, in her words, "to make a boat part of a wave." In doing so she has as much as realized in freestanding, if low-lying, sculpture a standard exemplar of metaphor itself often given in studio talk and art poetics: "The ship ploughs the sea." The curling gunwale of *Swell* is indeed in itself wavelike, while the whole seems not so much "taking on water," or swamped, as *taking a wave,* broadside. Everything about the piece, including its seemingly pliant bulges, corroborates a sense of flexing, unpeaking *swell*: putting it this way risks evoking a caricatural gush more appropriate, say, to heavy popular "art glass," with its gratuitous molten peaks and ripples; but then *Swell* could be said to show the unforced, ultimately Baroque conviction from which even such wares derive.

Two medium-sized pieces from 1986 present themselves as mythological in an orthodox classical sense: witness their titles, *Charon* and *Styx*. Thoughts of mortality here take virtually erotic shape—as is often the case in the Metaphysical poetry of John Donne and others in the Baroque era. These are in a sense empty, podlike vessels, but affirmatively cavernous, with utterly labial rims; the cavities around which their edges curl are, as it were, phallic in negative (not unlike the status of the lump of dental cement into which Duchamp slipped the little bronze element of his *Wedge of Chastity*). Inside, at the bottom, *Charon* is as much as salaciously lined with black lace, while on the exterior ripples like elegant silken drapery folds resemble fine convolutions in marble works by Louise Bourgeois—but also Bernini. The inside of *Styx* has exposed silk, while outside a vivid aquamarine band girds the "hull." In making *Styx* the artist recalled the experience of floating on a smooth pond with algae all around the edges, an interestingly circumscribed, reasonably person-sized experience of "oceanic" peace. Floating and death (and art) were comprised in a broader meditation, metaphysical enough, on whatever might finally be remembered as "continuing to exist after one is gone."

Fibrillation (1986), too, is a meditation on death, as well as a plastic pun on the heart as governing the system of blood "vessels" (Harvey's understanding of the circulation of the blood being one of the milestones of Baroque natural science). The title refers to ventricular fibrillation, an irregular, nonrhythmic pumping of the heart in coronary attacks, which interests Connor from reading in the scientific literature of chaos—especially on the breakdown of pattern or rhythm. It is at least not inappropriate that the cloth over which this piece is modeled and molded in wax and plaster is a crumpled woolen sweater, that is, a garment for covering the torso, which is to say, the chest and heart. Typologically, the piece might even relate to the sculptural urns for the hearts of French kings by artists of late Mannerist times.

While Connor's sculptures are shaped and elaborated, their concentration on permanently fixing materials that are pliant and temporarily molten has connections, in the artist's generation, with certain Minimalist sculpture and the general tendency of "process art." Connor's sense of "process," however, embraces natural process as a matter of life. Even the *povera* quality of her work, naturalizing in means and effects, is part of an achieving or attaining of an abstract "naturalism" by human agency.

By now, of course, everything *merely natural* has already been claimed, by industry or art, to a point where primitivism, in the sense of high-cultural retreat to some less alienated state of nature, is an impossible fantasy, more symptomatic than therapeutic. Connor calls attention to the 1965 prophecy, now expired but more than fulfilled, in which Claude Lévi-Strauss, comparing the relation of industrially advanced culture to the rest of the world with a virus only alive in relation to host organisms, predicted that by 1985 "the morbid hunger which drives us to gulp down all forms of past and present art in order to elaborate our own will experience a growing difficulty in satisfying itself."[2] Significantly, when she incorporates actual microorganisms into works of sculpture, as with actual pond algae (reminiscent of her experience of peaceful suspension that inspired *Styx*) in the pulpy substance of a large boatlike piece, Connor might almost be embedding microorganisms, at least temporarily, in a "culture" in the biologist's sense.

---

2. Claude Lévi-Strauss, "Art in 1985" (1965), in his *Structural Anthropology,* vol. II, trans. Monique Layton (Chicago, 1976), 281–83, here 283.

By the same token, any "Baroqueness" in Connor's work is freshly attained and not simply historicizing. Is it possible that a new artist's work might in some sense recapitulate not merely certain physiognomic traits but some sense of a like morphology as well—not just so many characteristic words, figures, or even their syntax, but something of a historical "grammar" itself? Even such a seemingly anomalous feature of Connor's work as (otherwise feminist) concrete-abstract projects in ironing cloth into complex geometrical forms, a few years back, can be considered in relation to the conventionalizations of (originally) Baroque etiquette. At any rate, an essentially Mannerist sense of literal, yet exotic nature permeates works by Connor of the mid-1980s, of concrete over cloth, where what is basically a drapery study assumes a peculiarly vermiculated or pocked, coral-like surface (coral having its own "process" aspect, as interfacing peculiarly between zoological and geological structure). So, too, the visibly direct embedding of cabbage leaves in the concrete but in itself also leaflike shape of *Cicada's Dream* (1985) is Manneristic in the sense of *Naturabguss,* the direct casting and incorporation of natural plants and animal elements in Mannerist ornamental art. Likewise, the incorporation of wheat mold in *Robe de Jardin,* also of 1985 (and is the mold still growing, in which case the piece could be dated, for the time being, "1985–?"): here a twisted swag of drapery hangs, Manneristically enough, upside down from a wire, its original point of hanging now *en pointe* on the floor. Thus it is out of just such "Mannerism" that the "Baroqueness" of Connor's new vessel-like work, which is generally more voluptuously engaged in the interplay of human and natural vitality, has sprung.

All Connor's recent wax-and-concrete pieces, none of them huge, could easily have been made as *wax "for" bronze* and "scaled up" for monumental casting. In the Reagan period, we saw a too easy and compromising desire to effect in inflationary, overscaled bronze sculpture an unearned, unachieved grandiloquence.[3] Connor's pieces can only seem all the more true and just, in scale, material, and workmanship, by comparison. How her new work concerns the humane grandiloquence of the Baroque is not a matter of grandeur of scale. It does concern nature in heartily active human possession in that great earlier age of science, and individual artistic integrity and aspiration in an age at least as notorious as ours for its open political strife and utterly planetary ambition.

---

3. President Reagan himself was absurdly pompous when he meant to be grandiose, but then how the grandiose is akin to the magnanimous would be difficult for such a Weberian Calvinist type to comprehend.

10

ROBERT GOBER'S NON-READYMADES

Robert Gober appeals to partisans of tough, *thingly* yet also intellectual abstraction as well as to fans of certain alternative, revisionist modes of artmaking. Gober's best-known works look like, but are anything but, heavy-duty industrial sinks. You might think they were gross in the sense of "gross weight" (or as a sculpture teacher might say, of gross mass as opposed to pure volume), although they also carry just a tinge of the gross in that other sense of the baldly uncouth. Really, they are not sinks at all but completely artificial and, if anything, understated, chunks of pure, modeled sculptural shape in relief. The true irony is that as such they can be so subtle and reticent precisely as sculpture.

It is remarkable how varied are these curiously poetic reliefs. Along with otherwise quite different new works, Gober has produced further variations on the *non*sink conception. One such piece, conceived for the out-of-doors, consists of a pair of sinklike units, side by side, like husband-and-wife tombstones, embedded, for gallery exhibition, in a wide planter of real turf—presumably with the funerary aspect extending as far as the problem of "perpetual care." (Somehow the usual Goberesque rigor seemed compromised in at least one installation, the effect being too cartoony.)

However, another double-barreled work, a pair of nonurinals, elucidates the mutely Duchampian aspect of Gober's overall work as by no means superficial. The pair of elements hangs in obvious homage to Duchamp, whose notorious *Fountain* (!), that actual, industrially made (supposedly by Mott Iron Works) urinal signed "R. Mutt," dates from 1917 (yet also "c. 1915" as a plumbing fixture?). Indeed, more than a few of Gober's works allude to just such Duchamp "readymades"—those once manufactured, and subsequently artfully "found," objects, displaced from the realm of utility and baptized as full-blown works of art. Just arch enough for the 1980s is the tinge of oblique nefariousness implicit in the mutual adjacency of a pair of urinals, which would not have escaped Duchamp himself, while the urinal-*like*ness of the paired elements is more deeply connected with modernist sculptural thinking from Rodin to Roni Horn than one might suppose.

Furthermore, the wall-boundedness of both his sink and his urinal conceptions returns Gober's thought back to the absolute condition of relief. In pencil studies for sink-type pieces, drawings that show an alert and nicely flexed touch on behalf of such ostensibly simple proposed shapes, Gober unself-consciously indicates a horizontal floor line, so that the forms do not float scalelessly on the page but are anchored, already at this stage, in a relief conception.

Now there are also noncribs (Fig. 17), nonplaypens, and other freestanding pieces of nonfurniture, including a would-be dog's bed and a chair you wouldn't sit in, if only for fear of soiling or mussing it. Both dog's bed and chair look suavely odd in hand-painted, chintzlike slipcovers of that kind of impacted "good taste" that as it were bulges out, or at least threatens to, in an extremism of self-repression. Call it Calvinist kitsch, perhaps specifically the *yuppische* WASP kitsch of the 1980s, which included many thousands of otherwise reasonably straight-looking men wearing tassled loafers to the office. The dog's bed is a similar, corollary specimen of life-style too, in, say, a prissified L. L. Bean, coed Ivy League mode—but distractedly, mind-wanderingly refined, or else aimlessly *sensitif.* Maybe all Gober's sculptures are really, as one used to say, "head stuff."

Gober's plain, almost inane, criblike and playpenlike pieces deserve some close reading. You expect a baby crib to rise, like a cage, a kennel or a little jail cell, from a rectangular plan. Well, what if somebody builds one on an *X* plan instead? Otherwise generic wooden baby furniture mutates into disengaged and strangely, almost mistakenly "pure" prismatic structure, this enameled, innocuously enough, a plain glossy white. As to the

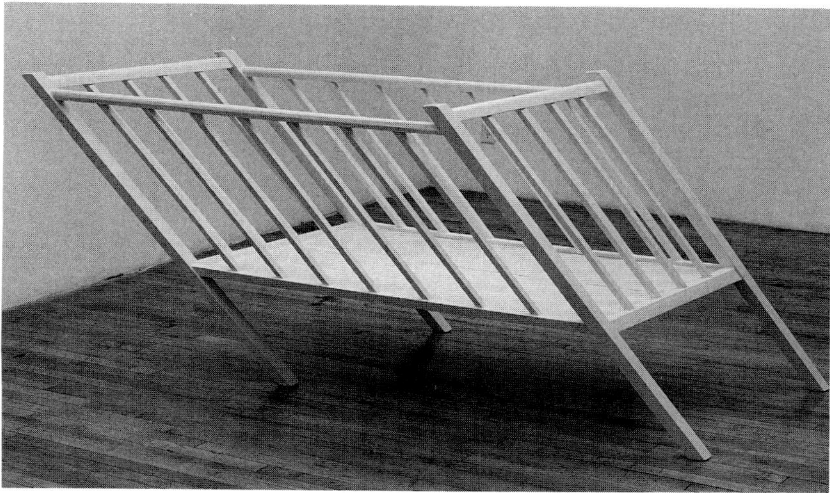

Fig. 17   Robert Gober, *Pitched Crib,* 1987, wood with enamel paint, 38¼ x 77 x 52 inches.

topologically screwy, antifunctional design of these sculptures: what one small kink in the regular formula can do, as if genetically, to such a simple construct! The workmanship is too spiffily plain for the result to seem at all ineptly hobbyistic. For sculpture's sake, you can consider such a construction a structural circumlocution, purposefully roundabout, that is *anything but* a baby crib or playpen.

For the enamel paint job as well as for the quietly "freaked" grillwork of wooden slats, these pieces are second cousins to Marcel Duchamp's "corrected readymade" *Apolinère Enameled,* done in New York in 1916–17, that touched-up little shallow, stamped sheet-metal advertising relief showing a little girl inanely painting the slats of a bedstead, each a different color of "Sapolin" enamel. Here, in a hilariously literal form that manages to extend the thought of Duchamp's original piece, Gober sends up the favorite snow job of Western representational *painting,* perspective rendering.

Gober's deadpan skewing of a playpen, or rather what *might have been* a playpen, would surely have amused Duchamp. But let's get one thing straight: none of Gober's sculptural objects actually is a readymade. His Duchamp allusions are precisely that, allusions, effected by objects made as full-fledged sculptures. Has any sculpture that did not eschew matter (as in

Conceptual Art) ever been as practically *invisible,* or at least as overlookable, as this?

Like Duchamp before him, Gober plays on stereotypic masculinity. An elusive but telling example is an oblique, enigmatic, and thoroughly demanding piece called *Plywood*—which must also be a comment on the Minimal Art that now serves the purpose of old-masterism in Gober's generation. Now this is no shelf item. Any American handyman would have to notice that the thing is decidedly not the usual 4-by-8-foot sheet of ⅝-inch fir plywood leaning against the wall, but is "off" standard just enough, at 94¾ by 47 inches, to seem at least "custom." Even he might not be prepared to notice that it has also been built up, in lamination, by hand. Whatever else it is "supposed to be," our handyman would have to acknowledge it as something willfully destandardized and unique, that is, rather like an artwork and perhaps equally impractical or "useless." Aesthetically, however, it really sort of *does a job,* leaning against the wall and sagging under its own heft, while also, admittedly, doing a number. Weird, some would surely insist, though still having to concede that the guy must be good with a power saw.

If Gober is also taking the poker-faced constructs of Minimalist sculpture for a ride, he certainly seems to know where he is going. It is all too easy for sculpture to amount to little or nothing more than an annoyingly arty, three-dimensional equivalent to mere prose, like all the rest of the world's hardware—and junk. But what Gober produces is a rather shyly, but nevertheless essentially, poetic object. His sculptural voice is virtually a whisper, but a strong one indeed—clear, articulate, distinct.

Gober's work becomes more and more convincing as true abstract sculpture planted, pretty much incognito, in the world of ordinary things. If for now it still looks light, well, just turn to the "sinks" that aren't sinks, whose more voluptuous abstraction is no less pure. One way or the other, you can't expect to settle in with slippers, pipe, the evening paper, and the family dog.

Photo-Ideas

While photography is generally "of," or at least "out of," the world, with its own materialist excitements, it is also *of* the mind and mentality, if rarely "spiritual" (*geistlich*). The sheer physical thinness of the photographic emulsion, its apparent negligibility as almost mere residue of medium, sends its image almost electrolytically to the brain. In putting the matter this way, I must be influenced by an essay that I have long considered one of the best of all speculations on photography, George Santayana's "The Photograph and the Mental Image" (written between 1900 and 1907), in which the American aesthetician suggests, a generation before Surrealism, that the photograph strikes us as if it were a memory image of our own.

Clearly, the first-generation photographer Henri Le Secq appeals to me because his inescapable *mentality* is so rationally constructive; some would reduce this to the formalism of a painter's sense of composition, but Le Secq's consciousness shows a deeper poetic suffusing even his most takeable-for-granted props. Paul Strand is indeed beloved of formalists, but my essay on his *Cristo with Thorns* considers how detached this image of a religious image may or may not be from its ostensible subject and from artistic tradition.

There is formalism and there is formalism. It was around the time I was writing the Strand essay, and teaching at Harvard, that in Boston I discovered the "Starn Twins" (a tag I suggested for David Wojnarowicz's poster for a group show I arranged, their New York debut), which led to their first article ("Of One Mind: Photos by the Starn Twins of Boston," *Arts Magazine,* March 1986) and my abiding admiration for their art.

THINK-SHOTS: HENRI LE SECQ

Jean-Louis-Henri Le Secq Destournelles studied painting with the academic Paul Delaroche and is said to have learned photographic technique from Gustave Le Gray, another Delaroche pupil, but his photographs are anything but academic. While Le Secq's work is known to fans of nineteenth-century photography, he tends to get anthologized as a landscapist or an architectural specialist rather than for his fanatically rigorous vision of still life, in which appears something resembling the critical cerebrality and utter "linguistic" concreteness of Cézanne—not unlike photography today that freshly engages the artificiality of the image so as to provoke alertness to concept. Le Secq's best landscape photographs, done like the rest of his work around the midpoint of the century, are tantalizingly vacant *photographs,* affirmatively enough, *of nothing*—if "nothing" can cover the plain world as rendered transparent to reason, as with a famous picture of a dwelling built right into the side of a quarry, which would have fascinated Cézanne. In his official photographic documentations of the French cathedrals Le Secq did indeed pioneer the laying bare of the sheer, quasi-"abstract" structurality of architectural form, notably but not only as regards aggressively cropped images of building details. It is, however, precisely the deeply mental "abstraction" of his own photography, not any superficial formalism, that Le Secq's (wonderfully) contrived still lifes of the 1850s not only share with his arguably "pure" landscapes but show forth outright.

Le Secq probably knew the photography of W. H. Fox Talbot (his album publisher worked to improve Talbot's printing methods) as well as that of Gustave Le Gray, and he would readily have taken to Niépce's works, such as a view of Parisian rooftops as shifting, Cézannean planes, or, even more to the point, a still life, *Set Table,* with a rigid, tall/short/medium/short/tall array of isolated, silhouetted objects punctuating the luminous white field of a tablecloth in dressy formality. But however inspired or confirmed he may have felt by anybody else's work, Le Secq developed a kind of still life in which objects as tokens of rational manipulation and exchange take carefully deliberated places in a lucid mental structure of more than formal relations that looks back to Chardin and forward to Cézanne in French painting.

Household items are Le Secq's still-life props (as with Jan Groover's kitchen still lifes today), including, for instance, a vessel holding a spoon cocked at a Chardinesque angle or a knife angled off a table edge in just the way that Cézanne, too, pays respect to Chardin. And Chardin above all would have understood Le Secq's cultivated, rationalistic enchantment with finely crafted things (like his own works), things by no means on loan from the state of nature. Hence flowers and fruit are played down, almost as possible contaminants of a more mathematical intellection, not unlike the more complex way Cézanne would struggle bravely with his apples to attain a stable permanence (= immortality?).

Since Le Secq was also an etcher, and a photographer of contemporary artists' paintings, his objectifying handling of still-life motifs can be seen in the light of nineteenth-century "reproduction" artwork, first in engraving and etching and later in photography—that bourgeois portraiture of *objets d'art* which perhaps announced the "age of mechanical reproduction." I have a typical album of such engravings, with tastefully "artistic" images of arms and armor, decorative art and the like, from the Louvre and other sources, by various graphic artists, all handsomely but mostly monotonously printed by the ubiquitous "Delâtre." (Needless to say, such albums, as early coffee-table books, anticipate not only the "museum without walls" but also the "Nelson Rockefeller Collection" of synthetic stand-ins for masterpieces.) Although as a rule the items appear singly, sometimes several objects are composed into tidy still clusters, as with "tie-ins" in modern merchandising. Again, one cannot overlook in such albums the sense of a merchandise catalogue, as if in anticipation of the commercialized art merchandising now all too common in museums (witness an actual bridal registry at the Metropolitan).

Most like a Le Secq still life here, with its familial, intimately known elements, is an image by one of the brothers Lièvre of a faience *vase à parfums* and a footed, covered cup of Venetian glass, both from the Rothschild collection, with a knife placed contrivedly between them. The rotund perfume jar sits slightly in front and to one side of a delicate, transparent covered goblet: as with Chardin (here perhaps summoned up in a pedantically antiquarian way) and Cézanne—and also Le Secq—a conceptual opposition and complementarity prevail, between something short, spherical and opaque, and something tall, cylindrical and transparent, both being covered vessels.

Le Secq may parallel this order of highbrow illustration in a still life of a metal ewer and a footed metal cup or chalice. But the heavy, Victoria-and-Albert clunkiness of such metalwork, often even stuffier in "reproduction" prints, is overridden by a distinctly photographic perception of light as physically playing onto shiny yet artfully variegated surfaces: ornament is, so to speak, taken literally, or rather substantially, as the occasion of a superseding aesthetic transformation. Compositionally, a few posies around the foot of the cup help it to counter the massiveness of the ewer, with the leaning spoon modulating between the heights of the two vessels. Le Secq shows subtlety in the spacing of the two main elements as well, for the close juxtaposition of their profiles calls inquiring attention to the extent to which their comparable ornamental bands do or do not correspond.

The depth of field of Le Secq's lens produces effects simpler than, though hardly unlike, Cézanne's give-and-take between volume and the plane. Unlike the "reproduction" graphics, but much like Cézanne in still life, Le Secq goes right for the structural forthrightness of simple objects, which he then extends to utterly lucid relations between them. Were this for either artist a question of simplistic purism, it would exclude the painted decorations and other "unnecessary" formal inflections that both artists can be seen to welcome into still life as compatible evidence of the play of artistic intellection.

*　*　*

When Chardin, Le Secq, and Cézanne include crafted objects, even elegantly crafted ones, in their still lifes, they show real sympathy with them as at once the finished product of somebody else's workmanship and the starting point of their own artistic thought and handwork. For his part, Le Secq's still life of an elegant painted vase compares, say, with Chardin's *Bouquet with White Procelain Vase with Blue Decoration* (Edinburgh). A broad band of crisscrossing diagonals around Le Secq's vase is internally in tune not only with his presentation of the corner of the tabletop up front (thus allowing the sides to veer off unexpectedly to the left and right), but also with the larger sense of a governing structure of sheer thought (not mere consistency of pattern) that Cézanne might well have acknowledged. Further, Le Secq is sometimes pleased to offer categorically folkloric elements—typically, pleasant "country" motifs—such as the chanticleer and stylized floriated ornamentation on certain crafted items. These motifs are, typically, cheerfully but not dumbly painted. Instead of capitalizing on anything anonymously folkloric, much less patronizing it, Le Secq seems to entertain such motifs, pleased to convey the modest artistry he finds, filtered through, rather than censored by, his own sophistication.

Another of his still lifes, which were published as "Picturesque Fantasies," can exemplify Le Secq's intellectual comprehensiveness. All in the usual line-up, as if at attention, are two filled crystal glasses, a dark spirits bottle with white label, and a photographic lens (Fig. 18). Yes, yes, we know: the lens is an internal reference to the medium; but it also appeals more pervasively to analytical intelligence, as one, perhaps the chief, element in a family of things all related by appeal to sensitive and accomplished (much more than only luxurious) craftsmanship—even as regards, presumably, the spirits contained in what must, at that, be a *hand-blown* bottle.

Moreover, we are welcome to infer that inside the lens casing is another highly refined piece of glasswork, even as we know for certain that the bottle contains a liquid that might well *look* solid, even like glass. The lens is categorically similar to the bottle not only for its cylindricality and its shiny, reflective smoothness, but also in that the concave and hollow lens cap structurally both matches and counters the bottle's cork, itself convex and solid, as a cylindrical closure for a cylindrical opening. The one closes on the outside of a cylinder, the other on the inside, even as both tripartite objects (vessel, contents, and closure) join in an alliance of categorical difference as against the pair of interchangeably *like* glasses.

If the lens is at all privileged in this quartet of objects, it is no doubt

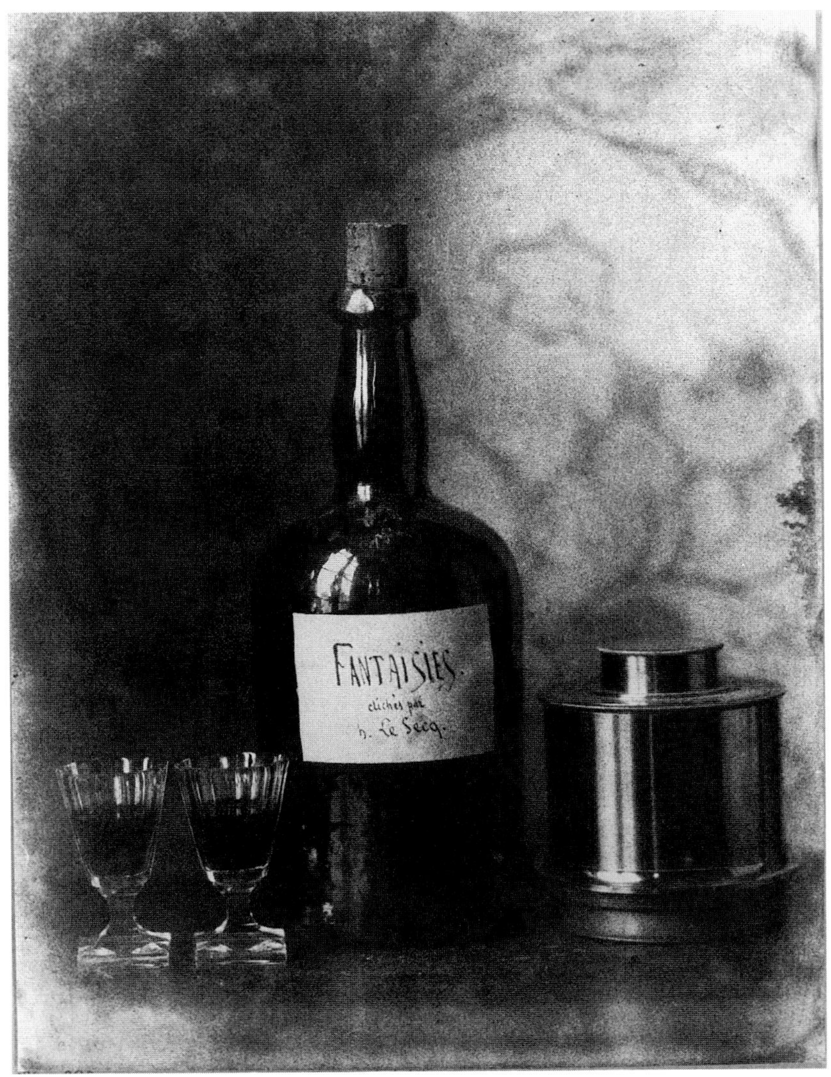

Fig. 18   Henri Le Secq, *Still Life with Bottle, Glasses and Lens,* c. 1855 (1930 print), photograph, 13½ x 10 inches.

because, bespeaking the exceptional beauty of nineteenth-century technical equipment, it is the motif to which the photographer's own dignified workmanship is specifically anchored. Equally human and personal is the way the very life-style of the socially privileged artist can be inferred, what with the instrument of artistic work resting convivially beside the bottle and the poured pair of drinks. Le Secq's well-heeled aloofness may not be too different from Cézanne's private introspection, either, though it happens he gave up photography by the end of the 1850s, when, it seems, it was getting so easy that any boob could do it, whereas Cézanne (whose old pal Zola took enough photographs to fill a recent book) shocked Émile Bernard with what Bernard thought an excessive enthusiasm for photography. In any case, on the label of his bottle Le Secq has inscribed in an amateurish hand, and in such a French way, too, the title of his larger still-life project, like some private vintage: "Fantasies. / clichés par / h.LeSecq."

Le Secq's special task in still life may have been to borrow things from the human world of things made with mind and hand, of thought manifest in material—in order to constitute more distanced, yet for that more comprehensive, concrete formulas of visual thought. Like Chardin's, Le Secq's still lifes are highly "conceptual" structures that nevertheless can tolerate being thoughtlessly apprehended, even if one might wonder to what gain (there is no turning back from consciousness, not since Adam). To that extent only, they may compare with the polite inconsequentialities of Fantin-Latour or something more pre-Cézannesque yet merely stiff by François Bonvin. But they also anticipate the more intransigent intellectuality, so demanding of consciousness (and may not critical consciousness be a redeemed form of guilt?), of Cézanne's related works—works that condense and intensify in the sublimating enfleshment of the painter's metahandwork the most intimate affinities of things of the world. For what Le Secq's smaller enterprise, with its roots in the tradition of Chardin, prepares for, and what Cézanne makes so fantastically rich and profound, yet all the while so lucid, is precisely the mutuality of resemblance and distinction in the visible and imaginable. Like a *philosophe* of visual form and structure, Le Secq isolates the germ of just what Roger Fry would one day celebrate in Cézanne: "The intellect is bound to seek for articulations. In order to handle nature's continuity it has to be conceived as discontinuous; without organization, without articulation the intellect gets no leverage."[1]

---

1. Roger Fry, *Cézanne: A Study of His Development* (1927), 2d ed. (New York, 1958), 40.

PHOTO-GLOSS:
ON PAUL STRAND'S
CRISTO WITH THORNS

Paul Strand's photograph *Cristo with Thorns, Huexotla, Mexico,* taken in 1933 and published in his 1940 *Mexico* portfolio, offers a would-be holy figure, or rather a holy would-be figure, in an interior space with part of a plant intruding into the field. (Fig. 19).[1] Simply to notice the fragment of plant is already to sense an element of succulent vitality, if only in contradistinction to the intrinsic fixity of what has to be a statue. Photographic, in contrast to sculptural, stillness is "natural" here—any stir in the leafage would only qualify it. Only a child could mistake this for a photographic portrait of Jesus taken in A.D. 33; on the other hand, the fact that a child might well do so concerns the theology of images, something not usually at issue in photography. One can imagine adults being led into trouble by the photographic fundamentalism of an image like Frederick Holland Day's *The Crucifixion,* staged with a model in 1898. Strand's figure of Christ, however, is actually a doll-like Mexican "santo," that is, a specifically devotional

---

1. This is a much expanded version of an essay for which I received honorable mention and a Reva and David Logan Grant in Support of New Writing on Photography, through the Photographic Resource Center at Boston University, in 1985.

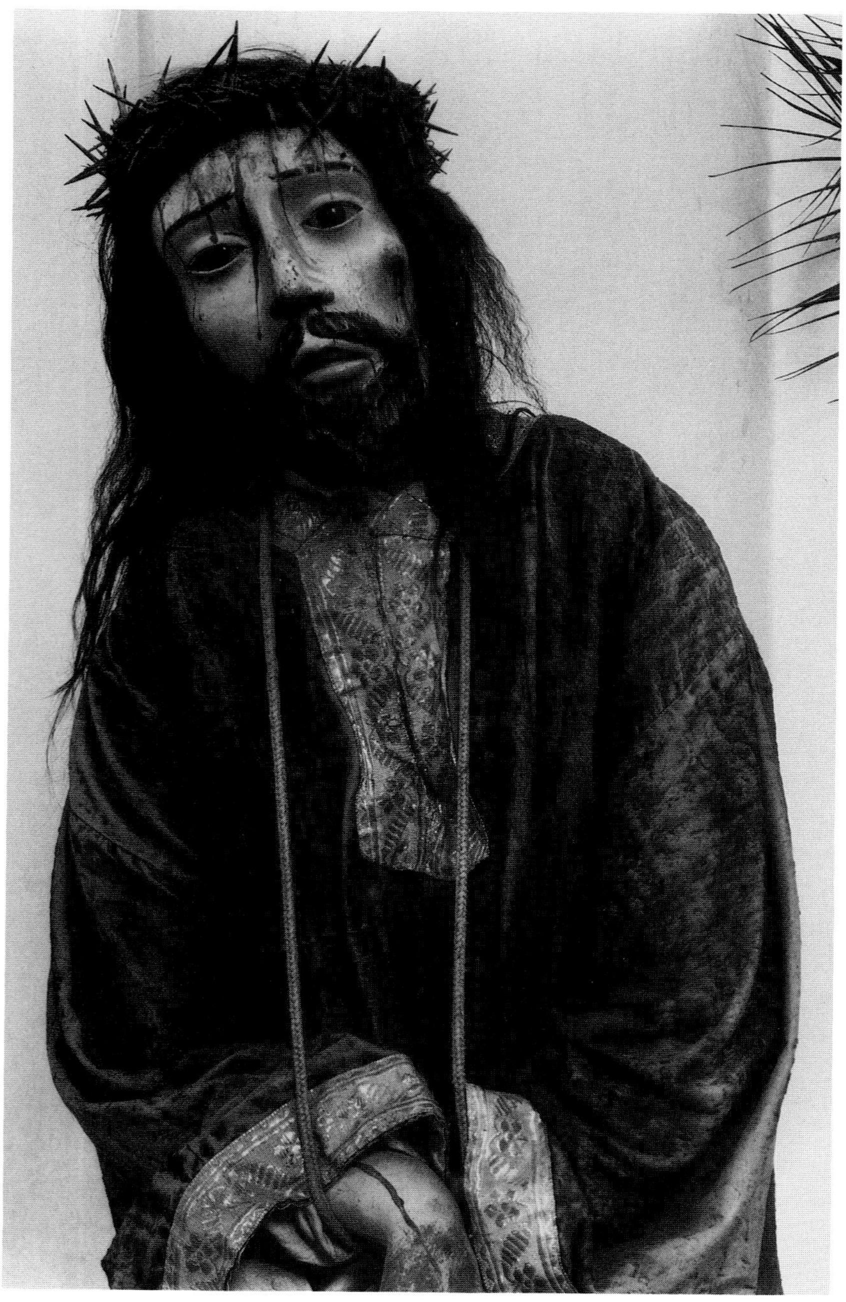

Fig. 19   Paul Strand, *Cristo with Thorns, Huexotla, Mexico, 1933,* copyright © 1940, Aperture Foundation, Inc., Paul Strand Archive.

object. As such, it has a fascinating double status, as mere "prop" yet also as sacred art in relay.

Having admired Strand's *Cristo with Thorns* for years, my sense of it has only recently become clear in relation to another image, the lithograph *La Sainte et le Chardon* (The Saint and the Thistle) by the Symbolist painter Odilon Redon, published in an edition of fifty in 1891 (Fig. 20). The print shows a haloed woman, a generalized Virgin Mary, head bowed; cropped below the waist (as is Strand's *Cristo*), she stands behind a plain parapet while half-clasping one hand to her waist. Redon's entire image, figure and all, seems ambivalently sacred and profane, owing to the conjunction of a wan moodiness in the figure and the prickly, weedy rawness of the thistle.[2]

Redon's *Sainte* has literariness written all over it. The artist had already dwelt vividly on the spikiness of the Crown of Thorns in another lithograph, *Christ* (1887)—a head only, with suffering eyes and a particularly prickly thorn crown, plus a single long thorn stabbed into Christ's forehead. In scriptural conjunction, thistles and thorns are twin images of arid, spiritless life;[3] the thistle itself betokens austerity, and in the case of Redon's *Sainte* suspiciously so, as if asceticism might be just another posture or "attitude," exchanging an odor of sanctity for a peculiarly entrancing perfume. That Redon's thistle can also connote misanthropy only corroborates hints of pervasive fin-de-siècle archness, a testy repressiveness presenting itself as ultrasensitivity. In Strand's photograph the santo represents Christ as the Man of Sorrows, whereas Redon's woman seems to be playing a role. While her halo stays put in the plane, her head pivots coyly in space, rather more make-believe than deeply Byzantine, not unlike some wayward detail on a person in drag.

The foliage, such as it is, in Strand's and Redon's images is structurally crucial. I am likewise struck, thanks also to the Strand photograph, by a

---

2. The structural role of Redon's plant is quite as relevant to Strand's *Cristo* as his figure is, and can be referred back, for its form and placement, to two famous paintings, of about a generation earlier, one categorically sacred and the other profane. In Dante Gabriel Rossetti's *Ecce Ancilla Domini!*, 1850, an upright embroidery frame holds a flat, stylized textile rendering of a symbolic lily stem in bloom, this coexisting with a "real" lily stem elsewhere in the picture. In Manet's *Woman with a Parrot,* 1866, the prongs of the parrot's perch splay out like the leaves of Redon's thistle even as they shy away, in the picture's surface design, from the irregular edge of the woman's gown. This unambiguously secular painting also serves to illuminate the structural role of Strand's fragmentary plant in relation to the architectural context. For the actual *Cristo* in the photograph is seen beside two intersecting whitewashed walls, with the sharp, palmy leaves of the plant projecting crisply dark against the right-hand plane.

3. Gen. 3:18; Is. 34:13; Hos. 10:18; Mt. 7:16; Heb. 6:08.

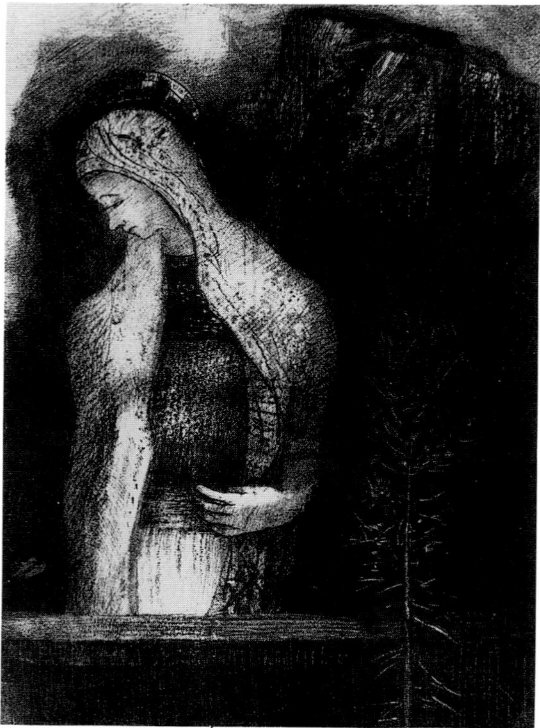

Fig. 20   Odilon Redon, *La Sainte et le Chardon*, 1891,
lithograph, 11⅜ x 8¼ inches.

pile-up of forms along the central vertical axis of Renoir's *Dance in the City*
(1882–83). There a dancing couple—the gentleman tall, dark, and in
evening black, the lady shorter, fairer, and contrastingly light in her gown—
intertwines before a background polarized into opulently decorative vege-
tation at left and the crisp plainness of classical architecture (an engaged
column and a stretch of untrimmed white marble wall) to the right. By
a kind of spillage, some fanning fronds of potted palm cross over from
the left in silhouette, garnishing the paired heads and shoulders of the
intertwined dancers (these fronds also relate understatedly to the male
dancer's tousled hair). Renoir's punctuation of the fulcrum of an otherwise
workaday composition by means of the palm fronds seems more than
incidental in light of Strand's photograph: I can almost imagine Renoir

being led to develop his hingelike join among halves, foliage, and blank wall, here conveniently muffled, into what in a more modern painting might amount to an "internal edge" with essentially modern intimations of the experience of discontinuity. Today, for example, an abstract painting by Stewart Hitch, *Private Dancer* (1985), compares, after the fact, with Renoir's *Dance in the City*,[4] as well as Strand's *Cristo*—and *Amaryllis, Paris,* a photograph by Robert Mapplethorpe—for its vertical bisection and the palmy or fernlike leafage that springs out along it, as if through a split or cleavage. Hitch's leafy forms comprise a weedy turf of "pure" brushwork. The structural similarity between Renoir and Hitch makes only more vivid the expressive difference between untroubled bourgeois pleasantry, in the case of Renoir, and in Hitch a lyricism accomplished, without force, against the grain of the way things are. Together, the earlier and later paintings help me to get at Strand's intruding fronds as structurally yet also expressively significant.

It is mainly Redon's print that serves my understanding of Strand's photograph. Photography, after all, is only a slightly younger form of printmaking; both are planimetric processes concerned with the tonal articulation of images in black and white (despite the development of color processes in both mediums). Both make possible image replication in large volume while also reserving, for economic or other purposes, the alternative of master-printed limited editions. The problem of print editions, of which we hear so much today in respect to photography, already pertained to graphics at the turn of the century, when an enthusiast of old-master and modern prints could complain that lithography was becoming vulgarized by the publication of large editions.[5] Now it happens that on this score Paul Strand might prove a special case: as Hollis Frampton once put it, "What Strand actually made, during 53 years, was a large number of negatives,"[6]

---

4. Hitch was not conscious of Renoir's picture while painting *Private Dancer,* whose title comes from a Tina Turner song. However, he has been interested in Ambroise Vollard's relay of Renoir's sense of the verb "to appropriate," with respect to Japanese prints, as reported in the dealer's *Renoir: An Intimate Portrait:* "No people should appropriate *(s'approprier)* what does not belong to their own race, if they don't want to make themselves look ridiculous"; trans. Harold L. Van Doren and Randolph T. Weaver (New York, 1934), 67.

5. In Frederick Wedmore, *Fine Prints,* The Collector Series (London, 1897), lithography is called "one of the more recent fads in Print Collecting . . . , far less important, indeed, and far less interesting than Etching, far less historic than Mezzotint" (221). Wedmore reports this comment by an artist-connoisseur: "You do not need to vulgarize lithographs by making too many impressions" (236).

6. Hollis Frampton, "Meditations Around Paul Strand," *Artforum,* February 1972, 52.

even though his *Cristo with Thorns* was printed in gravure for the *Mexico* portfolio—itself a limited edition that has subsequently been reprinted in a larger but still limited edition.

Both Redon and Strand studied the craft aspects of their respective graphic arts with specialists, namely Rodolphe Bresdin and Lewis Hine, who placed technique in the service of a literary-descriptive concept of subject matter. In this sense Bresdin's teeming, phantasmagoric, secular displacement of the visionary parallels Hine's otherwise very different pressing social documentary. Redon and Strand nevertheless managed to surmount the grossly technical—Redon with images that, however illustrational, amount to self-sufficient visual tone poems; Strand with images so objectifying that form and pictorial structure seem discovered as properties of visibility itself.

Early on in his career, Strand may well have fixed upon form as an antidote to literariness—possibly to a compensatory formalistic extreme. In the *Cristo with Thorns* this may be mitigated in part by recourse to a principal motif capable of implying that what is taken as seen ("figuratively" or not) comes, here at least, already invested with making and consciousness.

Modern photography, in its revolt against the "pictorialist" mystique, had precedents in earlier but already definitively modern painting. In this regard, consider Strand's well-known *The White Fence,* an unfadingly fresh study in space, tonal contrast, and balanced yet altogether unconventional composition, published in the June 1917 number of *Camera Work.* Here the fence of the title functions structurally as something more than a component of graphic design, depending for its scale, as does the entire image, on its implied relation to a house beyond in space. Yet the very independence that enables the fence to function as a form (a patch of crossing bands) and as a barrier seen in space manages to extend a specifically Symbolist tradition in modern painting that includes not only Gauguin's *Bonjour, Monsieur Gauguin* (1899), but also Kandinsky's *Improvisation No. 27 (Garden of Love II)* (1912)—and there is, interestingly enough, a photograph of the latter by Alfred Stieglitz in the Kandinsky Archives in Munich.[7] It should by now be obvious that to recognize such a pedigree is by no means to denigrate *The White Fence* as derivative, at least not in the old simplistic sense. On the contrary, new art (re)activates old, "retroactively."[8]

---

7. Hans K. Roethel and Jean K. Benjamin, *Kandinsky: Catalogue Raisonné of the Oil-Paintings, 1900–1915,* I (Ithaca, N.Y., 1982), cat. no. 430 on p. 422, with illus. after Stieglitz photograph.

8. The literary critic Harold Bloom is most responsible for elucidating how a later poet's

Strand's *Cristo with Thorns* merits closer regard, in part because it transforms rather than simply negates the more exclusively formal emphasis of *The White Fence* and other earlier Strand photographs. Its peculiarly high-voltage subject allows for other ways of acknowledging the intervention of the photographer's consciousness than formal contrivance alone. Strand was in Mexico as a documentary filmmaker for the Mexican government—only a year or so after Eisenstein left—and the *Cristo* shows a nice "documentary" forthrightness in its presentation of the santo as a cultural specimen bearing, for better or worse, the impress of colonial culture. One gets to apprehend the santo—an anonymous work made to be spiritually utilitarian—on its own terms: Strand shows the santo as it "really" is, even as he makes something personal of it.

In Strand's representation of a representation, the tilt of Christ's head off the vertical is compensated by the spikily interjected leaves in expressive if distanced analogy with the Crown of Thorns. With Strand's understated fringe of leaf-points along the right-hand edge, there is even perhaps the suggestion that, like the beard-rimmed face of Christ, his entire, incorporating image, conceived as likewise fringed, might present itself as visagelike (and thus perhaps with echoes of frontal images of an artist himself as Christ-like, such as those of Dürer or Blake). An astute complementarity would then hold between the leaf-points centripetally poking in, like some visual garnish, à la Renoir, and the very concept of a Crown of Thorns as a radially or centrifugally spiky thing. In any case, the *Cristo with Thorns* is a work, whether of "fine art" or of proudly humble technical application, that deals sympathetically with another work, also ambiguous as to art or craft. A fine example of a type of popular sculpture assumed to be more or less anonymous, the actual santo is, as such, of documentary or ethnographic, as well as aesthetic, interest.

Whereas Redon's poetic Symbolist religiosity hardly seems serviceable to religion, Strand's utter devotion to the artistic (re)presentation of a functionally devotional artifact leaves the motif much more spiritually intact. Here its stereotypic status is important. In French one can pun in saying that photographs make *clichés* of things, since "cliché" is also a term for the photographic negative. Upon being photographically "taken," things tend to stiffen into specimens in rigor mortis, and the resultant pictures of them can likewise stiffen into stereotypes.

---

work can "influence" an earlier one's. I have considered "retroactive influence" on several recent occasions: see, in the present volume, the section "The Play of Texts."

The santo already had a certain intrinsic stereotypicality when Strand confronted it; and in the political circumstances of revolutionary Mexico, it is significant that one cannot tell by internal evidence whether the statue is seen in a church or in a museum, even some "museum of atheism." Nevertheless, if anything, Strand's "taking" of it more than "captures" the object with its built-in spirituality intact; and, at least artistically, his own art or craft sympathetically animates, enlivens it.

That Strand was Jewish, and the sculptural image at stake categorically Christian as well as technically "graven," may suggest, whatever his theology, Simone Weil's extraordinary articulation of the position of a penetratingly sympathetic outsider.[9] Such a view amounts to little if it does not transcend sentimentality, as Strand manages to do. Indeed, if there is any irony here, it is that the *Cristo* is probably most likely to touch with religious affect the unchurched, "cultural" Christian, or the believer afloat in doubt.

That the santo shows Christ specifically as the Man of Sorrows necessarily entails an idea of animate, soulful life beyond the wooden stiffness that stamps the end of suffering mortal life. For the Man of Sorrows stands outside or above Gospel narrative as a figure of the Savior undergoing in a consolidated way the linear-sequential Passion. Here a Christ is encountered whose wounded humanity appeals to the divinely merciful in whoever beholds him, even in the civil strife of 1933 (or now). Actually, the Man of Sorrows is a contemplatively static rather than scripturally illustrative type whose popular diffusion stems ultimately from Northern European *devotio moderna,* as it is termed, of the late Middle Ages, in which the emphasis is always on direct, meditative identification with the figure, a willing scapegoat suffering on the individual sinner's behalf.[10]

Such a figure presupposes a spectator—here, the photographer at first, then oneself—with a responsive interior life, with the kind of "heart" that

9. For example: "We must have given all our attention, all our faith, all our love to a particular religion in order to think of any other religion with the high degree of attention, faith and love that is proper to it. In the same way, only those who are capable of friendship can take a real heartfelt interest in the fate of an utter stranger." Simone Weil, "Forms of the Implicit Love of God," in *Waiting for God,* trans. Emma Crauford (New York, 1951), 184.

10. See Gertrude Schiller, *Iconography of Christian Art,* vol. II, *The Passion of Jesus Christ,* reading, in part: "So direct is his confrontation with the spectator that the suffering Son of God and the sinful man seek one another in their love. Christ who has mercy on mankind himself implores mercy: 'Have done now.' Yet this entreaty is also an admonition from him who is to judge"; trans. Janet Seligman (Greenwich, Conn., 1972), 198.

is essentially holy (in an age of vapid religious "pluralism," this is perhaps the one meaningful common denominator). Notwithstanding Calvin (for to abolish metaphoric representation altogether as much as enshrines the fallen world), the santo offers unusual potential for immediate spiritual gain to the unschooled in its summary relation to the scriptural Man of Sorrows. Compared with this motif, the Crucifixion itself, self-evident as it might be thought, presupposes some modicum of New Testament understanding, however indirect, as anyone who has ever tried to explain it to a child is aware.

A sense of narrative becalmed, implicit in the Man of Sorrows theme, must have been artistically satisfying to Strand. In James Thrall Soby's words, "Strand's vision proposes for the most part a serene and motionless plastic order."[11] What better motif, then, than a statue, and a statue, at that, of a figure suspended between contradictions: this image of a "king" abased, of the divine enduring the most grossly inhumane, is concerned with both death and eternal life. So, too, the inanimate while naturalistic "statue morte" in some sense attains more "life" than ever in quotation, as relayed by the sympathetic photographer. Indeed, photographically defused of its naive gravenness, even the sophisticated believer for once gets to approach it in a quasi-naturalistic way. Recall how Cézanne, that genius of *nature morte,* was also fascinated by the statue figure as a representational motif: for him it became possible to negotiate the muscular male—and *pagan*—nudity of Puget's *Milo of Crotona,* not to mention the very figure of Eros, at such a remove.[12]

In producing his own imaginal redo in black-and-white of the vivid Mexican santo, a sculpture too fine in its own right to be reduced to condescending generic charm, Paul Strand as much as discovers some real working poetic affinity with the anonymous sculptor, not just some common ground that he might have claimed, imperialistically enough, for his own purposes. Whether that sculptor be considered an artisan or a fine artist matters little, except that Strand himself might have appreciated the ambiguity. This is a more-than-charming image of loving folkloric devotion,

---

11. James Thrall Soby, "Two Contemporary Photographers," in his *Modern Art and the New Past* (Norman, Okla., 1957). He also speaks of Strand's "Portraits of single figures or groups, architectural scenes and landscapes, revealed in the quiet essence of their being and monumental in definition" (173).

12. Of the Eros and a drawing of another statue (an *écorché*) that appears in *Still Life with Plaster Cupid,* c. 1895, Meyer Schapiro, in his *Paul Cézanne* (New York, n.d.) writes, "they are works of art, and as such represent the erotic and the suffering in a transposed form" (34).

presented as more than a curiosity,[13] and if Strand aestheticizes it some, he draws on the best that he, as craftsman and artist, has to offer. Especially telling is the way the figure gets to "bleed" out of frame by being cut off at the level of the hands, the agents of creative manipulation, which hang restrained in a sling—in contradistinction to the breezy intrusion, into the image, of lively leaves or leaflets, above. That the leafy plant is, appropriately for the Passion theme, a palm, seems less important than the innocent vitality with which it accompanies the "dead" stillness of the statue, like some slight rustle in a long still-shot in a motion picture. Perhaps, too, some element of "gringo," as well as modernist, reserve helps to steady things, much as a quasi-classical composure informs the great *Man of Sorrows* painted by Guido Reni around 1640. "Shot" and "bagged" without harm, brought home without exploitation into the sphere of modernity, Strand's *Cristo* is like some translation or poetic "imitation" at least as beautiful as its "original."

At the same time, *Cristo with Thorns* is a souvenir. It is also, deferentially enough, and Strand's creativity notwithstanding, a documentary photo. In fact, the photographer's cultural distance from the piece posed the risk of a detachment great enough to lose spiritual content.[14] Strand's deference toward the santo as a piece of nuts-and-bolts salvific hardware, however, issues in a "documentary" image that does not compromise the metapragmatic potency of the original. An ordinary tourist photograph, by comparison, only sustains sentimental association, while documentary photography strives to minimize the inevitable necessity of interpretive response.

In Strand's photograph, not only the santo but also the white walls are a local feature seen, noticed, and shown by a sophisticated outsider. As whitewashed, and thus also as photographically soaked with the bright, "true," local Mexican light, these walls project as a pair of ambivalently joined planes that might as well parallel the image surface, except, significantly, for their contribution to the sculpture's presence as a space-displacing object. The sculpture gets to display its material presence even

13. Weil: "Some . . . have faith exclusively in one religion and only bestow upon the others the sort of attention we give to strangely shaped shells" ("Forms," 184).

14. Which is often the case with contemporary advertising images which "deliberately exploit a confusion of truth and falsehood, because the possibility of 'distancing' from the subject that is set up in this way has an amusing and catchy effect"; Mark Roskill and David Carrier, *Truth and Falsehood in Visual Images* (Amherst, Mass., 1983), 64. In the same way, chic magazines sometimes flirt with low culture, and religion too, as trapped safely under a protective sheen.

as, due to truncation by the lower edge of the "frame," its specific location in real space is downplayed. Only the slight but consequential ambivalence as to the walls' corner being concave or convex allows the pointy fronds poking in at the right (in a clump at the top and several sharp pricks down the right-hand edge) to read as a pattern of sharp and irregular graphic inflections. Claims to (sculptural) space and (pictorial) surface overlap where Christ's left sleeve at once takes up volume in a nichelike cranny and graphically punctuates the right-hand or nearer wall with a compound curve.

But the whitewashed walls also entail the question of taste—"low," "high," or "slumming"—because they contribute to making Strand's picture, in an appropriate American socioreligious distinction, both plain and fancy. For in one sense this is a culturally "plain," as well as photographically "straight," image of a colorful ethnic item; in another, more complex sense, the santo overflows into the tasteful cosmopolitanism that imports it into "fancy" culture in fulfillment of aesthetic, but not unlikely also unconfessed spiritual, needs.

Strand uses the pristine walls to set the santo off in a way that suggests the urbane contemporary enthusiasm of Le Corbusier for not only the whitewashed folkloric architecture of the Mediterranean world, but whitewashed urban vernacular architecture as well. In fact, the architect was inspired to formulate a "law of whitewash," which he opposed unrelentingly to the "impurity" of decorative art.[15]

Whitewashed walls provide an ideal neutral "culture" for things of various origins, including, potentially, even Strand's print, in which the otherwise possibly *too* colorful santo floats in an ahistorical white present. Yet there is a history to this very attitude, this pleasure in presenting exotic, colorful, even specifically Mexican folk artifacts in specimenlike isolation in settings of otherwise "tasteful" restraint—notably as part of

---

15. Reyner Banham, *Theory and Design in the First Machine Age* (London, 1960), 218. Elsewhere, Le Corbusier, who romanticized the very process of making whitewash, is quoted as saying, " 'If the house is all white, the design stands out without any possible transgression: the volume of things is clear-cut; the color of things is categorical. Whitewash is absolute, everything stands out from it or goes down on it absolutely, black or white: it is forthright and straightforward. Set objects against it that are unclean *(malpropres)* or in bad taste: you see them at once for what they are. It is a kind of x-ray of beauty. It is an Assize Court sitting in permanent judgment. It is the eye of Truth. Whitewash is extremely moral. It is the wealth of the poor man and the rich man, just as bread, milk and water are the wealth of slave and king alike' " (Maurice Besset, *Who Was Le Corbusier?* trans. Robin Kemball [Cleveland, 1968], 16–17). I am grateful to Eduard F. Sekler for directing me to Le Corbusier's thoughts on whitewash.

the life-style of an intelligentsia in more or less conscious symbolic solidarity with supposedly less alienated, or at least less "developed" peoples.

Eisenstein, who had worked in Mexico in the early 1930s on the film *Que viva Mexico!,* conveys as much in a reflection on color: "How pleased I am when the striped ribbon of Filipino lace curls about and lies across the bright Uzbek bedspread. Or the embroidered Mongolian pattern stretches across the dark crimson background of the wall that is so effectively punctuated by the Mexican white paper emblem of All Souls' Day, and the other black mask with its bloody wounds, unexpectedly found this far from the semi-ritual world of the Mexican Indians."[16] In addition, one can think of the whitewashed buildings of the Greek islands as admired by architectural students in recent decades but really dating from the time of World War I, when the Greek "Tourismos" association had walls whitewashed, even over mural paintings.[17] And today, in Mexico itself, the calculated irregularities, the pronounced "photo-receptivity" and the subtly vivid coloration of Luís Barragán's elegantly "intellectual" houses carry on, no doubt with sophisticated self-consciousness, this modern "high Mexican-esque."

Strand's *Cristo with Thorns* evidences such taste at an early, formative stage, when the Mexican mural-painting revival was calling progressive cultural attention to the social revolution in Mexico. Probably more like Orozco than Rivera among the muralists, Strand resists ideological oversimplification, as much on grounds of taste as of religion. Possibly this is because the santo struck this highly cosmopolitan photographer, a native New Yorker of Bohemian descent who would eventually live in France, with just the right timbre of sentiment—in analogy, one might even guess, with the usually "gaudier" Infants of Prague. At any rate, the *Cristo* both is and is not a holy picture: without blasphemy or fanfare, it lets the santo be. Even as it can be taken neutrally as to creed and can be consulted credally too, under the personal and ideological circumstances this image abets neither idolatry nor political reaction.[18]

---

16. Sergei Eisenstein, "One Path to Color: An Autobiographical Fragment," in Lewis Jacobs, ed., *The Movies as Medium,* trans. Jay Leyda, (New York, 1970), 209.

17. Ronald Crighton, "Theophilos," in John Lehmann, ed., *Orpheus: A Symposium of the Arts,* II (London, 1949), 150–57, esp. 155.

18. For the possibility of a kind of porous ideological integrity, it may be worth considering how another great American photograph from the time of Strand's *Cristo,* Dorothea Lange's *Migrant Mother, Nipomo, California* (1936), may extend, without distortion in more "liberal" circumstances, the less escapable ideological conviction of the widely known lithographs of Kathe Kollwitz, in Germany. This possible influence was suggested to me long ago by William

*   *   *

As much as possible, all affirmative understandings—religious, spiritual, humane, aesthetic—are congruent in Strand's photograph, unlike the evidence of artful, though arty, Surrealist blasphemy in some practically contemporary photographs by Manuel Alvarez Bravo, a Mexican.[19] Bravo's *Alicia, desnude academico* (Alicia, Academic Nude), of about 1937, presents a woman seated, cross-legged, stable, and statuesque in the manner of the pre-Columbian figurines that Bravo admired and photographed for picture books. In 1938, stimulated by the use of bandages in the costumes of a visiting foreign dance troupe, Bravo had a doctor bandage the hips, abdomen (except for the pubic area) and ankles of the same model, for *La buena Fama durmiendo* (Good Reputation Sleeping), an image made for André Breton for the cover of a Surrealist exhibition catalogue. The still, recumbent nude suns herself on a blanket, accompanied photo-glamorously by four *abrojos*—bulbous lobes of thorny cactus, like peculiarly arch beach balls. On impulse, Bravo also produced a less calculated image, in some measure parodic of the Resurrection, *La Desvendada* (The Unbandaging), with the same model standing and unwinding her body bandage in a doorway. Much later in his career, *Las Tentaciones en la casa de Antonio* (Temptations in the House of Anthony, 1970) shows a standing female nude posed under a suburban clothesline, her head and shoulders masked by laundry, in a conception that can only extend the Symbolist, and proto-Surrealist, naughtiness of Odilon Redon's lithographic suite after Flaubert's *Tentations de Saint Antoine* (first series 1888).

In the spring of 1938, after Strand took the *Cristo with Thorns* but before he published it in his Mexican portfolio, Graham Greene had the experiences recounted in his *Another Mexico* (1939), a book offering a decidedly alternative view of the condition of the Catholic religion under the ostensibly radical socialist (but oddly freemasonic) Mexican revolution. As a Catholic, Greene was understandably angry over the persecution of the Church, not to mention political hypocrisy.[20] "Between November 11, 1931

Brimmer. Art historians who need the security of making things as deterministic as possible might care to note that Lange grew up in a family that included several German-trained lithographers; see Robert Coles, *Dorothea Lange: Photographs of a Lifetime* (Millerton, N.Y., 1982), 9.

19. The present discussion is based on Manuel Alvarez Bravo's untitled essay in Jain Kelly, ed., *Nude: Theory* (New York, 1977), with fig. 5 on p. 11, fig. 1 on p. 6 and fig. 4 on p. 10, respectively.

20. Graham Greene, *Another Mexico* (New York, 1964): "There is still an inclination to defend the Mexican Government on the part of labour organizations. But Mexico does not follow accepted ideological lines, as may be seen in the recent oil deals with Italy and Germany": 78n; next two quotations: pp. 69, 174.

and April 28, 1936," the novelist reports, "four hundred and eighty Catholic churches, schools, orphanages and hospitals were closed by the Government or converted to other uses." In the State of Chiapas he saw "the statues . . . carried out of the church while the inhabitants watched, sheepishly, and saw their own children encouraged to chop up the images in return for little presents of candy." Greene pays special, scrupulously unpatronizing respect to the many faithful Indians from the mountains and to the people of the towns who persisted (as in seventeenth-century Holland and under the "Penal Laws" in Ireland) in the sacramental practice of the faith, at risk, in secret. As for the Indians, the question of how orthodox or how superstitious their approach to a santo like the one Strand photographed might have been is academic in face of a totalitarianism that makes all believers kindred fugitives. One may even think of the *ecce homo* aspect of Strand's Man of Sorrows as a Christ under arrest and in custody.

Greene met up with one clandestine Catholic who happened to be a portrait photographer. At another point in the narrative, his description of one kind of photography, other than workaday portraiture, that held popular appeal, provides a counterpart to Strand's distanced, "outsider's" view of the Cristo as both exotic and sympathetic. It seems that the Mexicans were fascinated by pictures of themselves fictitiously planted almost anywhere but in their own habitat. In Mexico City, "at every corner photographers stood with their old hooded cameras on stilts and their own antique screens—an early steamship, a train, a balloon, improbable aeroplanes out of Jules Verne, and of course the swans and lakes, Blue Danubes and roses, of that nostalgic period."[21]

   Orozco once asked the painter Jean Charlot, a European Catholic artist who also knew the Mexican "scene," if he thought Rouault might have been influenced by "Mexican things" such as "the santos in the churches" or "the flogged Christ of the Holy Week."[22] Later comments by Charlot help give wider bearings on Strand's *Cristo* image. Reviewing an album of Mexican photographs by George Hoyningen-Huene, Charlot sees images of "ex-votos and clothed sculptures . . . , sacred dolls . . . so intent . . . on performing convincingly their sacred mimicries that it is difficult to think

---

21. Ibid., 99. Had Greene traveled a decade earlier, he might have visited the small portrait studio, in Mexico City, of Edward Weston, who worked and exhibited in Mexico in the mid-1920s, in the circle of Rivera and Orozco.

22. Jean Charlot, "Orozco in New York" (1959), in *An Artist on Art: Collected Essays of Jean Charlot,* 2 vols. (Honolulu, 1972), II, *Mexican Art,* 301.

of them in terms of *objets d'art.*" He thinks Hoyningen-Huene takes these objects too flippantly: "Blood oozes lavishly from wounds in all-over patterns whose brutal and holy meaning is neutralized by the photographic refinements of an unusually selective eye. Beautiful as are some of these plates, one may feel that the derivation from the original exegetical meaning toward decorativeness has been only too successfully realized. As one appreciates the delicate tracings drawn in red on white by the martyr's blood, one remains callously unaware of the meaning of martyrdom."[23]

Charlot himself made a sympathetic retrieval, namely a hand-drawn copy in ink of one of the categorically ordinary Mexican popular prints, a nineteenth-century *Man of Sorrows* (Metropolitan Museum of Art). Tied-back curtains, portière-like and suggestive of theatrical display, frame a Christ in a long, plain, simply bordered gown, slumping under the more-than-symbolic weight of a long knotted noose. This rope itself resembles the "cord," or simple rope belt, of the Franciscans who evangelized Mexico from early times, and for whom Charlot detected honest respect in Orozco's otherwise secularist art.[24] The three slipknots and two looser loops can be likened to the five knots of the Franciscan cord, said to refer—apropos of the Man of Sorrows—to the five wounds of Christ in the Passion. Lively, in its paired clashing textures (rope and drapery swag, gown and curtain, decorated garment hem and patterned paving), Charlot's typically fluent drawing only points up, vis-à-vis Strand's photograph, how the very "limitation" of black-and-white can heighten a pressing evocation of "colorful," instead of specifically colored, effect—thanks in part to a generic sense of Mexican santos as far from reserved in their polychrome.

If in modern culture most pictures, including old ones, tend to be seen neutrally, with implacably cultic images in a special class that barely

---

23. Charlot, "Mexican Heritage" (1947), in *An Artist on Art*, II, 72.

24. Drawing illus. in ibid., 134. In "A Review of Alma Reed's *J. C. Orozco*" (1956), Charlot writes: "Simplifications are attempted on the religious plane. Even in his lustiest anti-clerical days, filled with the spirit of priest-baiting and church-sacking, Orozco never pretended to moral or philosophical originality. When the free-thinking plebs he had fought for came out on top and launched a religious persecution, the painter, in a typically bold turn-about, frescoed pious incidents from the life of St. Francis. Alma Reed extolls the pagan martyrdom of Prometheus as a supreme achievement, but the Christian martyrdoms that Orozco painted towards the last, and his noble Crucifixions, are silently bypassed. . . . Either . . . [his later] clerical patrons—as did Father Couturier in France—prized genius over faith, or else and more probably, being in themselves Mexican, they allowed for tantrums between a child and his mother, be it his Mother the Church" (*An Artist on Art*, II, 319).

overlaps with art, there might also be a category of "unholy pictures." The Redon of effete Catholicity is borderline, with Manuel Bravo and his naughty nudes well inside. Today, Robert Mapplethorpe reviews fin-de-siècle perversity in an "eccentric" *décadence* of overwrought rigor, an aesthetic unholy less for its frigid and joyless sexual fetishism than for its idolatry of force (to consider strength as good, power as vulgar, force as wrong).

A certain unusually vacant image by Mapplethorpe, his 1977 photograph, *Amaryllis, Paris,* published in a portfolio entitled *Y,* relates structurally to Paul Strand's *Cristo with Thorns.* The image consists of two white walls meeting in a corner that vertically bisects the field. It is not easy to settle on reading this join of two uninflected planes as concave rather than convex (as is the case in Strand's photograph), but Mapplethorpe's stripped-down view is lyricized by the intrusion, into the field at left, of three languid, palmy leaves. Here is the steely inhibition of Mapplethorpe's "romantic agony" in an unspecified state. As languid as they are spiky, the leaves project into a scrupulously bare setting, almost as if in decorative application of Le Corbusier's antidecorational whitewash idea (the pristine white planes might be large vertical slats or louvers rather than walls; no matter). The moodily tonal gloom of Redon's *Sainte* with intruding thistle plant might be said to have given way to a subtle deployment of leaves interjected into the stillness surrounding Strand's santo and then, in Mapplethorpe's image, to a primped and airless interior.

It was not, after all, that Strand's *Cristo with Thorns, Huexotla* owes anything—as if out of limited capital—to Redon's *La Sainte et le Chardon,* or any other work. On the contrary, Redon's lithograph only becomes more rewarding in the reflected light of Strand's photograph. There is no resembling until there is a second thing; and how bound up creation, beholding, and resembling really are. It is even possible, before Strand's image of the Mexican santo, to think of the passage in the epistle of John (1 John 3:2) where it is said of the twice-removed prototype of the *Cristo* itself—a man who was himself the Image (or "icon") of the Father, as Christians are meant to be "images" of him—that "we shall be like him because we shall see him as he is."

MIKE AND DOUG STARN: PHOTOEXHIBITIONISM 1930/1990

When Delacroix, himself a photographer, said in his *Journal* entry for 1 September 1859, that in truly striking photographs "the very imperfection of the process as a matter of absolute rendering leaves certain gaps,"[1] he was onto something that resounds in recent theory, where a historical shift is seen in the avant-garde of the 1920s and 1930s from photocollage to a photography of monolithic, even grandiloquent, single-objectification.[2] Critically, this has concerned me in terms of a sculpturesque (versus pictorial) tradition in photography, which, within or without the argument about photocollage, is obviously relevant before the new works of the Starn brothers, Mike and Doug. Despite having produced many concretely constructive photo-objects, even a kind of *photographie collée,* the Starns have never practiced photocollage proper (with its disjunct scales or spaces discouraging doubling or mirroring); and most of their new works are

---

1. *The Journal of Eugène Delacroix,* trans. Walter Pach (New York, 1961), 645.

2. Benjamin H. D. Buchloh, "From Faktura to Factography" (1984), in Richard Hertz and Norman M. Klein, eds., *Twentieth-Century Art Theory: Urbanism, Politics and Mass Culture* (Englewood Cliffs, N.J., 1990), 81–111.

categorically *reliefs,* whether the enlarged source motifs are graphic or solid-objective to start.

These two artists have always been objectifiers, even in their Romantic-bohemian aspect. In their many portraits of themselves and of each other, which in their case is practically the same thing, the twins have seemed if anything exhibitionistic rather than narcissistic, as if exploiting the generosity potential in exhibitionism itself (on the museum wall, the otherwise swooningly narcissistic self-represented Courbet opens himself to all hearts). The nineteenth-century undertones in their work all along only confirm a rootedness in the photographic medium as itself historically modern now that ongoing experimentation with materials and presentation has led into a new mode. With them, framing was always actively presentational; but the Starn brothers' very poeticism has also issued in a poetry of "real materials" in Constructivistically direct, forthright, and sometimes quite understatedly clunky manipulations in the actual print. Most of their big works of 1989–90 present themselves on double-barreled curving panels that may even evoke the pasteboard curl of the old binocular stereopticon card as well as the now milky, curved Celluloid planes of classic Constructivist sculptures.[3] Still more important, I tend to think, is László Moholy-Nagy's sense of the curved material plane as "light-modulating," alike in sheet-metal sculptures and on a more purely optical, experimental level: witness a how-to-do-it article with photo-illustrated instructions for variously curling a sheet of paper as interestingly light-reflective.[4] At any rate, with already thingly images on hefty transparent film sheets that also bulge like viewing screens, the very question of a photographic sculpturesqueness opens up, as it were, in relief.

Around the same time they did *The Big Chair* (1985) a single-object photo of a 1950s "functionalist" chair (by Harry Bertoia) that I have already considered on its own,[5] the Starns took their first trip to Europe, where they photographed *Notre-Dame Interior* (1985), showing ranks of rush-seated chairs in the Paris cathedral. There the camera looks along a row of the

---

3. For curled planes in Surrealism as well as Constructivism, here is an interesting sequence of materialization and dematerialization: Man Ray's paper *Lampshade,* 1919, destroyed, redone in white-painted tin, 1921; then, after Moholy's *Nickel Construction,* 1921, Man Ray's painted "Lampshade" form in *La Retour à raison, III,* 1939, with title borrowed from a 1923 film.

4. László Moholy-Nagy, "Make a Light Modulator" (1940), in Richard Kostelanetz., ed., *Moholy-Nagy,* Documentary Monographs in Modern Art (New York, 1970), 99–104, with illus.

5. Joseph Masheck, "Of One Mind: Photos by the Starn Twins of Boston," *Arts Magazine,* March 1986, 69–71.

plain wooden chairs facing right, locked top-to-bottom in the field of vision with a row of chair backs to the right and a thinner slice of seat "fronts" at the left. One might not expect such pieces to reference an object-study from the period between the World Wars like Raoul Hausmann's *Spanish Chairs, Ibiza* (1933–36): that photographer's care for the actual chairs as made things is documented by an admiring description in his novel *Hyle* (begun in 1926) of the painstaking and distinctly constructive process of a carpenter's making one, having it caned, and placing a cluster of them in a large white room near a white staircase, much as in his photo.[6] But already *Notre-Dame Interior,* with its chairs in neat and silent rows, has a museum-esque air. Indeed, besides *each other,* crafted things (including paintings) already on display constitute a major category of the Starn brothers' output, in recapitulation and extension of the nineteenth-century tradition of "reproduction" artwork.

Two recent series from the beginning of the 1980s "take" directly after antique sculptures—manipulatively, at that, though only as regards cropping and mounting. The older source is an acrobatic Minoan *Bull-Leaper* or *Bull-Jumper,* gold and ivory, of about 1500 B.C., from the palace of Knossos, in Case No. 56 of the Heraklion Archeological Museum, on Crete (Fig. 21). Like Yves Klein leaping so photographically into the existential void,[7] this is an airborne figure in intense yet ever-arrested action, its fragmentary condition only heightening its sportively self-possessed detachment. Enlarged and mounted, however, some Starn "Bull-Leapers" are markedly *present* in their very detachment, precisely as caught in the museological web of the cubical glass case whose inside corner projects as an evenly divided *Y,* with hazy "zip" of a closer-up vertical corner, fuzzy, to the side. The visual construct recalls not only sketches by Degas of glass-cased antiquities in the Louvre but also, more tellingly, Moholy-Nagy's *Structure of the World* (1927), with bathing-beauties (divers?) perched like a troupe of Rockettes on a construction scaffold, not to mention Rodchenko's photogenic divers of the early 1930s. Still more to the point, however, as this

---

6. Quoted in Andreas Haus, *Kamerafotografien 1927–1957* (Munich, 1979), 22, from Raoul Hausmann, *Hyle: ein Traumsein in Spanien* (Frankfurt, 1969), 45–46; photograph, pl. 56. Such chairs were still admired in the 1960s by the architect Sert, a disciple of Le Corbusier, for their "happy marriage of the natural and the man-made": J. Prats Vallés, ed., *Ibiza: fuerte y luminosa,* photographs by Joaquim Gomis, text by Josep Lluís Sert (Barcelona, 1967), 21 (Engl.), with pl. lxix (close-up of single chair on sunny floor); also, pls. lxxii (three chairs against whitewashed wall with steps) and lxxiv (row of chairs against whitewashed wall with steps).

7. See Marjorie Welish, "The Specter of Art Hype and the Ghost of Yves Klein," *Sulfur,* no. 12 (1985), 22–28.

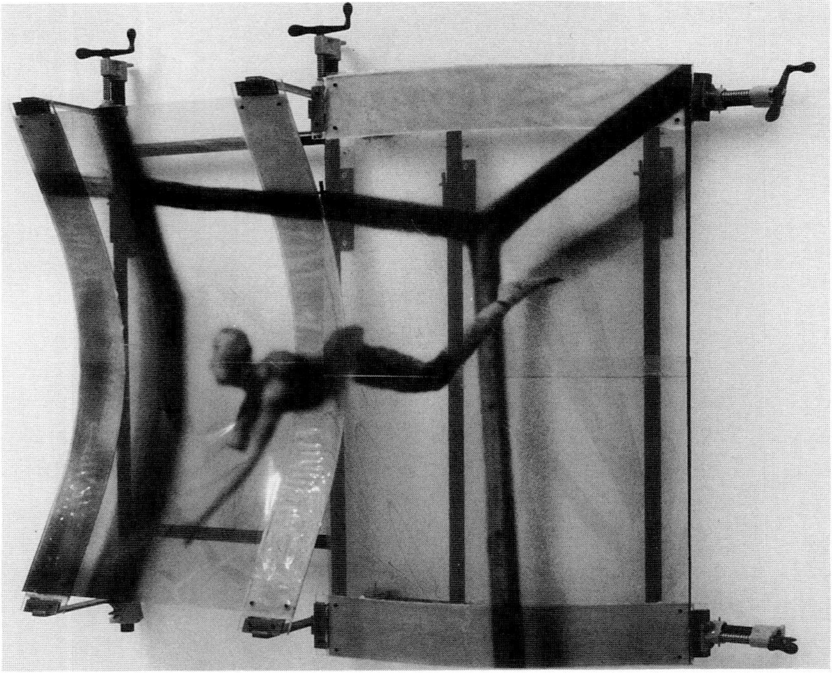

Fig. 21   Doug and Mike Starn, *Convex, Concave Bull-Jumper*, 1989–90, Ortho film, wood, silicon, Plexiglas, pipe clamps, 47 x 60 x 12 inches.

image is itself subsumed into the large bent film sheets and metal structural armatures of the Starns' reliefs, is a particular Rodchenko *Pole-Vaulter* (1937), with (now old-fashioned) bamboo vaulting-pole delicately intersecting with the still in-place horizontal bar.[8] It is as if the Starns' ancient layer of reference were merely the occasion for an open, modern-historical layering.

Likewise the other pieces taking off from the Hellenistic *Horse and Rider of Artemisium,* of the second century B.C., in the National Archaeological Museum at Athens, whose marble elements, if not originally made for each other by now share a history of having been *spliced* together. Some Starn pieces detail only the mighty looming horse; others include the surmounting figure like a child emperor. Either way, there reverberates, from classic

---

8. Illus., Evelyn Weiss, ed., *Alexander Rodtschenko: Fotografien, 1920–1938* (Cologne, 1978), pl. on p. 164.

modern cinema, Vladimir Nilsen's Eisensteinian "dynamic foreshortening" of Falconet's equestrian *Peter the Great* (1766–82) in Leningrad.[9] For its part, at least one unmounted work made from a detail of the similarly art-object(ive) *Bull-Leaper* shows the upper, or rather forward, torso of the diver, with outstretched arms, on two skewed sheets of film tacked to the wall, not unlike one of Nilsen's own cinematographic diagrams.[10] At the same time, the tense horizontal leap of the figure in the Starns' relief produces a kind of flying-C or leaping curve formation that follows forward from preclassical Greek,[11] eventually through modern American, sculpture—Frederic Remington; Theodore Roszak; the David Smith of *Albany III* (1959). Here, as well as with the modern film, is the "classic" in its relative sense.

In their own right, the Starns' long metal pipe clamps that keep these large photos hanging bulged tautly in relief recall the importance of hardware as appearing, more significantly even than in the *Large Glass,* in Duchamp's *Glider Containing a Water Mill (in Neighboring Metals)* (1913–15), all the more in its own "prop" appearance in Man Ray's photo of the piece with Duchamp himself holding it up from behind (hinge edge horizontal), *Duchamp with His Glass* (1917). The actual handyman's C-clamp holding together the slats of Man Ray's sculpture-object *New York,* first made in 1917 and remade in 1966, also deserves notice. After all, "alternative" forms participate in history too, even if with them what seems pressing is the structural point of such witty forays into experimentalist construction in a surprisingly Constructive mode of exhibitional *mounting for display.*

Together, the Starns' initially museological imagery and their adoption of hardware mounts manifest a preoccupation with implications of display that finds telling East European precedent around 1930. Within Constructivism, El Lissitzky was particularly important for the explicit development of exhibition design from as early as 1926, when his "Demonstration Rooms" with movable wall panels fulfilled Vavara Stepanova's vision of the museum as transformed from treasury to archive, and which Lissitzky later considered his most important work as artist.[12] Lissitzky's involvement with "transparency" and transparent image overlap is established within photog-

---

9. (Or now, Saint Petersburg.) Vladimir Nilsen, *The Cinema as Graphic Art (On a Theory of Representation in the Cinema),* trans. Stephen Garry (1936, repr. New York, n.d.), 67–104.

10. Ibid., fig. 7 on p. 33, a composition from Eisenstein's *October* (1927) by his cameraman Edward Tisse.

11. E.g., a bronze *Silenus* of the late sixth century B.C. from Thebes.

12. Treated in Buchloh, "Faktura," esp. 88–89, 96.

raphy itself as well as in photographic display. According to Herbert Bayer, at Leipzig in 1927 and at Cologne in 1928 Lissitzky used "large suspended photomontages and enlargements . . . held by a thin and barely visible wire netting . . . as well as [N.B.] cellophane . . . in such complete relativity that the visitor was irresistably drawn into the exhibition and forced to exercise his energies."[13]

This is not the first time, either, that I have felt Moholy-Nagy as pertinent to the Starns' larger project, at a deeper level than surface style. Under one of "The Eight Varieties of Photographic Vision" listed in his "A New Instrument of Vision" (written 1932; published 1936), Moholy, who by the way also worked with curved Plexiglas, speaks of "simultaneous seeing by means of transparent superimposition: the future process of automatic photomontage." He recommends a "series" approach, with sequences of images of an object: "The series is no longer a 'picture,' and none of the canons of pictorial esthetics can be applied to it. Here the separate picture loses its identity as such and becomes a detail of assembly, an essential structural element of the whole which is the thing itself. . . . The true significance of *the film* will only appear in a much later, less confused and groping age than ours."[14] A decade later Moholy offers (reformed) photography as enabling a new "integration," no less, against "our specialist age . . . built upon a multiplicity of visual information pounded relentlessly into the individual by the daily press, magazine, radio and cinema," wherein the more the individual "knows in this superficial way, the less he is able to understand, because he has not been taught to relate and integrate his casual and scattered information." Now, "binding different space and time levels together, we shall find that reflections and transparent mirrorings of the passing traffic in the windows of motor cars or shops belong in the same category. In photographic rendering they usually appear as superimpositions."[15]

Historically speaking, the development of the exhibition as a contrived super-construction seems to imply no single progressive path, any more than does the Starns' productively ad hoc development. Bayer himself was

---

13. Alexander Dorner, *The Way Beyond 'Art': The Work of Herbert Bayer,* Problems of Contemporary Art, 3 (New York, 1947), 199n.

14. Moholy-Nagy, "A New Instrument of Vision," trans. F. D. Klingender and P. Morton Shand in Kostelanetz, *Moholy-Nagy,* 50–54, here 52, 54 (emphasis mine).

15. Idem, "Space-Time and the Photographer" (1942), op. cit., 57–66, here 58, 63, continuing—"Mirroring means in this sense the changing aspects of vision, the sharpened identification of the inside and outside penetrations."

responsible for the even, regimental tilting of mounted, unframed military photographs in "Road to Victory," an exhibition at the Museum of Modern Art in 1942,[16] while the strung partitioning cords of his "Airways to Peace" photo-exhibition for the museum in 1943 were possibly only a tidying application of Duchamp's "string" installation in the New York Surrealist exhibition of the previous year. It was in that year too, 1942, that Frederick Kiesler had produced the famous interior of Peggy Guggenheim's Art of This Century gallery (demolished 1947) with movable panels and unframed paintings suspended out from curved wooden walls on sawn-off baseball bats. Alexander Dorner then took up Bayer's cause, publishing a Bayer diagram relevant to the Starn brothers' new large images, some doubled, of one of their single eyes[17] (and a strange cross of paths between the architecture of Ludwig Mies van der Rohe and the painting activity of Jackson Pollock[18]), that in turn led to the projection outward of paintings on steel rods in the original disposition of Frank Lloyd Wright's 1959 Guggenheim Museum.

With these brief notes I mean to suggest how the work of the Starn brothers inherits a significant poetic of the material and its material *setup* in Constructivist art, including, especially lately, the artistic concern with exhibitional mounting. As to "exhibitionism" in the ordinary sense: perhaps we can begin to overcome the black-hole exhibitionism of Andy Warhol's emptily insouciant persona. The Starns' recent images of the *Hindenburg*

---

16. Making an otherwise worthwhile point about the pseudo-pictorial isolation of blown-up details in antiquities exhibits, Rosalind E. Krauss shows some such as rectangular and *mounted*. But she describes them as "framed" though they appear *unframed*, only to define on this evidence an "Institution of the Frame": "Sincerely Yours" (1982), in her *The Originality of the Avant-Garde and Other Modernist Myths* (Cambridge, Mass., 1985), 174–94, esp. 191–93, with illus.

17. Dorner, *Way Beyond "Art"*: e.g., Bayer's "Diagram of Extended Vision in Exhibition Presentation," a cubical room in which a man with a single large eye for a head stands, hands in pockets, on one raised panel, surrounded fore and aft, above and below, by empty panels variously angled to his gaze: "The modern visitor does not want to be confirmed in one revealed immutable truth, or in the chaotic absolutism of ever-new and yet still eternal truths which are all equally true and necessarily result in mutual paralysis. He wants a suggestion for the improvement of the present ways of feeling and thinking. He wants to see the wrestling between obsolete and new forces, their whole relative penetration" (199, with fig. 138).

18. When Ludwig Mies van der Rohe's 1942 project for an ideal museum (or "Museum for a Small City") inspired Peter Blake to interest Pollock in working on a similar project in the summer of 1949, Pollock would have been challenged in his idea of hanging his paintings unframed in free space by the fact that in a collage perspective drawing Mies uses a reproduction of Picasso's *Guernica* to show the muralistic scale of the exhibits as well as by Mies's previous Resor House project, 1938–40, on the Resor Ranch, near Wilson, in just the next county from Cody, Wyoming; see Masheck, "Reflections in Onyx on Mies van der Rohe" (1986), in my *Building-Art: Modern Architecture Under Cultural Construction* (Cambridge University Press, forthcoming.)

disaster, however seemingly closer as art to Warhol's "Disaster" paintings than, say, to Vladimir Nilsen's earnest German documentary film *The Mooring of an Airship* (with parallel columns of men hefting the mooring ropes as seen from above[19]), might as well be fresh metaphors of the Weimar Republic exploding. They convey a spiritual Lisbon Earthquake in the wrenching apart of a once optimistic and universalizing Constructivist beauty.[20]

Warhol's *129 Die in Jet (Plane Crash)* (1962), the big *New York Mirror* front page with tattered airplane wing seen dangling from a rod or pole and retouched officials milling in the foreground (if not some of the electric-chair "Disasters" of the mid-1960s) seems genuinely dumb when one turns to the Starns' new mounted "DEAD" photos. These derive from an illegal, surreptitious execution photo of Ruth Snyder—who, with her lover, Henry Judd Gray, murdered her husband—that is supposed to have been taken with a tiny camera on a shoe and was published on the front page of the *Daily News* on Friday, 13 January 1928. I am struck by the double strength of these Starn images, gripping where *129 Die* looks anxiously air-headed, and as hospitable to historical consciousness as Warhol was busy being history's slavish *tool*. Here one can even discover the ancient seated figure of national personification—such as Roma, Britannia or, more to the point, "Columbia"—mortified, like the seated statue of Czar Alexander III being toppled by guy-ropes in Eisenstein's *October*. Not that the Starns (would have) had to contrive such a thing; but too many of the theoretically inclined today would rest content with the *idea* of the museum as archive, whereas the Starn brothers actually engage it.

19. Illus., Nilsen, *Cinema*, fig. 57 on p. 107.

20. In the Museum of Modern Art *Art of the Twenties* catalogue, ed. William S. Lieberman (New York, 1979), are four photographs from a souvenir album of *Airship 127; the Graf Zeppelin* (1928) under construction, these, as it happens, donated by my cousins and me in memory of our grandfather, Daniel E. Cahill, who as an industrial engineer was rather more optimistically fascinated by the sheer structural beauty of the craft's infrastructure under *construction* (illus., pp. 66–67).

Preexpressionism to Neoexpressionism

The historical moment of circa 1983, when I began frequenting the new artworld of the Lower East Side, in New York, still seems poignant. By temperament I was drawn to the more conceptually oriented of the new storefront galleries (Cash, Nature Morte, International with Monument); yet my own bruised spirits in the early *Reaganzeit*—being dumped by Barnard College soon after having *Artforum* sold out from under my editorship—also disposed me toward Expressionism and a fluorescing Neoexpressionism. At least at first, I found some renewal of an *alternative* spirit of the Lower East Side in the 1960s; besides, it was all the better now that nothing, not even rock 'n' roll, was more important than painting.

It was also at this time that Francesco Pellizzi, the editor of *Res: Anthropology and Aesthetics,* encouraged me to finish one chapter of a complex project on which I had been working for years, an expansion of my essay "The Carpet Paradigm: Critical Prolegomena to a Theory of Flatness" (*Arts Magazine,* September 1976). Not mysteriously, the part I was most inclined to develop concerned Romantic primitivism and German Expressionism, which I reprint here, as knotty as it would prove for fireside reading. The reader of it may also be interested in "Expressionist Fantasias," above, and vice versa.

On the contemporary side: Polke was well established when my brief notice functioned as a belated appreciation of this remarkable painter who as a figure connects abiding Expressionist tradition with the original 1960s and, otherwise different, 1980s outlooks. In America, Rifka's boppy Parthenon paintings had already provoked an article, "Judy Rifka and 'Postmodernism' in Architecture" (*Art in America,* December 1984) when I gained the opportunity to sketch out more broadly how for me this painter, whose very archness is solid, embodied the hot spirit of the Neoexpressionist moment in New York.

(T)RAPT IN TVILIGHT: ON SCANDINAVIAN "SYMBOLISM"

The subtitle of the "Northern Light" exhibition that traveled to Washington, New York, and Minneapolis in 1982–83 was "Realism and Symbolism in Scandinavian Painting, 1880–1910." Just what that ought to mean was never made certain or vivid, however, despite an ample catalogue. With even Realism and Naturalism left undiscriminated, the task of crystallizing any specifically Scandinavian *symbolisme* was undermined. Maybe Ingmar Bergman might have had something to say, not to mention Kierkegaard. Left to their own devices, the paintings too often seemed to be passing off sentimentalism for the spirituality without which no definition of Symbolism can altogether do—as, for starters, with *First Snow,* 1891, by Louis Sparre, almost a Finnish Wyeth, if not Norman Rockwell.

Out of some hundred works, the one having most ostensibly to do with spirituality was telling: Niels Bjarre's 1897 *The Prayer Meeting, Harbøre (Children of God).* Here was a picture of six meditating pietists in a state of mind-wandering transport so doggedly committed to external description that the viewer was torn between a sense of an intensified reality and a more quotidian sense that there might be something wrong with the sitters.

The catalogue notes that Bjarre's "Children of God" were followers of one Nicolai Grundtvig, but no hint is given that Grundtvig's religiosity stemmed from the (Anglo-Catholic) Oxford Movement: according to Edmund Gosse's essay "Four Danish Poets" (1877), collected in his enlightening *Northern Studies,* to which I shall return, Grundtvig even went to Oxford to imbibe at the Tractarian source. With Scandinavian religiosity pretty much confined to this lone cell of devotees, one would have no idea that any other Scandinavians, notably the Swedes, were (and remain) in fact ecclesiastically "High."

Any attempt to squeeze out of the art in "Northern Light" some Symbolist tincture or essence has to have been problematic. Avant-garde was made to socialize—no hard feelings, mister?—with conservative art. With religion downplayed, it should have been urgent to confirm any proto-abstract transcendentalism. Anyone who knows my work will understand that it is hardly political of me to call upon the words of Michael Fried for a good suggestion of what I have in mind: "the discontent with the denotative faculty of language which one senses throughout Symbolist literature is intimately related to the deep distrust which others besides myself feel in our time for the representational faculty of painting."[1] But Kirk Varnedoe, who organized the exhibition, did not pursue that tack either. In "Northern Light" the whole proto-abstract aspect of Postimpressionism was lost in a smorgasbord of cultural-historical ideas that, in the catalogue, now and then melts down in doubletalk. For example, "Although the coincidence of psychological and social implications in Scandinavian Symbolism is only another episode in the dialogue between Romantic ideas of the individual and the nation-state, the particular forms and motivations of National Romanticism that underlie Nordic art of the late nineteenth and early twentieth centuries seem fraught with implications for modern politics." (Like what?)

The centerpiece of the Brooklyn Museum installation of the exhibition was Richard Bergh's *Nordic Summer Evening* (1899–1900). This is a picture, in the drabbest sense of that term, of a gent chatting up a lady, or rather, not really doing so. The gent happens to be Eugen, "Prins"—and this usage in an American catalogue seems either uppity or too familiar, the latter in the sense of a family tag or the name of a pet—of Sweden, himself the royal dauber of three somewhat vacant, overscaled canvases in the show (evidently H.R.H. didn't skimp on materials). Here he and his equally wooden

---

1. Michael Fried, "Some Notes on Morris Louis," *Arts Magazine,* November 1963.

companion stand so far apart, bracing the posts of a porch and, with them, the large composition, that to communicate they would almost have to wave. Perish the thought that any of Mr. Munch's unpleasant angst should ruffle the Hathaway poise of their ennui, which would be too much like sweating instead of perspiring (not that perspiring is, anyway, more truly "U"). The frigid blandness of these two figures might have been emblematic of "Northern Light" itself, where anything at all radical had a way of looking welcome only, so to speak, at the buffet and not at the sit-down supper. Sorry, but zombie stares, preciously switched-off, sterling-silver inhibitions and long-winded, post-Barbizonian sunsets are not, in themselves, enough for a "Symbolism" of consequence.

Considering that Varnedoe already had a Gustave Caillebotte revival behind him before taking on the Scandinavian project, I found myself as it were backing Ibsen against his Bjørnson. Edmund Gosse, who introduced Hendrick Ibsen to the English-speaking world, has two essays on him in *Northern Studies* (1890). First comes Ibsen the satirical "realist," with Gosse commenting on the artistic failure of the play *Julian the Emperor* as a function of its subject: "Julian [the Apostate] was not the voice of his time. . . . In his brief life was exemplified how much can be done by one whole-hearted man in stopping the civilization of the world."[2] But the second Ibsen essay (1889) shows the critic, too, exceeding himself; Gosse, who had liked the dramatist's earlier lyrical plays enough to have tried to get Ibsen to reconsider giving up rhyme, learned to grow in response not to Ibsen's failures but to his "masterpieces of a new sort of writing."[3] Now he can comprehend the very middlebrow resistance that Ibsen's genius helped him to transcend: "Those to whom the most modern spirit . . . is distasteful, who see nothing but the stitches of the canvas in the vast pictures of Tolstoï, would reject Ibsen, or would hark back to his old sweet, flute-like lyrics."[4]

Further, Gosse notes Ibsen's anarchism, quoting a letter to Georg Brandes, who appeared in "Northern Light" as the lecturing subject of Harald Slott-Møller's starkly compelling *Georg Brandes at the University of Copenhagen* (1890) and on whom Sven Møller Kristensen wrote a good brief essay for the catalogue. In the letter, Ibsen tells Brandes, "Undermine the idea of the State, set up in its place spontaneous action, and the idea that

---

2. Edmund Gosse, *Northern Studies* (London, 1890), 74.

3. Ibid., 78.

4. Ibid., 104.

spiritual relationship is the only thing that makes for unity, and you will start elements of a liberty which will be something worth possessing." As for the mature and challenging Ibsen, he is "indisputably superior" to the more conventional, hence reassuring, Bjørnsterne Bjørnson with his "ill-regulated zeal for moral health"—this despite Bjørnson's "grace of touch and occasional felicity of expression."

Read Munch for Ibsen, and Gosse's thinking helps to account for something insufficiently critical, thus all the worse for being didactic, in "Northern Light," where a simplistic gentility seemed to have rummaged after all charming things of a certain taste. There was an embarrassing proliferation of "den" pictures, not unlike what they used to sell in the gallery at the old Abercrombie & Fitch: unreformed pictures of "regular guys" doing Eagle-Scout things like whittlin', fixin' fishnets, workin' on the railroad (real neat and clean) or else just having one with the fellas—not to mention posturing at a balconied window down in Gay Paree. All this threatened a cocky down-to-earthedness that is precisely what *Peer Gynt* makes fun of in its title character (Gosse, incidentally, points up the rather Brechtian fact that between Acts 3 and 4 the enterprising Peer makes a fortune in the American slave trade and also by selling idols to the Chinese!). And just for being so hyper-O.K., as clonedly normal as "yuppie" culture of the 1980s, the works that I refer to as den pictures reminded me of Le Corbusier in *When the Cathedrals Were White* (1938–39) on Princeton athletes: "I am attracted by the pathos of life and danger; much less by the assurance of spoiled papa's boys, well fed, well washed, well buttoned up."[5]

A subcategory of artists' frat-house stag parties included Peder Severin Krøyer's naturalistic *Artists' Luncheon* (1883), a tiresomely cramped little group portrait. An earlier but very similarly structured Krøyer of women at work in a *Sardine Cannery at Concarneau* (1879) only made one think of Gauguin and his crew in the same town afterward. Speaking of *them*: neither Francesco Mogens Ballin nor Jens Ferdinand Willumsen, two Danes treated by Wladyslawa Jaworska in her important *Gauguin and the Pont-Aven School* (1971; English edition, 1972) was included in "Northern Light."

On the other hand, one of the rewards of the exhibition was Karl Nordström's *Varberg Fort* (1893), which might have been drably Böcklinesque had it not been slapped so vigorously onto rough canvas. The catalogue does pick up on the painting's Gauguin evocation, noting Nordström's

---

5. Charles-Édouard Jeanneret (called Le Corbusier), *When the Cathedrals Were White,* trans. Francis E. Hyssop, Jr. (New York, 1947; repr., 1964), 139.

exposure to Gauguin's work in Copenhagen in the preceding year. Actually, *Varberg Fort* is nicer than some rickety early Gauguins hanging in the Copenhagen museum.

But wait a minute! People hated Gauguin in Copenhagen, and in retaliation he hated them back, as pinched, puritanical squares: worse than the Jesuits, he said! In a letter of May 1885 he wrote that he couldn't even get picture frames made, since any carpenter he was known to patronize thereby lost business—and "This, in the nineteenth century."[6] For a sense of the unwarranted arrogance that Gauguin was up against in the "northern light" one need only turn to Christian Krohg's *Portrait of Gerhard Munthe* (1885), proffering that ol' "witty and exclusive conservative," as we are told in the catalogue, although he looks more like the kind of local grandee who might have ordered his underwear from Paris. Amazingly, Krohg was an inspiration to Munch. Gosse observes of Ibsen's *Pillars of Society* that "the main disease treated" is "a certain local and peculiarly Norwegian species of hypocritical respectability," the "pathogenic sign" of which is a "cautious lying silence which holds its tongue so carefully in small social circles, and wraps around its consciousness of guilt garment after garment of false propriety, spurious indignation and prudent hypocrisy." What is Krohg's *Munthe* but a stylish, arty case of the same malady? In realms like these the likes of Sargent could have passed for genius.

What I really wanted to ask of this exhibition was: *Did Manet paint in vain?* Even if modernity were defunct, it will have amounted to something more than just another *option*. Entertaining so "liberally," on par, the hip and the square—in "Northern Light" or anywhere else—can only take place at the expense of the real struggles of the heroes, artists of the caliber of Ibsen and Munch and worthy aspirants.

Much of the art at least conveyed a sense of the world that made Munch scream. The master himself was represented by no fewer than eight paintings, some major, including the astounding 1895 *Self-Portrait with Cigarette* (and something like an update of Krohg's *Gerhard Munthe,* of 1885), with its wonderfully daring brushwork. And what blues in blues in blues! The curling cigarette smoke alone is headily evocative: I think of Alice Meynell's opulently sultry analogy between "the smoke of the cigarette"

---

6. *The Writings of a Savage: Paul Gauguin,* ed. Daniel Guérin, trans. Eleanor Levieux (New York, 1978), 7. In January of 1890, however, van Gogh would tell his brother Theo, "Gauguin wrote me that he had exhibited in Denmark and that this exhibition had been a great success"; *The Complete Letters of Vincent van Gogh,* 2d ed. (Boston, 1978), III, 254 (Letter 626).

and the wavy forms of Oriental art as "more sensitive in motion than breath or blood, . . . its waves so multitudinously inflected and reinflected, with such flights and such delays," as "it flows and bends upon currents of so subtle influence and impulse."[7] Perhaps all the more because the portrait, which is dark, has to look less spectacular in reproduction, here at last was an intense sensitivity managing to get someplace in expressive terms. The painting also turns out to sport a punchy intimacy, notwithstanding elegance, that is akin to Max Beckmann's somehow graciously sassy *Self-Portrait in Tuxedo,* of 1929. This fantastic work by Munch would alone justify a visit to Oslo, despite "Northern Light's" tendency to submerge it into a practically ethnic typicality into which, however, it can never quite be dissolved. Indeed, here's the crucial problem: the *symbolisme* in Munch is atypically astute, while his vital Expressionism exceeds the limits of Symbolism altogether.

Dark horses are always interesting, although, of course, while we disinterestedly survey, commerce impatiently waits. A certain kind of collector must love the guy who painted like that present-day American depictor of prissy society interiors from which the maid has just retreated (why glorify either name), this old Scandinavian dissolving everything into the soupy grisaille of some "Cream of Mood" that desubstantializes everything but his contrivedly Vermeery compositions. Well, I'd take Eugène Jansson, a Swede, especially, if not only, for his leanly lyrical 1901 *Self-Portrait.* There, what looks like a cutting from one of Monet's "Wisterias" (or perhaps, in our time, a brushy interface between zones in one of Nicholas Marsicano's paintings), a long bright arc snaking its way through a nocturnal sky, segmented, screenlike, in four tall windows behind the standing figure, is really the urban glow of Stockholm at night. How refreshingly civil, too. The same artist had then already painted *The Outskirts of the City* (1899), something between van Gogh or Signac—the creeping tentacles of some turn-of-the-century industrial city that might as well be Newark—and the *Deserto rosso* vacancy of Boccioni's 1908 *Self-Portrait* with its sort of Co-Op City looming behind the artist. Jansson also did the similarly Postimpressionistic street scene *Hornsgatan at Night* (1902) and the more stagey *Österlånggatan* (1904), a nocturnal street in Stockholm's old town. But it was with the *Self-Portrait* that one met this unfamiliar painter looking so thoughtfully up to the business of painting.

Still, it was really Munch who stood out in "Northern Light." Resisting

---

7. Alice Meynell, "The Plaid," in her *Essays* (New York, 1914), 152–55.

any dissolve into typicality, he was the true *fauve* in roomsful, mostly, of would-be "Donatellos." Generally, the Scandinavian painting of the fin-de-siècle that one saw amounted to a homegrown, semiconscious Postimpressionism by no means unlike much American, Canadian, and other provincial material of the time. In Brooklyn, to get to the exhibit one passed first through a room hung with "Ash-Can"–type American work that proved a bracer for much of what lay ahead. At least some Americans of around 1910 knew they were semiliterate provincials intimidated by Europe (yet they could see Ibsen's plays performed in New York, as a matter of fact). Unwilling to kowtow to academicism, they plunged right into painting with the same risk of producing an elusive localism that just doesn't travel.

Confronted by an exhibition such as this, where the juggling of academic and ostensibly harmless entertainment values reduces to showmanship, I had to notice that even the travel interests now happily chipped in just as endowed and official support for disinterested scholarship dwindled and public institutions conveniently became corporate-commercial. I still believe that criticism can only play along with the status quo in an uneasy peace, thanks to the higher values of art itself. A century ago, in May 1883, Camille Pissarro sent his son Lucien a copy of Huysmans's then new collection of essays, *L'Art moderne.* Lucien wrote back in complaint, "he only looks at the subject. [And] . . . what about Delacroix? I . . . find that he is critical of Puvis de Chavannes but too indulgent with Caillebotte. But here's the explanation: they are boating partners, and 'oarsmen' protect each other. He is also too gentle with Raffaelli and not gentle enough with Monet."[8] The parallel here may not be complete, but, yes, what about Munch?

We cannot all be so careless of our own historical moment, or so swept up in its apparent confusion, as to retreat to revisionist fairs of charming, de-overlooked historical resuscitations. "Northern Light" was an exhibition of painting from one of the most florescent of all the European periods. Where, one deserved to ask of almost all but Munch, was evidence of that which could ever be held up—to resort to a very big Lutheran concept, widely comprehended in Scandinavia—in *justification* of us all?

---

8. Camille Pissarro, *Letters to His Son Lucien,* ed. John Rewald, trans. Rewald et al., 3d ed. (Mamaroneck, N.Y., 1972), 363.

15

RAW ART:
"PRIMITIVE" AUTHENTICITY
AND GERMAN EXPRESSIONISM

Every vital and productive germ with which the Germans inoculated the Roman world, was due to barbarism. Indeed, only barbarians are capable of rejuvenating a world laboring under the death throes of unnerved civilization.

—Engels

Prehistoric or primitive, Gothic, Romantic, and even folk arts might have little in common other than exotic appeal as specimens of unclassical eccentricity.[1] As unrelated allies, all have served the modern cause, espe-

1. On the general European *invenzione* of primitive art, see Robert Goldwater, *Primitivism and Modern Art* (1938), rev. ed. (New York, 1967), especially pt. 1 with chapter "The Evaluation of the Art of Primitive Peoples," 15–50; A. A. Gerbrands, *Art as an Element of Culture, Especially of Negro Africa,* Mededelingen van het Rijksmuseum voor Volkenkunde, XII (Leiden, 1957), chap. 2; "Some Aspects of the History of the Study of Non-European Art"; Douglas F. Fraser, "The Discovery of Primitive Art," *Arts Yearbook,* 1 (1957), 119–33. Peter Selz, *German Expressionist Painting* (Berkeley, 1957; repr. 1974), has been extremely useful in the present investigation. Also the essays in the XX Olympiad exhibition catalogue, *World Cultures and Modern Art: The Encounter of Nineteenth- and Twentieth-Century European Art and Music with Asia, Africa, Oceania, Afro- and Indo-America* (Munich, 1972; English ed.), especially those by J.-L. Paudrat, W. Schmalenbach, and M. Schneckenburger.

The present essay is a development from my article, "The Carpet Paradigm: Critical Prolegomena to a Theory of Flatness," *Arts Magazine,* LI/1 September 1976, 82–109. For their encouragement with the project, I want to thank Edward Albee and the Edward Albee Foundation, Andrew Attaway, David Carrier, and Arthur C. Danto. For his generosity in commenting on a draft of this essay, I owe gratitude to Joseph Rykwert, reserving responsibility for errors to myself. Francesco Pellizzi and Annabel Sherk were most patient and helpful with editing and typing.

cially in opposition to academicized classicism. For classicism presumes to universality, taking as normative a culturally determined ideal of the "beautiful" in nature as purified and essentialized in previous classic art, in stable and enduring forms assumed to ring true always and everywhere— or at least in the always and everywhere of an advanced and dominant people. So the "beautiful" classical *whole* inevitably confronts the "interesting" nonclassical *particular*. By this account, alternative forms of art constitute, at best, unrelated exceptions to the classical rule, each so lacking in anything more than idiosyncratic tradition or merely local continuity as to be strange even to the other. From Winckelmann to Wölfflin, art history perpetuated this view up to modern times, with exceptions permitted only so long as primitive or anticlassical art kept its place as an exotic affair.

Germanic Expressionist art emerged as part of a complete reconsideration of such presumptions. A new understanding of the primeval past of mankind, including a sense of the Neolithic Age as distinct from the "nature-bound" culture of the Paleolithic Age and, consequently, of the sophistications of surviving primitive peoples; a new acknowledgment, in art history (especially by Franz Wickoff and Aloïs Riegl, in Vienna), of the virtues of phases of Western art previously considered decadences from classical perfection; and an appreciation of Gothic art, as testimony to a singularly Germanic artistic potentiality, reviewing progressive nationalist enthusiasms of Romantic times: such diverse and apparently unruly historical currents all advanced a rationale as intelligible, if not as normative, as that of classicism itself. Now a positive premium, not merely an anticlassical adversary value, accrued to signs of vitality and free growth, which confirmed new expressive possibilities within the fine arts even as it called artistic attention to previously unworthy, normatively "primitive," forms. Hence the productions of tribal cultures encountered in the course of European colonial expansion might claim the specifically aesthetic regard once reserved for the classical masterworks while contemporary artists pursued a freshly direct, even sometimes transcendental, spontaneity, at least partly in response to alienation from the conventions of high-industrial culture at home. All at once the primitive assumed more than specimen interest, the Gothic reaffirmed its Northern identity, and Romanticism itself achieved its modern historicity.

Gothicism and Modern Primitivity

Soon after 1905, when the painting of a new generation of Postimpressionists came into view in France, the art of these "Fauves" (Wild Beasts) was met by emergent Expressionism in Germany. To both these movements tribal art was a vital inspiration, but in typically, even traditionally, different ways. African wood sculpture, especially, encouraged in French painters a formal freedom, as did the already primitivized Gauguin in a freely ornamental play of color. Fauve primitivism was tropically exotic and refreshingly beyond "taste," yet still an essentially aestheticizing affair. And soon the Cubists, too, would find reinforcement for their own formal experimentation in African sculpture.

In Germany a dissatisfaction with by then conventional, so-called Impressionist, "modern" painting is apparent in Wilhelm Worringer's 1909 criticism, just before the institution of a "New Secession," of the "bourgeois portliness" of exhibitions with "the same atmosphere of saturation, the same crystal-palace ambience, the same marketable works."[2] Already, in *Abstraction and Empathy* (1908), Worringer had elaborated a categorical opposition between arts in (more or less naturalistic) harmony with the surrounding world ("empathy") and arts withdrawn into a formal realm ("abstraction"). Then, too, in 1910 Germany saw its first exhibition of Cubist painting,[3] something structurally and expressively different *both* from French Fauvism and from the Germanic Expressionism (including primitivism) that Worringer himself substantially encouraged. Even so, the chunky masses and fixed poses of nudes in, at least transitional, Cubist figure paintings still manifest a definitely statuesque solemnity that is, ironic or not, ultimately classical. That could only heighten, by comparison, the definitively Germanic approach of the Expressionists. At least by the time of Paul Fechter's *Der Expressionismus* (1914), Cubism and Expressionism were evidently parallel, but with the French movement as distinctly cerebral and the German as emphatically emotive.

To the Germans, rather, and in a way that revived Romantic ideals of tapping into the lifeblood of nature, primitive art seemed to offer the possibility of emotional release from a sometimes excruciating discontent, feeding a spiritual, if sometimes quasi-pagan, longing for freely externalized

---

2. Worringer, in *Kunst und Künstler*, vol. VIII (1909), 369–70, quoted in Klaus Lankheit, "A History of the Almanac," introduction to his edition of Wassily Kandinsky and Franz Marc, eds., *The Blaue Reiter Almanac*, trans. Henning Falkenstein et al., The Documents of Twentieth-Century Art (New York, 1974), 11–48, here 11.

3. See Ann H. Murray, "Henri le Fauconnier's 'Das Kunstwerk': An Early Statement of Cubist Aesthetic Theory and Its Understanding in Germany," *Arts Magazine*, December 1981, 125–33, especially for Fauconnier's preface to the 1910 Neue Künstlervereinigung exhibition catalogue, which may have been translated by Kandinsky.

feeling. This also involved a primitivizing life-style in seeking liberation from inhibitions of bourgeois civility. Kirchner's enthusiasm for painted reliefs from the Palau Islands, in the Dresden ethnographic collection (at the Zwinger Palace), is often paralleled with Vlaminck's response, in 1905, to Dahomey sculptures in Paris, but by 1912 in Germany tribal art was being exhibited as *art,* at the Museum Folkwang, Essen. Some German artists took to the field to encounter tribal art *in situ* as part of primitive life: Emil Nolde was working in New Guinea (a German territory since 1884) in 1913–14 on an official expedition; Max Pechstein stayed in Palau (German since 1899) in 1914–15.

If such was the special mission of modern German art, it had also the advantage, by the early 1900s, of a whole new vision of prehistoric and primitive art, in addition to an entire North European legacy of preeminent "content" and *intensity* in representation, as against all classicizing beauty of "form"—especially as a (Romantic) "Gothic" alternative to any normative Franco-Italian classicism. For here, too, was an enthusiastic embrace of Gothic "barbarity," so different from traditional French rationalizations of the Gothic style.

That Gothicism as an affirmation of primitive "crudity" ("Gothic" in the sense of the Goths) might hold specifically Germanic aesthetic potential was a notion contemporary with the rise of modern Germany itself. Since Vasari's *Lives of the Artists,* in the mid-sixteenth century, Italianate art theory had derided Gothic architecture and Northern art generally as crude and barbarous.[4] Dürer's early fascination with the more exotic than "primitive" pre-Columbian Montezuma treasure was an early symptom of Germanic enthusiasm for categorically nonclassical art. But Goethe helped precipitate a wholesale Romantic-nationalist ideal with his essay "Von deutscher Baukunst," of 1772.[5] Wilhelm Wackenroder, the aesthetician, reprinted his

---

4. Vasari, whose sense of the barbarity of German architecture was in the Italian air at the time, usually speaks of the *maniera tedesca,* or "German manner," of Northern Europe, especially for architecture and sculpture; sometimes he says *maniera dei Goti,* likening the, to him, crudity of the North to that of the Byzantine Greeks, though he never uses an adjectival form, "Gothic." For him, architecture *alla moderna,* in the new Renaissance style, was but a restoration of an ultimately Greek sense of proper form. See T. S. R. Boase, "The *Maniera Tedesca,*" in *Giorgio Vasari: The Man and the Book*, A. W. Mellon Lectures in the Fine Arts, 1971 (Princeton, 1979), 93–108. Boase wisely suggests that the seemingly inordinate attention devoted by Vasari and other littérateurs to the paintings of Pisanello, which teem with otherwise "Gothic" detail, stemmed from the fact that the pictures "lent themselves to the detailed descriptions that were the humanist critics' form of appreciation and opportunity for rhetorical variety and display." The matter reaches a peak with Dürer, whose prints were then influential in Italy (112).

5. See Georg Germann, *The Gothic Revival in Europe and Britain: Sources, Influences and Ideas,*

"Recollections" of Dürer, written for the journal *Deutschland* (1796), in his famous *Heartfelt Effusions of an Art-Loving Monk,* of 1797, a work that itself would occasion an essay by the influential Munich art historian Heinrich Wölfflin (1893). According to Wackenroder, "when Albrecht was still painting, Germany's art had a distinctive character as compared with other nations of the world," and this was "the only time when Germany could speak with pride of its own native art."[6] Even the young Hegel betrays a quasi-gothicizing sense of proliferate detail, as against monolithic classical unity: "The German Empire is a kingdom, like the kingdom of nature in its productions, unfathomable as a whole and inexhaustible in detail."[7] Notable, too, are Friedrich Schlegel's writings on German art and architecture from an anti-French point of view, in his journal *Deutsches Museum* (1812–13).

Well before 1900, collections of ethnographic art could be found all over Europe, though only a few, including that at Dresden, were organized in a rigorous way.[8] One important German collection from early on was that of

trans. Gerald Onn (Cambridge, Mass., 1973), 89, on Goethe's limited enthusiasm for the facade of Strasbourg Cathedral, but, nevertheless, its (Romantic) influence on Ludwig Tieck, in the Nazarene circle.

6. From the excerpt quoted in Robert M. Wernaer's still lively *Romanticism and the Romantic School in Germany* (New York and London, 1910), chap. 15, "Patriotism and Cosmopolitanism; or, Middle-Ages, Renaissance and Neo-Romanticism," 303–20, here 305.

7. "The German Constitution" (drafted 1799–1802), in *Hegel's Political Writings*, trans. T. M. Knox, introd. Z. A. Pelczynski (Oxford, 1964; repr. 1969), 143–242, here 150.

One of the most compelling instances in English of the Germanic primitive-Gothic-Romantic, and almost the Expressionist too, as a complex of interrelated notions, must be the paragraph in Carlyle's lecture "The Hero as Priest" (1840) characterizing Lucas Cranach's portraits of Luther. The very topography of the North is evoked in the description of the "rude plebeian face; with its huge crag-like brows and bones, the emblem of rugged energy." To Carlyle, this Luther is a "Great Man"—but "Great, not as a hewn obelisk; but as an Alpine mountain,—so simple, honest, spontaneous, not setting-up to be great at all. . . . Ah, yes, unsubduable granite, piercing far and wide into the Heavens; yet in the clefts of it fountains, green beautiful valleys with flowers!" Thomas Carlyle, *On Heroes, Hero-Worship and the Heroic in History* (1841), The World's Classics (London, 1974), 186–87.

8. In England, prehistoric and primitive, Gothic, and even European folk art were in close association, not to say confusion, from the very founding of the British Museum, which developed as a sort of attic for the expanding British Empire. For anthropology was long part of the "British and Mediaeval Antiquities" department. Sir Hans Soane, whose collection formed the basis of the museum (1753), collected folk crafts of Scotland, Lapland, and the Pyrenees alongside non-Western items; Henry Christy, whose collection passed to the museum in 1863, had collected tribal art in order to explain European prehistory (this despite the fact that Sir John Lubbock was one of his trustees); even O. M. Dalton, important in the department at the turn of the century, wrote ambidextrously on African and Early Christian art. See H. J. Braunholtz, *Sir Hans Soane and British Ethnography*, ed. William Fagg (London, 1970), 33 (with plates), 38, 40.

Gustav Klemm, which came to form the nucleus of the Museum für
Völkerkunde at Leipzig. Klemm had behind him a *Handbuch der germanischen
Alterthumskunde* (Handbook of Germanic Antiquities; Dresden, 1836) when
he began to produce his sweeping, ten-volume *Allgemeine Cultur-Geschichte
der Menschheit* (General Cultural History of Mankind), of 1843–52. There, in
the first volume, comprising "The Prelude and the Primitive States of
Mankind," he notes that until the time of a "new poetic outburst," in the
Gothic period, earlier medieval Germanic buildings, like classical architecture, lay in ruin; then, in the age of the Hohenstaufen monarchs (twelfth
and, mainly, thirteenth centuries), came a fantastic outpouring of new
Germanic Gothic production, with architecture in a most integral *(innigsten)*
unity with sculpture and painting.[9] In volume 4 (1845) of the same work,
covering "The Primitive States of the Mountain and Desert Peoples of
Active Mankind and Their Dissemination over the Earth," Klemm, relying
on Captain Cook's reports (and taking a special interest that would have
appealed to Gottfried Semper in native plaited mats and body
ornamentation[10]), maintains that, charming as the natives are, "the art of
the South Seas is still in its childhood." This notion, which may depend on
Vico, would become problematic under the influence of evolutionary
theory. Klemm's own explanation sounds virtually Heideggerian: not having
"loosened *(losgelöst)* itself from its native soil," and so not yet risen to self-
sufficiency, art still "clung *(haftete)* to man himself, to his implements and
weapons, to the objects of his awe *(Verehrung),*" though just so it shows "a
certain artistic value."[11]

In recent echo, the variously primitivizing voices of Gottfried Semper
and William Morris were still heard in modern art circles in the later
nineteenth century. Even Wölfflin was stimulated by Semper in the famous
dictum from his *Renaissance and Baroque* (1888): "We judge every object by
analogy with our own bodies." In context, Wölfflin appears to move
empathy theory in the Expressionist direction, claiming that by projection
"we interpret the whole outside world according to the expressive system

---

9. *Allgemeine Cultur-Geschichte*, vol. I (Leipzig, 1843), 217. Klemm had studied medieval
cultural history and was also interested in European folk culture (Italian, in particular). After
writing his *Allgemeine Cultur-Geschichte*, he produced an *Allgemeine Culturwissenschaft: Die materiellen
Grundlagen menschlicher Cultur* (General Cultural Science: The Material Foundations of Human
Culture), of 1854–55. See F. Schnorr von Carolsfeld, "Gustav Friedrich Klemm," *Allgemeine
deutsche Biographie*, vol. XVI (Leipzig, 1882), 152–53.

10. *Allgemeine Cultur-Geschichte*, vol. IV (Leipzig, 1845), 278–79.

11. Ibid., 400.

with which we have become familiar from our own bodies," as with any "expression of severe strictness, taut self-discipline or uncontrolled heavy relaxation"[12] (note the un-French extremism). Worringer, partisan of the new art, refers to Semper in *Form Problems of the Gothic* (1910)—as it happens, to Semper's *avoidance,* in his architectural *practice,* of the Gothic style.[13] Semper himself was generally important for his concern, however mythic, with primeval art (despite his obsessions with material and technical process).

Anyway, Worringer, who totally embraced primitive art as a live alternative to the conventional naturalistic conception of art left over from academicized classicism, advanced the new Expressionist aesthetic through his own critique of Semper. In his Gothic book he is enthusiastic, in a modern way, about the virtually Symbolist evocativeness of primeval (even Neolithic) planar forms: "Only in surface representation has man even in his earliest development possessed an invariable symbol for that which is denied him by the three-dimensionality of the actual, an invariable symbol for the absolute form of the individual object of the outer world, that is, for the form purified from all accident of apprehension [a distinctly anti-Impressionist remark] and from all spatial confusion with other phenomena." But Worringer also indicates a functionally Expressionist emphasis on carving (witness the Neo-Gothic woodcut revival), claiming that sculptural modeling, by comparison, belongs "not to the history of art, but to the history of handicraft."[14] The Gothic, offering as it does such a transcendence of materiality, is seen to spring from and to extend the enduring primitivity of the North, even up to the Expressionist present: "The art of the whole Occident, as far as it has not immediately participated in the antique Mediterranean culture, is Gothic in its inmost essence and remains so up to the Renaissance, that great turning point of the northern development. . . . [Even] northern Baroque is in a certain sense the flaring up again of the suppressed Gothic form-will under a strange mask. So *Gothic* as a term of style psychology extends further than the school term *Gothic* toward the present also."[15] Reacting against what he saw as Semper's

---

12. Heinrich Wölfflin, *Renaissance and Baroque*, trans. Kathrin Simon (London, 1964), 77, with reference to Gottfried Semper, *Der Stil in den technischen und tektonischen Künsten*, vol. II (Munich, 1879), 5 (treating the Greek *hydria* vase as balanced on the head).

13. Worringer, *Form Problems of the Gothic*, 3d ed. (1912), trans. (New York, n.d.), 126, says that Semper, "with his classical prepossession," had "first coined the term 'petrified scholasticism,' and he thought to discredit the Gothic thereby."

14. Ibid., 33.

15. Ibid., 44.

mechanistic notion of primeval art production, Worringer thus reopened the Gothic issue, in tune with the new art of Germany.

As for William Morris, whose well-known medievalism was a radical politicization of Ruskin's aesthetic: his influence is apparent in the diffused form of a general concern with handicraft in the several "secessions." It was, indeed, as a craftsman whose theoretical work has obvious consequence for fine art that the critic Meier-Graefe took special interest in Morris's work and influence.[16] Ernst Ludwig Kirchner paid homage to Morris as a graphic artist with his woodcut manifesto for the Dresden "Brücke" group, a broadsheet of 1906 whose carved text recalls one of Morris's craft masterpieces, the title page of the *Kelmscott Chaucer* (1893).[17] Besides, Morris himself had adumbrated the Expressionist revival of interest in the ostensibly crude medieval woodcut, collecting Flemish and German, as well as French and Italian, examples.[18] Here, too, Dürer, as the genius of woodcut, was again a principal "pro-Gothic" hero, as he had been in Romantic times (even if Expressionist radicality would eventually come up against a conservative cult of the German "Renaissance" master). The English Pre-Raphaelites and Victorians had trod a similar path since at least 1869, when the painter William Scott published his life of Dürer.[19] The architect Matthew Digby Wyatt mentioned Scott's then new book in one of his Slade Lectures,[20] lectures that a generation before Worringer begin

16. Julius Meier-Graefe, *Modern Art: Being a Contribution to a New System of Aesthetics* (1904), trans. Florence Simmonds and George W. Chrystal (London and New York, 1908), esp. vol. II, 235–46.

17. Selz, *Painting*, 94–95, with illustration (Kirchner).

18. Walter Crane, "William Morris and His Work," in his *William Morris to Whistler: Essays and Addresses on Art and Craft and the Commonwealth* (London, 1911), 3–44, esp. 29.

19. *Albert Dürer: His Life and Works; Including Autobiographical Papers and Complete Catalogues* (London, 1869). One might go back further, considering as part of the general earlier eighteenth-century English influence on the Continental Enlightenment, the discovery of a "primitive" strength and force in the Old Testament and in Homer. Thomas Blackwell's *Enquiry into the Life and Writings of Homer* (1735) "stressed the emotionally expressive elements, which he likened to those of the utterances of Arabs, Turks and American Indians"; Robert Lowth's *Lectures on the Sacred Poetry of the Hebrews* (1753) maintains that poetry "derives its very existence from the more vehement emotions of the mind"; these lead to Johann Gottfried von Herder's *Vom Geist der hebräischen Poesie* (1782), "in which can be seen the beginnings of an extensive theory of folk poetry as self-expression." For convenience I quote here from the interesting essay by Vincent Freimarck, "The Legacy of Eighteenth-Century Primitivism," in the Harpur College exhibition catalogue *Primitivism, Folk and the Primitive* (Binghamton, N.Y., 1962), 7–13, here 10, owing my larger sense of such connections (especially Shaftesbury's notion of the "natural" in relation to the classical) to the lectures of my late mentor, Rudolf Wittkower, some fifteen years ago.

20. *Fine Art: A Sketch of Its History, Theory, Practice and Application to Industry: Being a Course of Lectures Delivered at Cambridge in 1870* (London and New York, 1870), Lecture 10: "Painting: Theory," 265–89, esp. 266.

to suggest an escape from Semperian determinism toward something like expressive form; much of what Wyatt said would not have sounded out of place, half a century later but in a descendant tradition, in the Bauhaus lecture hall.[21]

The Gothic as Germanic-Primitive

Kandinsky and Marc's *Blaue Reiter Almanac* testifies, inadvertently as well as deliberately, to the Romantic-Gothic appeal of the woodcut for modern German artists as a legacy of the "barbarous" North. Along with the numerous old woodcuts reproduced, the *Almanac* has an extraordinary page on which a woodcut of a knight appears, accompanied by a quotation from Goethe that anticipates early modern art theory in suggesting a quasi-musical consideration of the underlying elements and structure of images, beyond representation: "In 1807 Goethe said: 'In painting the knowledge of the thorough bass has been missing for a long time; a recognized theory of painting, as it exists in music, is lacking.' "[22] That the woodcut of the knight, however, is really a forgery, dating, appropriately enough, from the Romantic period,[23] only exposes the nationalist Gothicism to which Goethe himself had contributed. In Worringer's modern study of the early woodcut as a characteristically Germanic ("Nordic") art, from the Middle Ages through Holbein and Dürer, a contemporary thrust is urgent again: the woodcut is distinctly an art of imaginary conception rather than an art about the *appearance* of the world, as in Italy.[24]

The modern relevance of Romantic-Gothic tradition could only have been enhanced by the 1906 Berlin centennial exhibition of German painting from 1775 to 1875, organized by Hugo von Tschudi, who was an advocate

---

21. Although on design Wyatt can sound like Ruskin and Morris, he clearly sided with the industrialists. See Nikolaus Pevsner, "Matthew Digby Wyatt" (1949), in his *Studies in Art, Architecture and Design*, vol. II: *Victorian and After* (London, 1968), 96–107.

22. Kandinsky and Marc (*Almanac*, 112) give as their source for the remark *Goethe im Gespräch* (Munich, 1907), 94. A "thorough," or "ground," bass is the same in music theory as a *basso continuo*.

23. *Almanac*, 39, Lankheit's n. 21.

24. *Die altdeutsche Buchillustration* (Munich and Leipzig, 1912), introduction, esp. 27 (*Vorstellungskunst* vs. *Anschauungskunst*). Kurt Pfister's beautiful later album, *Die primitiven Holzschnitte* (Munich, 1922), points up the woodcut's "primitive" appeal in its very title. Max Picard uses the word "expressionistic" in his title for a similar album. See note 80.

of the Expressionists in the museum world and to whose memory the *Blaue Reiter Almanac* of the Munich Expressionists would be dedicated. Tschudi, the author of studies of Böcklin (1901), Manet (1902), and Menzel (1906), was a living link with non-Western and also Romantic art: he was the son of Johann Jakob von Tschudi, an early ethnographer of pre-Columbian Peru, and the grandson of the Romantic painter Ludwig Schnorr von Carolsfeld.[25] The younger Tschudi began his museum career under Böde in Berlin and was from 1891 to 1907 at the Berlin National Gallery, where he worked on behalf of modern art especially; from 1909 until his death he was in Munich, at the Staatliche Gemäldesammlungen. At least to the extent of firing a competitive spirit as regards modern French painting, of which the critic Meier-Graefe, notably, was a devotee, Tschudi's "Jahrhundertausstellung" was an understandably German enthusiasm[26] (Worringer, the Expressionist theoretician, has even been accused of racism for his doggedly Germanic enthusiasms[27]).

True, the recognition of France's role in the genesis of the Gothic was not exactly an obsession of the Germans, but Robert Delaunay found welcome in Germany, and *St. Séverin* (1909), his Gothic church interior, fits nicely in the *Blaue Reiter Almanac*.[28] Otherwise, an interesting ambiguity as

---

25. Friedrich Ratzel, "Johann Jakob von Tschudi," *Allgemeine deutsche Biographie*, vol. 38 (Leipzig, 1894), 749–52. On Hugo von Tschudi, see the standard German encyclopedias. The elder Tschudi worked with Mariano Eduardo de Ribero y Ustáriz's *Peruvian Antiquities* (trans. Francis L. Hawks [New York and Cincinnati, 1854]), first published at Vienna in 1851 with a beautiful atlas of color plates. Although not concerned with aesthetics, the book ends with a chapter on ancient monuments in which burial textiles are noticed and a stone head at Tiahuanaco is praised as bearing "no resemblance whatever to what is known of other nations" (296). Interestingly, the blood sacrifices associated with graven (wooden) idol worship are described as having superseded "the pure and abstract worship of the invisible Pachacamac" (288). According to Louis Baudin (*A Socialist Empire: The Incas of Peru*, ed. Arthur Goddard and trans. Katherine Woods [Princeton, 1961], 256), the text was by Ribero alone, and Tschudi disclaimed any unscientific hypotheses in it. Tschudi's own *Kulturhistorische und sprachliche Beiträge zur Kenntnis des alten Peru* was published in 1891 as volume XXXIX of the Viennese *Denkschriften der kaiserlichen Akademie der Wissenschaften*.

26. On the pertinence of German Romantic painting to the German Expressionists (and Edvard Munch), see Robert Rosenblum, *Modern Painting and the Northern Romantic Tradition: Friedrich to Rothko* (New York, 1975).

27. Walter Abell, "Toward a Unified Field in Critical Studies," reprinted from his *The Collective Dream in Art: A Psycho-Historical Theory of Culture Based on Relations between the Arts, Psychology and the Social Sciences* (Cambridge, Mass., 1957), in Milton C. Albrecht, James H. Barnett, and Mason Griff, eds., *The Sociology of Art and Literature* (New York and Washington, D.C., 1970), 724–36, here 734.

28. Lankheit, "History," 45, with reference to Ludwig Grote in the "Blaue Reiter" exhibition catalogue (Munich, 1949), 12.

to Germanic Gothicism and primitivity may be seen in Kirchner's *Two Women (Two Midinettes)* (Fig. 23), of 1911–12 (Los Angeles): an aggressively zigzagged interface between the two figures here recalls the wonderful zigzag archivolts separating the columnar figures of the "Adamspforte" (Fig. 22) of Bamberg Cathedral (c. 1230–40), but it happens to derive, without contradiction of this structural Gothicism, from a "primitive" (African?) textile hanging in the artist's studio.[29] In 1912, even before leaving for the Pacific islands, Nolde, planning an introduction to a book on primitive art, praised the latter over and against classical art, admiring the sculptures of Bamberg and other German Gothic cathedrals as worthily primitive.[30] Only in the face of the general losses to European culture at large from World War I does Max Dvořák seem to turn, in his *Idealism and Naturalism in Gothic Art* (1918), to a more traditionally, classicizingly French vindication of Gothic sculpture and architecture.[31]

Less acknowledged, perhaps, than the (neo-)Neo-"Gothic" aspect of German Expressionism is the relevance of new scientific thought on prehistoric and surviving "primitive" culture[32] (no doubt partly a function of the German term *Naturvolk* as applied to a primitive people). Already around 1890 the long-standing confusion of the prehistoric with the surviving primitive was being dispelled. Facilitated by the distinction framed a generation earlier by Sir John Lubbock (Lord Avebury) between Paleolithic and Neolithic culture, prehistory was finally separated from the question of

---

29. When Kirchner moved to Berlin, tribal textiles, sculptures, and other carved wooden objects filled his studio. Prominent in paintings of the time is a long painted cloth split vertically in two with large roundels on each half, this seemingly represented with or without a vivid zigzag pattern. Donald E. Gordon, in his *Ernst Ludwig Kirchner* (Cambridge, Mass., 1968), refers to this motif in other paintings as "part of a Brücke studio drapery, modeled after a primitive (presumably African) ornamental design" (66). From Kirchner's own photograph of a black male nude model, since published in Erika Billeter's *Malerei und Photographie im Dialog von 1840 bis Heute* (Bern, 1979; fig. 250, p. 99), it can be seen that there were really two cloths hanging in the studio doorway, one with roundels, in front, and the zigzagged one, separately, behind.

30. Selz, *Painting*, 126, with reference to Nolde's *Jahre der Kämpfe* (Berlin, 1934), 172–73.

31. *Idealism and Naturalism in Gothic Art*, ed. and trans. Randolph J. Klawiter (Notre Dame, Ind., 1967), 26. The German army had taken Rheims and Amiens mere weeks before a cosmopolitan, international survey of the "afterlife" of Gothic in European architecture down to the turn of the century appeared, this by Hans Tietze, art historian and friend of new art. Tietze's essay closes with the claim that although later "Gothic" manifestations are conditioned by their times, there is nevertheless a Gothic "spirit" that is "immortal and without end" ("Das Fortleben der Gotik durch die Neuzeit," *Mitteilungen der k. k. Zentral-Kommission für Denkmalpflege* [Vienna], XIII [1914], 197–212, 237–49, here 249).

32. See the interesting review of modern prehistoricism in Otto Rank, *Art and Artist: Creative Urge and Personality Development* (New York, 1932), introduction and passim, with references.

primitivity as a relative state. Now an almost "Gothic" enthusiasm can be seen to carry over in German theories of the eminence of Northern Europe in earliest times. Ernst Krause maintained (in *Die Trojaburgen Nordeuropas* [1893]) that the prehistoric North had even influenced the Mediterranean basin, and in the heyday of Expressionism there appeared Carl Schuchhardt's (Semperian) *Alteuropa* (1918), a study in "Cultural and Stylistic Development," drawing an artistic contrast between prehistoric Northern and Southern Europe not unlike those of the Renaissance and later times. Becoming more politically chauvinistic about primitivism, Leo Frobenius, a pioneer in the study of African art in the 1890s, would even agitate for the restoration of the German overseas empire: during the 1920s and beyond he embraced an ideal of African strength as opposed to the "oriental lethargy" connoted by rugs, silks, porcelain, and even drugs, which he took as essentially akin to the "feminine" French.[33]

Primitive (vs. Prehistoric) Sophistication

But it was the fundamental notion of art as having developed *from* Paleolithic representation *to* Neolithic ornamental-abstraction that made it possible to

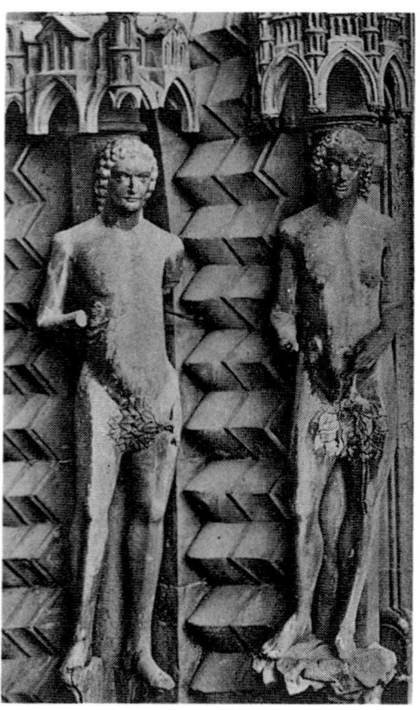

Fig. 22   Bamberg Cathedral, "Adamspforte," right jamb, Adam and Eve, c. 1230–40.

---

33. Goldwater, *Primitivism*, 29.

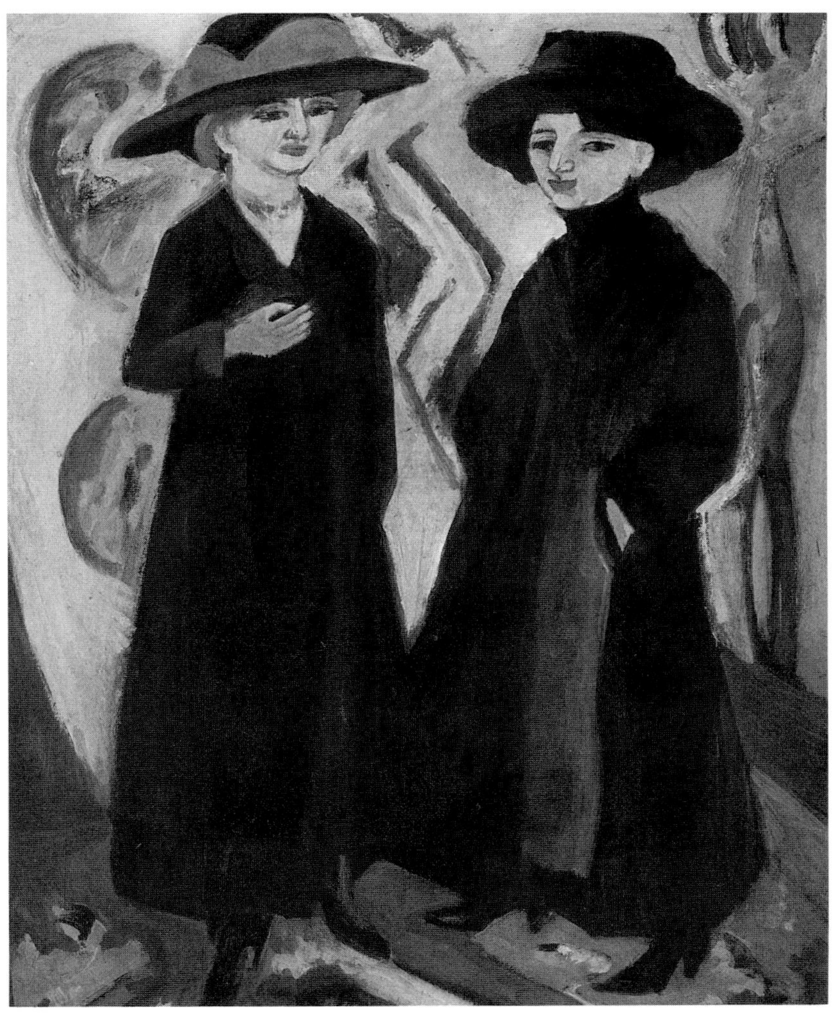

Fig. 23   Ernst Ludwig Kirchner, *Two Women (Two Midinettes)*, 1906 (according to museum), 1908 (Kirchner Archive), or 1911–12 (Gordon), oil on canvas, 59 x 47 inches.

see contemporary "primitive" art as neolithically continuous with modern European, and specifically Germanic, culture. To lend nonfigural forms of "mere ornament" serious aesthetic regard, all the more as a development *from* or improvement *on* pictorialism, required a comprehension of primitive art as much more than a matter of "ineptitude" left over from the "childhood" of humanity.

Crucially, Paul Ehrenreich's 1890 report of an expedition to the Brazilian Indians made it possible to think that apparently nonobjective ornamental forms might have images generatively behind them, that is, that they might even have submerged iconographic significance.[34] Although in one sense this extended the nineteenth-century search for describable representation, in a more radical way it definitively confirmed the approach to abstract-ornamental form as a positive *sophistication*. Ehrenreich found that designs painted by the people of the Xingu River basin as seemingly nonobjective architectural ornaments actually reflected motifs of nature, mostly animals (or such special items as little triangular G-strings worn by married women). This was a pivotal case of "realistic degeneration," to borrow Pitt-Rivers's conception of the abstractedly decorative designs on Papuan canoe paddles[35]—objects already admired for their formal beauty in Owen Jones's *Grammar of Ornament* (1854). Ehrenreich considered a form thus derived a *Tiernachbildung,* or "animal after-image," something that was "hardly just a geometric figure." Inescapably, this amounts to an acknowledgment of human transformation—rather than any quasi-natural process of formal simplification by wearing-down or decay—as, for example, in the rendering of an anaconda as a line wavering over and under a row of dots.

Knut Hjalmar Stolpe was one of many ornamental theoreticians of the late nineteenth century influenced by evolutionary thought, yet his studies show the new awareness that representational art developed, through stylization, into ornamental-abstraction. In an 1890 essay on "evolution" in the art of primitive peoples *(Naturfolkens),* translated from Swedish into English (1891–92) and then into German (1892, for the Viennese Anthropological Society), Stolpe traces the derivation of an apparently nonobjective ornamental pattern, a band of rectangles with zigzags running inside, along top and bottom, from a motif of crouching human figures in a row, the

---

34. "Mitteilungen über die zweite Xingu-Expedition in Brasilien," *Zeitschrift für Ethnologie,* XXII (1890), 81–98.

35. A. Lane-Fox Pitt-Rivers, "The Evolution of Culture," in his *The Evolution of Culture and Other Essays,* ed. J. L. Myres (Oxford, 1906), 41–42, with pl. 4.

zigzags being vestigial limbs in the "last degree of dissolution."[36] The term "dissolution" hardly seems pejorative here, merely descriptive. By 1927, in his foreword to a new English edition of this and another of Stolpe's papers, Henry Balfour seems old-fashioned in saying that "the domination of material and technique is well illustrated by the coarse textile fabrics, which impose a certain conventional angularity upon all would-be curvilin-ear designs,"[37] which sounds more like a misfortune than Stolpe has it. Soon Stolpe would find confirmation of his approach in the researches of Ernst Grosse, as acknowledged in his own "Studies in American Ornamen-tation: A Contribution to the Biology of Ornament" (1896).[38]

Grosse's *The Beginnings of Art* (1893) indeed calls attention to a pictorial significance behind ornamental forms to show that such art is not naively inept. Grosse admits to a certain lack of resolution as to the precedence of ornamentation or representation. Where he notes textile seams as an occasion for ornamental elaboration,[39] he seems beholden to the specula-tions of Semper, though, significantly, there is also a sense that Semperian insight is limited. In line with Semper, Grosse may wonder whether the tattoo designs of Eskimo women (known from examples published by Franz Boas in the 1880s) derive from embroidery,[40] but then, more in tune with Aloïs Riegl's aesthetic critique of Semperianism, he pursues a more affirmative notion of *creative surface elaboration.* Why should primitive paintings on skins suggest "resemblance to a woven piece" in a (surviving) culture that does not employ naturalistic rendering in other artwork? Grosse is prepared to propose a rather Schopenhauerian explanation of why tribal artists should resort to artistic stylization. Because the style cannot be a simple matter of craft ineptitude, "it must be referred to the will."[41] As it did for many a modernist, the whole question of stylization reminds Grosse of "the designs on our parlor carpets." This is because he has an eye for pattern, as, again, where he says of a belt from India, "the oblique strokes on the girdle are repeated, just like the flowers on the carpet, at regular intervals, and, like the flowers, form rhythmical series."[42]

---

36. "On Evolution in the Ornamental Art of Savage Peoples," in his *Collected Essays in Ornamental Art*, trans. Mrs. H. Colley March (Stockholm, 1927), 1–57, here 29.

37. *Essays*, v.

38. Ibid., 61–128.

39. *The Beginnings of Art* (ed. New York, 1900), 101, 130.

40. Ibid., 80.

41. Ibid., 140. The closing sentence of Grosse's book reads: "The art of Plato, teacher of Peoples, is the opposite of the art of Schopenhauer, deliverer of men" (316).

42. *Beginnings*, 149.

Grosse is fully prepared to refer aboriginal murals and rock carvings to the European fine-art tradition, and vice versa: "While the works of this kind correspond to the fresco paintings and reliefs of European ornaments, our canvas paintings also have their analogies in Australia in the drawings which the aborigines make on soot-blackened pieces of hide."[43] Even conventional painting, that "simplest form of moveable decoration," itself "most eminently represents the original form of decoration."[44] Such an idea of the self-sufficiency of decoration as somehow nonobjective underlies even Kandinsky's speculations on abstraction.

Ironically, Ehrenreich's 1890 report was mobilized by the Russian materialist aesthetician G. V. Plekhanov, who was strongly Semperian and ideologically committed to the proposition that work purely and simply precedes play, with all aesthetic operations deriving from labor processes. Plekhanov's series of "Letters without Address" began to appear in 1899, when the young Kandinsky had already given up law to pursue art in Munich: although Plekhanov's (rather undialectical) materialism would have rubbed Kandinsky, with his irreducible spiritualism, the wrong way, Kandinsky himself was at home in the *Jugendstil* milieu and closely involved with craft work. Out of an intent to be scientific, Plekhanov turns to Ehrenreich's 1890 Xingu study and the related work of Karl von den Steinen (1894). Because he seeks blunt *fact,* Plekhanov comes to a halt in interpreting Ehrenreich's principal intuition. The sixth and last of the "Letters" (posthumous) opens with a Semperian treatment of the technical derivation from plaiting or weaving of the ornaments on primitive combs, axes, and pottery. Plekhanov, feeling in his element, generalizes: first designs arose in weaving and then "they soon became very widespread."[45] Here, however, the original manuscript has a passage that, the Russian editors explain, is crossed out: "I hasten to note . . . that by no means all 'geometrical' designs can be referred to the source I have indicated. Ehrenreich's and von den Steinen's observations on the art of the Brazilian Indians show that there yet another 'factor' played no less important a role, if not a greater one—to wit, nature."[46] Possibly this was deleted to stress Stolpe's idea that geometric ornament developed specifically from human

---

43. Ibid., 174.

44. Ibid., 54–55.

45. "Letters without Address," trans. Eric Hartley, in Plekhanov, *Art and Social Life*, ed. Andrew Rothstein (London, 1953), Letter 6, 130–39, here 131.

46. Ibid., 131 n. 3.

and animal, *rather than vegetal,* motifs.[47] In any event, according to Pelkhanov, "depictions of this kind lose their original form insofar as they become *stylized,* and often rejoice the heart of the idealist research worker by their apparently abstract character."[48] Not until the time of Expressionism was it fully clear that such stylization was a genuine sophistication in primitive ornament.[49]

Well before Expressionism emerged as a movement in Germany, primitive art was showing itself in modern painting. Edvard Munch exhibited with the Berlin avant-garde as early as 1892, the year in which he painted his famous *Self-Portrait beneath the Mask* (Oslo). In that painting, the artist's head and upper torso, seen slightly off-center against a loosely painted red field, are boldly surmounted by a primitive mask centered in a friezelike band along the upper edge: by the play against symmetry, which depends on the masklike frontality of the artist's own image, and within the decorative flatness of the whole, Munch sympathetically equates his own visage with the anonymous mask. Despite certain disclaimers, Munch must have influenced the "Brücke" artists of Dresden.[50] This self-portrait and other works by Munch would obviously have appealed to the Germans.

Yrjö Hirn stands clearly on the modern side of an artistic divide for his antidepictive stance in *The Origins of Art: A Psychological and Sociological Inquiry* (1900): "The painter's ideal can no longer be confused with that of the story-teller, nor the sculptor's with that of the actor."[51] Hirn knows that prehistoric and primitive art is not pointlessly nonrepresentational,[52] and not merely interesting but aesthetically gratifying. He can sound like Freud (whose own *Lustprinzip* likewise traces back to Gustav Fechner's "psychophysics"): "The life-preserving tendency which, under the feeling of pleasure, leads us to movements which intensify the sensation and make it more distinct for consciousness, compels us in pain to seek for relief and deliverance in violent motor discharge. In either case the activity is expressional, and it seems difficult to avoid this equivocal usage."[53] As

---

47. Ibid., 132, with 132–33 n. 5, quoting Stolpe, *Entwicklungerscheinungen in der Ornamentik der Naturvoelker* (Vienna, 1892), 23: "The plant world, strange as this may seem, appears to have provided primitive peoples with considerably less material for stylization."

48. "Letters without Address," 138.

49. Noteworthy is the dissertation of Elisabeth Wilson, *Das Ornament auf ethnologischer und prähistorischer Grundlage: ein Abschnitt aus den Anfängen der Kunst* (Leipzig, 1914), covering ornamental studies since Semper. Thanks to Meyer Schapiro for this reference.

50. Selz, *Painting*, 81–83.

51. *The Origins of Art* (London, 1900; repr. New York, 1971), 3–4.

52. Ibid., 10–12 and passim.

53. Ibid., 42.

regards pleasure, there are all the "secondary manifestations, by which we try to sustain every pleasure, to make it more distinct for consciousness, and thus enhance it by expression"; if this, in itself, sounds aesthetically French, pain, on the other hand, leads man to "strive for relief in diversion or in violent motor discharge."[54] Note that for Hirn *both* are matters of "expression": while there is an "expression for expression's sake—as when a child laughs or dances for mere joy,"[55] it is nevertheless "more in conformity with ordinary usage—and also with etymology—to apply the word expression to those active, outward manifestations by which . . . inhibition is relieved," that is, to distinguish "between the expression which enhances and the expression which relieves"[56]—or, one might add, between Matisse's Fauvism and the Expressionism of the Germans. For failing to draw this distinction Hirn criticizes William James's chapter on the emotions in the great *Principles of Psychology* (1890); but more urgent, here and now, is the relevance to the equal-and-opposite aspects of Fauve and Expressionist painting of his opposition, even if Hirn does not pretend to have the last word (besides, "it is . . . impossible to decide in individual cases whether an activity of expression . . . serves to enhance a pleasurable feeling or to relieve a pain"[57]).

Consider, in the same light, the alternative aesthetic possibilities offered by the oriental carpet as a motif in early modern art, especially as ostensibly "tribal," nomadic types begin to relate to the new expressive values. Such a carpet serving as a backdrop for a cluster of swords in a late nineteenth-century etching by J. F. Jacquemart anticipates, in some measure, Matisse's decorative interest in non-European textiles, though as yet only in the terms of conventional still-life and drapery studies. Toulouse-Lautrec still overlooked the decorative potential of a similar textile source encountered in 1887: painting a portrait of his friend François Gauzi, he left out a strongly patterned, apparently nomadic rug hanging behind the figure in the photograph from which he worked.[58] Early in the 1890s the more sophisticated, high-class oriental carpets became objects of serious curatorial interest to Riegl, in Vienna, and to Julius Lessing and (the anti-Expressionist) Wilhelm von Bode, in Berlin; by the turn of the century

---

54. Ibid., 72–73.

55. Ibid., 47.

56. Ibid., 52.

57. Ibid., 68.

58. R. Huisman and M. G. Dortu, *Lautrec by Lautrec* (New York, 1964), 48, with photograph and color plate.

these refined types abounded in conventional Central European bourgeois domestic furnishings. But in prewar Germany the "cruder" carpets, in particular, with their aggressive angularity and often vivid color, appealed to rather bolder tastes. Kirchner uses a sketchy but florid oriental carpet as a foil for posed figures in *Two Girls on a Rug* (1905), now in Essen, an opulently loose tempera painting in which two languid nudes punctuate the carpet pattern; two years later, however, in a woodcut, *Nudes on a Carpet,* a more nomadic-looking carpet contributes lustily to a scene of uninhibited bodily display, its already schematic zigzag pattern seeming tauter still for the brutal gouging and tonal extremism of the woodcut. Soon the more vivid oriental carpet, typically Anatolian or Caucasian, came to signify the (suspect) bohemian freedom of the artist's life. Carl Hopf ends a middlebrow book on *Old Persian Carpets and Their Artistic Values* (1913) with a bright color plate of an example from the South Caucausus, only semihumorously calling "daring hotspurs" the enthusiasts of these less tasteful rugs flaunting "color full of joyous life and strength."[59]

Graven Idols in Modernist Paintings

Works of primitive sculpture sometimes appear within the Expressionist work of the "Brücke" artists of Dresden. Kirchner, who already knew the Dresden ethnographic collection, had spent previous summers with Erich Heckel and Max Pechstein and their models in earthy, lakeside rusticity, when he took his first Berlin studio. In *Summer,* a woodcut of 1911, the zigzagging of a carved Melanesian work is picked up not only in an overall jaggedness of form but also as a specific ornamental motif, in the canvas pattern of a modern deck chair.[60] Among the paintings showing primitive artwork of one sort or another, Kirchner's *Two Nudes with a Sculpture,* of the same time, can be mentioned for the unusually Gauguinesque way a standing female nude, seen from the back, divides the composition left and

---

59. 2d ed., English trans. (Munich, 1913), 36, with pl. 8. Hopf's book appeared in German, French, and English versions. The subtler irregularities of the Anatolian carpets described by the contemporary composer Morton Feldman ("Crippled Symmetry," *Res* no. 2 [Autumn 1981], 91–103, esp. 93–94) concern the (usually more French) issue of decorative variation. This deserves mention here insofar as such rugs still evoke an avant-garde.

60. Selz, *Painting,* 255, with fig. 32.

right.[61] Heckel also shows primitive sculpture in his work. In the ambitious *Convalescent Woman* triptych, of 1912–13 (Harvard), a standing statuette of carved wood (or possibly a figure taking such form), at the far left, opposes sunlamplike sunflowers at the far right, as though both might alike be capable of radiating onto the ailing woman the restorative vitality of nature.

The independent Nolde, who had studied art in Paris at the turn of the century, was also familiar with the tribal art in Dresden by 1910, well before his Pacific expedition of 1913–14. Nolde participated briefly (1906–7) in the "Brücke" group, along with Kirchner, and also showed with the Munich counterpart, "Der Blaue Reiter," in 1912. An interest in James Ensor, the proto-Expressionist Belgian artist, makes itself especially felt in Nolde's images of masks and masklike faces.[62] Several paintings by Nolde of Russian and also Slovenian peasants, done between about 1911 and 1915, parallel, however knowingly, generalized images of folk types by Larionov (1909), Goncharova (1910), and Malevich (1912), in Russia, which makes him seem less different than might be expected from Kandinsky, who already knew about modern West European primitivism when he returned to Russia in 1910 and there renewed his sense of native Russian arts.

Certain paintings by Nolde juxtapose tribal and European folk art, as if in equation. His *Still Life D (with South Seas Fetish and Porcelain Figurines),* of 1914 (Hanover),[63] shows what looks to be a Melanesian, shieldlike figured board together with an apparently ceramic blue bird and a European figurine group of a standing woman with another bird. On the wall behind, and likewise equated, are a figured Oceanic board and a patterned textile. Nolde would seem here to be (re)integrating his exposure to primitive art and culture with his own European heritage on a common ground, especially since the quaintly splotched painting of the figurine has the character of folk work; the "marvelous bird," moreover, is a widespread motif in East European folklore (witness Brancusi and Stravinsky). A related painting also recalling his South Seas experience is Nolde's 1915 *Still Life*

---

61. It is as if the pose of Gauguin's *The Moon and the Earth* (1893; Museum of Modern Art) were combined with the general disposition of his *Where Do We Come From? What Are We? Where Are We Going?* (1897; Boston). I cannot, however, conclude from the tiny illustration of the (then missing) Kirchner (in Gordon, *Kirchner*, cat. no. 195, with fig. on p. 293) whether the third figure is a "sculpture" or another person.   ·

62. On the idea of the mask as an image not of deceit but of veracity in artifice, in Emerson, Nietzsche, and Oscar Wilde, see Lionel Trilling, *Sincerity and Authenticity* (Cambridge, Mass., 1972), 112, 119–20.

63. Color plate, in Georg Schmidt, *Die Malerei in Deutschland 1900–1918*, Die Blauen Bücher (Königstein im Taunus, 1959), 26.

with Uli Figure (Seebüll), where the wooden image of an androgynous deity of creation, one such as Nolde himself apparently brought home with him from the Pacific, appears before what is probably not two (presumably both female?) "lovers who are turning toward each other," in extension of a primitive androgyny theme,[64] but rather a European ceramic figure group on a table covered by a vividly rendered tribal textile with bright green irregular stars in a dark field.

Max Pechstein, a member of Die Brücke from 1906 until 1912 (when he was expelled for dividing his institutional loyalty), also shows primitive sculpture in his work. Pechstein is sometimes considered less aggressively Expressionistic than others, but his drawings and woodcuts can carry over energetically the vitality of tribal art. Thus the faceted head in *Eibedul* (1917), perhaps based on a Sepik River figure from New Guinea, gains a high-strung tenseness from the struggle with the wood. Likewise, the cover for Pechstein's *Holzschnitte 1919* (Woodcuts 1919), of 1920, itself a woodcut, owes its ferocity at least as much to Cameroonian wood sculpture on which the image is based, as to the raw directness of the woodcut medium.[65]

From the Decorative to the Spiritual

For Die Brücke, in (Protestant) Saxony, tribal culture seems to have served as a quasi-pagan, or at least untranscendental, tonic. Rather differently, Kandinsky (who was Russian Orthodox) and Marc, of Der Blaue Reiter, in (Catholic) Bavaria, tended to pursue a kind of spirituality or transcendence seeming to offer itself in the unexploited mythopoetic integrity of primitive art. Of course, any antithesis of this kind can be forced: a significant exception here is the remark of (the Protestant) Nolde, in a letter to his mother from the Pacific, in 1914, in which he regrets that probably within twenty years "the primitive spirituality that we today so frivolously and

---

64. Charles Wentinck, *Modern and Primitive Art*, trans. Hilary Davies, Phaidon Twentieth-Century Art (Oxford, 1979), pl. 11b (in color), caption (with *Uli* figure from New Ireland, Melanesia, now in the Hoogstraate collection, Amsterdam, on pl. 11a, facing). Carl Einstein saw a lesson of sculpturality in African art: "La Sculpture nègre" (1915), trans. in *Méditations*, III (1961), 93–114.

65. In Orrel P. Reed's catalog for the Frederick S. Wight Art Gallery, University of California, exhibition *German Expressionist Art: The Robert Gore Rifkind Collection: Prints, Drawings, Illustrated Books, Periodicals, Posters* (Los Angeles, 1977), cat. nos. 147 on p. 94, 151 on p. 97, with illustrations.

shamelessly destroy" would be lost.[66] Yet the contemporary critic Theodor Däubler's attempts to elaborate on an ascetic element that he claimed to observe in "Brücke" art have been found overstated.[67]

It may help to understand the Munich mood to consider how Hirn's *Origins of Art,* for instance, might have appealed to the Symbolist in Kandinsky in precisely the way it could not have affected Plekhanov, his nine-years-older materialist compatriot. For Hirn the "natural aim" of the "expressional impulse" is nothing less than "to bring more and more sentient beings under the influence of the same emotional state." Indeed, "as a result of this craving the expressional activities lead to artistic production. The work of art presents itself as the most effective means by which the individual is enabled to convey to wider and wider circles of sympathizers an emotional state similar to that by which he is himself dominated."[68] Hirn is aware of the aesthetics of Vernon Lee, in England: "The formative and decorative arts may, by compelling our eye to follow a regular arrangement of lines and figures, transmit to us an emotional excitement by the mediation of rhythm. Ornament, that purely popular art, may therefore be compared as to its psychological effects with simple popular dances and melodies."[69] Prevailing European painting, as Hirn finds it, is compromised and, in some as yet unknown way, unfulfilled: the "mimetic principle tends to be lost among the descriptive elements," so that the result loses "the direct transmission of feeling." Clearly, Hirn's insights into early "ornamental" art help point the way, via *symbolisme,* toward a freely expressive and truly modern art: "The mimic movements which are the psychological counterparts of distinct emotion may be, so to speak, translated into lines and forms. . . . Thus even an object of handicraft—a vase, for instance—may, by the suggestiveness of its shape,

---

66. *Briefe aus den Jahren 1894–1926*, ed. Max Sauerlandt (Berlin, 1927), Letter of March 1914, quoted in Theda Shapiro, *Painters and Politics: The European Avant-Garde and Society 1900–1925* (New York and Amsterdam, 1976), 100. Nolde did hope for the success of the German Empire, however (see 99n.).

67. Selz, *Painting,* 74. Here, for instance, is Däubler on Gauguin's influence: "With him the new art, already filled with innocence and delighted charm, emerged as a highly poetic, spiritual revelation" (*Im Kampf um die moderne Kunst,* 3d ed. [Berlin, 1919], 19, quoted in Shapiro, *Painters and Politics,* 94n.). In 1914, however, Apollinaire wrote of tribal sculptures themselves: "Ces fétiches qui n'ont pas été sans influencer les arts modernes ressortissent tous à la passion religieuse qui est la source d'art la plus pure" ("Sculptures d'Afrique et d'Océanie," *Les Arts à Paris,* 15 July 1918, in his *Chroniques d'Art* [1902–1918], ed. L.-C. Breunig [Paris, 1960], 441–42).

68. *Origins,* 84–85.

69. Ibid., 91, after Vernon Lee and Anstruther Thompson, "Beauty and Ugliness," *Contemporary Review,* LXXII (1897), 559.

affect our emotional life in an almost immediate way. And geometric ornament has an equal, if not even greater, power of conjuring up in us emotional states, which we read into the angles and volutes."[70]

New expressive possibilities might be inspired by the supposed inertness of applied or decorative art at the very time of Kandinsky's emergence, in the context of the (first) Munich secession. An affirmation of decorative value per se was widespread by 1900, even among those who resisted modernity in its more threateningly individualistic and expressive manifestations, thanks in part to the unassumingly subordinate and frequently anonymous character of craft work. Even the grandest European mural paintings might thus be admired for their rhythmic sweep, as where Wölfflin, the high priest of classical orthodoxy in Munich, sees Raphael's commanding frescoes in the Stanza della Segnatura of the Vatican under the aspect of "decorations in the grand style." And right here, in subsequent editions of his *Classic Art* (first published in 1899), Wölfflin seems pleased to show his awareness of decorativeness in the sense of contemporary, though hardly perilously avant-garde, painting, observing in a footnote that Böcklin "already uses the phrase" and that one Rudolf Schick had described the "decorative grandeur" (*Gross-Dekorative*) of Raphael's Vatican frescoes in his journal (1900).[71] That Wölfflin should have cared to mention Böcklin at all is understandable in light of bourgeois Böcklinism (vaguely evocative, tasteful escapism) around the time of the painter's death in 1901, despite, again, an aesthetic far-right that thought even Böcklin too radical.[72] In 1905, Reinhard Piper, soon to be the quasi-official publisher of the Munich Expressionist movement, copublished Meier-Graefe's *Der Fall Böcklin* (The Case of Böcklin), a modernist attack on the artist.[73]

Certainly the *Gross-Dekorative* is a different matter from Kandinsky's aspirational *Epoch des Grossen Geistigen* (Epoch of the Great Spiritual). Yet

---

70. *Origins*, 96–97.

71. *Classic Art: An Introduction to the Italian Renaissance*, 8th ed., trans. Peter and Linda Murray, 3d ed. (London, 1968), 87 with n. 1, referring to Rudolf Schick, *Journal* (Berlin, 1900), 171. Wölfflin had written gushingly on "mood" in Böcklin's art in 1897, saying his inventions are "impregnated with the particular character of the momentary mood, and so are altogether inimitable and untranslatable" (quoted in Goldwater, *Symbolism* [New York, 1979], 57–58).

72. H. G. Evers, *The Art of the Modern Age*, trans. J. R. Foster, Art of the World (New York, n.d.), 148–51, mentioning the difficulties of even Jacob Burckhardt. On the cultural politics of Böcklinism, see now Peter Paret, *The Berlin Secession: Modernism and Its Enemies in Imperial Germany* (Cambridge, Mass., 1980), 170–82.

73. *Der Fall Böcklin und die Lehre von den Einheiten* (Stuttgart and Munich).

Kandinsky could well have known the second volume (1906) of Theodor Lipps's *Esthetics,* titled "Esthetic Contemplation and Fine Art," which opens with a consideration of "Empathy and 'Expression.' " Lipps was of great importance to Expressionism for his understanding of how we "feel into" forms. In view of the Bauhaus emphasis on mural painting as collective and utilitarian, and of his own little folklike *Hinterglasmalerei* work (painting on the back of glass, which he would take up again as late as 1936), Kandinsky could have found, in particular, Lipps's interesting discussion of decorative wall painting as being similar to stained glass for its affirmative planarity. As with the glass, Lipps says, so too with the plaster ground of the fresco painter: far from being insignificant, the ground amounts to a "bearer of life," as an integral component of the overall life of an architectonic whole. Compared with this, the opague pigmentation of easel painting is a different matter altogether, something conventionally more dominated by the subject: "One calls oil painting on canvas figure, animal or landscape painting. One never calls it canvas painting."[74] Kandinsky's quest for the "Great Spiritual" was part of a wider search for spiritual significance in which the admiration of unspoiled, *bauerlich* strength of primitive hardihood was (in line at least with Kierkegaard, Tolstoy, and even Heidegger, if not with Whitman and Nietzsche) a distinctly and unavoidably *spiritual* longing.

Heightened interest in folk roots in Central and Eastern Europe was manifest with the approach of Franz Josef's sixtieth anniversary, in 1908. From the turn of the century on, Eduard Fuchs, a scholar and collector, saw folk and popular art as a liberating alternative to the academicized bourgeois-classical aesthetic and the cult of established masterpieces and canonized artist-geniuses. Later Mircea Eliade would look back on the achievement of Brancusi, emphasizing that even the Parisian sophistication of his art depended on a *descensus* into his own Romanian folk primitivity, a rediscovery or archaic *presence,* whether that of "a hunter of the lower paleolithic or a framer of the Mediterranean, Carpathian-Danubian or African neolithic."[75] In his *Karikatur der europäischen Völker* (1901–3), Fuchs, whose studies of caricature and erotic art interested Freud, displaced the authority of art as idealized reality in favor of the forceful immediacy of

---

74. *Ästhetik*, vol. II: *Die ästhetische Betrachtung und die bildende Kunst* (Hamburg and Leipzig, 1906), 628–29.

75. "Brancusi et les mythologies," in Petru Comarnesco, Eliade, and Ionel Jianou, *Témoignages sur Brancusi*, Collection Essais sur l'Art (Paris, 1967), 9–18, esp. 12; thanks to Roger Lipsey for a copy of this essay. There is, as well, the matter of the earnest study of native folk music by Bartók and other modern composers.

caricature, with primitive art for corroboration. By this reckoning, caricature is "in a certain sense the form . . . from which all objective art takes its beginning. A single glance into the ethnographic museums furnishes proof of this statement."[76] More closely pertinent to Kandinsky, however, is the fact that, as Walter Benjamin points out, in a 1908 study of erotica, Fuchs—inspired by the art of Rodin and, in Germany, of Max Slevogt—anticipated a new aesthetic *spiritually* greater than even Greek art: "Where antiquity was only the highest animalistic form, the new beauty will be filled with *grandiose spiritual* and emotional content."[77] Rudolf Czapek, in a 1908 treatise, *Fundamental Problems of Painting,* reviewed by Worringer in 1910 and known to Kandinsky, claimed that the gradual development of painting suggests its coming to "offer the eye what by today's standards would seem pure ornamental decoration," but which would have "inestimable inner significance"; this was only possible thanks to finding in "the direction of the decorative spirit a spiral of symbolically effective ornament."[78] Comparably, in Hungary, Georg Lukács, who was less likely to engage Symbolist-spiritual phraseology, nevertheless also felt that "Impressionism turned everything into a decorative surface," and called for an expressive breakthrough: "Impressionism always came to a stop at the discovery of possibilities of expression"; it was for a "new art . . . of going the whole way" to "destroy all the anarchy of sensation and mood."[79]

Under the circumstances, the old woodcut as well as the, in Kandinsky's day, still surviving Bavarian folk *Hinterglasmalerei* tradition plays a part, all the more importantly for its affinity with the sophisticated Russian icon tradition of Kandinsky's homeland. Such folk images were being collected

---

76. Vol. I: *Vom Altertum bis zum Jahre 1848* (Berlin, 1901), 4–5, quoted in Walter Benjamin, "Eduard Fuchs: Collector and Historian" (1937), trans. New German Critique, in Andrew Arato and Eike Gebhardt, eds., *The Essential Frankfurt School Reader* (New York, 1978), 225–53, 356–62 (notes), here 237. Lipps was at the time about to consider caricature one species of aesthetic stylization (*Ästhetik*, I: *Grundlegung der Ästhetik* [Hamburg and Leipzig, 1903], 261).

77. *Geschichte der erotischen Kunst* (1912; repr. Munich, 1922–28), I, 125, quoted in "Eduard Fuchs: Collector and Historian," 234–35, Slevogt's 1905 *Portrait of Eduard Fuchs* is a good example of Expressionism emerging out of Naturalism (illustration in Hans-Jürgen Imiela, *Max Slevogt: eine Monographie* [Karlsruhe, 1968], color plate on p. 97).

78. *Grundprobleme der Malerei: Ein Buch für Künstler und Lernende* (Leipzig, 1908), 108–9, quoted in Peg Weiss, *Kandinsky in Munich: The Formative Jugendstil Years* (Princeton, 1979), 114 (and in the original German, 207 n. 69). Worringer's review appeared in *Kunst und Künstler*, 4 January 1910, 236.

79. "The Ways Have Parted" (1910), trans. George Cushing, in the Hayward Gallery catalogue *The Hungarian Avant-Garde: The Eight and the Activists* (London, 1980), 106–8, here 108. Lukács was then studying under the sociologist Georg Simmel in Berlin (Georg Lichtheim, *Lukács*, Modern Masters [London, 1970], 14).

by Klee and Gabriele Münter, Kandinsky's mistress, one of whose items became the frontispiece of the *Almanac*. Likewise, Kandinsky's own works of *Hinterglasmalerei* are said to have facilitated his overcoming of an originally "quasi-impressionist technique" by releasing "a more direct form of expression."[80] All along, the old woodcuts, with their aggressively gouged, angular forms and, often enough, their flat patches of blaring color, also appealed to Kandinsky who, as early as 1903–4, had produced, still in Russia, an album of woodcuts, *Stikhi bez' Slov'* (Poems without Words). In 1913 Kandinsky's prose poetry with woodcuts, entitled *Klänge,* would be published by Piper (for Kandinsky a *Klang,* or sound, suggested in a Symbolist way a poetically convincing resonance). Of Kandinsky's woodcuts the critic Wilhelm Michel remarked, in terms virtually indistinguishable from the artist's own, that "the material is the vehicle of the spiritual."[81] As one way out of decorativeness and toward lively expression, the direct carving of the woodcut seemed to have just the right *Klang* implicit in the very medium.[82] A relevant comment in *Concerning the Spiritual in Art* (1912) calls to mind not only specifically the carved Palau beam in Dresden that charmed Kirchner, early on, but even Brancusi's approach to wood carving: "A rudely carved Indian column is an expression of the spirit that actuates any advance-guard work."[83]

Paul Klee, who came to Munich in 1903, offers a telling parallel case. In 1902 Klee had found himself at a point where "upon awakening . . . I lie in

---

80. Hans K. Röthel, with Jean K. Benjamin, *Kandinsky* (New York, 1979), 68. For a more extensive discussion, including inconography, see Röthel's introduction to the Solomon R. Guggenheim Museum exhibition catalogue *Vasily Kandinsky: Paintings on Glass (Hinterglasmalerei)* (New York, 1966). Max Picard, in the introduction to his album *Expressionistische Bauernmalerei* (2d ed. [Munich, 1918]), with images as charmingly homely as those of *Biblia pauperum* woodcuts, and quite like Kandinsky's *Hinterglasbilder,* strains to make Expressionism derive from Impressionism and not the Gothic. To him the avant-garde Expressionist's concern with the spiritual is a merely intellectual affair, whereas the naive folk painter shows a heartfelt zeal in his religious images. Interestingly, the explanation may anticipate the conception of God as the "Ground of Being" in the theology of Paul Tillich (then an army chaplain), who was to have his own difficulties with Expressionist art in America (*Theology of Culture,* 1959): for Picard the flat figures of the Bavarian folk paintings are so profoundly isolated, so devoid of shared contextuality, that they only stand "together" in implicit mutual relation to God (25).

81. "Münchener Graphik: Holzschnitt und Lithographie," *Kunst und Dekoration* (1905), 440, quoted in Röthel, *Kandinsky: Das graphische Werk* (Cologne, 1970), 128.

82. *Kandinsky,* 127.

83. Wassily Kandinsky, *Concerning the Spiritual in Art and Painting in Particular,* trans. Michael Sadleir et al., Documents of Modern Art, no. 5 (New York, 1947), 52. Eliade was interested in Brancusi's "crudeness" in carving as being "spiritually earnest" (see his *No Souvenirs: Journal 1957–1969,* trans. Fred H. Johnson, Jr. [New York, 1977], 167, 218–19, 291–93).

a complicated position, but flat, attached to the linen surface. I am my style."[84] Luckily, so supine a decorative flatness did not continue beyond the time when Worringer's book *Abstraction and Empathy* appeared: then Klee could note, "I am at last finding my way out of the dead-end of ornamentation where I found myself one day in 1907!"[85] Soon primitiveness, per se, was of pressing importance to Klee, who by at least 1911 was concerned with the art of children and the insane as well as with tribal work. This also went along with a developed aesthetic sense of handwork, as when Klee admired Expressionist embroideries executed by Frau Niestlé to designs of Campendonk, Macke, and Marc.[86] With Klee's own later paintings, of around 1921, which have been called "crystalline" for their underlying grid structure, "we are immediately reminded of weaving, where the network of warp and weft provides the structure within which forms can move. . . . Then we remember that Klee was summoned to the Bauhaus to take over the teaching of weaving and glass-painting."[87]

Worringer's Willful "Abstraction"

The premier theoretical text of the whole German movement was indeed Worringer's *Abstraction and Empathy: A Contribution to the Psychology of Style*, published by Piper in Munich in 1908. This, Worringer's dissertation, had been sparked by a crucial encounter with primitive art at the Trocadéro, the Paris ethnographic museum, where it happens that Worringer was also looking at casts of medieval sculpture.[88] Significantly, in the foreword to his

---

84. *The Diaries of Paul Klee 1898–1918*, ed. Felix Klee, trans. Pierre B. Schneider et al. (Berkeley, 1968), 124, entry for 22 June 1902.

85. Ibid., 232, entry of late November or early December 1908.

86. Ibid., 363.

87. Werner Haftmann, *The Mind and Art of Paul Klee* (New York, 1967), 167. Even after 1926, Klee's work shows "parallel configurations . . . spread across the surface of the picture as if it were woven, thus creating a rich rhythmic pattern (like knots in weaving or embroidery on lace)" (175).

88. *Abstraction and Empathy: A Contribution to the Psychology of Style*, trans. Michael Bullock (New York, 1967), foreword (1948), viii–ix. It was in fact while looking at these that Worringer had run into Georg Simmel. Before the turn of the century, Simmel had already been influenced by German ethnologists of the Romantic period, including Karl Friedrich Vollgraf, with his nostalgia for primitivity, and Johann Jacob Bachofen, who, with Julius Lippert, saw matriarchy as a recurrent primeval state (Paul Honigsheim, "A Note on Simmel's Anthropological Interests," in *Georg Simmel 1858–1918*, ed. Kurt H. Wolff [Columbus, Ohio, 1959], reprinted in Simmel et al., *Essays on Sociology, Philosophy and Aesthetics* [New York, 1965], 175–79), and, likewise, by the American Lewis Henry Morgan, a lawyer who joined the Seneca Indians and whose tripartite distinction of savagery, barbarism, and civilization (*Ancient Society*, 1877) influenced Friedrich Engels (*The Origin of the Family, Private Property, and the State*, 1884) as well as Marx, in Germany.

third edition (1910), Worringer says that to revise the book would too complicatedly involve his new *Form Problems of the Gothic,* "the direct sequel to the present book and . . . an attempt to apply the questions it raises to that complex of abstract art which is closest to us, namely the stylistic phenomenon of Gothic." It seems more urgent to make the contemporary point, for: "The most recent movement in art has shown my problem to have gained an immediate topicality, not only for art historians . . . but also for practicing artists striving after new goals of expression. Those misconstrued and ridiculed values of the abstract artistic volition [an obvious Rieglism], which I sought to rehabilitate through scientific analysis, were simultaneously—not arbitrarily, but from inner developmental necessity— re-established in artistic practice as well."[89]

Theoretically, *Abstraction and Empathy* refracts Wölfflinian polarities, as though using Riegl (who was intimately concerned with "barbaric" and folk art) as a new anticlassical, or rather nonnormative, lens. It depends, beyond Wölfflin, on the "psychological" aesthetics of Robert Vischer and Theodor Lipps, as well as on Riegl's: on Vischer, ultimately, for the concept of *Einfühlung,* or "empathy," announced in an 1872 discussion of, significantly enough, *medieval* art. Vischer's empathic principle may have had a limited applicability insofar as Worringer was concerned with the "abstract" (angular, antinaturalistic) alternative, but it was helpful with regard to the precocious idea, elaborated by the students of prehistory, of abstract ornament as a *sophistication* rather than a symptom of (prenaturalistic) crudity. Interestingly, when he quotes Vischer in the new modern context, Worringer has to qualify an embrace of decorativeness pure and simple that had been progressive enough for the preceding generation:

> All pictorial art has a subjectivist propensity, which leads it to a relatively independent attitude toward the given natural model and seeks expression in purely formal terms, in forms as such; hence all pictorial art has a profound relationship to decoration and a greater or lesser inclination to the playful refashioning of natural structures, as it were toward drowning the sound of singing with orchestral music. Thus the artist came gradually and quite simply to impose upon the living figure the character of surface ornament. The total appearance of the human figure, giving expression to its autonomous, closed organic life, was now replaced by an harmo-

---

89. *Abstraction,* xiv–xv.

nious conglomerate of particles [*ein harmonisches Konglomerat von Teilchen*] in which the aim of giving an illusion of life takes second place to the aim of achieving an autonomous decorative effect [*einer selbständig dekorativen Wirkung zurücktritt*].[90]

Vischer was useful in overcoming the Semperian sense of material determinism in ornament, in the sense that ornament, no matter how primitive, could never be simply the collective excretion, as it were, of some specimen *Naturvolk*: "The detailed and brilliant analysis of Byzantine art given by Semper in his *Stil*," Worringer observes, "was, of course, based entirely on his materialistic theory; it linked up the peculiar quality of Byzantine art with carpet-weaving, without pausing to consider that a particular technique was selected because it was in closest accord with the artistic volition."[91] Because Vischer has already revised the issue, Worringer can defer to Semper for "one of the great acts of art history, which, like every intellectual edifice that has been grandly erected and thoroughly worked out, stands outside the historical valuation of 'correct' or 'incorrect,' "[92] even as he proceeds to hail Riegl for transcending an accrued materialism in Semper's diffused influence.[93] The shift from Semper to Riegl is thus seen as a shift from a nineteenth-century criterion of technical necessity (the *automatic*) to a more modern idea of will in relation to the range of possibility as exposed by Riegl. Even Worringer's admiration of "crystalline" beauty, it turns out, is borrowed from Riegl.[94]

Worringer's pursuit of a "psychology of style" is symptomatic not only of Riegl's influence but also, probably, of Lipps and his then new *Esthetics,* subtitled "Psychology of the Beautiful and of Art." Lipps's first volume, on "Foundations of Aesthetics," treats empathy as the "inside" *(Innenseite)* of artistic imitation. In an extended discussion resorting, interestingly enough (in light of Kierkegaard, Nietzsche, and Rilke), to imagery of acrobatic performance, Lipps describes how empathy plays on an internal sense of bodily movement, apart from any actually executed movement. Perfect, or full, empathy involves a consummation of this sense of animation in the finally optical perception of art, an "inner imitation" *(innere Nachahmung)*.[95]

---

90. Ibid., 100; in the original, *Abstraktion und Einfühlung: Ein Beitrag zur Stil-Psychologie*, 8th ed. (Munich, 1919), 131.

91. Ibid., 99.

92. Ibid., 8.

93. Ibid., 9.

94. Ibid., 19.

95. *Ästhetik*, II, 125–26.

Lipps also devotes considerable speculation to the issue of stylization, not mentioning primitive art but, once, calling attention to the imitative conviction of children's schematic chalk drawings. Indeed, nature is seen not as a range of singly representable entities but, rather, as rich in potential for artistic transformation: loosely speaking, "all possible geometric or ornamental forms" might conceivably be derived from a single natural form.[96]

But Worringer also stands on the shoulders of the students of primeval art, especially for the explicitly modern view that "art does not begin with naturalistic constructs, but with ornamental-abstract ones." This is precisely why "the eminent artistic gifts of a few particular primitive peoples, which have been exercised in a purely ornamental field, have naturally been passed over by the view of art history that is directed solely toward the naturalistic and have only very recently received the appraisal they merit." Hence, "anyone who looks upon approximation to reality as the criterion of art must regard the cave-dwellers of Aquitania as artistically more advanced than the authors of the Dipylon style [of Greek vase painting]."[97]

Much, too, comes down from the earlier historical dichotomy between Northern, or Gothic, and Southern, or classical, European cultures. Echoes of Nietzsche's version (*The Birth of Tragedy*, 1872) may even be discernible: "The lucid consciousness of the impossibility of knowledge, absolute passive resignation, had led the Oriental artistic volition to that expressionless tranquility and necessity of the abstract; here in the North, however, there is anything but tranquility, here an inner need for expression desires, in spite of all the inner disharmony—or rather all the more because of it—to speak itself out."[98] Furthermore, the Northern spirit requires an "intensifi-

---

96. Ibid., 264.

97. *Abstraction*, 54–55 (all three passages).

98. Ibid., 108–9. Compare this on the proto-Gothic North: "The need for empathy of this inharmonious people does not take the nearest-at-hand path to the organic, because the harmonious motion of the organic is not sufficiently expressive for it; it needs rather the uncanny pathos which attaches to the animation of the inorganic" (77). If Nietzsche's notion of the Apollonian as something possible only after or beyond the primeval Dionysian—to which culture must sometimes return for strength—partakes of the modern idea that (Paleolithic) representation *preceded* (Neolithic) quasi-abstraction, then it is possible to speculate on the relevance of Nietzsche's friend Erwin Rohde, who argues, in his *Psyche* (1894), that the Dionysian came *after* an Apollonian outlook (see E. R. Dodds, *The Greeks and the Irrational*, Sather Classical Lectures, 25 [Berkeley, 1951; repr. 1973], 68–69). For an early parallel to Worringer's dismissal of Semperianism and embrace of Riegl, involving the modern affirmation of stylization as a sophistication, see Anthony M. Ludovici, *Nietzsche and Art* (Boston, 1912), consisting of lectures delivered at University College, London, in 1910. Ludovici is concerned largely with Nietzsche's posthumous *Will to Power* (1901) for the idea of a human *appropriation* of nature; he attacks such "evolutionary" naturalists as Balfour and A. C. Haddon.

cation of . . . resistance" (a phrase that recalls Riegl's own "coefficient of friction") lacking in the organic. "And so," Worringer explains, "that hybrid formulation comes into being: abstraction on the one hand, and most vigorous expression on the other."[99] Interestingly enough, while Worringer's own writing might seem impetuously expressive or only "poetically" philosophical, it struck a perfect chord: in February 1912, when a second *Almanac* was being planned, Franz Marc, reading *Abstraction and Empathy,* wrote to Kandinsky (who may have read the book in 1909) that Worringer had "a good mind, whom we need very much. Marvelously disciplined thinking, concise and cool, extremely cool."[100]

Marc and Kandinsky's first, and only, *Blaue Reiter Almanac* includes Roger Allard's "Signs of Renewal in Painting."[101] This is in one sense a report from the aesthetically remote Cubist front, but in context it seems as much like a description of a parallel struggle as possible. The illustrations to Allard's essay include a fourteenth-century German embroidered religious image (since destroyed) and children's drawings, together with two odd, early decorative "seasons" paintings by Cézanne and the vivacious 1910 (Saint Petersburg) version of Matisse's *The Dance.* Allard's project does, in fact, parallel Marc and Kandinsky's insofar as it concerns a final overthrow of Impressionism. Lacking a working concept of Postimpressionism (an English term for which, ironically enough, Roger Fry first considered employing "Expressionism"), Allard nevertheless sweeps aside the Neoimpressionism of Seurat's contingent as, now, "nothing but a concealed restoration" and "an art for gourmets." Cubism, on the other hand, as though it must defend its own sophisticated primitivism, is "no new fantasy of 'savages,' no new scalp dance around the altars of 'officials,' but an

---

99. *Abstraction*, 109. Whatever the status of Worringer's treatise as a "Contribution to Psychology," it has fascinated psychologists. C. G. Jung, who goes into detail on Lipps and Riegl in relation to Worringer in *Psychological Types* (1921; trans. R.F.C. Hull, rev. H. G. Baynes, Bollingen Series, xx/6 [Princeton, 1971], 289–99), tends to favor "empathy" as being more "extroverted" than "abstraction," but concedes that both are necessary for "any real appreciation of the object as well as for artistic creation." Otto Rank, closely concerned with both Riegl and Worringer in *Art and Artist* (note 32), passim, claims that even Worringer, like all estheticians, overlooks a specifically "individual need for expression" (93). Others interested in Worringer include Franz Alexander, a Freudian who appears to have adopted his polar categories without acknowledgment (Jack Spector, *The Aesthetics of Freud: A Study of Psychoanalysis and Art* [New York, 1973], 163–64, with reference), and Zevedei Barbu, a psychohistorian who applies Worringer to the development of Western civilization at large, in analogy with individual ego development (*Problems of Historical Psychology* [New York, 1960]).

100. Quoted in Lankheit, "History," 30 n. 2.

101. *Almanac*, 104–11.

honest search for a new discipline." Despite what Delaunay may have gained from Postimpressionism, he is seen as safely beyond it for having "conquered the arabesques of the plane," achieving "the rhythm of great, infinite depths" (within a year or so of this Delaunay would exhibit in Berlin and publish an essay in *Der Sturm*). Here Allard the Frenchman sounds like Kandinsky, the *Almanac*'s Russian emigré coeditor; so, too, when he ends, like a polite guest, on this cosmopolitan note: "The new spiritual movement is also no longer solely French. The same search for renewal in art resounds abroad. . . . Against worn-out aesthetics," a "new canon . . . shall give our life style an inner beauty."

Kandinsky's Sublimated "Spiritual"

Kandinsky's own experience with craft in an originally *Jugendstil* context facilitated his pursuit, at first through decorativeness, of an independent and somehow transcendentally abstract art. Already in 1903 Peter Behrens asked him to teach decorative painting.[102] In 1904–5 Kandinsky designed a carpet with "stylized crinolined Biedermeier ladies around the border,"[103] and in 1906 he exhibited a number of craft items, together with prints (which also count as craft manufacture), drawings, and paintings. Then, also, he designed several dresses for Gabriele Münter. His decorative work links the artist's early *symboliste* experience, in the circle of the poet Stefan George, with his search for expressive abstraction in painting. Moreover, by the time Kandinsky produced *Concerning the Spiritual,* the Germanic arts and crafts movement was of concern even to the French: young Le Corbusier, himself fresh from architectural study with Behrens in Berlin (1910–11), expressed his enthusiasm in an official report on German craft developments, which, he knew, derived ultimately from Ruskin and Morris in England.[104] Still, however helpful decorative design might have been for

102. For this entire matter, see Weiss, *Kandinsky* (note 78). On Behrens's own sense of expressive value, again involving a denial of Semperiansim and an embrace of Riegl, see the interesting essay by Stanford Anderson, "Modern Architecture and Industry: Peter Behrens, the AEG and Industrial Design," *Oppositions*, no. 21 (Summer 1980), 78–97.

103. Johannes Eichner, *Kandinsky und Gabriele Münter: Von Ursprüngen moderner Kunst* (Munich, 1957), 75, quoted in Weiss, *Kandinsky*, 119.

104. Charles-Édouard Jeanneret (called Le Corbusier), *Étude sur le mouvement d'art décoratif en Allemagne* (La Chaux-de-Fonds, 1912; repr. New York, 1968), especially pp. 11, 14, 44. Although Apollinaire had reviewed the decorative arts exposition of the 1910 autumn salon in Munich, he didn't like it, partly out of chauvinism ("L'Exposition des arts décoratifs de Munich," *Les Marches de l'Est,* 15 November 1910, in his *Chroniques* [note 67], 130–31).

overcoming the limitations of pictorialism, decorative value could not in itself answer the profound need felt by Kandinsky for a positively spiritual content in abstraction.

In *Concerning the Spiritual in Art and Painting in Particular* (1911; also published by Piper), Kandinsky comments on the limitations of decorative beauty, notably in the passage starting, "If we begin at once to break the bonds that bind us to nature and to devote ourselves purely to combination of pure color and independent form, we shall produce works which are mere geometric decoration, resembling something like a necktie or a carpet."[105] A painting of Kandinsky's own, entitled *Composition II,* had already been criticized, in 1910, by an unsympathetic critic who wrote that a better title might have been "Color Sketch for a Modern Carpet."[106] The point is that "mere" decoration is a kind of formal play that has either lost meaning (as with Ehrenreich's *Tiernachbildungen?*) or else never had any: "Beauty of form and color is no sufficient aim by itself, despite the assertions of pure aesthetes or even of naturalists obsessed with the idea of 'beauty.' It is because our painting is still at an elementary stage that we are so little able to be moved by wholly autonomous color and form composition. . . . It must not be thought that decoration is lifeless. It has its inner being, but one which either is no longer comprehensible to us, as is the case of old decorative art, or seems illogical." This suggests a "jumble . . . where material accident reigns, not spirit."[107] Personally, a dissolved kind of Christian Apocalyptic imagery was important to Kandinsky, while his theosophical side is well known.[108] One way or another, as decorative, or *empty,* "abstraction" came to seem superficial.

The later work of Kandinsky and the other Expressionists, Brücke as well as Blaue Reiter, is mostly not at issue here, but perhaps Kirchner, in the North, can supply an instance of postwar continuation of "primitive" consciousness of the early period. Kirchner seems to have renewed his interest in the brazen vitality of nomadic carpets after having met Lise Gujer, a weaver, in 1922. In a letter to Henry van de Velde's daughter, written in the summer of 1919, he describes the sixth-century Indian Ajanta caves, which he had admired for several years, in terms of their

---

105. *Spiritual,* 67–68.

106. Georg Jacob Wolf, in *Kunst für Allen,* 1 November 1910, 68–70, esp. 70; quoted in Weiss, *Kandinsky,* 196.

107. *Spiritual,* 68. In the last phrase a Semperian overtone seems inescapable.

108. Thanks to Sixten Ringbom, *The Sounding Cosmos: A Study in the Spiritualism of Kandinsky and the Genesis of Abstract Painting,* Acta Academiae Aboensis, ser. A, XXXVIII/2 (Åbo, 1970).

(tapestrylike?) muralism: "They are all plane and yet absolute mass and, accordingly, they have absolutely solved the mystery of painting."[109] His Davos house of the time (1919–23) sophisticatedly combined just such decorative furnishings as boldly patterned carpets with Islamic ornamental tiles and pseudo-Cameroonian furniture. Anyway, Kirchner actually designed tapestries that Gujer wove, including *Ascending the Alp and Ages of Man* (1927–28), with interlocking figures and Expressionist zigzags whose edges are tiny steps, responding to the rectilinear weave. True, the painter was surely struck by the "distinctive manner by which forms in depth are made to fuse on the surface" in tapestry, just as he had already appreciated the elegant, "high-culture" planarity of the Ajanta murals (in reproduction).[110] Yet there is also meaning in the cottage-industry aspect of the work.

It was during this experience with Gujer that Kirchner painted *Modern Bohemia* (1924), a scene of studio life that exhibits the society of sentient outsiders, individualist refugees from bourgeois conformity, finding solidarity in a room decked out with primitivizing cultural properties. *Modern Bohemia*, of which Kirchner also made a woodcut in 1924 (Fig. 24), is said to exemplify a " 'tapestry' style," especially for the way the limbs of the nude model participate in the interlocking angular pattern of a rug; indeed, "the very brushstroke placements, in their horizontal and vertical variations, heighten the similarity of picture surface to textile weave."[111] Actually, at least three rugs appear in the picture, all possibly of nomadic design. Such nomadic weavings would have been cheaper than finer orientals (bohemian poverty) while also carrying over the earlier Expressionist bohemian élan. Artistically, their stiffly textural, angular forms are appropriate motifs for the rough, jagged gouging of the wood block, as admired by the Expressionists in medieval prints. But so are their implications: tribal rugs as stubbornly handmade, in the face of industrialism—in analogy with the alienated modern artist's role of executing, as far as possible, unalienated work on his own and others' behalf?

Generally, Expressionism might seem to have lost radicality in the 1920s. In 1921 Worringer himself delivered a "funeral oration" for the Expressionist movement at a meeting of the Munich Goethe Society. Inevitably, the

---

109. *Briefe an Nele* (Berlin, 1961), 21, quoted in Gordon, *Kirchner*, 22.

110. Gordon, "Ernst Ludwig Kirchner: By Instinct Possessed," *Art in America*, November 1980, 80–95, here 94.

111. Gordon, *Kirchner*, 128.

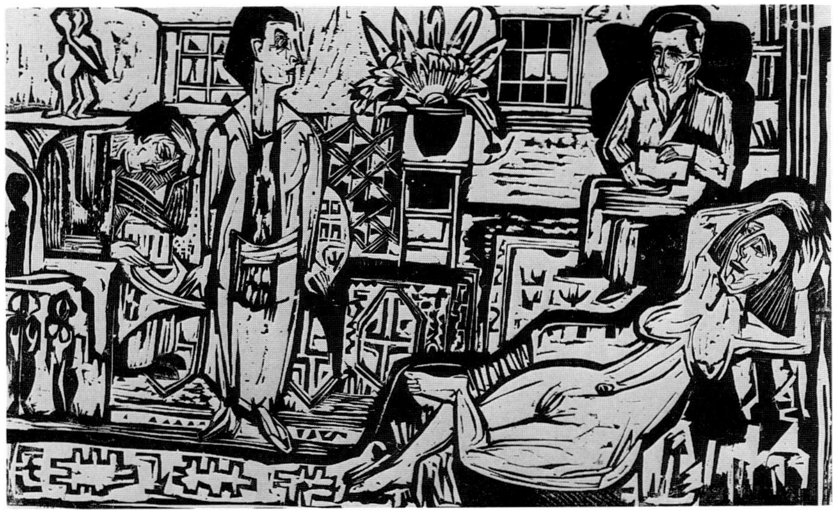

Fig. 24   Ernst Ludwig Kirchner, *Modern Bohemia*, 1924, woodcut, printed in black,
21¼ x 33¼ inches.

radical moralism implied by Fuchs at the time would have been blunted,
once the "sexy," "unspoiled" barbarism of primitivity came more easily:
"Art is sensuality, become visible. At the same time, it is the highest and
noblest form of sensuality."[112] Then Wilhelm Hausenstein might echo
Fuchs, but exaggeratedly, in a passage on primitive art from *Barbaren und
Klassiker* (1922) quoted, in our own day, in an antimodernist attack on
Riegl's influence: "Only lust is the bridge between maker and object. The
root of the shaping hands thrusts itself down into the loins of figures who
squat and kneel. . . . Lust turned into art—that is creative power."[113]
Fuchs, by then, was studying grotesquerie in Tang dynasty ceramics,
normally a field for suave connoisseurship. Even so, in his *Tang-Plastik* (1924)
he seems to discover a vantage point for observing the ambivalence of his

112. Fuchs, *Erotische Kunst*, I, p. 61, quoted in Benjamin, "Fuchs," 361 n. 53.

113. *Barbaren und Klassiker: Ein Buch von der Bildnerei exotischer Völker*, 2d ed. (Munich, 1923), 9–
10, quoted in Philipp Fehl, *The Classical Monument: Reflections on the Connection between Morality and
Art in Greek and Roman Sculpture*, Archaeological Institute of America and College Art Association
of America Monographs on Archaeology and the Fine Arts, 24 (New York, 1972), 87 n. 27. One
may think of the Nazi *Entartete Kunst* (Degenerate Art) campaign, with its demeaning equation
of primitive and Expressionist art on grounds of unwholesomeness; cf. Paul Schultze-Naumburg,
Kunst und Rasse (Munich, 1928; repr. Berlin and Munich, 1938).

own historical moment, saying that what looks grotesque can be seen either as "an expression of the teeming health of a time" or else as an indication that "the problems of existence have taken on an appearance of unsolvable complexity."[114]

An aspiration of passionate naturalness, of being grounded like some supposed peasant in the true, raw earth (consider D. H. Lawrence, Heidegger, and others), was abroad in the new decade. In 1921 Walter Gropius built, with Adolf Meyer and the help of Bauhaus apprentices, his idiosyncratically rustic Haus Sommerfeld, near Berlin. True, Gropius had been running the Bauhaus *woodworking* workshop, which also made this an exercise in truth-to-materials, and the building likewise reflected the (in its own way Whitmanesque) "Prairie" aesthetic of Frank Lloyd Wright; besides, there was expressive appropriateness in the fact that the client was a timber merchant. Nevertheless, the result, in the achievement of which the students supplied highly original fixtures and furnishings, was nothing but a great log cabin, much more ostensibly *bauerlich* than Bauhaus.[115] A few years later, in France, the painter Gleizes tried, for the second time in his life, to establish a rural, utopian artists' and craftsmen's commune, "Moly-Sabata," at Sablons, only to have its back-to-the-soil ideal preempted by the fascists.[116] It is as if European culture had become saturated with sophistication, after the first phase of modernity, and needed to regain a more bracing spirit. A later comment by Eliade on Brancusi, whose *Maiastra* (Marvelous Bird) form was likened to the stylized figures in Romanian peasant carpets in 1913, suggests the appeal of the sculptor's carved work even after the overthrow of academic art: "Brancusi was a peasant who managed to *forget what he had learned in school* and thus rediscovered the spiritual universe of the Neolithic age."[117]

It would probably be a mistake to suppose that when Kandinsky went to the Bauhaus, in 1922, his earlier Expressionist passions faded. Kandinsky taught in the interdisciplinary foundation course, there being no painting instruction per se until the school moved to Dessau in 1925 (and even then

---

114. *Tang-Plastik: Chinesische Grabkeramik des VII. bis X. Jahrhunderts*, Kultur- und Kunstdokumente, I (Munich, 1924), 44, quoted in Benjamin, "Fuchs," 238.

115. Most conveniently: Gillian Taylor, *The Bauhaus* (London and New York, 1968), 58–60, with illustration.

116. Daniel Robbins, "Albert Gleizes: Faith and Reason in Modern Painting," in the Solomon R. Guggenheim Museum catalogue *Albert Gleizes 1881–1953: A Retrospective Exhibition* (New York, 1964), 12–25, esp. 23–24.

117. *No Souvenirs*, entry for 10 July 1962, 167 (emphasis in original). On the *Maiastra* and the peasant carpet, see Barbu Brezianu, *Brancusi in Romania* (Bucharest, 1976), 235, with reference.

painting kept up an applied-art rationale). His *Point and Line to Plane* (1926), springing directly from this teaching, thus shows Kandinsky tailoring his once less avoidably transcendental approach in a newly rational theory of the "Basic Plane," or "BP"—this defined in *Point and Line* as "the material plane which is called upon to receive the content of the work of art"[118] (shades of an Annunciation). This may have been more than a work of Bauhaus pedagogical utility, even as the setting must have helped push Kandinsky actually to spell out how painting works.

Whether or not the fact that the BP has a vitalistic character, even in its elemental state, recalls Theodor Lipps, Kandinsky speaks of it as a "somewhat primitive and yet living organism," something " 'breathing,' " whose "frivolous abuse" is "akin to murder." The BP has to be approached with love: "The artist 'fertilizes' this being and knows how obediently and 'joyfully' the BP receives the right elements in the right order."[119] Aware of the antithesis between "the elements lying firmly (and materially) on a solid, more or less hard and, to the eye, tangible BP and . . . the elements 'floating' without material weight in an indefinable (immaterial) space," Kandinsky affirms that the habit of according "exceptional esteem" to the material plane, together with all its ramifications, grows out of a "sound, indispensable interest in handicraft," that is, in technique and material.[120] Kandinsky was speaking from experience, not merely adjusting an idealist message to a materialist school, there being no transcendence without material conditions *(felix culpa!)*. Painting, it turns out, needs its materiality for that very "dematerialization" that shows "the road from the external to the inner."[121] In broader terms, art needs its "primitive" roots for the very health of its developed refinement.

---

118. *Point and Line to Plane*, trans. Howard Dearstyne and Hilla Rebay (New York, 1947; repr. 1979), 115.

119. Ibid., 116.

120. Ibid., 144.

121. Ibid., 145. Ringbom (*Cosmos*, 166, with reference) mentions Vladimir Soloviev only in the general context of apocalyptic imagery in Russian Symbolism. Soloviev had influenced Rudolf Steiner, the eminent Theosophist, as early as 1909, and the poet Andrei Bely wrote enthusiastically of Soloviev to Alexander Blok, in 1912: see Rose-Carol Washton Long, *Kandinsky: The Development of an Abstract Style* (Oxford, 1980), 34–35; and also 37 (impact on Nikolai Berdiaev) and 105 (Soloviev's "Divine Sophia" and the theme of love). But the famous late nineteenth-century mystic may have been less obliquely influential on the distinguished author of *Point and Line to Plane*. Edith Klum (*Natur, Kunst und Liebe in der Philosophie Vladimir Solov'evs: Eine religionsphilosophische Untersuchung*, Slavistische Beiträge, xiv (Munich, 1965]) explains the Soloviev-ian classification of the arts into three types: "direct or magical" (music and, in part, the lyric), "indirect," and "negative indirect" (epic, tragedy, comedy). As "indirect," the plastic arts (with,

The genuine and integral "primitivity" of the Expressionist artists is, after all, just what makes prehistoricism, primitivism, Gothicism, and also the Romantic and folkloric all similarly relevant to their original artistic affirmations and not merely miscellaneously anticlassical, ahistorical stylistic parallels. Likewise, there were not, as it were, two Kandinskys: a spiritualistic Expressionist who, in changing circumstances, might have passed into an antithetical Constructivism. After all, the Neolithic itself had arisen out of (and against) the Paleolithic, as Postimpressionism had out of (and against) Impressionism; conceivably, the closed case of either earlier, more primitive and perceptual phase is itself a grand *myth* of its more conceptual successor, framed under a new, self-conscious mentality. In any case, the words of Saint Paul would have carried all along for Kandinsky a powerful testimony to the importance of truly transcending, not attempting to evade, the rude, "Gothic" strength of the primitive state. The thought is Nietzschean, and the quotation Tolstoy would have had readily at hand; but the words can apply to Kandinsky, the one Kandinsky, himself: "Take note, the spiritual was not first; first came the natural and after that the spiritual" (1 Cor. 15:46; N.A.B.).

---

to some extent, the lyric), and especially landscape painting, offer the ideal aspect of complex natural appearance in a poetically condensed, intensified *(verdichteter)* state, "purified" of three-dimensionality (155–56). In a huge footnote Klum also discusses an 1898 discourse on Auguste Comte by Soloviev, referring to the positivist's "Grand Etre" (i.e., "l'Humanité") as supreme being (262). She presents the following symbolic scheme: (1) POINT = person; (2) LINE = family; (3) PLANE = nationality *(Volk)*; (4) GEOMETRICAL BODY = race; (5) PHYSICAL BODY = mankind (260–61 n.). *Point and Line to Plane*, it is here worth considering, is the incomplete realization of a larger project that Kandinsky had envisioned, growing out of his Bauhaus teaching. Otherwise, Comte himself maintains that, while point, line, and plane *can* be conceived of abstractly, we really think of them as pertaining to the three-dimensional world (*Cours de philosophie positive,* vol. 1 [Paris, 1830], 354–57; for the "Grand Etre," see his *Système de politique positive: ou, traité de sociologie instituant la religion de l'Humanité,* vol. IV [Paris, 1854]). Comte's mentality was obviously remote from Kandinsky's, but Soloviev's symbolic version may well not have been. The latter-day mystic Thomas Merton, lifelong friend of the abstract painter Ad Reinhardt, was interested in Soloviev: see a 1964 letter to the poet Robert Lax, in their *A Catch of Anti-Letters* (Kansas City, 1978), 40.

16

A NOTE ON POLKE

Painting can never be just another activity, nor, probably, just another art. Sigmar Polke is among the most important of those artists who actively paint today after having first cleared a special zone for themselves from a wider turf on which painting, if not exactly disqualified, was only conceded to be one game. But you either paint or you don't paint; and even if you sought only to make anti-paintings of some kind, you would nevertheless have to risk getting hooked. Polke's recent paintings may be as outrageous, in some sense, as ever, but they would also be extremely impressive as paintings, whether he liked that—as an evident engrossment in the sheer activity of painting suggests he does—or not.

Maybe Polke is most remarkable for managing to carry over a fundamentally sixties-ish Pop, or really Euro-Pop, aesthetic into the realm of abstract painting proper. Frankly, I don't think American Pop was very well understood in Germany, to go by certain embarrassing generalizations misconstruing the art of Warhol and others, crudely confounding it with garden-variety kitsch, and ten years late anyway, in the *New German Critique* in the late 1970s. But to see Polke's drawings from even the 1960s is to discover something isolated, provincial, yet on its own fermenting, like sourdough, into true contemporaneity.

An example of such "translation," in the root sense, from Pop mentality into abstraction, is *Ata-Ata,* a large canvas from 1982 hallucinogenically subtitled *Psilocybe Freunde* (Psilocybin Friends), in which three large and seven smaller splats of runny, yogurtlike white acrylic have been, well, deposited upon, a watery, wiped blue field that by itself might look like something put aside by Constable for another *Stonehenge.* Absurdly nonobjective, but articulately so, in the manner of some suave late Surrealist, these curdling patches are plopped onto the surface like many other plastered-on elements in Polke's work at large. Instead of just letting them sit on top like junked old motifs from whenever abstraction was confidently "deep," Polke at least sets them into a spatial context by wiping a wet puddle of drippage in the lower right. Quite a mess all this is, as we would once have been expected to think with some ritual outrage, yet also perfectly gorgeous for anybody who just can't get enough of the thrills of paint. If the subtitle suggests rumpled, bohemian intimacy back in the age of "acid," and not untenderly, the actual painting—which almost rustles with silky refinement, if one cares to see—addresses itself to us grown-up junkies of paint.

The later paintings I have seen are of two types: "hearties," one might say, and "aesthetes." The hearties, ironically enough (and since everything can be ironic in Polke, at last you don't have to *worry* about irony), start with decorative textiles but then really work them over with paint: if such yard goods must "signify" the female, then this must be ladies' wrestling. In his 1986 *Never Seen* (Fig. 25), pigment drips in stringy lines, more sideways than top to bottom, while reckless deposits of color get desperately "fixed up" with undisguisedly compensatory touches. A large dotted area, black on white, could have been painted through a stencil or screen. So blotted is it that whether the "holes" now count as positive or negative is hard to tell—which Polke must like, because he heightens the already rather overloaded effect with extra black dots all around.

Spirals, also of 1986, is painted on a pair of stretched fabric panels of zigzag design. It amounts to a study in black-and-white oppositions: in the textile ground, in drippy black paint on white and vice versa, and in the embracing relations of the two panels themselves, taken together. Here must be a very knowing, concocted "spontaneity," skeptical from the start.

Paintings on the "aesthete" side are thinner and more indulgent, indeed, seductively so. Snatches of languid, doodling, curlicue arabesque are muffled

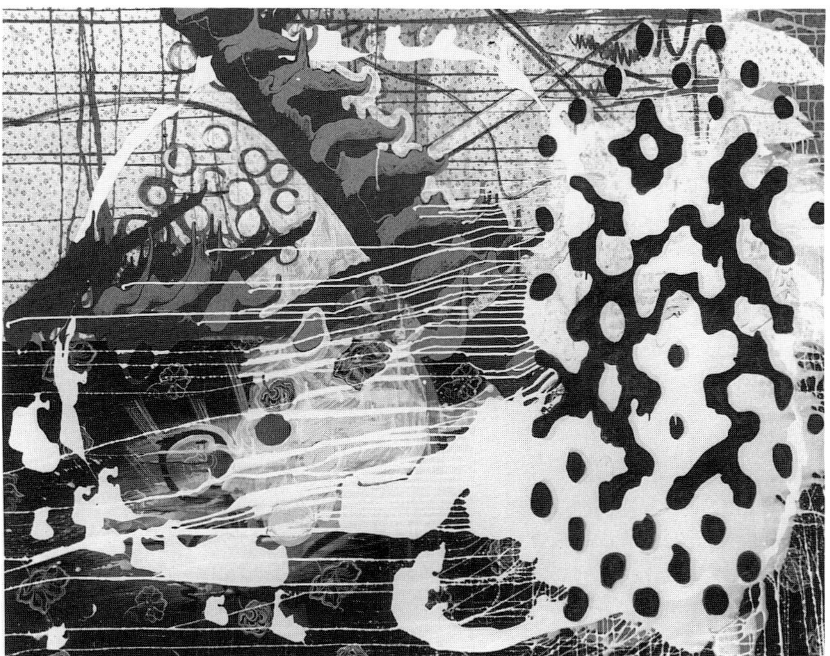

Fig. 25   Sigmar Polke, *Never Seen*, 1986, oil and lacquer on fabric, 59 x 70¾ inches.

in large cloudy "skies," with more earnestly wrought complex curves atop. These spirals, loops, and flourishes are like aimless melodies, melodic lines that, rakishly, have time on their hands. Where may one have seen like patterns before—in eighteenth-century engravings? Books of designs for Rococo ornament? How such forms have become transparent formulas, pure stylistic "information," is fascinating, in a way. Here they may work as charming caricatures of style itself or, especially when dotted instead of continuously drawn, as mirages of stylishly "abstract" ornamental form.

Art as willfully "lightweight" as this, so shamelessly caught up in the sweep and follow-through of the meaningless curve that it might be "stoned," is bound to meet with resistance. But to dismiss whatever is ornamentally thin or thinly rhapsodic as kitsch can be a boorish defense. There are times when the "Incidental Music for *A Midsummer Night's Dream*" is no less than—as only the Germans have a word for it—"wonder-beautiful." The moral, if necessary? Perhaps that it is weakness to identify only with what appears powerful.

So much of the latter-day German so-called Neoexpressionism is over-blown and pseudo–avant-garde—not "atonally" modern at all, just so many more oompah bands playing out of tune. Polke's recent works, however, which build on two decades of painting with as much subtlety (and, I imagine, love) as wit, are demanding in their utter refinement. However slapdash Polke might still feel like making them (and may he keep his gift), a strange elegance makes itself desperately felt.

No doubt the supposed frivolity of the Rococo curlicues is telling. We Americans like to make such a point of bridling at such things; but when the Germans first ate up the French Rococo in the eighteenth century, it turned out to be the first course of the Enlightenment itself. At least it cannot be said that Polke's paintings simply mirror the decadence around us. Oh, no: their decadence is much more beautiful than that.

17

STREET WISDOM:
JUDY RIFKA
AND GRAFFITI CULTURE

Supposedly, the modern urban consciousness has an atomized character, although those who belabor the fact sometimes betray a desire for reassuring uniformity, with everybody contentedly, domestically alike and all the commuter trains running on time no matter what. To an outlook threatened by the lively and spontaneous, by signs of creative animation and loose control, nothing could be more different from all reassuringly clinical, belated Constructivist sculptures sitting mute and sphinxlike in the plazas of antiseptic office buildings than Judy Rifka's utterly agitated paintings. But Rifka's wit, which luckily keeps up with her anxious agitation, entails putting high care into a "careless" look. And in a world charged with contending impersonal forces, this is like advertising in reverse, "pushing" the individual consciousness in all its brave fragility.

Individualism, per se, has its own limits and its functions, including safely utopian dreaming. If much is often made of the raucously iconoclastic Punk music that drew in young New York painters at the turn of the 1970s, the high-cultural revival by the Metropolitan Opera of Bertolt Brecht and Kurt Weill's *Rise and Fall of the City of Mahagonny* (1930) in November of

1979 is equally symptomatic of the frustration, but also a certain camara-
derie, of the time. Not unlike Brecht's opera, Rifka's archly iconoclastic
paintings suggest that utopias come cheap, which it may be responsible
rather than necessarily cynical to face up to. That, after all, idols are for
shattering, pertains generally to Rifka's work as I see it, to her single,
smaller canvases having one "unscrewed" image on its own as well as to
her big-band muralistic works, those sweeping cascades, Niagaras—to be
as hyperbolic as they are—of images fragmented and atomized.

Rifka's is so distinctly an urban art that, in its most characteristic aspect,
it may not travel well, except from one downtown to another. For one
thing, city culture has had a bad name in America from Puritanism onward,
though it has become easier for outsiders to tune in, at least on a plane of
caricature, thanks to the media. Given the daily experience of an open
landscape, true city art must look pinched—the opposite for us in the big
town being the void evoked by all the moaning songs about truck drivers
abandoned in trailers by waitresses. Seriously: it is too easy to forget that
the weight of European culture, ever since the rise of the medieval market
town (of which Los Angeles may be a gigantic survival), has rested on the
sheer human density of life in the capital and that this has been by no
means unfortunate for cultural life. I notice in the *Introduction to the Devout
Life* (1609) of Saint Francis de Sales a suggestion for a rather vivid meditation
on hell as "a gloomy city burning with sulphur and foul-smelling pitch and
filled with people who cannot escape from it." All the more because
Francis goes on to evoke as the opposite a landscape vision of heaven's sky
in beautiful night and day, it is easy to jump to the false conclusion that he
is evoking first the (bad) city—in terms that as much as anticipate even
Frank Lloyd Wright's caustic jibes at New York—and then the (good)
country, whereas he actually assumes that the beautiful sky and light
pertain to, yes, Jerusalem (1.15f).[1]

Georg Simmel, the philosopher and founder of modern sociology, says
much in a lecture on "The Metropolis and Mental Life" (1902–3) that
illuminates Rifka's art as fundamentally urban and, here and now, of the
New York moment. First comes the itchy unanchored agitation so characteristic, no doubt, of the modern cultural capital itself. Speaking of how
the city encourages an intellectual and quantitative, rather than sentimental,
consciousness, Simmel holds that "the psychological basis of the metropol-

---

1. Francis de Sales, *Introduction to the Devout Life,* trans. John K. Ryan (Garden City, N.Y.,
1972), 64–65.

itan type of individuality consists in the *intensification of nervous stimulation* which results from the swift and uninterrupted change of outer and inner stimuli." It's not merely the pace, but the expenditure of attention and response: "Lasting impressions, impressions which differ only slightly from one another, impressions which take a regular and habitual course and show regular and habitual contrasts—all these use up, so to speak, less consciousness than does the rapid crowding of changing images, the sharp discontinuity in the grasp of a single glance, and the unexpectedness of onrushing impressions."[2] We are accustomed to such an essentially urban consciousness as manifest in the Impressionists' painting of the hustle-bustle of nineteenth-century Paris, and even, in a more abstracted way, in relation to Mondrian's boogie-woogie vision of New York in the 1940s. What Rifka's jumpy images expose is a still edgier, more anxious and testy, late twentieth-century version of a like mentality.

Where Simmel speculates on the far-reaching chaos that would ensue if all the clocks of Berlin were stopped for a single hour, I am reminded of a remark made by Edit de Ak, the New York art critic who has done so much to relate the work and world of the real subway "graffiti" artists, and Punk musical culture as well, to the New York artworld. Describing how difficult it is to keep moving on both fronts at once, de Ak commented that the time-consuming "hanging out" entailed by discourse in the one sphere is bound to be shattered by the clock-dominated, business life of the city, so that, after hanging out for, maybe, three days with the young outsider artists, she would have to break off contact at an inevitably promising point in order to keep, just late enough to manage, some mainstream appointment. Historically, one might even think of Baudelaire, in the nineteenth century, who, as Walter Benjamin points out, maintained apartments in three different neighborhoods of Paris at once!

Interesting, too, in light of the rootless float of Rifka's human figures, which might be taken as acquiescently bobbing around in a gravity-free space, is Simmel's conception of the "blasé" attitude that marks the modern city dweller. For in a life structure "of the highest impersonality" what develops is "a highly personal subjectivity" at the heart of the defensive or even aversive urban personality. Today, Simmel's pseudo-physiological terms may sound quaint, and amusingly so, yet his thought is nevertheless telling: "The blasé attitude results first from the rapidly

---

2. *The Sociology of Georg Simmel,* ed. and trans. Kurt H. Wolff (New York, 1964), 409–24, here 409–10; emphasis in original.

changing and closely pressed contrasting stimulations of the nerves. From this, the enhancement of metropolitan intellectuality, also, seems originally to stem. Therefore, stupid people who are not intellectually alive in the first place usually are not exactly blasé." Hectic, Baudelairean nightlife has its part in this, including even, by extension, ear-splitting rock music nowadays: "A life spent in boundless pursuit of pleasure makes one blasé because it agitates the nerves to their strongest reactivity for such a long time that they finally cease to react at all." Battered by otherwise "harmless impressions," the nerves are torn "so brutally hither and thither that their last reserves of strength are spent, and if one remains in the same milieu they have no time to gather new strength." This results, as Simmel sees it, in "an incapacity . . . to react to new sensations with the appropriate energy," just what "constitutes that blasé attitude, which, in fact, every metropolitan child shows when compared with children of quieter and less changeable milieus."[3]

Pop Art, psyched-up urban if not urbane, brought fast city culture and its "life-styles" (the term was used by Schopenhauer, not that there was time to notice) to the artistically conscious surface. However, Rifka's fitful shifts of attention from one theme to another—a bunch of these, then a bunch of those—amount not to a passively reflected contemporary dizziness but to a more dogged stalking of the fickle and elusive modern consciousness in its very agitation. More than Andy Warhol, who was content by and large with impassive registration, Rifka goes after and nails down the sprinting temper of the time, bagging it, as it were, not just taking bird-watcher's notes. Because the emotive texture of her work is so honestly, defensively ironic, "street-wise," and because in her judo-like, flexible (instead of flexing) strength there is a feminism so clear as to be transparent (and as such almost unnecessary to remark), she shares something of what must have been the polite sass of the prolific Rosalba Carriera, in the eighteenth century, at least in a quip by that painter that strikes me as more Rifkaesque than Warholean: "I am charmed with every thing I do, for eight hours after it is done!" (this as quoted by the once-famous "Mrs." Jameson.)[4]

Rifka's work is embraced with delight by the aware young, even if, to put it in New Yorkese, these kids today don't know from history. Andy Warhol is somebody they encounter in art history classes. Understanding

---

3. Ibid., 413–14.
4. [Anna] Jameson, *Sketches of Art, Life, and Character* (Boston, 1866), 360.

this concerns Judy Rifka's work fundamentally. Far from regressing into a childish realm, safe from fuller consciousness, her painting assumes its historical weight so ably that I imagine it as downright educational for the kids themselves, whose own dilemmas they might well have thought inarticulable even though, since the Beatles, their fraternity is effectively worldwide. No art that simply mirrored the way things are could be as capable as Judy Rifka's of crossing a definite line of consciousness and then also managing to re-cross it, reporting back from what to most adults might as well be Oz.

Popularly, there is in ever later industrial culture a premium on expert invention in the sense of coming up with the workable new trick, with the special gleam of fine art reserved as a consolation prize for moral drabness and conformity. Thus even the grand Victorian phrases, all sort of upholstered, practical and elegant, with which Carlyle toasts "The Poet as Hero" (in *On Heroes, Hero-Worship, and the Heroic in History*), can begin to sound like the poet or artist as tycoon in a marketplace of things warmingly spiritual, or even as a mere star, one who has found a way to "make it" at some mass-marketed game that requires its quantum of upbeat "sincerity." Rifka gets into this through her assumed posture of offhandedness, inadvertency, insofar as that appears as an act—not phony, either, but an act as such, her number.

What would it mean to say that Rifka's posture is no pose? At one extreme, that the artist "couldn't help" producing her art as the result of a certain syndrome, helplessly, even pitiably (Arbus); at the other, that the artist was such a dandy as somehow "genuinely" to be *all pose,* with art as a pseudonatural by-product (Warhol). The trouble is that both can be "acts" and marketable as such, especially in a populistic American way. For example, the cartoons of Peter Arno are an act, broadcasting within bourgeois society, with a lightness that cannot threaten but can only assuage, a drawing style developed with committed passion in German Expressionism by Ernst Ludwig Kirchner and which originally had deep roots in consciousness. Rifka's outright accessibility differs from the populism of an Arno, however, precisely because it encourages a consciousness of superficiality as such, and that is *not* a superficial thing. Oscar Wilde might have seen this as victory of the critical, over the creative, intelligence; yet there is its ultimate genuineness *as art,* something more than a theatrical spinoff of pose.

That the leveling, democratic American temper that Wilde himself found bracing here, at least for a few weeks (!), also charmed later European moderns, pertains historically to Rifka's art. For one thing, her picture structure sustains a post-Cubist jumble that is, as Theodore Roosevelt might have noted in his famous critique of the 1913 Armory Show, not so unlike that of the "crazy quilt"—so symbolically American as well as female and domestic (but also feminine-collective), despite its historical sources in European folk art. Even Rifka's high-art appropriations of the image of the Parthenon, touching base with the European classical tradition at its most hallowed point, are as utterly American as the home-grown "Parthenon" of Nashville, which in the most literal way is sportier, in so much better shape, than its long-infirm European model (Fig. 26). Besides,

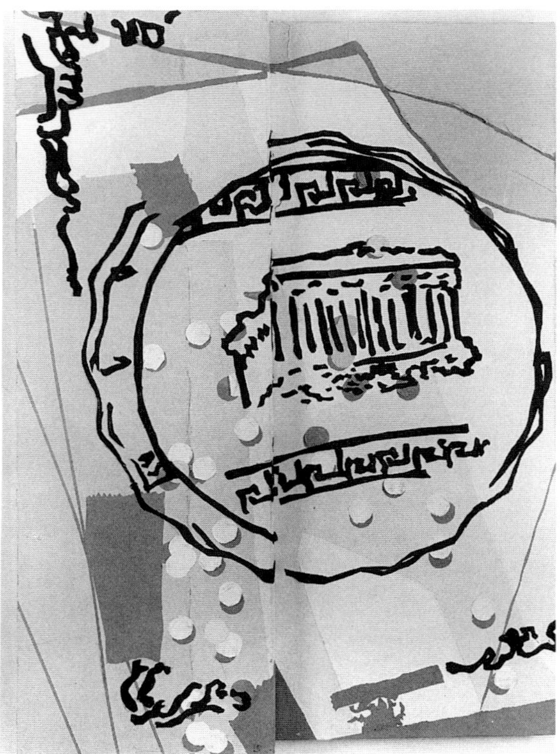

Fig. 26   Judy Rifka, *A. Museum*, 1982, oil on linen, 72 x 48 inches.

what could be more gutsily wrong-headed than the way the Nashville building (an art museum and hence an unashamed temple of culture) doesn't mind being parked as it is, like some big 1950s sedan, on a flat lot in the world's capital of popular country-and-western music? Most like Rifka's art must be the sense of doing "it," naive or not, *anyway,* maybe even doing a whole bunch, as Rifka has done with the Parthenon image in her "Museum" paintings. Yet even more important, I should add in a hurry, is the real cosmopolitanism this art may belie (shucks).

Rifka's painting is altogether in tune with the interest taken by earlier modern European artists in just such American esprit, especially in regard to New York. The cultural importance of New York as the big hometown of American art deserves more understanding in a suburbanized postwar America. It may seem incredible, but when we war babies were born, something like five percent of the entire population of this country lived within the City of New York. This city epitomized urban excitement to everybody from G. K. Chesterton—who said the neon signs of Times Square would look wonderful if one couldn't read English (my chauvinistic grandfather included these in his periodic tours, but tried to drive by fast enough so that we kids *couldn't* read the racy ones—to Mondrian—who took up boogie-woogie. It was a floating congress for everybody with ideas and, well, gumption. Bostonians may have said crude ambition, jealously enough, after the publishing industry moved to New York in the nineteenth century; yet there is a beautiful early photograph by Steiglitz of Manhattan, with the smokestacks of buildings and ships steaming away, just arrogantly enough entitled *City of Ambition.*

Of various between-the-wars paintings I could cite, one of the most Rifkaesque, Stuart Davis's *New York to Paris, No. 1,* painted in 1931 (University of Iowa, Museum of Art), has transatlantic cultural contact with the jivey Paris of Léger as its overt theme. In a hurry and jumble that anticipate Rifka, Davis intertwines a fishing boat with nets, a New York "el," a cliché–Parisian café, telegraph pole and wire, the Chrysler Building, and a luggage tag hanging down into the cheerfully reckless composition. This whole cluster of emblematic items is dominated by a big, sassy, silhouetted, American-in-Paris "gam," to recall a popular term of the time of World War II, strutting by in stocking and high-heeled shoe. In the next decade, the war itself displaced major artists, among them Duchamp and important Surrealists but also Mondrian, to New York, where, within a few years, American painting would for the first time challenge and even exceed the artistic claims of Europe. Already here, however, in 1931, with Stuart Davis being so American even in grooving on Paris, is an intimation of Rifka's rather more anxious and fretful urban jitterbugging. Not that everything is quite *that* simple or causal: in a subtler way in Rifka's work of only a few years ago, even the Abstract Expressionism of the booming postwar years reverberates, notably in a kind of twirling drawing-in-paint apparent in, especially, latter-day works by de Kooning. Yet, without being deterministic, Davis's painting does offer one way into Rifka's altogether Nowsville art.

The various multiple images that flit so seemingly irresponsibly, or with anesthetized disengagement, across so many of Rifka's canvases, come from a stock of sorts. They are so distilled, in the processes of being drawn on transparent acetate sheets and then jiggled around in opaque projection for placement as forms in the painting, and too digested, as such, to amount to simple appropriations. What they do have in common with an aesthetic of appropriation prevalent today is their air of being initially pulled down, rather than elevated, in the hierarchy of images: unlike the high-culture appropriation of primitive and folk arts, early in the century, many an imagery of mass distribution is now borrowed from the technical realms of the media, including television (this we hear much of) but also the visual parlance of slickly calculated advertising. Such is a *broadcast* imagery in the root sense, one scattered far and wide. Appropriating becomes an issue of qualifying the sometimes almost magically authoritarian character of images as coming from on high, that is, from the same high stratum, ironically enough, in which works of fine art stand as special tokens of cultural ultimacy.

In a way, this advances a tactic first pursued less critically by the Pop artists of twenty years ago, as when Roy Lichtenstein took over comic-book imagery and transformed it abstractly into high art. And now that appropriation has a sharper critical thrust, Henri Zerner's discussion of Lichtenstein's *Bobby Kennedy* cover from *Time* magazine seems keen: Zerner points out that the *Time* cover, for which, significantly, Lichtenstein made the color separations himself, is, even though it constitutes an edition in the millions, "*more* of an original print than so many Braque or Chagall lithographs that are merely gouaches skillfully reproduced by professionals and signed by the master."[5] Now one might think, further, of Rifka's generative use of drawings on transparent acetate sheets in analogy with the reproductive transparencies of Lichtenstein's color separations, in which sense she makes monoprints, of a sort, from her own stock.

---

5. This in the Harvard University Fogg Art Museum catalogue *The Graphic Art of Roy Lichtenstein* (Cambridge, Mass., 1975), introduction.

Picture Rifka juggling her acetates to the beat of rock music and you have some idea of her approach as extending Léger's with-itness and even Stuart Davis's and Mondrian's flying in the very face of the European disrepute of jazz as (overstimulating) "low" music.

What is easily forgotten here, given the popular sense that in history things merely *happen,* like the weather, is precisely that texture of conviction wherein if nothing goes against the grain enough to grate, something must be wrong. This has generally to do with modern culture as critical, even adversary, culture: complete inoffensiveness probably means innocuousness. Nevertheless, not even all the partisans of modernity have had an easy time with the jazz aesthetic. In an essay called "Plus de Jazz" (1921), collected in his *Since Cézanne,* the distinguished art critic Clive Bell considers jazz childishly anti-intellectual and beneath the dignity of high culture; wittily enough, Bell dismisses the prose style of Virginia Woolf as insufficiently *"gavroche"* (ragamuffin) to offer a literary parallel to jazz syncopation and discontinuity.[6] At the end of the same decade, a brief notice by George Bataille entitled, in English, "Black Birds," treating "Lew Leslie's Black Birds" at the Moulin Rouge in 1929, goes for jazz as primitive and decadent, which would hardly have encouraged taste-minded skeptics.[7] Later, in the very time of Pop Art, Theodor Adorno, dating jazz's European impact to about 1914, would lash out at the whole mode in an essay, "Perennial Fashion—Jazz," where jazz is found pseudonatural, pseudovital and full of clichés and conventionalized variations anyway, not to mention its being psychologically regressive along sadomasochistic lines![8] If in extending a new "jive" in painting now, Judy Rifka might run into some of the same flak, she would at least be in good historical company.

The way Rifka will do whole lots of one thing and then of another, piles as it were of each, sometimes interchangeably, is itself like the reiterative culture of phonograph records playing over and over again. It's funny how a piece of music on a record got taken to heart: the record wore down, however imperceptibly, with each successive play, even as it was inscribed more and more vividly in memory—not too differently from the way Rifka's images partake of the schematic concision. In either case, the unaccustomed spectator may be stumped by abbreviation, whereas a

---

6. Clive Bell, *Since Cézanne* (New York, 1928), 213–30, esp. 224.

7. Georges Bataille, *Oeuvres complètes,* II, *Premiers Écrits, 1922–1940,* ed. Michel Foucault (Paris, 1970), 186.

8. Theodor W. Adorno, *Prisms* (1967), trans. Samuel and Shierry Weber (Cambridge, Mass., 1981), 119–32.

buildup of familiarity tends to help in the negotiation of complexity—as I can still remember from first learning to hear not only the music of Bach, but then also, more broadly, the "motor rhythm" of rock 'n' roll.

Artistic richness turns out to be more important than where something ranks on the totem pole of culture. Besides, it becomes difficult to tell in modern culture what "high" or "low" origin is, as musicologists found out when they wondered whether "Annie Laurie" was a folk song or a song composed in folk manner by a sophisticated person; Donald Francis Tovey affirmed the latter, claiming in an essay on "Normality and Freedom in Music" (1936) that "its first seven notes are obviously the work of a lady or gentleman picking out sweet appoggiaturas on the pianoforte."[9] What gives "Annie Laurie" away, it seems, is its reliance on standard harmony, much as the classic subway "graffiti" art of the turn of the late sixties through the 1970s related to the preprocessed graphics of certain more hard-nosed, post-naive comic books. It could be maintained that graffiti-type art inevitably achieves a special lowbrow status *within* sophisticated highbrow culture just because it is so pre-tailored to a special, limited satisfaction, much as, say, the winning songs in the annual middlebrow "Eurovision Song Contest" have often fallen back on nonsense tra-la-las that will sound catchily "cute" in any language. Only an art as sophisticatedly rooted as Rifka's is prepared to transcend limitations of this kind.

What is at stake with graffiti art is a complex affair, but Rifka's work does raise the issue. Precisely *as painting* (and thus as deeply linked with our earliest life experiences of control over mess-making), such an artwork constitutes an unconventional and clearly potentially threatening outburst of individuality in the public context, one that any authority would prefer to control, not to mention hoi polloi for whom any prospect of freedom is a threat of instability. Furthermore, the literary culture is always unwilling to see such artwork, whatever its virtues, on its own terms as visual art. This is complicated by the technical terms "writer" and "writing" for the graffiti artist and his macho artwork (only one female muralist of the subway cars seems to be mentioned). It is more helpful when these terms are reserved for younger aspirants starting out with the justifiably offensive and *much more textual,* unpictorial "writing" applied to the insides of subway cars, the problem being that the same terms became used more broadly to include the eventually ever rarer, extravagantly visual exterior murals.

---

9. Donald Francis Tovey, *The Main Stream of Music and Other Essays* (New York, 1959), 183–201, here 189.

Curiously enough, in Dominican monasteries of Savonarola's day, the manuscript artists were called not *miniatori,* or miniaturists, but *belli scrittori,* or fine writers.[10] Generally relevant, too, is surely the literary bias that American culture probably inherits from the British Isles. In the first mainstream album of subway graffiti art, the novelist Norman Mailer's *The Faith of Graffiti* (1974), a glossy picture book with art-historical pretensions, the color photographs show not a single large, coherent, exterior car mural.[11] There is, beyond, a historical problematic as well.

Because practically all organized attempts to "beautify" the city with outdoor murals result semiautomatically in innocuous art, it is worth considering that such public works recall the utopian attempt of modern artists under the Weimar Republic to apply "bright paint . . . to the facades of petty-bourgeois houses in German provincial towns, to hide the shame of their structural disgrace and the emptiness of their eclectic ornamentation."[12]

These considerations may seem to ramble, but only, perhaps, in a way like that by which Rifka's painting sustains relentless transformation. For her, one thing leads on to another in a fertile stream of ideas that seems tinged, knowingly enough, by the anxious, "hyper" urgency of life on the run. Yes, in a general way this has to do with the Joycean stream-of-consciousness (and in Ireland too, by the way, as no doubt even in the smallest nation, slower folks affect to disdain the fast pace of the cultural capital). Let it not seem, however, that this indicates a stream of ideas in any *verbal* sense, of thoughts first presenting themselves in programmatic form, *except insofar as* James Joyce himself, as Vladimir Nabokov insisted, was concerned with an *essentially visual* stream of "images." This is important because it rules out any bracketing of Rifka's work within the special but inevitably inferior category of illustration, even illustration that can be patted on the head for special astuteness, as when Baudelaire does just that for Constantin Guys in the famous essay called "The Painter of Modern Life" (1863). No, understanding that this painter's self-consciously stylish, with-it work is not "literary," and pertains, if anything, to a musical, rather than verbal, culture, makes it possible to see how, as painting, it is, perhaps

---

10. Ronald M. Steinberg, *Girolamo Savonarola, Florentine Art and Renaissance Historiography* (Athens, Ohio, 1977), 11.

11. Norman Mailer, *The Faith of Graffiti,* photographs by Mervyn Kurlansky and Jon Naar (New York, 1974); for a much later but much more visually aware treatment, see Craig Castleman, *Getting Up: Subway Graffiti in New York* (Cambridge, Mass., 1982).

12. Hellmut Lehmann-Haupt, *Art Under a Dictatorship* (New York, 1954), 23.

most ironically of all, also visually *abstract*. No wonder that, to the extent that they are "motifs" at all, Rifka's images come and go in packs, like extras having few or no lines, whose role is simply to advance a general hubbub.

The set of twelve somewhat graffiti-like gold panels called *Surface Tension*, from 1981, is telling. Here is a figure that has to be the artist, however generalized it also is, struggling with a stretched canvas, which is to say, with *art* and, at that, with the capacity of representation to show the very struggle of art. The gold is thinly and "sloppily" smeared, in a way capable of alluding to a certain kind of gustatory abstract painting a decade ago but that also advances, now, a post-Pop sense of deliberately superficial mock-luxury like certain lowbrow home furnishings. At the same time, the irony that such paintings themselves are capable of becoming tokens of luxury might as well be a comment on tiresome formalist reflexivity. Most typical, looking way back three whole years, is the slight female figure contending, with a witty clumsiness, against the awkwardly physical resistance of a supposedly mainly mental kind of work.

Doubts may come and go about the facile effect versus the studied facility of the means advancing it. With *Dracula's Mirror* (1982), it is at least as funny as it is aesthetically serious to see the stand-in, representational aspect of painting, by reference to the mirror of reality, put on rolling casters, like a (Duchampian?) suitcase full of pure thought equipped with wheels. As the aesthetical trapeze artist in *¡Eso si Que es!* (1982) might understand, Rifka's large *Valley of the Queens,* of 1983, can charm one even by the ironically delicate glitzy dazzle of light bouncing off the rabbit-skin glue with which the linen is primed. But doubt can only return once it has departed, and if there may well be a temptation to make a facility seem profound—art as offering an easy time—that can only keep happening because the "heavy" is in fact made to *seem* light.

If you had only raw physical data on Rifka's hefty paintings, such as the facts on their materials, size, and weight, you might suppose that they made a Constructivist point about displaying the concrete materials and single-minded pragmatic of the "real world"; yet to know them in the flesh is to understand how funny that misconstrual would be. Once paint is nothing but paint, as such, we know that painting's own poetry, just what we were after, has slipped through our fingers. In this sense, what Rifka really exploits is a potential for *ironic* concreteness: painting fighting back against gross matter. Her art has strata of irony, including historical sophistication, as well as a (sometimes preposterous) mechanics of parts adding up to wholes. It displays a brass-tacks shoptalk even as it opens the possibility of aestheticism, while, from a slightly different angle, by its very iconoclasm it shows that aestheticism is not necessarily escapist.

In an impressive installation of 1984, at the 51X Gallery on the Lower East Side, titled *Why Die,* Rifka put together a mélange of wall-drawing, painted drapery (even on the ceiling) and images on canvas, the whole comprising a comment on militarism and looming holocaust that was all the more powerful for not simply collapsing art into a journalistic gesture. On balance, the project was a Goyaesque outburst of beauty as much as of rage, managing to articulate frustration itself (no mere irony, that). Inevitably, the "Mercenaries" series of Leon Golub was recalled; yet I am also struck by the fact that Golub's big, unstretched images, especially of man-to-man cruelty as embedded in sanguine fields of red, in turn relate to the abstract Philip Guston of *The Tormentors* (1947–48; San Francisco Museum of Art) and to the large tradition of such protest within "pure" painting in which loom Robert Motherwell's "Elegies to the Spanish Republic" (and his later Irish equivalents), themselves abstract progeny of Picasso's *Guernica*. Significantly, in light of Baudelaire's fascination in the "Modern Life" essay with military nonchalance, Rifka's individual paintings of soldiers keep urgent the matter of macho swagger in relation to cruelty and violence, while in more ostensibly aesthetic terms, their brown-and-green "fatigue" palette even recalls the direct involvement of certain Cubists in the development of camouflage during World War I. Rifka's installation was not immune to the problem of what might be called hot-headed pacifism, but its sheer gusto, as William Morris, Brecht, and perhaps some Dionysiac musicians of our day would have been pleased to see, showed that an art of peace is not condemned to wear a dreary face.

That Rifka is prepared to deal with themes along the lines of nuclear holocaust as well as the dizzy, nerve-end excitement and delight of rock music and dance says something about her moral range that tends to get lost once an artist becomes typecast with more or less trademarked images in the processes of cultural distribution and consumption. Factors that operate on the receiving end seem to include an understandable human preference for whatever strikes home as against whatever may be challengingly alien; a desire to have things simpler than they are, if only by avoidance of contradiction; and a quasi-pornographic fascination with the "bad" as titillating from a safe distance. I say this because if the 51X installation was Goyaesque, Judy Rifka is more generally Hogarthean. Consider, in general, the "Rake's Progress" aspect of her painting, but also, in particular, the case of a famous Hogarth print. Hogarth's *Gin Lane* is actually one half of a didactic pair, its pendant being another engraving called *Beer Street:* everyone recognizes *Gin Lane,* with its spectacle of individual and social degeneracy through heavy drink, while only specialists seem even to know of *Beer Street,* with its contrasting display of a mellower life of kinder social relations. What deserves not to be lost sight of, in the bargain, is Rifka's exemplary ability to handle the bad without being stung by it, which is the moral aspect of an artistic range that by itself might have seemed merely dizzy and all-over-the-place, instead of sweeping, as comprehensive as Hogarth's distinctly sensible and middle-class take on eighteenth-century London.

As I originally wrote this essay, a certain popular song of the moment, German in origin, captured something of the spirit of Rifka at 51X, but by means of a radical sentimentality that calls up the utter freeze of childhood terror. The song, "99 Luftballoons" (translated as "99 Red Balloons"), by "Nena," is about the sudden, sweeping horror of thermonuclear war, for which a certain mentality has, with shockingly childish *un*reality, pseudo-rationally prepared itself; important to its effect is Nena's blasé bounce and cynically "innocent" lilt. This seems relevant to Rifka's contrivedly childish, pasted-together, whistlingly preoccupied approach, even when her absorption does not spill out naughtily onto the wall. For her work is more than uncritically infantilistic and critically transitory thanks to its calculatedly raw, adult edge (this seems distinctly American in comparison with the taint of bitterness in the German song). It is as though, just as when Pandora opened the famous box everything escaped but hope, it might somehow, someday, be possible to look back on our present condition as dated because of its having been overcome. That said, what is most adult is—again the raw edge—that we need to be reminded that wishing will not make it so.

What an uphill battle it seems nowadays to make spiritual ends meet! How helpful, in the circumstances, to have an art that may look superficial, or at least forward, in its dizzy recklessness, but that will not let us off lightly. Such has to do, I think, with nothing less than the redemptive power of art. There is no turning back from consciousness—sentimental art is bad only because life is short and death awaits. And once we are sentiently conscious, only yet more sentient consciousness will do.

THE PLAY OF TEXTS

Around 1980 I was concerned, in teaching even more than as yet in writing, with what I consider retroactive influence, having always subscribed to T. S. Eliot's notion that whoever understands cultural tradition "will not find it preposterous that the past should be altered by the present as much as the present is directed by the past" ("Tradition and the Individual Talent," in *The Sacred Wood,* 1920). I had before treated more "normal," Baroque influences on *Guernica*—"Grandeur Mobilized" (1967; revised, 1981), now in Ellen C. Oppler's *Piccasso's "Guernica"* (1988)—and had the notes on textual influence under way, when I wrote "Two Blasts-from-the-Past" and "Observations on Harking Back (and Forth)" (*New Observations,* no. 28, 1985).

At the time, "appropriation art" had special appeal. Mike Bidlo had his 1983 non-Schnabel behind him (and Julian Schnabel himself, a redone Rodchenko of 1980) when I responded to a ridiculous article by Schnabel, "The Patient and the Doctors" (*Artforum,* February 1984) with textual parody. Pseudonymously, I also produced paintings, full-scale copies of mod masterworks executed by mail-order in Hong Kong, one of which was exhibited by Jeffrey Deitch in "The New Portrait," at P.S. 1 in 1984, describing all this in a rather lame narratological experiment, "China Trade" (*Arts Magazine,* September 1986).

Peter Halley's annoying lecture showed how naive even a very articulate writer-artist can be in respect to prior art and influence. As to the larger project of Bidlo and some other appropriationists, it reminds me of something James Agee wrote in one of his *Letters to Father Flye:* "I would suspect a chemical rule on reading as in 'influence,' 'imitation,' and 'plagiarism': that in reading or being influenced 'successfully' one does as much work as the authors did originally" (10 August 1939; Braziller ed.).

18

TWO BLASTS-FROM-THE-PAST IN PICASSO (AND YES, MARCEL, YOU TOO)

In Memoriam Mary Ann

"Years ago as a boy I saw in the Royal Museum of Brussels a similar figure that has remained vivid in my memory." Thus, in a beautiful thought, one perhaps a little reminiscent of Freud's "Disturbance of Memory on the Acropolis," Meyer Schapiro recollects the image of Augustus listening to Virgil read from the *Aeneid* in Ingres's *Tu Marcellus Eris,* of 1819, while thinking of Picasso's 1905 *Woman with a Fan* (Washington).[1]

Warm blood of youth, health of all that will ever be truly classic. Consider Picasso's 1901 *Evocation (Burial of Casagemas)* as a juicy remake of Cézanne's *Apotheosis of Delacroix* (1873–77?). There, the romance of the artist-hero, à la Carlyle; yet more, too, for heroes have their heroes, not to mention God—whom Carlyle himself may have found rather antique, or at least not very British. But "Remember also your Creator in the days of your youth, before the evil days come, and the years draw nigh, when you

---

1. Meyer Schapiro, "Picasso's *Woman with a Fan:* On Transformation and Self-Transformation," *Essays in Archaeology and the Humanities in Memoriam Otto J. Brendel,* ed. L. Bonfante and H. von Heintze (Mainz, 1976); repr. in his *Selected Papers,* II, *Modern Art: Nineteenth and Twentieth Centuries* (New York, 1978), 111–20.

will say, 'I have no pleasure in them'; before the sun and the light, and the moon, and the stars are darkened and the clouds return after the rain; in the day when the keepers of the house tremble, and the strong men are bent, . . . and those that look through the windows are dimmed, . . . and terrors are in the way; . . . and desire fails; because man goes to his eternal home, and the mourners go about the streets" (Ecclesiastes 12: 1–3, 5).

How death begets death. First Casagemas's suicide; six months later, in the summer of 1901, *that* as a theme; next, in the autumn, Toulouse-Lautrec's death and influence; and then, on top of it all, the Blue Period proper. And, too, the human circumstances: the other dude, the one with the rent money, suffers impotence. Imagine having to compete with P. P. There is Casagemas in *La Vie* (1903; Cleveland)—and why don't we just call it *"Life,"* which in English has just enough c'est-la-vie in it? Differing life-styles: equivocation either as inhibited or as spendthrift (Hamlet had money). There stands Casagemas, "like a modern Hercules, choosing between two types of love," says a nineteenth-century scholar.[2] Sure enough, even if Choices of Hercules (more on him later) generally come out of a more professedly classicizing bag.

But with the *Woman with a Fan,* Schapiro affirms how the figure, compared with that in a nice but hesitant, even limp, drawing that leads up to it (Oberlin), evidences "a new personality, one that assumes a role, facing the world with a certitude lacking in the other," and, more, how like this is to Picasso's own coming into enlivened self-possession. Has Casagemas somehow paid for that as well? Grief as debt. May the grief of genius repay all?

Now, in *Les Jeux du cirque et la vie foraine* (Paris, 1889), by Hugues Le Roux, a book with by no means un-Lautrecesque illustrations by the painter Jules Arsène Garnier (1847–1889), there is a male figure in effectively the same posture as that of Picasso's girlish woman. The man is apparently one Billy Hayden, a British performer noted for transforming the conventional Pierrot character, as still in Cézanne's contemporary *Mardi Gras* (1888; Moscow, Museum of Modern Western Art), into the modern circus clown. Actually, Hayden had started off "barbouillé de noir" (in blackface). His career only took off once it occurred to him "s'enfariner comme Pierrot," that is, to dust himself with flour, like Pierrot. Hence only in making himself *look* more ostensibly like Pierrot did he manage to break the Pierrot mold.

----

2. Theodore Reff, "Themes of Love and Death in Picasso's Early Work," in John Golding and Roland Penrose, eds., *Picasso in Retrospect* (New York, 1973), 4–30.

As with Picasso's own anticipating sketch, to turn from Garnier's clown image to the *Woman with a Fan* is to sense something coming out of hiding, released from self-restraint, with the touchingly sad clown's gesture as inhibitively shaping, or else hypothetically shaping, like a mime's shaping in thin air. Picasso's figure is not only female but specifically maidenly, "Corinthian" and not yet "Ionic." So from Garnier's clown to Picasso's young woman we also pass from a "childlike" guy to a *gal* still ripening in her womanhood, slim and firm and no doubt "leggy." Also, she is active, spirited, athletic in sustaining the angular positions of her arms; for the firm hold of the pose is supple and gymnastic more than statuesque, and, just so, partakes of a charming transitivity. Excuse me: Lessing says, "Charm is beauty in motion" (*Laocoön,* xxi). How effectual this makes her, like some crack choir mistress; or, too, hers might as well be a gesture of blessing. At any rate, the difference of sex allows too, as with Schapiro's Augustus, for a transformative analogy between an objective "subject" and the "subjective" artist as active objectifier.

Jules Garnier's almost too pretty, bourgeois-Rococo tints disappear from the otherwise same drawings in the English translation of A. P. Morton, with its comedown, squarer, title *Acrobats and Mountebanks* (London, 1890), which I saw first. Only a year later, the reprinted illustrations look practically like Xeroxes. Here, indeed, I consult my actual black-and-white photocopy of the tinted French original, where the figure appears—in a *pink* suit with *blue*-and-white, broadly striped sleeves and leggings. The very suit can be seen as shakily, unstably intermediate in look, as if part belted tunic but also part ruffled tutu. One also thinks of gestures of the kind in association with Nijinsky, as in *L'Apres-midi d'un faune* (1912), with faun and nymphs both.

Finally, apropos of the pal, Casagemas: in Egyptian art such gestures as this occur in funerary contexts, notably with wailing women. All the more interesting, perhaps, is the exceptional case of a woman in this posture who is serenading her husband on the harp, which, according to Mrs. Frankfort's once-famous *Arrest and Movement,* happens to be "a unique instance of something approaching an erotic scene."[3] Recall, in light of this, the playful heavenly girlfriends in the oddly but cheerfully Greco-like (that D. P. *to* Spain), as well as Cézannesque, empyrean of the *Evocation (Burial of Casagemas)* painting.

---

3. H. A. Groenewegen-Frankfort, *Arrest and Movement: An Essay in Space and Time in the Representational Art of the Ancient Near East* (London, 1951), 42 with pl. xviiib.

Truth always grows in the midst of difficulties and gets stronger in conflict because it then shines forth more brilliantly.

—*Savonarola*

Well, let us turn now, ahem, to a piece by Antonio Canova, his *Ercole furioso* (or Hercules Furious), of 1801 (Fig. 27), a clay relief in the Gipsoteca Canoviana at Possagno, the sculptor's home town (at that, one smaller than Malaga). Yes, right, Picasso did go to Italy with Jean Cocteau in 1917. But if I didn't have to go to Possagno to run into Canova's image a couple of years ago, why, once every doorknob in Italy had been photographed by the Alinari or by Anderson, if not both, should Picasso necessarily have had to? Rather than run off at this point to trace the possible dissemination of the *Ercole furioso,* one might better reflect on what a density of circumstantial fact could prove, or, more likely, seem to prove. It would be puny, jealous, to want to cut a masterpiece down to size by treating it as some more or less redundant reiteration. With *Guernica,* even Anthony Blunt seems too glad where he can just, almost, *practically* prove that on a certain afternoon Picasso could easily have glanced at a lucky page in a current magazine.[4]

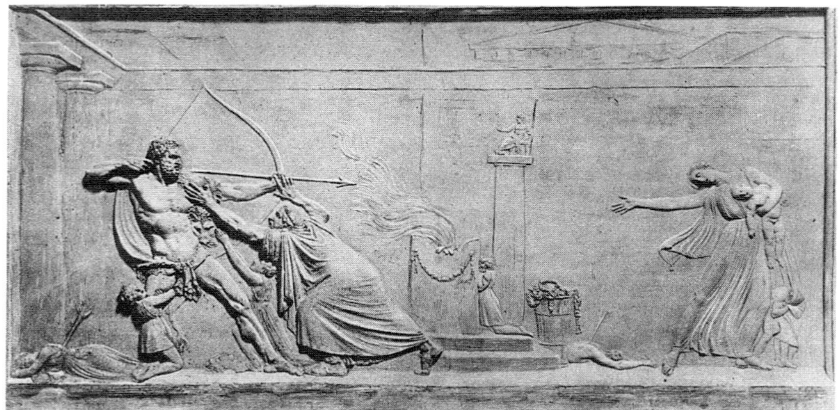

Fig. 27   Antonio Canova, *Ercole furioso,* 1801, plaster.

---

4. Anthony Blunt, *Picasso's Guernica* (New York, 1969); for my own 1967 article on *Guernica* "sources," see now Joseph Masheck, "Grandeur Mobilized," in Ellen C. Oppler, ed., *Picasso's Guernica: Illustrations, Introductory Essay, Documents, Poetry, Criticism, Analysis* (New York, 1988), 305–9.

Some things in the Canovan *Hercules Furious* match suggestively with *Guernica* (1937; Prado), while others do not. The relief, which illustrates a particular scene in tragic drama, is more contained in scope as well as far smaller in scale. Still, most vital is the temper of the whole; some temper, too. If anything gets elucidated in this conjunction, instead of grossly explained away, it is *Guernica*'s high-voltage torment as expressively laid bare and paraded as such, engaged with yet overriding, bursting out of, Laocoön-like, a stolidly classical and specifically pedimental architectonic common to both images.

Norbert Lynton once wrote of Picasso and his *Guernica,* "He is so successful that we have to discipline ourselves lest the bombing itself should be diminished by his picture into little more than a . . . prerequisite for it," wondering, nevertheless, if we would "remember the event at all if it had not occurred just when Picasso was debating how to use the commission for a large public mural."[5] True enough; but is this any less true of the heroic-herculean demands that Michelangelo inherited, together with the partly carved stone, with the *David* job? Give the guy a break, at least since, as Savonarola put it, even when "God wants something done, He still wishes fit means for the conditions of the times to be used."[6] No, this was something more than luck; it was a rising to an occasion. Now that the *Guernica* has returned to Spain, Mike Bidlo has painted a full-scale copy, not so simply "appropriating" it as, at once, lessening its aura but also reaffirming the work as something we still need.

Take note, in the sphere of Latin culture, of the two Senecas, both, incidentally, Spanish-born. Junior based his play *Hercules furens* on the *Heracles* of Euripides, this even though dad was "suspicious . . . of Greek culture."[7] "So," as Gertrude Stein might have said, making everything sound so naturally consequential, the Spanish Republicans had appointed Picasso director of the Prado.

Euripides' *Heracles,* according to Philip Vellacott called a *Hercules furens* only by Latinizing pedants, bespeaks deranging horrors of civil war and tyrannical usurpation. Any anti-fascist potential would have been vivid in 1937, at least, say, to somebody like Bertolt Brecht:

---

5. Norbert Lynton, "Art and Violence," *The Guardian* (Manchester), 18 November 1967.

6. Girolamo Savonarola, "The Compendium of Revelations" (1494), trans. Bernard McGinn in his edition of *Apocalyptic Spirituality* (New York, 1979), 192–275, here 236.

7. C. J. Fordyce, "Lucius Annaeus Seneca," in *The Oxford Classical Dictionary,* 2d ed. (Oxford, 1970), q.v.

> The king has as allies many poor men,
> Though they seem by reputation to be prosperous,
> Who have created party strife and have destroyed the city
> For the sake of plundering their neighbors, while what they have at home
> Wasted in expenditures, has been dissipated by idleness.
>
>   (lines 588–92)[8]

The person of Madness herself comes to describe the bearing of the once-heroic Heracles, the crushed, ex-"pro" hero who "tosses his head [as if] at the starting gate," "rolls his fierce, crazed eyes, / And, like a charging bull, . . . does not check his panting / But bellows fearsomely" (lines 867–70). Even the fallen, broken, equestrian-chivalric statue on the ground in *Guernica* finds an analogue of sorts where Heracles refers self-reflexively to Hera as having succeeded in "upending from his very pedestal the first man of Greece" (lines 1306–7). Public meaning has its personally human roots. In the closing lines of Euripides' tragedy the mature and aware and distraught Picasso, awakened as an emigrant to the urgency of life in his Basque and Spanish homeland, might well have felt echoes of the life and death of his old compatriot in those early days in Paris, more than thirty years before:

> We go with laments and much weeping,
> Having lost the greatest of friends.
>   (lines 1427–28)

Sometimes He inspires what He is to predict in the prophet's intellect without any images, the way He gave wisdom to Solomon and the way David prophesied; other times He imprints in the imagination different figures and images that signify what the prophet is to understand and predict. From the power of this same light the prophet himself clearly understands the meaning of these visions; otherwise he would not be able to say, as is written in Daniel, "There is need of understanding in a vision."

—Savonarola

Just what is it that is so often mistakenly uncritical about concern with artistic antecedents, as if the most extensive and thorough genealogy could ever yield the substance of history? There is a photograph of a reclining young female nude, taken by Robert Demanchy around 1898, that might very well have been Matisse's immediate "source" for the splendid *Blue Nude* (1907; Baltimore), right down to the painting's frond-patterned textile

---

8. Translations of this and the following passages from Euripides' *Heracles,* by David Murphy.

backdrop, as well as the figure's upward-swelling hip. Don't run to the library over it, however, because it will not explain how Matisse got the hip into such sublimatedly passionate relation with his souped-up palm fronds—which now throb with lush life, unlike the demure drapery motifs of their "source."[9] In other words, do not look to Demanchy for the gift of Matisse (not that there may not also be a *gift* of Demanchy), except to see it missing, like the soloist's part on those music-practice phonograph records that used to be known as "Music Minus One."

Duchamp's case may be peculiar, but it is relevant for the way his work vamps before the miscellaneous masters, as if always out to pick up the best "influences" it can attract. Only a few years ago, a certain, let's say, squarely established art historian got all upset because I had proposed in print that Charles Willson Peale's 1795 portrait *Staircase Group* (Philadelphia), with its actual wooden stairs, had, however anachronistically, *as much as influenced* Duchamp in the drawing *Encore à cet astre* (1911) that, provoked by a poem of Jules Laforgue, is the acknowledged compositional starting point of Duchamp's various Nudes Descending Staircases.[10] (I believe that some almost constitutionally oppose such speculation because they need to affirm generational control over historical periods, which is a way of refusing to see history as a whole, with themselves embedded in it instead of safely off to one side if not grandiosely over and above it.) My point at the time was that the Peale connection might allow for an interactive circuitry of relations—in one sense dia-, in another, synchronic—between old and new art, something more reciprocal than the utterly mechanical sense of causality employed by art historians who may tip their hats to Kubler's *The Shape of Time,* of a generation ago, yet to this day do nothing to overcome a nineteenth-century mechanical understanding with, at least, some more electrical one. To me it was all the more interesting that Duchamp had probably *not* simply seen and, as if on a one-way street, been conventionally "influenced by" the old American portrait of (N.B.) *an artist's two artist brothers.* You might think, at least in connection with the oddball Duchamp, that the claim of a certain freaking of normal causality might have been entertained. I see now, moreover, that Malcolm Cowley,

---

9. Demanchy's photograph, which I have discussed in classes and in public lectures many times in relation to the *Blue Nude,* can be found in Oliver Mathews, *Early Photographs and Early Photographers: A Survey in Dictionary Form* (London and New York, 1973), pl. 228.

10. Masheck, "Chance is zee Fool's Name for Fait," introduction to my edition of *Marcel Duchamp in Perspective,* Artists in Perspective (Englewood Cliffs., N.J., 1975), 1–24, esp. 7–8.

testifying on the formative influence of none other than Jules Laforgue on American moderns from probably T. S. Eliot's Harvard days (class of 1910) into the 1920s, has observed, "In talking about literary sources, we always run the danger of assuming that because something is *post hoc* [after this] . . . it is also *propter hoc* [because of this]."[11]

A retroactive influence need not involve an *un*likelihood or *im*possibility that the later artist might have known some earlier artist's work. The point is not the precipitation of the later work at all, but the opposite, the way the later work influences the earlier one, casting back onto it a reflected light that can enliven latent meanings that, needless to say, may never have been prosaically intentional anyway. A subtler instance than that of Peale's *Staircase Group* might involve not simply the prior image, but also its historical absorption of subsequent responses, as with several by now conceivably Duchampian aspects of Chardin's *La Fontaine de cuivre* (The Copper Water Urn), apparently painted around 1734 (Louvre), and the relentlessly notorious urinal readymade that Duchamp christened *La Fontaine* in 1917. At least once one is acquainted with the Duchamp piece (and with his related, onanistic *Sad Young Man on a Train* [1911]), in Chardin's *Fontaine* an imaginably torsolike samovar dribbles, by means of a rather penile little faucet, into a container below. A 1737 inventory description, appropriately businesslike in tone, of the Chardin painting, may evoke other classic motifs in Duchamp's oeuvre as well, including the coffee grinder and water mill, and, hence, the great *Large Glass* (1915–23; Philadelphia) itself, into which they became incorporated: "A copper urn equipped with its cover and rings, containing two water compartments with its faucet of pinchbeck, resting on wooden legs." A critic, Paul Mantz, commented in 1870 on the painting's "witty rugosity of manner," something it is safe to say that Duchamp would have liked. This was in fact, we are told, one of the most copied of all Chardin's paintings after 1871, and Pierre Rosenberg observes, in a comment that could differently yet also just as aptly and categorically apply to Duchamp's readymades, that here, as often in the earlier master's work, the objects of still life seem chosen "for their humility."[12] (And are not Duchamp's readymades sculpturesque still lifes

---

11. Malcolm Cowley, "Laforgue in America: A Testimony," in his *And I Worked at the Writer's Trade: Chapters of Literary History, 1918–1978* (New York, 1978).

12. Pierre Rosenberg's Cleveland Museum of Art catalogue *Chardin 1699–1779* (Cleveland, 1979), cat. no. 53, 184–86 with plates, for all three quotations. In a lecture at the Museum of Modern Art in November 1985 I related both Chardin's and Duchamp's *Fontaines* to Kasimir Malevich's *Samovar*, c. 1913 (now in the Museum).

of very single, "bachelor" objects lacking the familial contextuality of even the lone object as it presents itself in painting?)

Both *Fontaines,* Chardin's and Duchamp's, relate in retroactive influence at least because once Duchamp's has been an object of consciousness it is likely to insinuate itself, like some association that one will always make with a certain tune, into the apprehension of Chardin's. This is like a "soft" kind of influence as long as we tend to think of such associations as disposably subjective; but they can make more intersubjective sense than that once noticed, since anyone else who also knew the Duchamp work and thought about it might very well just as automatically and reasonably recall it before, or through, Chardin's. Those who are annoyed by the way such thinking, even in the soft form, runs against the supposedly one-way grain of gross causality are no doubt most disturbed that something later but less distinguished might be seen as responsible for any worthy sense of something earlier and clearly more distinguished.

Surely much worse, however, are all the cases of workaday influence where insignificant things just plod flatfootedly on down the historical road toward significant things: unless they lead to a heightened sense of the originality of the supposedly influenced work, these are the really trivial instances. Many art historians do seem to love them, as if pleased to diminish the gratitude deserved by genius and, at the same time, to rob present art of its power to affect the past, its crucial say in whatever "history" is to be about. Such observers would neglect to thank Matisse for lending reflected charm to Demanchy, being in such a hurry to withdraw, so to speak, from Matisse's account whatever might have been borrowed, if not stolen, from Demanchy. Fortunately, everything is really much simpler: the later, greater thing lights up, conducts sympathy back to, the earlier, lesser thing, which, in this sense, it can really be said to "influence," affecting its own subsequent transmissions. By comparison, trying to pin this or that causal source on somebody like either Matisse or Picasso can be as pathetic as trying to track down the name of the dude's barber or tailor.

Square that surely is, which in a word is just what Wittgenstein proves Sir James George Frazer of being, in his *Remarks on Frazer's "Golden Bough."* Wittgenstein says, "An historical explanation, an explanation of an hypothesis of the development, is only *one* kind of summary of the data—of their synopsis. We can equally well see the data in their relations to one another and make a summary of them in a general picture *[in einallgemeines Bild zusammenzufassen]* without putting it in the form of an hypothesis regarding the temporal development" (and while we're at it: Frazer's "explanations" of "primitive observances" are found "much cruder than the sense of the observances themselves").[13] In a different way, my teacher, Rudolf Wittkower, once called attention to Horace Walpole's defense of Sir Joshua Reynolds when the painter was accused of plagiarism for deriving portrait ideas from the masters. Walpole's remark that "a quotation from a good author, with a novel application of the sense, has always been allowed to be an instance of parts and taste" is easy enough to take—somewhat easier, to this day, than the fuller implications of the rest of his claim, which is that a mobilized quotation can "have more merit than the original."[14]

Despite the art-historical bookkeepers, Harold Bloom manages to show, in *The Anxiety of Influence,* how a poet can, in Bloom's words, "hold open" his poem to that of a precursor, and how, for examples, Milton can be said to be influenced *by* Wordsworth, Wordsworth *by* Keats, Wordsworth and Keats *by* Wallace Stevens, Shelley *by* Browning, or Whitman *by* Hart Crane.[15] In life we do not, anyway, run into works of art that affect us in the chronological order in which they were created; so, unless one considered a finished work of art more like something dead than something alive, why should it be closed to subsequent influence? More simply, all works of art that are of more than specimen interest offer themselves fully in the here and now; they always have and they always will. Maybe Picasso did know the little circus illustration or Canova's Hercules relief, but that cannot be as important now as the way the *Woman with a Fan* redeems something touching from mortal anonymity or the way the *Guernica* attains a communion with the immortals. Mortally enough, with my copy of the reprint of *The Anxiety of Influence* came an errata slip that includes a beautiful thought, apparently lost in typesetting, proofreading, whatever, as though somebody's telephone had just happened to ring at the wrong moment: "Freudian sublimation involves the yielding-up of more primordial for more refined modes of pleasure, which is to exalt the second chance above the first."

---

13. Ludwig Wittgenstein, *Remarks on Frazer's "Golden Bough,"* ed. Rush Rhees, trans. A. C. Miles and Rhees (Retford, Notts., 1979), 8E (German, 8).

14. Rudolf Wittkower, "Palladianism in England," *The Listener,* 18 May 1950.

15. Harold Bloom, *The Anxiety of Influence: A Theory of Poetry* (New York, 1973; repr. 1975).

19

NOTES ON INFLUENCE
AND APPROPRIATION

This Is Not Original

It is two decades, now, since I published a note under the title "Samuel Johnson's Uttoxeter Penance in the Writings of Hawthorne" in *Hermathena: A Dublin University Review* (no. CXI, Spring 1971). It seems that in the marketplace of Uttoxeter, in Staffordshire, in 1784, a then seventy-five-year-old Johnson performed the self-imposed penance of standing bare-headed in the rain for an hour on the spot where his father's bookstall had been, in order to atone for having half a century earlier been too proud to help his dad sell books. Johnson's hardly-instant replay of lifetime struck me as telling, all the more for its structural resemblance to the "Revelation" episode in Nathaniel Hawthorne's *Scarlet Letter* (1850), where when the so literally "marked" principal is exonerated by the confession of the preacher, she stands on the very spot where she had been as much as framed, a nice round seven years before.

Well, it turned out that Hawthorne was indeed concerned with Johnson, and above all with his Uttoxeter penance. His seven-year cycle imposed upon Hester Prynne does more than likely echo Sam Johnson's freewill expiation of fifty years of personal guilt. In a children's book he has the penance represent Johnson's character completely. Much later, after writing a campaign biography for Franklin Pierce's successful election campaign and becoming American consul at Liverpool, he made a pilgrimage. Uttoxeter wasn't far away; neither was Johnson's town of Lichfield, where since 1838 stood a Johnson monument by the sculptor Richard Cockle Lucas, this bearing a relief commemorating the Uttoxeter penance, which provided Hawthorne with a nice occasion for reflection on the favored theme ("Lichfield and Uttoxeter," in *Our Old Home, 1863*). In between, at precisely midcentury, came *The Scarlet Letter.*

This much I detailed in 1971, but more recently I ran into something else. Brousing in a work by one of the few utter geniuses of American culture, I came upon a heady account of a conversion experience. The speaker says he was walking along with friends when he saw "three steeple-spires and they struck at my life" (shades of van Gogh?). On asking his companions the name of the town, a detail with its exact counterpart in Hawthorne's pilgrimage account, "They said Lichfield." Next he remembers receiving a divine call, leaving his shoes behind, and going on a holy rampage; "and as soon as I got within the city, the word of the Lord came to me again, saying: 'Cry, "Wo to the bloody city of Lichfield." It being marketday, I went to the market-place, and to and fro in the several parts of it, and made stands, crying as before, 'Wo to the bloody city of Lichfield.' " He had seemed to see blood coursing through the Lichfield streets and flooding the marketplace, and on leaving the town wondered why he had been moved to do such a thing. Lichfield had been taken by each side in the Civil War, but it wasn't said to have seen all that much bloodshed. "But afterwards I came to understand, that in the Emperor Diocletian's time a thousand Christians were martyr'd in Lichfield. So I was to go, without my shoes, through the channel of their blood, and into the pool of their blood in the market-place, that I might raise up the memorial of the blood of those martyrs, which has been shed above a thousand years before, and lay cold in their streets."

All I have just quoted might be framed in a further set of quotation marks. The original passage is from the journal of George Fox, founder of the Quakers, but given here *as already found quoted* in the opening lecture (1901) of William James's *Varieties of Religious Experience* (1902). Hawthorne had read Johnson; James, Hawthorne, and Johnson, too, for that matter, could all have read Fox, whose *Journal* had been published in 1694 with, interesting enough for any American, a preface by William Penn. At a certain point, one begins to wonder, How much can it really matter in what sequence the relay runners ran?

If the provisionally ultimate account of Fox is enough to send one back further, say, to Bede, it would no doubt be better to ask what's really going on in such a network of connections. Writers share the discovery of their presence in the world and time with the dead and those to come. What is so false about the conventionally causal notion of literary and artistic influence is its illusory simplism, whether sustained by an intellectual sort of three-card monte, with *X* as cause and *Y* as effect, or, worse, by fuzzy talk about "affinities." In reality, artistic influence is more complex than one billiard ball banging into another—something in its own right by no means simple, at least according to David Hume. Maybe instead it's like a wild break in pool, with English on the cue ball and plenty of cushion activity. Better still, it is more like something electrical than anything mechanical, a conduction that either flows in opposite directions at once or else doesn't flow at all.

The writer or artist may find what he needs in the past, or at least may usefully think he does (the dream as most fully realized in its telling); but in gazing back he also lights up whatever he sees with a beam of his own tint. All writers, after all, are readers, and all readers are human beings. Then again, however ironic it might seem, to be human is, categorically, to be unique. The same James makes a similar point as "Transcendentally" as wittily in his same lecture: "The first thing the intellect does with an object is to class it along with something else. But any object that is infinitely important to us and awakens our devotion feels to us also as if it must be *sui generis* and unique. Probably a crab would be filled with a sense of personal outrage if it could hear us class it without ado or apology as a crustacean, and thus dispose of it. 'I am no such thing,' it would say, 'I am MYSELF, MYSELF alone.' "

This Is Not a Pipe

Some would say that there is appropriation and there is appropriation. Traditional academic art historians, especially, may resist the idea of appropriation as plagiaristic and exploitative. Hardly separate from the old romance of "originality," however, is an obsession of some such art historians with in effect *negative appropriation,* undercutting the apparent originality of even famous works of art by rendering them less extraordinary than one is supposed to have supposed. At the least, many art historians still fall back on an unquestioned, essentially mechanistic, "Newtonian" conception of cause and effect. If they may resort to the default category of "affinity" in the absence of adequate (essentially "diffusionist") evidence of causality, they nevertheless expect to be able to trace back from a work of art to actual and potential sources, hoping to expose by elimination the je ne sais quois by which some (more) creative mind actually *made something of* its inheritance. There is an air of envy whenever a contemplative type, not impossibly stunted in creativity, cuts down to size the apparent originality of a man or woman of action.

Yet some may also be thinking about what it would be like to have their own defenseless intellectual work ripped off, which might after all be different from the appropriation of one worked *object* for another—as if, say, concrete works of art were more like public personalities in libel law. The conventional historical mentality does seem otherwise preoccupied, and uneasy with revisionist forms of influence—including what I consider "retroactive influence"—or appropriation. Whether or not this could indicate hovering guilt over vague, perhaps long-standing and undischarged intellectual debts, fear for one's own intangibly intellectual property must come into play.

I can speak from the experience of more than once suspecting my written thought had been appropriated, which nevertheless does seem somehow different from what goes on in appropriation *art,* and not, I trust, merely because that is somebody else's problem.

English-language readers of Michel Foucault's little Magritte book, *This Is Not a Pipe* (first French edition 1973), as translated by James Harkness (Berkeley, 1982), may well come away with a connection between Magritte's famous "pipe" motif that isn't a *pipe*—in *The Wind and the Song* (1928–29)—and the symbolic briar pipe serving as a symbolic colophon at the very end of Le Corbusier's *Vers une Architecture* (1923). Now increasingly, Michel Foucault's name has entered into this connection. (Note too, by the way, how the question of Magritte's possible "source" in Corbusier is here superseded by the question of the source of the critical *idea* of that artistic source.) In actual fact, the Corbusier idea occurs *not at all* in Foucault's text; it was interjected by Harkness, the translator, which of course means that the problem I am describing would still be unknown in France or in

Magritte's Belgium at least until new accounts in English were summoned into French or Belgian arguments.

Harkness himself claims to rely for the point on Robert Hughes's *The Shock of the New* (1981). Next question: What about Hughes? I myself had illustrated and discussed the Corbusier–Magritte parallel in an article in *Artforum* for May 1974, this eventually reprinted as "Magritte in an Imagist Light," in my *Historical Present* (1984). Furthermore, the article in question was based on a draft I had shown to Peter Townsend, the editor of *Studio International,* in London, to whom I had just been introduced by my friend, the late Barbara Reise. That was in 1967, right around the time Peter introduced me to Robert Hughes—wittily enough, I remember, as "the most promising young art critic in Australia." Here any art historian would feel on pretty firm ground in positing influence. The larger problem I see in this, my own case, is the utter submersion-erasure of a contribution to the more specialized literature (here, *Artforum*) by a popular book— something for which every intellectual field must have some protocol.

If I were researching this at some time in the twenty-first century, I would certainly entertain the supposition that someone named Hughes had preempted someone named Masheck, and that, thanks to one Harkness, from 1982 on the whole thing was handed over to a certain Foucault (except, oddly enough, not in France!) by people who only read, but not very carefully, his English edition. But that is still not all there is to it. What if, for instance—just what if—one of these other writers thought of the idea independently, like, on a rather grander scale, Leibniz and Newton each discovering the calculus?

I know *I* didn't cheat, but that only means I honestly remember not using any unacknowledged source. Could even I, in this case, ever know whether or not I really was "original"? I, who knew and loved Le Corbusier's book since my teens, and who was myself surprised to notice I quoted it more often than any other source in the essays I collected in my *Historical Present.* I know I was innocent of knowledge (= ignorant) of any prior statement of the Magritte relation.

Yet I also know now that there was a study contemporary with Foucault's original French edition, an interesting little monograph published in 1973, which, reporting remarks by Patrick Waldberg that I have failed to trace, relays that "Patrick [*sic*] Hughes" suggested the connection: André Blavier, *Ceçi n'est pas une pipe: Contribution furtive [!] à l'étude d'un tableau de René Magritte,* published by the Fondation René Magritte (*Temps mêlé,* Opinions et Documents, no. 1; Verviers [Belgium], 1973). Now, is this "Patrick Hughes" a slip-of-the-pen, and, if so, was it Hughes or Waldberg? Blavier knew of my original *Artforum* article by the later 1970s, when he kindly sent me a copy of his monograph inscribed with a request for a copy of my publication.

While we're at this, allow me to add a bit more on the Corbusian pipe. In the Romantic proto-modernity of the mid-nineteenth century the motif of the smoking pipe occurs more than once as a metonymic figure, an inanimate object but one so personally affiliated as to connote the artist's musing intimacy with himself: thus from Courbet's sultry *Self-Portrait with Pipe* and, remarkably, the opening line of the poem (xxi) "La Pipe," in Baudelaire's *Fleurs du mal* (1857ff.)—"Je suis la pipe d'un auteur"—to van Gogh's allegorical self-portrait with his own pipe and tobacco pouch on his so humble chair. While it was against the grain of such craftlike personalism that the rigorously anonymous Purist *objet-type* would be proposed, the once sleekly new look of such urbane, briar but (nonfolkishly) "uncarved" and rather manufactured pipes already during the time of Baudelaire and Courbet ought not to be neglected.

In *The Evolution of Designs: Biological Analogy in Architecture and the Applied Arts* (1979) Philip Steadman mentions Samuel Butler's novel *Erewhon* (1872), in which the pipe exemplifies " 'vestigial organs' in artefacts," plus the pipe as a motif in William Morris's *News from Nowhere* (1891)—there, however, as an object occasioning carved, individualizing ornamentation. As to the later, definitive modernism of design: Reyner Banham discusses Le Corbusier's closing image, taken as a specifically English briar pipe, as epitomizing the favored *objet-type,* or *objet-standard,* in his classic *Theory and Design in the First Machine Age* (1960). And, apropos of the pipe conceived in this ultramodern way: in Paul Valéry's dialogue *Idée fixe* (1932), written in 1931, the man of letters says to his physician friend, "Plato's pipe . . . [*sic*] but it would have been made in Tanagra, or Myrina" (trans. D. Paul, 1965).

Frankly, I have always found it curious that another suggestion of mine in the same Magritte essay has *not* been appropriated, at least not to my knowledge, in the art literature on Magritte, namely, that the painter's footnotelike legend "This Is Not a Pipe" itself finds remarkable adumbration in the very title of a story by Diderot: "This Is Not a Story." And now Francesco Pellizzi points out in a 1986 lecture at the Cooper Union, "Adventures of the Symbol: Magic for the Sake of Art" (published as a booklet), that, according to C. Christov-Bakargiev, an artist by the name of Alighiero "once saw an oriental . . . rug with the image of a flowery wood and with the Arabic inscription 'This is not a carpet, it is a garden.' "

Finally (?), a large bronze sculpture by Saint Clair Cemin, hilariously brontosaurian in form yet stubbornly entitled *This Is a Pipe* (!), not long ago appeared, sitting in the quadrangle right outside my office at Hofstra University.

20

SNAKE-OIL FROM
JULIO SCHNITZEL (A PARODY)

Halt' den Schnabel!

Hi, fellas. Suffer today? The best part is when it just starts to hurt, just enough to seem like, you know, no pain, no gain. Then it's an OK feeling and you can get good art. Really putting your all in it makes your butt sweat, so suffer right till your butt starts to sweat and you know you'll do fine.

Up,

down,

all around;

the hurt, the smart, the self-satisfaction (are the gradations of different plays. You could say they are the same one thing, which can be one huge fake-out).

It's your head that does it:

whatever they tell you, it has to be big;

you have to keep it pumped up
to use for feedback,

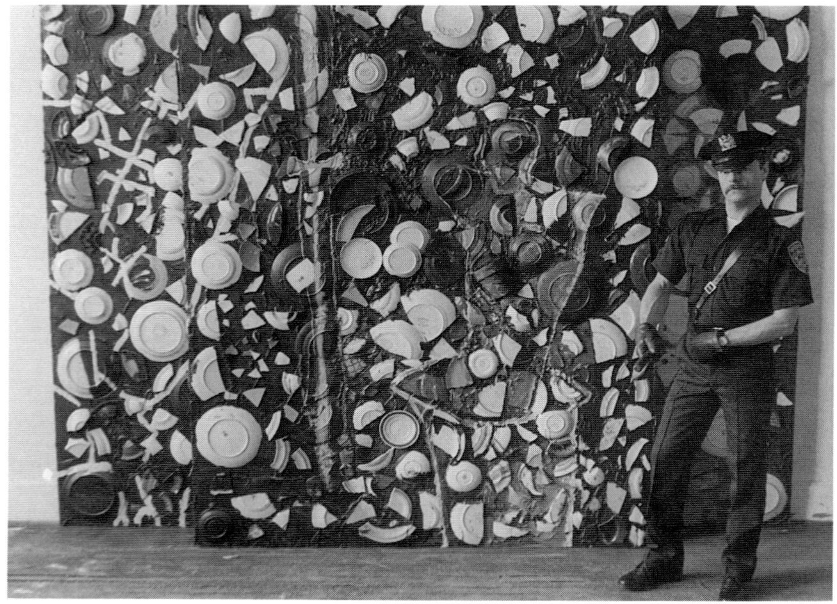

Fig. 28   Mike Bidlo, *The Original Schnabel Simulacrum*, 1983, as installed at the Institute for Art and Urban Resources (now Institute for Contemporary Art), P. S. 1 Museum, Long Island City, New York.

like a chimp in a lab or one of those rubber blood-pressure gizmos, or a CB radio when you hear yourself making yourself yell too loud to get cold feet.

Fans are funny.

Take it from me, getting your face on throwaway mags is nothing, what with their ceaseless upsets and all the sociopolitical orbits spinning at once like crazy tops.

Don't play for the fans; play for yourself, number one:
anyway, just take their minds off stocks and give them something else to bet on and they'll beg for more.

Not just art, but life, the big game, has penalties for walking, so just picture what it means to go running backwards or something. You will have to learn that even old pals won't see their way to give you the time of day.

But the stats, the bottom line, this is the true artist's comforter to blanket
his sprained soul snugly
in the lonesome casket

that is the void caused by the gushing up and flushing over of the artist's
relation to time.

As I myself once said to an old star, "Since a convergence is the same as a
start, and style is as quantitative as any symbol (watch how I don't stop
[dribbling, I mean]), the best I can do for you, mister, is to look you over
and take some pointers for the good of all concerned."

There is truly a mistake about the causes of why the plays an artist makes
are a lot of times like ones by him or her or somebody else. One thing is,
if you don't read too much, chances are you can't be doing "quotes," as
they call it; and if you do make a mental note of everything, really
everything they say, you couldn't even put "quote" marks in if you wanted
to. Some people, such as pacifists, hate to make literary allusions, no less
quotings, whilst others hold all members of art alike, going just by feel;
others still have the total record for one whole collage that they can recut
up and reput together again to give a little kick to any normal love affair
with art. Having a similarity go for an interpretation also diminishes
because it just might be only a sprain in your other leg from a different day
altogether. As Buff Buffon said, way back when, having style proves your
very own type of gumption. Try old plays over for yourself: it can be a
help, a trick, a total joke, maybe even a total gas. But remember, get it to
look like it just started opening up those glands. So many American guys
keep ignoring the obvious depth of Yves Klein that wipes me out. With
similar plays you can keep up the game of life over and over, though.

My own supposedly expressionistic plays

really are that way but not for why people think; no way. See, you have to
be so big that it's like the whole world feeling inside just your own gut;
like, if you could be the king then everybody could have you being sad for
him or her and not just for your selfish sad self.

This feeling is true greatness in all art; it kinda tingles too. What is truly
modern and way up there forever is not what you think. It is not about
getting some canvas stretched neat so the weave is as squared-away as the

seams of nylons on a correct female person's legs, or with boiling wax to make your every move look kind of sucked, smack-tight, against a blackboard. No, being modern has to seem like true heartburn and no less. You'll know when this seems to happen: all of a sudden it will look fine.

Never do I myself tire of playing reruns in my own mind of all I have already done at my age.

This is like watching a cute hamster, or getting slobbered with wet affection from another pet source.

It's funny that I can't tell where I am unless thenceforth I shall have removed myself elsewhere.

Such is what the time does tell, heedless of all cause and effect. Upside down or right-side up has little bearing, being fine inside or out, either way. Frankly the bigger I get the more there is sweet to go around, at least once I can be sure I have enough to be really big. I will be big enough to take the entire world's temperature at one time, front or back.

I have a wife and kids.

and a beach house and a bunch of lookers for buddies:

what more could any stud want?

Just plain everybody is talking about me; in fact, I hear America singing, not to mention Europe, and of me they sing. Yet do not read me wrong, since oftentimes they will all talk about everyone.

They do buy it too, all of it,

like there's no tomorrow
and comparisons are odious,

which just goes to make me bigger; and the bigger I get the happier they are too, just to see me seem so happy, making the game so great. I get to feel like some gas balloon, bigger and happier all the time. I think I like this feeling, yes, I am practically sure.

Already I can do anything I want.
If I wanted, right now, I could set up New Wave laundromats everyplace, or open an exclusive restaurant serving huge steaks, all ultra-rare, with unlimited champagne and only famous people and quiet agents, sitting nude, maybe, on red velvet banquettes. Who knows what I can do, who

can say. My freedom is yours, guys; look, it has no limits. I am famous, famous, famous, real big-league, blue-chip. This I feel makes me feel wanted. Nowadays I almost have to grit my teeth to break a plate, it's so gross, even though I used to break them all the time from nerves, overworked in a little hashhouse, nowheres. But even I have to worry because it might get harder and harder to keep myself psyched up so I can spread my chest, I mean my wings. I fear that some day I, even me, shall no longer be able to suffer even mild heartburn on behalf of the whole huge world, being perhaps too dead to care.

That's enough, though. No more, thanks. I feel a little stuffed already. But when I am really big, do not thank me, boys, I mean me personally. Just think about what matters in the great big game that will probably keep going on even after the likes of me:

just remember my plays,

my great hysterical plays,

and most of all my big gorgeous scores.

21

PETER HALLEY ON THE NATURE, BLAH-BLAH-BLAH, OF ABSTRACT ART

Fifty years before, in 1937, Meyer Schapiro, now professor emeritus of art history at Columbia University, had published his classic essay on "The Nature of Abstract Art" in the *Marxist Quarterly*. His Columbia colleagues celebrated the anniversary with talks by four artists. Peter Halley, who had exhibited his boxy, spackled, Day-Glo paintings for some time already without much hint of maturation, presumably started things off because the powers that be decided he was the season's hottest item.

Before introducing him, Professor Rainer Crone announced that the series also marked the launching of an "archive" of contemporary artists' observations. These are to be transcribed for posterity, said Crone, so that scholars will not "fall victim again to dry, academic explanations"—henceforth they will get their wisdom straight from the horse's mouth, "not mediated through written articles and the like." His words seemed strange coming from an art historian, especially with so much marketing effectively bypassing critical discussion nowadays. Not that the several dealers present were about to object.

Halley began by paying respects of sorts to Schapiro's essay—that is, borrowing whatever he could use as a lead-in to a slide show of his own work. For him to praise Schapiro's "predictive and prescriptive powers," however, was wildly inappropriate: "The Nature of Abstract Art" is almost entirely retrospective and historical; only toward the very end does Schapiro touch—and then with care and reserve—on the art of the day. Halley said he liked the "anti-formalism" of the essay, which is fine, except that the complexity of the formalist debate (going back to the early twentieth-century Slavs) obviously escaped him. Overall, the artist took advantage of Schapiro's openmindedness, as if finding doors left open by mistake.

Addressing his own work, Halley betrayed a breathtakingly naive grasp of representation. He simply *stated* several times that one of his most characteristic motifs, a centered rectangle cut into by vertical bands, *is* a cell (the penal variety)—even though it could also read as, say, an egg slicer, a drain, the symbolic attribute of Saint Lawrence, a bit of floor planking, or an air mattress. (Perhaps this is why the archive is necessary.) When an atypical blank white "cell" appeared on the screen, Halley assured us it was a "windowless cell"—why not the old white swan eating marshmallows in the snow? Another work was called *Freudian Painting,* because it has one larger and one smaller square: Get it? That it obviously matters little to Halley whether his works are representational or abstract made his enterprise seem something remarkably akin to Roger Price's "droodle" cartoons of the 1950s.

Referring to his slides, Halley admitted in deference to the audience that he himself would "probably find it hard to decipher what this is about" if he didn't, as the artist, happen to know. Near the conclusion of the lecture, he showed a solid black panel: This, ladies and gentlemen, was the first Halley in five years without a cell; it contains only an "empty or dead conduit." (At least he didn't say it showed mystic "thought-forms.") As to the iconography of his pictures in general, Halley commented, "It takes me a while to come up with all that after I have painted them."

Halley is one of too many youngish artists whose sense of art reflects a total of about two influences: Marcel Duchamp and Andy Warhol. I have said before that this is like taking Victor Borge for the world's most important pianist. I often wonder how some individuals find their way into art in the first place—unless, like new irreligious nuns, they now know a good thing when they see it. Actually, there once was a time when even Halley felt he was getting nowhere. Then it suddenly came to him: His work needed "ideas put in." That is a direct quotation. One had to wince, there in Meyer Schapiro's old lecture hall.

Halley apparently believes that anything blatantly geometrical counts as abstract form, and that the claims made for transcendental abstraction—art purporting to convey a nonvisual reality—are nothing but delusion and/or intellectual hype. Mondrian he dismissed ("utopian," of course). The modern artists who passed muster with Halley did so precisely because he discovered some personal use for them at last. The same with architects: No problem quoting Louis Kahn's "A brick is a brick," yet one would have expected Halley to come up with a little dialectical rub in applying Kahn's doctrine of "using materials for their own sake" to his own purpose of "using simulated materials in a real way" (instead of just talking fast).

"I like to refer to Jasper Johns," Halley said, singling out that artist's creation of "literal space." As for himself, he announced, "The way I make space must remain diverse"—this from an artist whose output is about as diverse as so many factory-baked doughnuts. Susan Rothenberg got dragged in, for no discernible reason other than her implied "success."

Barnett Newman figured more importantly: The backdrop of his work enabled Halley "to create the signs of a transcendental situation and then deny it" (thanks for being my straight man!). If Halley's painting is as refreshingly untranscendental as he hopes it is, I wonder what compels him to misappropriate as many transcendental moderns as he can. He even likened his "amphetamine" colors (as he was amused to call them) to the "technological glow" he sees in Mark Rothko.

Why be so hard on Halley for playing so fast and loose with history and criticism? For one thing, his lecture was offered in displacement of both. The worldly interests who set it up—and lapped it up—think of criticism as either marketing or party-pooping intellectualism. History? Merely a servant to enshrine whatever those with money eventually want to dump at a high price, or in new wings of museums they control.

Perhaps worse, Halley's freewheeling, "artist's" grasp of history is a little too convenient. For instance, it is fair to note that one standard pitch makes Halley out to be an emerging Frank Stella. What he neglects to mention is that his paintings owe more to a strain of queasily abstract, paint-smothered reliefs in the shape of little cottages—they're actually more arresting than this sounds—done by Ralph Humphrey about a decade ago. No need to get into a dither over the relative importance of "influences"; the point is that Halley not only takes what he wants, he smokescreens out the rest.

His two-fisted literalism may be nothing more than Halley's way of coping with the absurdity of acting totally cool and ever so "hot" simultaneously. He seems to think that embodying the synthesis of these two goals makes him Mr. Moment; I tend to think it makes him part of the problem.

Values mean nothing to Halley, despite some initially interesting published writings in which he represented his theme as a statement against social oppression—prison cells, conduits that restrict communication, and so on. In person, he offered his cell motif as cute rather than urgent. One must assume he has never known anyone who has been jailed unjustly. Or that in his view the culprit is bad taste.

When Halley looks beyond his art, all he sees is style, "attitude" (almost as if people sleep on sidewalk gratings because they are "into" air-baths). Halley said he tried painting on a surface of fake-brick siding, but the result was too "European," so he decided to go "suburban industrial." Fixated as it is on a vocabulary of simplistic and unarticulated "signs," his work cannot describe our society, let alone criticize it.

For many in the artworld, including artists, social power has become the predominant obsession, overshadowing aesthetic concerns. No wonder the likes of Halley have found a ready market, contrived with mirrors by greedy collector-investors and art pimps. But there is more authentic culture in a roadhouse jukebox than in the lives of many of these art fans, and their latest pet diversions won't help anybody.

Halley was the seasonal mouthpiece, and his output, flagship wares, of the cynical big-bucks art business. His principal colleagues are: Ashley Bickerton, who in a recent press release opined that "watching two dogs fuck must be the purest form of structuralism"; Jeff Koons, the former commodities broker famous for mercury-filled basketballs suspended in aquariums and other "sports" pieces; and Meyer Vaisman, whose once-witty photographic pseudopaintings have lately come stacked and nailed together, lumbering under the weight of their whoopee-room carpentry.

I sometimes wonder if all this isn't *husband's art:* it must have been a drag just writing checks for hoity-toity items; besides, placing a bet on an artist can't be too hard if wives have been doing it—you simply get on the phone and drum something up!

According to Halley, a "world of idealism" has somehow resulted in the existence of "art commodities." Gee, then what about selling the stuff for time-and-materials? Ileana Sonnabend, who as a dealer used to maintain a standard of intellectual dignity, but who gave Halley & Co. their big breakthrough show, said in *New York* magazine that if these artists are manipulators, well, they're only children of their time.

Making art that calls attention to its commodity status was not, of course, Halley's single-handed innovation. Was his contribution to insinuate an extra axiom: the dumber the better? Against all that Meyer Schapiro has ever taught, this new prophet denied that it is still possible to believe art can transcend alienation (although, in a weak moment, he did allow that "only the artist can hope to bring some understanding to the maze of mediations" that traps each of us). To care about artistic significance and true value is, by his lights, to waste time that could be better used, before the earth blows up, becoming rich and famous. In the clear vision of Halleyism, all the careful complexity of Meyer Schapiro's thought on art—which, by the way, has always advanced a politics of social democracy—turns out to be more of that ol' moonin' utopian humanism.

Twenty-four years previously, I couldn't help remembering, I used to sit in that same lecture hall, in almost the same seat, listening to Meyer Schapiro himself unfold the "spectacle" (his word, not yet trademarked) of Impressionism. We mostly pre-med–type scholar-jocks sat in the back, the pedants scrambled for the front seats, and in the middle were the downtown art folk with airs who kept asking things like how to spell "Helmholtz." What a luxury that was, then and in retrospect. Being young, we no doubt had an "attitude problem" too; but how proud we were that Professor Schapiro was one of us. Halley, the smug Yalie, the complacent young art tycoon, would have had a much harder time in those days, either from the podium or from the back of the hall.

22

MIKE BIDLO AS PABLO

Mike Bidlo went and redid some seven dozen, no less, of Picasso's paintings of women (1901–71), hand-painted in oil on linen, actual size, almost all in 1986 and 1987. Nobody would deny the sheer doggedness of doing that, or the cleverness of Bidlo's rendering blue-chip, gilt-edge art accessible again. But whereas merely serviceable paint jobs would have sufficed for stunt or gimmick purposes, Bidlo's "Picassos" are painted with a perceptible devotion to their admired prototypes—not that this artist, who has publicly played Pollock and Warhol as well as redone their paintings, has ever shied away from "performance." The affirmative, enthusiastic aspect of Bidlo's paintings specifically precludes satire, unlike the work of some simulationists who have set their caps against the so-called utopianism of modern art in its early and classic phases. And what could be more classic than Picasso?

In the eighteenth century Bidlo would have been called a *virtuoso,* a technically astute renderer but also a sympathetic admirer of worthy art. The art historian Henri Focillon makes a nice distinction between the imitator and the virtuoso: "With a mere imitator a reliance on memory narrows the field of metamorphoses; with a virtuoso such a reliance does

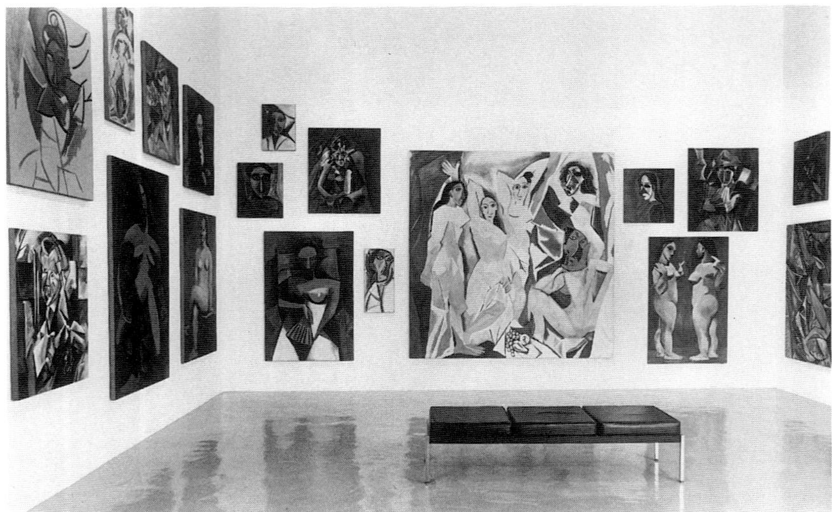

Fig. 29   Mike Bidlo, "Picasso's Women," installation of paintings at Leo Castelli
Gallery, New York, 1988.

not necessarily diminish their intensity in any way."[1] Without getting into
pedantic detail on the concept of the virtuoso, one can say that in its
modern sense it is perhaps as equivocal as Bidlo's "original copies."
According to the early modern Russian critic Anatoly Lunacharsky, the
virtuoso is so much a performer that he is practically part of his
(presumably musical) instrument.[2] Focillon himself says, "the virtuoso is
above all else a kind of tight-rope walker. So absorbed is he in his mastery
over equilibrium that his daring is but the endless repetition of the same
step—a step whose rhythm he is in constant danger of losing as he slides
back and forth along his thin, taut wire."[3]

---

1. Henri Focillon, *The Life of Forms in Art,* trans. Charles Beecher Hogan, George Kubler, and
S. L. Faison, Jr. (New York, 1948), 48. It would be interesting to see how those who eschew
connoisseurship entirely would deal with any one painting by Bidlo.

2. Lunacharsky writes, with some hostility: "Outstanding virtuosi are often men of average
intellect, but a virtuoso is, primarily, an impressionable individual who easily falls under
hypnotic-like influence, one who may be likened to a magnificent instrument, and naturally,
you would never demand that a wonderful violin have an intellect as well. . . . When a true
virtuoso or a sharp-sighted artist tries to create something original, i.e., something fantastic, for
instance, something that has not been dictated by Nature or [N.B.] a great master, the result
will inevitably be shabby." Anatoly Lunacharsky, "Heroes of Action in Meditation" (1909), in
his *On Literature and Art,* ed. A. Lebedev, English ed. (Moscow, 1965), 268–69.

3. Focillon, *Life,* 37.

The "real" Picasso seems to have been quite conscious of himself as a virtuoso. In remarks recorded by Hélène Parmelin, to which Bidlo has called my attention, Picasso throws a typical curve on the subject. "What does it mean," he asks, "for a painter to paint in the style of So-and-So or actually to imitate someone else? What's wrong with that? On the contrary, it's a good idea. You should constantly try to paint like someone else." And here the ball begins to curve: "But the thing is, you can't! You would like to. You try. But it turns out to be a botch." And, finally, the strike: "And it's at the very moment you make a botch of it that you're yourself."[4]

Bidlo may have his virtuoso, Paganini aspect, as a performer of passionate set pieces; it is significant, however, that as a simulationist artist he is not inclined to do repeat performances of any *paintings,* whereas he has shown no hesitation to produce several versions of readymade objects by Duchamp and Man Ray. This distinction suggests that Bidlo has some modicum of self-investment in execution when he paints, even if it is less apparent than in his early public "actions" *as* other artists. He always works from color reproductions, usually by projecting a slide or an opaque plate; sometimes, especially with a smaller piece, he will proceed simply by squaring a color plate and copying it freehand. I have seen him postpone direct scrutiny of an accessible painting by Picasso until his own sense of the image was sufficiently achieved, much as a musical performer, even a virtuoso, might avoid listening to a recording of a composer's own rendition until a certain point.

The "Picasso" series began before the fact with a single major Picasso redo, the full-scale *Les Demoiselles d'Avignon* (1983), followed by the even more formidable *Guernica,* painted in Los Angeles in 1984. It was during his preparation of the canvas of the *Demoiselles* at P.S. 1—he had a studio there but was preparing a couple of unwieldy canvases in the auditorium—that I happened to meet Bidlo; in fact, I wound up giving what was to be the *Demoiselles* a coat of gesso while he worked on another canvas as we talked.[5]

---

4. Trans. in Dore Ashton, ed., *Picasso on Art: A Selection of Views,* The Documents of Twentieth-Century Art (Harmondsworth, 1977), 53.

5. Soon after, I made a painting, otherwise "original" I guess, following Bidlo's improvised instructions over the telephone. This and related tales are told in my "China Trade: Discourse with W. D. Barnes, *Arts Magazine,* September 1986, 74–77. The name "Barnes," a pseudonym for myself, was borrowed from a character in "Dallas," a friend of the founding patriarch who, although sometimes mentioned, has to my knowledge appeared only in a special ur-"Dallas" episode. Otherwise, I see that the notorious aesthete John Addington Symonds was pleased, as a young man, to discover friends referring to him by the code name "Barnes" (*Memoirs,* ed. Phyllis Grosskurth [Chicago, 1986], 119).

Bidlo appreciated my long-standing interest in Duchamp, but Duchamp, for once, was not all there was to it. It was Bidlo's notion of modern-historical resuscitation that was especially appealing then, as few younger artists seemed to understand much about earlier art, at least beyond the work of Duchamp and Warhol.[6]

Bidlo's actual making of his "Jackson Pollock" paintings (much more than, say, his act of pissing into a mock-up of Peggy Guggenheim's fireplace) ought to have been a clue to something this painter's huge new array of "Picasso's Women" now makes more obvious. Thanks to its honest middle-class respect for the modern "classics," Bidlo's art offers, in the context of our prematurely fin-de-siècle culture, the gratification of the second chance—a special, matured pleasure of the second time around. The immediate point is not the naive idea that Picasso's art is no longer possible to *do,* but that, on the contrary, it has attained the leather-bound standing of earlier classics, including those of the Renaissance and even of antiquity itself. No need to dwell on the potential conservatism in that—as when some, early in our century, clung to Rembrandt as they tried to fend off modernity, including Picasso's. No, the vital thing is not only that there *was* a golden age of modern culture, but that it now has the dignity once reserved for much older tradition, just as the study of "English," i.e., vernacular literature, first crowded into *literae humaniores* and then displaced Greek and Latin, with all reference to antiquity per se moved down to the basement. Bidlo's "Picassos" may seem to play on the idea of the end of modernism, but since he drives us back to Picasso, the hero of our great beginning, who knows . . . ? In any case, in Bidlo's hands Picasso is by no means just another big "star" artist, or, worse, artist "star."

By taking on Picasso's entire work, without regard to chronology or development, Bidlo enters a long, ongoing discourse about this particular master's multiplicity of styles.[7] Some people wonder if Bidlo has a style of his own. But, in 1939, Robert Goldwater asked the same question about Picasso: "In what sense are his various periods and their different styles the work of one man; in other words, does Picasso have an artistic personality

---

6. No wonder Bidlo became my idea of what was then called an "appropriation" artist. His work helped to precipitate my thinking, even as he began to get pigeonholed as the guy who had "done" Jackson Pollock.

7. This project followed Bidlo's extensive series of still lifes after that stylistic Johnny-one-note, Giorgio Morandi. See my "Tendering Rendering: 9 Notes Apropos of Still Lifes by Giorgio Morandi by Mike Bidlo," *Arts Magazine,* March 1986, 81–83.

as this has been understood by the connoisseur of older art; can we see the same hand throughout his *oeuvre?*" In that same review Goldwater observed, "Like all modern artists, Picasso is heir to . . . such a wide acquaintance with historical styles that direct, unallusive statement has become peculiarly difficult."[8] Take note, all who have trouble with Bidlo's style, such as it is—who find it perhaps all too quotationally "direct" and "unallusive" in its own self-effacing, altogether eclectic statement! According to Goldwater, it is precisely because of Picasso's unique eclecticism that "another artist cannot begin at the point at which Picasso ends."[9] Well, now, out of left field, comes one who has instead done over Picasso—just the kind of gesture that literary Borgesians have thus far only promised to realize.

Because it operates at two removes from nature as well as by virtue of its more simply "conceptual" aspect, all of Bidlo's work can be called "abstract," which puts a funny kind of body English on "abstract art." Somewhere along in his "Picasso" project Bidlo actually made the following remark to me: "Everything is mine except the form." In one obvious sense this means that the form is borrowed from somebody else, in this case Picasso; yet in a subtler sense it may mean that whereas Picasso painted the form of a woman, what Bidlo rather unassumingly represents is the form of that form (which then happens to resemble or not resemble that woman).[10] Bidlo runs the risk of having whatever is "his" overlooked except insofar as it might be less eloquent than Picasso—and, of course, except for his whole *idea,* which very insistently takes on the form of actual artwork.

---

8. Robert J. Goldwater, "Picasso: Forty Years of His Art," *Art in America,* XXVIII/1, January 1940, 43–44.

9. Ibid., 44.

10. What could correspond more closely to Kandinsky's definitive conception of abstraction—i.e., when, upon seeing one of his paintings leaning sideways against the studio wall, he felt able at last to "overlook the subject"? See Wassily Kandinsky, "Reminiscences" (1913), trans. in *Modern Artists on Art: Ten Unabridged Essays,* ed. Robert L. Herbert (New York, 1964), 32. Cf. John Dewey, *Art as Experience* (New York, 1934), 249: "It is a familiar fact that colors of a landscape become more vivid when seen with the head upside down. The change of physical position does not cause a new psychical element to be injected, but it does signify that a somewhat different organism is acting, and a difference in the cause is bound to make a difference in the effect." Kandinsky's epiphany of abstract painting occurred upon seeing one of his own works under an unusual and unexpected aspect; Bidlo, who has already redone several Kandinsky abstractions, is by definition "a somewhat different organism" from the master. More like the situation Dewey mentions is the practice of certain artists—Richard Artschwager and Malcolm Morley for two—who paint at least some of their (own) paintings upside down.

NEW ABSTRACT PAINTING

The most difficult selection of writings for me to make in the present moment has been this, on abstract painting. As Eliot reflects in "To Criticize the Critic" (1961), this must be partly due to the accidents of commissions. After all, some, only, of the critic's work gets written down—especially that of the critic who teaches—and some, only, of that sees publication.

Some may be disappointed that I do not attempt to expound a theory of painting, possibly based on my "Iconicity" essays, of 1977–79 (reprinted in *Historical Present* [1984]): at least they may find some useful materials here as well as in the "Foundations" section. Obliged to speculate on my sense of abstraction as open-ended, I sometimes turn for analogy to chess or sport. Art people do tend to fixate morbidly on "endgame" situations: cults of the "end" or the "last," however, seem to exercise a make-do, spoilsport version of the wish to stand without progenitors.

Those who love chess no more want or expect to kill off the larger game than they want or expect their own games to "reduce," like a sauce, to some *theory* of chess. Painting, abstract painting, is the only art I attempt to practice myself, needless to say "at the end," in any given moment, "of history" (!). So I tend not to see why modernity in painting and the other plastic arts shouldn't be so endlessly fecund, not simply so unendable (as if that were tedious), as chess or baseball; of course, like Mets' baseball, this may also mean it does have its long-haul ups and downs.

I discuss the different painters' work ad hoc, in different ways, though affinities are surely evident. Presented together, the various essays may at least suggest the lively circuitry of a *field* of potential interconnections and distinctions, instead of some new fake myth about where art is supposed to be "going."

23

PIECING THINGS TOGETHER:
A CONVERSATION WITH
SEAN SCULLY

Masheck: Do you think of your big relief paintings in terms of architectural
  planes?

Scully: When I first came to New York I did a lot of construction work,
  wall building. There's something extremely beautiful in making divisions
  in walls and covering up the wooden frame and leaving little windows
  and things. The most difficult, tricky part is the fastidious sheet-rocking,
  the taping and finishing. Of course, privately I was trying to make it fun
  for myself, so I was composing; after all, I'm an artist.

Masheck: Because this work simply had to be obediently executed?

Scully: Yes, although I'm not sure anybody ever does that. I think we all
  have a sense of beauty. If you're working on a construction site, you can
  see beautiful things all the time. They're throwaway; nevertheless, the
  people working there are satisfying the need for visual interest, or
  harmony, whatever, unconsciously. The only difference is, I was doing it
  consciously. Then I did tryouts for wall paintings, which led to these. It
  was pivotal that, in 1979, Peter Nadin had an experimental "space," and
  he asked me to do an installation piece. . . .

That "environment of painting" which I did, really out of friendship, has rewarded me in all these different pieces. . . . [Part of it] was an enormous brown painting that looked like a big bear in the corner! It was brown, black on dark brown, with the tape left in, embedded in it. The stripes, about two inches wide, were all horizontal. The painting went through some very interesting stages, because I used black masking tape. When the white wall was taped up it was wild! It was so optical, you couldn't even see there was a corner there. In a way, I'm sorry I didn't leave it in that state, it was so exciting. It's just that, at the time, my interest wasn't in that kind of extreme opticality.

Masheck: Was there an idea that the wall was already vertically articulated, by the "corners" of the room, so you should articulate it horizontally?

Fig. 30   Sean Scully, *Dark Face*, 1986, oil on canvas, 112 x 93 inches.

Scully: Yes, that's it, and this refers back to my early grid paintings. Thinking of a dynamic between verticals and horizontals is something that I've been interested in all along.

Masheck: Maybe there was also a negation of decorativeness: if you were using striped wallpaper, you'd never "hang" it horizontally.

Scully: No, you're not going to go against what's there, because that would make it perverse and disturbing—which is what I'm really interested in!

Masheck: The recent paintings, which are reliefs but which comprise only smoothly stretched, rectangular canvases, strike me as somewhat scenographic, like the ironically "light" concreteness of stage sets—at least when seen this way, in the studio, "off-duty." And they put me in mind of tremendous blowups, as if from parts of the earlier, utterly intimistic, narrow-stripe paintings. A texture of intimacy blown up as big as a billboard: this, then, reminds me of Léger, who loved the modern close-up.

Scully: This is to me a crucial issue in art. When you have something that's really sustaining as an artwork, it's big and small, or powerful and delicate, both at the same time. These paintings are about massiveness, but they also have to become extremely intimate. If a painting is just massive, then it's just a big painting.

Masheck: Imagine Léger's close-up on the screen of a drive-in movie, huge, but sort of evanescent. With your paintings, where one plane projects in front of another and a single band "folds" from one plane to the other, I was at first skeptical about your simply painting the exposed thickness the same color. Now I think of that as "projectional." Suppose you were projecting onto an irregular surface . . .

Scully: Precisely. That brings out a really interesting tension that's both physical and willful. It could even be stated as a kind of futile attempt to repair something, or to put right something which is split apart, made in a fractured way. The paint can be used to make it either more holistic or more fractured.

Masheck: When it's made "all right," it may even be better than if it hadn't been "broken" to begin with.

Scully: Sure, because it's not just perfect.

Masheck: It's got something *in* it then.

Scully: Yes. After a while I wanted to make paintings that were, somehow, comfortable in the world as things. If they get a little banged up, it doesn't matter that much; whereas, the other paintings I was making were based on perfection.

Masheck: Although they have a very constructional aspect, even a certain architectural bravura, these reliefs are "non-load-bearing." They are not trading in material masses.

Scully: I've always been concerned with something Johns did, and something that Beckett has done in some of his plays: the artist introduces a kind of jolt; what he says is "O.K., this is fiction and this isn't fiction." So the fiction is broken all the time. With Johns, it's broken in a seam, or with two balls stuck between two canvases. That is the reason I do it. It has nothing to do with the paintings as being overtly physical; I think, in fact, they're quite discreet, physically. I could make the projections much larger, getting into something else, like Stella; but I'm only doing this to break the fiction of the paintings. So they can be seen as similar to Romantic paintings, though they're not hopelessly Romantic—in the sense that I might have no critical or ironic ability to understand how ridiculous that is.

Masheck: Discontinuity is a principal thing.

Scully: It's the principal reason for the composition in the painting and the whole thing about what kind of impositions to give it, what degree of agreement or disagreement.

Masheck: You accepted my "scenographic" reading, but I'm sure neither one of us was thinking of the old theater of illusory "reality." If anything, the theater in question is always saving us from that, even by being "anti-theatrical." I know you love Beckett; but I'm also thinking about Brecht, and the whole idea of making things rough, and—despite a risk of affected roughness—of rougher as truer.

Scully: I don't ever paint in a way that would make for an uncomfortable relationship with the surface I'm working on. These paintings have to feel "true," physically, when I make them. It's really important that I don't have to slow down the brushstroke to take care of a certain part. In other words, if I can paint the whole thing like this, then this is the right way to paint it; and if I can't, it's the wrong way to paint it. It's a bit like having a thesis about something, and if it doesn't cover what you want it to cover, then that disproves the thesis. I try and paint the paintings in a way that's very direct. I paint them with big Italian house-painters' brushes, and they're done straightforwardly. To me, if you spend a lot of time getting a surface flat, making it perfect, that is aestheticizing, because that is not really the way the paint goes down. . . .

Masheck: You and I may have had rather parallel experiences teaching at Harvard, if in two different decades. Frankly, while I otherwise enjoyed it greatly, I noticed a pervasive Yankee, nuts-and-bolts materialism. Just recently I read an essay by John Updike on Emerson, who was *so* Harvard. Don't get me wrong: in my own way, I have my way of dealing with Emerson; let's just say that his "Transcendentalism" isn't very transcendental. Anyway, Updike points up Emerson the highbrow huckster who got a couple of bucks a head for packing them in to tell 'em, "You can do it, folks." It seems that idealism is expected to turn a profit. Got any thoughts on this?

Scully: Quite a lot. American art has a disarming way of being visually immediate. By that I mean, it's obvious that people come up with a product that's extremely organized, and that's charming, in a sense. It's as if a lot of problems—things that would stop a painter from being presented in a certain way—are emptied out of the painting: "Let's empty out all this stuff that obstructs the making of our product." Then, of course, one is left with a horrendous blandness. You've only got to look at some recent American painters compared to Anselm Kiefer. It's like "What I need in the painting surface is something material."

Masheck: You want material? Just look it up in the *Yellow Pages!*

Scully: Visual expediency does have its advantages, inasmuch as it makes for a tremendous impact on the viewer, and its effect is very fast. But the flip side is that the artwork may suffer from a lack of dimensionality, so that it can only be read very simply and gets exhausted very quickly. Philosophical complexity is drained out. What you have is a product, but the product has a blandness about it that makes it nonsustaining. . . .

Masheck: I'm imagining you there, at Harvard against the, well, backdrop, of the official Color Field Painting.

Scully: That was really funny. I'd make paintings that had color in them all right, but with all these *overlapping lines!* I was reconsidering illusionistic space. . . . I knew about American Color Field Painting. I'd studied it very well. But I also knew about the complexity of Abstract Expressionism, which preceded it. And I knew that Color Field Painting was a way of making a product, blanding out what had been done by the heroic painters before. But then I also knew about Cubism. And then, of course, I was going back *way* too far, since if you go back as far as the crossed lances in Uccello you must just be being ridiculous!

Masheck: I don't think any contemporary artist should have to rationalize an interest in Cubism. I don't want to get into the problem of period style, but it's certainly arguable that Cubism is the "style" of the twentieth century, even of the way we think, including the way things are interruptive. I would even say that to do art without understanding Cubism has become like trying to study science without calculus, meaning then you can only do "baby" science.

Scully: Everything does happen at once.

Masheck: That's not unknowable, either.

Scully: I was going down Fifth Avenue one day. I'm sitting in the car, and it's like, somebody's doing one thing in one car, somebody is doing something else in another car; there're people in office buildings doing all kinds of things. Everything is happening at once. And I thought— Yes, that's what is happening in my paintings: I'm taking this thing and this thing, and making them go like this, and maybe putting something else in as well.

Masheck: I believe that the first person really to grasp this may have been Georg Simmel, the founder of modern sociology, whose thought helps with understanding Cubism as essentially urban and concerned with "abstract" quantification. Look, in the country, everybody does pretty much the same thing at any given time: farmers will milk cows at the same hour, and fix fences in the same week of the year. . . . But in your work you can start anywhere, even in the middle.

Scully: I can start anywhere I want. I can start at the end, in the middle, at the top, at the bottom: I don't care. Yes, I absolutely don't care. Now this may go back to the fact that for so long I made allover paintings, which don't have a middle, really, or a top or bottom; so any place is as good as any other place to start.

Masheck: As a man who has twice been an immigrant, you have recommenced life twice. I am starting to consider the architectural aspect of these big relief paintings more psychologically. As someone who has lived for quite some years in each of three countries, I can't help thinking that with these works you have made pieces of stability, so to speak. They're architectural, but they could be moved readily. You've made portable walls, and maybe now you can have "home" be where you are.

Scully: I love that phrase, "pieces of stability." One of my objectives, one of the things I'm most interested in, is to make the paintings "classical" in one way—they do use a stable structure—but schizophrenic in another way—in the violence of the abutments. So what you have are "pieces" making up something they shouldn't really make up, but still making up a kind of reality.

Masheck: I'd say that you're making paintings that amount to would-be walls, and that it's as if, maybe, you're indicating or evoking a "room of your own."

Scully: That exposes a very deep need in me to make some security out of, in, my art, because the life that I've led has been one of great insecurity. I read an article on Rothko once, and it had a profound effect upon me. The writer was talking about the immigrant, what the immigrant is. He's always in outer space in some way. Now, I've been an immigrant twice. I've had three nationalities—Irish, English, and American. That's very exhausting!

Masheck: Such concrete discontinuity!

Scully: Exactly! You've got a great need to patch things up or make things whole. But the idea of making something like a house, or a room of one's own, is wonderful. I've always thought of a painting as something you can be in. And when you've got a painting that has an actual corner in it, it's great: you can practically be in the corner if you want to. The paintings are paintings, but they also have a lot of *places* in them, nooks and crannies. And yet they can be broken down and moved on.

Masheck: Yes, to the extent that they are architectural, they can be de-fabricated, packed up.

Scully: You bet! You're not nice to me? I can still leave! . . .

Masheck: I'd like to show you a photograph of an old work of art that strikes me as structurally interesting in light of these recent paintings. This is a fourth-century manuscript painting of an interior, as admired by Aloïs Riegl. See the doorway jutting in at the left and implying a wall plane out of whack with the dominant perspectival setup? Riegl finds that positively interesting and creative. This reminds me not only of the architectural issue but also of your extremism, particularly your going for a kind of torque, for a strain of incongruity.

Scully: Well, what you've got in this image is a situation with a doorway to another situation, and that's what I do. I ram things together in the paintings, things that really shouldn't be there together. I like an alarming change of scale. Something else I love to do is to paint a panel and leave it around for six months, knowing that in six months I won't be painting quite the same way, and then make a painting and put it into that painting. . . .

Masheck: What was particularly insightful on Riegl's part was to look at something like this, something that would have been thought inept, and to say, as it were, "Hey, wait a minute. This is pretty interesting. It shows that the guy is deliberately avoiding closure."

Scully: Yes.

Masheck: That keeps it alive.

Scully: That's what I'm doing. I'm avoiding closure. I'm not idealizing the situation in these paintings. That's why they have such *volition,* formally; because, instead of thinking about them formally, I think about what incongruities I want to strike, and *that* generates the form. . . .

24

A NOTE ON DAVID REED

Eighty years of diversity in abstract art should amply have testified by now that abstraction is something more than just another *style,* and certainly much more than an axis of fashions that wax and wane. Still, abstract painters often seem preoccupied with repetition and the possible inevitability of reiterating as farce what was high tragedy the first time around. Work that does not abstain by irony tends to be knowing to a point of defensiveness—as if *en garde* against the mass and inertia of the modern past.

Some artists do go to the extent of offering a contrivedly mock-abstract art product, like atheists selling death-of-God theology. Others, like David Reed, paint like believers in painting (and only believers have doubts), painting of the old tradition as well as the modern.

Already known as a rigorously abstract painter, Reed has developed his work not only in scale but in amplitude and richness of articulation. A graduate of his namesake institution, the distinguished college of the Pacific Northwest, he used to produce paintings of an elemental, if not exactly Minimal, logic. Typically, one or a brace of long, fluid, horizontal brush-

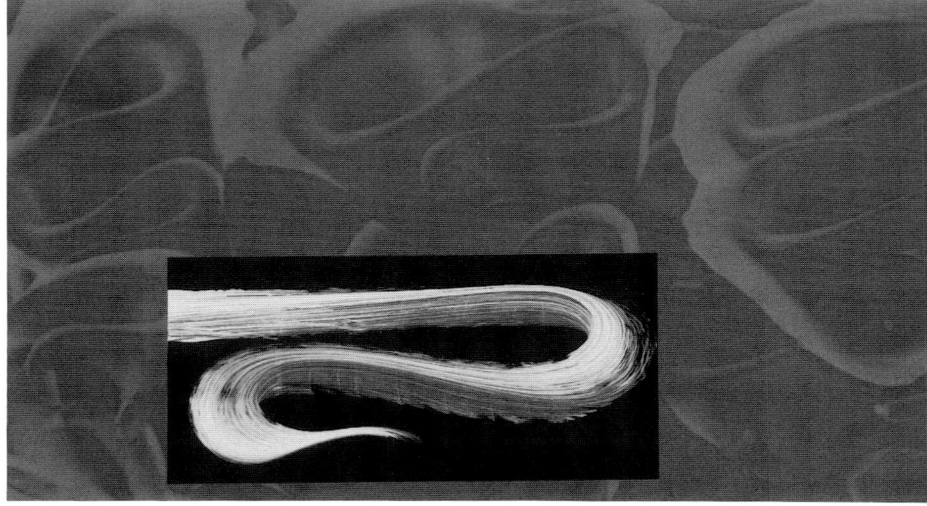

Fig. 31   David Reed, *No. 270*, 1988–89, oil and alkyd on linen, 27 x 202 inches.

strokes—not unlike Lichtenstein's detached, pseudo–Abstract Expressionist "Brushstroke" images only not switched-off, not ironic, and firmly
directional (left to right) and massively calligraphic in character—consti-
tuted an unexpressionistic statement of basic structural truth.

Reed was doing painting that set down clear and fundamental, but also
responsible, propositions. To wit: This canvas becomes a painting as soon
as this one long deliberate brushstroke reaches the end; or, These two
panels become one whole painting once a single considered swipe unites
them; or, A unique white stroke on a black field may compromise a
painting that somehow counts as chromatically complete.

Now that Reed's art has become more complex in technique as well as
image structure, his earlier paintings appear as already in their own right a
kind of recovery, a deconstruction implicitly implying, even initiating,
reconstruction, a starting of painting over again, initially and with initially
constructive rigor. There, too, all along, was the stroke on its own, as a
trace, indicator and even symbolic enactment of renewed possibility for
abstract painting—which many in the 1970s thought a dead issue.

All of Reed's later work is busier. The change reflects no arbitrary
stylistic shift but a gradual and conscientious personal evolution. Oblong
canvases, extremely tall or wide, are divided into rectilinear zones of
different area; the zones are defined not by lines or a regular, preexistent

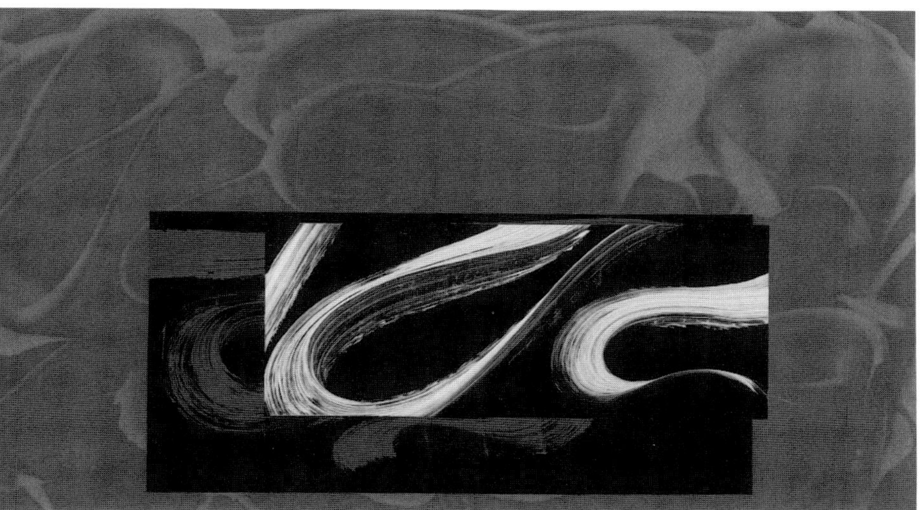

grid, but by dramatic discontinuities in brushwork and the comings and goings of various bright, strangely translucent glazes of color—sometimes liqueurlike, sometimes archly, even *automotively,* synthetic. And I know of no one, artist or art historian, so passionately attuned as David Reed to the wild color and structure of the Sienese (versus Florentine) early masters.

These paintings have an emphatically finished sheen, almost as if some body-shop fanatic had proudly and fastidiously Simonized them. (David Carrier's comparison of their surface effect to the technical gloss of photographic representation has understandably caught on in the critical literature.) That the shininess heightens the naked and unashamed bravura of the brushwork, too, like oil on the bodies of exhibition bodybuilders, renders it ironic only in advance: you'll get your frisson, but you'll have to acknowledge it as such.

Reed's slick surfaces are just bumpy enough here and there to certify that the relation of pigmented goo to silkily detached finish is precisely what he as artist takes responsibility for. And more evidence of this accrues in passages where paint application is linguistically negative, meaning, where the point is clearly that what you see is due to a material *scraping-away.* Willfully disembodied smears and splatters and self-consciously curling figure eights more than disrupt any laid-back Pop parody of the rhetorically heroic Abstract Expressionist brushstroke quite without pretending to resume a nowadays dubious heroic posture. Not that you have to be forewarned of all this to appreciate the lyricism: the ironic tinges are simply Reed's way of innoculating his images against retrograde misconstrual.

Despite their elemental simplicity, the earlier paintings were not altogether lacking in nuance, indicating possibility beyond a Square One of self-evidence or redundancy. In the sense that painting can truly be considered linguistic, Reed's development exposes its generative capacity, its possibility of creative statement in potentially limitless extrapolation within its own set limits, as when language is made to outstrip itself in poetry. This is a complex matter, as the newly complex paintings risk looking, if anything, sententious; still, they are more imaginatively complex, with give-and-take in the apportionment of zones, variety of facture, cultivated ambiguities of structure, as well as more chromatic orchestration.

Much more than a new "look," this newer work is a matter of artistic growth and maturation. Before, Reed's painting was easy to respect for its forthright display of analytical rigor. Now no less respectably, as authentic and no more cosmetic, it may be even easier to tune in on sympathetically. We Americans have to watch out for beautified products that channel desire into phony need and aggrandizement, but we can use all we can get of thought freely and richly elaborating itself in pleasurable works.

25

THOMAS NOZKOWSKI: PAINTING AND THE STRUGGLE OF ANALOGY

For D. C.

Everyone who paints must know a fulfillment tainted by doubt. Now and again, one finds a way out of some challenging problem only to face the new dilemma of whether this is now a way of discovery, development, satisfaction (should there be such a way, at least for the moment), or whether one now must "break through" (the term seems so naive) again and again, ever restless between brainstorms. As in life, one cannot know if something is a dead end until far enough along the way, and the point may be that every way is possibly a detour.

At one artistic extreme: the boringly enforced "unity" of an egotistically tailored and trademarked signature style; at the other: the exhausting "diversity" of egoistic indulgence in eccentricity. The polarity finds equivalents in postmodernist cultural theory; but it is rather as one to whom the very personal work of Nozkowski has personally appealed for a long time that I want to try to surmount a solipsism of mere identification that itself has a certain *Symboliste* historical origin. Needless to say, this makes for a bumpier ride than rehearsing how Nozkowski's abstraction is Symbolist- and also Surrealist-affiliated and how one might like picking up on that.

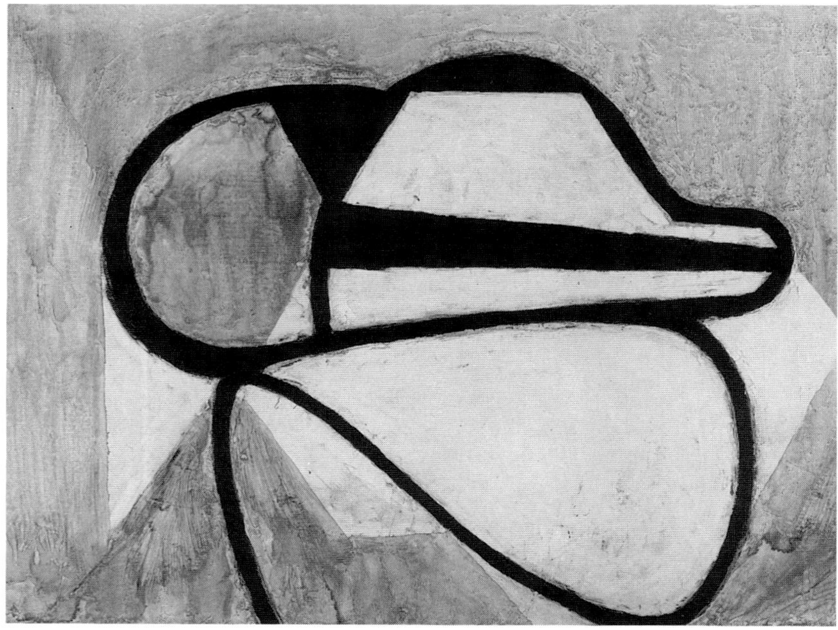

Fig. 32   Thomas Nozkowski, *Untitled*, 1987, oil on canvas board.

Somewhere in between the typecast product and the trivial nuance must be a focal point of identity, as when one can recognize a friend from a distance by gait or even footfall alone. Then what can it mean to expect of an artist's work, no less than the artist, that it remain familiar yet be fresh as ever? All the years I have known Tom Nozkowski's painting he has kept almost without exception to the same intimistic, "cabinet-picture" format—just what all overthrowers of easel painting have most hated—yet with the same (but is it?) relentless inventiveness. However wildly anticlassical in "style" his work may be, Nozkowski nevertheless thrives within a might-have-been classical limitation of parameters, and not simply of format. He has by now a repertory of characteristic elements, yet coming up with one more is incidental compared with a really urgent inventiveness of device, syntax, permutation.

The work's most characteristic traits, in other words, are found much less in quirks one might caricature—and insofar as Nozkowski is ironic, I believe it is for the purpose of fending caricature off—than, more elusively but more importantly, in its way of going about its business, its way of playing the game. Should "playing the game" sound unserious, let me say that I know of no other contemporary painter who more convincingly exemplifies the true Aristotelian sense of *mimesis* not as "representation," with all the theoretical flotsam that drags along after that word, but as *rendering*—including the sense of rendition, as any jazz soloist understands it (we might remember that Aristotle himself was considering a performing art whenever we transpose *mimesis* to the terms of painting).

The map of consciousness is always complete, yet also always under revision. In Nozkowski's case, a for me once adequate sense of his abstraction—all of it—as structurally resembling landscape or still life, has lately been enlarged by another metaphoric possibility, an architectural one. Not that, whereas I would once recognize echoes of nature or of little *things* of some elusive kind on a table or shelf, I now have *instead* to see structures referentially larger in scale, as nondescript and structurally incongruous as ever only planted upon the earth. No: more radically, I am made to see that the forms can often be read *in plan* and not necessarily only *in elevation*. Hence a field unbroken by a horizon might as well be any possible ground, not just a conventional expanse of empty space pretty much translatable, even in Suprematism, as "sky."

As a matter of fact, Nozkowski and I have often talked about architecture, which of course normally connotes rectilinear constructs, indeed, Constructivism itself, in painting. It took time to realize that, for instance, his fascination with the gaga, flimsoid-curvaceous Pop-moderne of Bruce Goff's buildings—including teardrop "styling," but also an understated theoretical commitment to the ad hoc—had more than witty pertinence to Tom's painting. That a more comprehensive architectonic, perhaps like that of the early Russian moderns, might be at work, is suggested by the way bulging, otherwise leafy planes in Nozkowski's work likewise compare with the now datedly interesting, schoonerlike tarpaulin structures of Frei Otto—something that even Winslow Homer, as a painter, would have admired, to witness his interesting study of a pup tent with its cusped planes, *The Tent (Summer by the Sea)*, c. 1873.

At least such thoughts will suggest how the real irony of certain gaga-flamboyant forms in Nozskowski's images is their structural seriousness, as when in actual architecture a pneumatic, spatial going-for-bulk of late Baroque structure informs the bulbous, interpenetrating bays of Saarinen's 1962 TWA Terminal at Kennedy Airport, recalling, retroactively, Guarino Guarini's work in northern Italy in the late seventeenth century. It might be interesting to inquire what it would mean to describe any of these structures—Guarini's, Saarinen's, Otto's, or Nozkowski's—as *scenographic,* but it is more urgent to see in Nozkowski's small imagic format, by virtue of the architectural analogy, an absurdly complex but true *geometry* unleashed in the flexible space of painting.

Substituting one formula for seeing for another would only be a trick: the point is to account for a (re)stimulation of what one has already seen and knows by an enriched evocative experience that hardly amounts to *more of the same.* So too with Nozkowski's paintings themselves as "pure" abstractions, the term *nonobjective* seems curiously apt: they seem to have set out as almost lost, "non-objectively" enough, only to find themselves in being painted. (How else to talk about this work except metaphorically?) There would be no use in attempting to replace any one code of reading by another because in that sense the images aren't coded at all, their play of forms (and irresistibly "atonal" chromas) being altogether undisguised. It is our encounter with them that stimulates the attempt to make them jibe with who we are.

We are also talking about the works' poetic polysemy, their capability, insofar as they refer at all, to reference a multiplicity of even contradictory things. Some of the more "elevational" images still also suggest personages or the head of one person. I have considered Nozkowski's admiration of Philip Guston before,[1] but wherever a lone headlike entity looms up, there is also the older example of Redon—by no means just another artist to the Nozkowski of catholic tastes but a special master of evocation. Yet a configuration, and sonorous hue, that evoke Redon can also call to mind, say, prehistoric "X-ray" images of the heart as seat of animate life. One painting of the turn of the 1980s even has a headlike form—seat of *consciousness*—swiped over by a rainbowlike triad of color smears, as if in a metaphor that just skirts the pun of having color *on one's mind.* I wish it were possible to write down thoughts like these without their sounding so literal. Must everything be worthy of being engraved in stone? (Nozkowski's painting may teach one the virtue of understanding this.)

Yes, quite instead of being relational in a formalistic sense, like just another nice flower arrangement, Nozkowski's configurations seem like lively presences, whether in intimate interaction or more complex (and

---

1. Joseph Mascheck, "Nozkowski: Pressing On" (1981), in my *Historical Present: Essays of the 1970s* (Ann Arbor, 1984), 271–78.

social?) aggregations. In fact, the whole body of this painter's work is itself familial, showing physiognomic throwbacks and attitudinal affinities over time. In this sense, the fecundity of his project is genetic, a matter of regeneration through endless recombination of traits. Various identities appear and reappear in and out of sequence: they might as well be known things or persons encountered under changed conditions. Still, each painting, whatever its few or many forms, has the wholeness of a complete aspect, is not a mere facet of some determinate thing. One infers a consistent personality thanks to the adequacy of this very wholeness in each, however oddball, case—as personality, stationed in this or that circumstance, carries its cargo of experience and association.

The expressive combination and recombination of elements into ever new wholes leads me even to think of Arnold Schoenberg's far from random system of musical composition, at once anti-hierarchical and obliging of a rigorous freedom. Although Schoenberg's modernist music, in which abstract "shapes" displace old-time melody in a specifically "musical space," has significant Cubistic features in theory,[2] for what could be called the *illyrical* thrust of its atonality alone it holds a central place in musical "Expressionism." Just how was such a systematic ever expected to produce, of all things, intensity of *expression?* Partly by virtue of an urgency of creative decision within a system that is rigorous in the sense of demanding, but by no means supposed to operate under absolute conscious control. And in this—not unlike the shape-clusters of Nozkowski's images—the posited musical "shape" complex acquires such (abstract) objectivity that, according to a classic exposition, it "rotates, as it were, in musical space, [and] takes on at each repetition a different form which is an individual one each time."[3]

The Surrealistic cast of Nozkowski's painting is more obvious than its structural rigor. Most neo-Surrealism evident in the later 1980s only paraded cliché stylistics as dead as the tropes of commonplace speech. You might think a lively variety would be easy to sustain, as if all one had to do

---

2. The subject deserves something like the serious musicological attention through which it was (finally) shown that Debussy is not really "Impressionist," in the art-historical sense, at all, but as much as Post-Impressionist, by Stefan Jarocinski, *Debussy: Impressionism and Symbolism* (1966), trans. Rollo Myers (London, 1976). Jack Beeson has pooh-poohed the importance of this, in conversation; but if one field borrows a term from another in which that term has an antithesis, it seems to me that the borrowed usage ought not to contradict the original one.

3. Josef Rufer, *Composition with Twelve Notes Related Only to One Another* (1952), trans. Humphrey Searle (New York, 1954), 138.

to be interesting were to resign from obligations of rationality and take it easy. No memory, however, no buildup of experience, not to mention history; which is to say, no accrual of meaning, as Nozkowski's metamorphoses imply. More technically: within the single painting a fleshly facture is advanced and sustained as much by thinly painted areas as by palpably pasty ones; indeed, scraped passages manage to imply a negative plasticity, for only what had been given in abundance or excess can have been stripped so physically away. All this is structural, and rigorous.

Nozkowski's painting is also heartily Nietzschean in the way it has to be faced as beautiful by some sort of vulcanization, as it were, in the struggle of experience. All beauty of the kind, seemingly immediately "lyrical," is really the antithesis of primping surface effect, and the order it attains exceeds its givens. In music, then, is not Schoenberg as fanatical as Bach in the fecund recombination of a set of elements? "In composing with twelve notes," we are told, "just as before, one must work hard before the 'unconscious' gives its blessing to the work."[4] For Nozkowski, likewise, this obliges at least a different "way out" every time. The way worth finding must mean something to the searcher (and to him or her who would follow), now not by self-conscious predetermination, but after the fact, like character itself.

---

4. Ibid., 140; see also 7–13 and passim.

26

ROSS BLECKNER'S *CHAMBER* AND THE LIMITS OF SUBLIMITY

O artist! Shun the light of heaven! Descend deep into the tomb, let the sepulchral lamps, with their wan, expiring gleams, light your way!

—Boullée

Given the departmentalized marketplace, what I'm supposed to say is that Ross Bleckner's work, in toto, is "sublime." Well, I don't really want to, not without resistance. That might only confirm the *bossa-nova* nihilism into which many have lately been backed. While I have cared about Bleckner's art for a long time, I have cared about the nature of the sublime for much longer; so what I want to do about Bleckner's supposed sublime is to refer it directly to the definitive eighteenth-century texts.

By Kant's standards, at least, *Chamber* (1985) and other of the categorically funereal paintings of Bleckner just might not count as sublime at all (Fig. 33). That *Chamber* happens to be beautiful will hardly serve to accredit it, since as a notion the sublime is, if anything, a distinct alternative to beauty. That the painting is quite *big* does count. Nevertheless, in the sense of Kant's *Observations on the Feeling of the Beautiful and Sublime* (1764), it probably does not rate because there the sublime "must be simple," whereas "the beautiful can be adorned and ornamented" (sec. i).[1] True, by

---

1. Immanuel Kant, *Observations on the Feeling of the Beautiful and Sublime,* trans. John T. Goldthwait (Berkeley, 1960), 48.

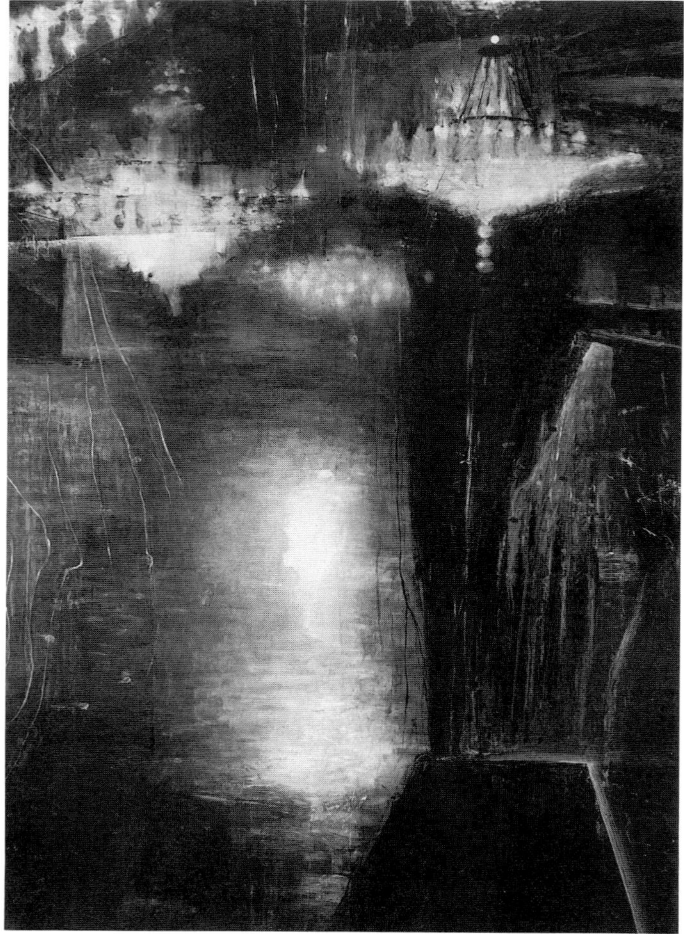

Fig. 33   Ross Bleckner, *Chamber,* 1985, oil on canvas, 87 x 60 inches.

now there is enough of a history of artistic simplicities to say that the
category of the simple is itself not altogether simple, and that *Chamber*
might well be relatively simple; but that would only go to show that we
were in too deep for *utter* simplicity. With *Chamber,* Kant could have
specified the chandeliers, not only a pervasive Goncourtesque-sentimental
neo-Rococo, as showing what he calls an *"esprit des bagatelles"* (sec. ii) that
testifies to fineness of feeling but that just isn't sublime. Being something

that overwhelms (as too in Kant's *Critique of Judgement,* 1790), the sublime has to be more, and other, than ingratiating.

Edmund Burke seems more telling in respect to this sort of "camera obscura" Bleckner (*camera* meaning "chamber"), versus his striped, perhaps "camera lucida" type paintings (more like opaque projection). Just what *is* sublime, quite before Kant, in the *Philosophical Enquiry into the Origin of Our Ideas of the Sublime and Beautiful* (1757)? "Whatever is fitted in any sort to excite the ideas of pain, and danger, that is to say, whatever is in any sort terrible, or is conversant about terrible objects, or operates in a manner analagous to terror" (I.vii).[2] Apropos of his "camera obscura" paintings, such as this, which Bleckner began to memorialize friends dying or dead of AIDS: significantly, Burke more than allows for anything having to do with death, including a subjective grief probably too private for Kant. Indeed, Burke's subjective sublime is predicated on the immediately personal experience of *terribilità.* Grief in general, Burke takes as a positive cessation of pleasure, which ought to be altogether understandable in the case of mourning: "The person who grieves, suffers his passion to grow upon him; he indulges it, he loves it: but this never happens in the case of actual pain, which no man ever willingly endured for any considerable time. That grief should be willingly endured, though far from a simply pleasing sensation, is not so difficult to be understood. It is the nature of grief to keep its object perpetually in its eye, to present it in its most pleasurable views, to repeat all the circumstances that attend it, even to the last minuteness" (I.v).[3] Note the permissibility of a "minuteness" otherwise unsublime, under such extreme sway of feeling.

If it might be reasonable to suspend knowledge of the personal elegiac feelings known to have motivated Bleckner in the interest of aesthetic judgment (a judgment then, however, concerned with "beauty" alone), it would be less justifiable to assume that a painting motivated by such strong sentiment was necessarily a merely sentimental work and, as such, disqualified from the sublime. In that the light flecks of "starry" heavenly domes of night in similar paintings are said to have been suggested by horrific lesions on the flesh of the terminally ill, they may conform to the Burkean sublime: although the merely "odious" (e.g., toads and spiders) is insuffi-

---

2. Edmund Burke, *A Philosophical Enquiry into the Origin of Our Ideas of the Sublime and Beautiful,* ed. J. T. Boulton (London, 1958), 39.

3. Ibid., 37.

cient for sublimity, extremely horrid smells and tastes allow for the sublime if "moderated, as in a description or narrative" (II.xxi), while the starry sky itself exemplifies a sublime magnificence, "an appearance of infinity by . . . disorder" that some fireworks, for instance, manage to attain (II.xiii).[4]

Actually, it has been suggested that an influence in Edmund Burke's own first intimations of the sublime, while still a teenager in Dublin in the 1740s, was "his acquaintance with a 'forsaken lover' who committed suicide."[5] If, then, we accuse Burke's *Enquiry* itself of sentimentalism, we shall have lost sight of what it—and perhaps Bleckner, too—is trying to teach us. Aware as I am of deferring to Burke's *Enquiry* itself as a "classic" text even in the matter of sentiment, I call attention to Burke's sentiment(ality) as that of one utterly grounded in classical decorum—which may or may not parallel Bleckner in relation to the modern tradition. Half a century later, when he holds up chivalric honor against the mundane pedants' and economists' view of life, and toasts eighteenth-century French culture with the grand phrase "vice itself lost half its evil by losing all its grossness,"[6] his now-classic remark may itself echo a schoolboy-classical text. For according to Tacitus, with Romanization the ancient Britons had acquired "the amenities that make vice agreeable" (*Agricola,* xxi).[7] So, I am thinking, Burke's traumatic youthful awakening to the sublime could have occurred to a mind just then busy absorbing classical order and decorum itself as *second nature.*

Maybe the sublime makes no real sense apart from some assumed classicism. And now what I want to know is whether, in respect to Bleckner, "classical" painting would mean classicism, old-time established pictorialism, or else some form of now itself "classic" modernity.

To modern eyes *Chamber* proposes a literalizing quasi-pictorial fiction, whereas Bleckner's quite different stripe paintings seem rather fictively

4. Ibid., 85–86, 78, respectively.

5. Ibid., Boulton's introduction, xvi.

6. Burke, *Reflections on the Revolution in France,* ed. Thomas H. D. Mahoney, Library of Liberal Arts (Indianapolis, 1955), 86.

7. Thus in the rendering of H. Mattingly: Cornelius Tacitus, *On Britain and Germany: A Translation of the "Agricola" and the "Germania,"* The Penguin Classics (Harmondsworth, 1960), 72. Tacitus's "paulatimque descensum ad delenimenta vitiorum," given by Maurice Hutton as "and little by little . . . were seduced into alluring vices," in *Dialogus; Agricola; Germania,* Loeb Classical Library (London and New York, 1925), 207 (Lat. on 206), concerns a dressing-up. My point is that the Tacitus who did appreciate native culture remarked the Gallic nice-ification of vice, and that this might well echo in the comment on vice de-grossified as Burke (in the complex position of an Irishman, vis-à-vis Norman and later British conquests) contemplated the smashing of French aristocratic civility. I thank David Murphy for advice.

literal. Its shimmering darkness is essentially prephotographic, and by *putting* darkness *into* his image with black, Bleckner only confirms Burke, who recommends "a judiciuous obscurity" (II.iv).[8] In a sense, such an image might really date from circa 1800. Taking it as a funereal landscape, I can imagine something related to it by, say, Coleridge's American friend Washington Allston. All Bleckner's paintings of the kind are, Romantically enough, paintings from the mind's "I," that little *camera* that gets filled with world, to overflowing. Yet virtual pictorialism, however inviting to any who have not attained modernity and strain to pass as "postmodern," *cannot* any longer *simply be.*

The true duality in Ross Bleckner's art entails a sensuous asceticism, or ascetic sensuousness. Notwithstanding sensuality as now suspect, painting is still allowed to indulge a "sublimely"—for once, sublimatingly—removed sensuousness. The novelist Huysmans, for one, in the earlier modern artworld, a man led literally to monastic religiosity by his passion for art, would have known a certain letter by Saint Bernard of Clairvaux against religious opulence. In terms that *Chamber* employs, Bernard had written of interiors "adorned with gemmed crowns of light—nay, with lustres like cart-wheels, girt all round with lamps . . . , candelabra . . . glistening. . . . O vanity of vanities."[9] That may or may not be officially sublime, yet for its sense of virtually hyperpicturesque overload it might well have overwhelmed even Edmund Burke.

---

8. Burke, *Enquiry,* 62: "even in painting a judicious obscurity in some things contributes to the effect of the picture."

9. Bernard of Clairvaux, " 'Apologia' to William, Abbot of St.-Thierry," trans. G. G. Coulton, excerpted in Elizabeth Gilmore Holt, ed., *A Documentary History of Art,* I: *The Middle Ages and the Renaissance* (Garden City, N.Y., 1957), 19–22, here 20.

27

PAINTING IN DOUBLE NEGATIVE: JONATHAN LASKER

To make paintings capable for good reason of being taken as vacant or exhausted abstractions; paintings prepared to handle underestimation as to "authenticity"; paintings that without being simplistically ironic are at once hyperdecorative and ultraintellectual: what a tall order!

Maybe a painting by Jonathan Lasker ought to be something of a cultural embarrassment. How glibly we speak before it of postmodernity, while it is hardly a generation since a distinguished old-master art historian could get away with claiming that Manet "pursued . . . [his] lesson in a direction that involved spiritual impoverishment"[1]—a statement that may be more right than Charles Sterling could have comprehended, though it would take a modernist to know. Even Bataille said that Manet "sounded the death-knell of rhetorical eloquence in painting," hardly hinting at his articulation of a whole new eloquence.[2] But for Baudelaire to have famously written to

---

1. Charles Sterling, *Still Life Painting from Antiquity to the Twentieth Century* (1952), trans. James Emmons, rev. ed. (New York, 1981), 122.

2. Georges Bataille, *Manet* (1955), trans. Austryn Wainhouse and James Emmons (New York, 1983), 92. Bataille is here addressing "that elegant thinness of the pictorial image, that flat

Manet "You are only the first in the decrepitude of your art"[3] now sounds like sheer poetry. Having followed Lasker's work enthusiastically since the early 1980s, I can see how squares might hate it even as revisionists rejected it for a buffered yet undeniable commitment to abstraction—as those mesmerized by the "economy of signs" show such small patience with what seventeenth-century French theory called the specific "oeconomie" of the single painting.

Allow me, then, to begin art-historically, as neither party will want to do that job. There is apparent in Lasker's work a certain High Disneyesque mode of surface display that is itself adumbrated in turn-of-the century Symbolism. I think, for instance, of the rubbery, kitsch-unforgettable shadows in the "Ave Maria" sequence of *Fantasia* (1941) as anticipated by shadows shifting across tree trunks and figures in Maurice Denis's *Procession Under the Trees* (1892), not to mention, as equally Laskeresque, jigsaw shifts of hatching with biomorphic zones in, say, Armand Séguin's engraving *A Summer's Day* (1894). Equally relevant to Lasker are would-be folksy images by Charles Filiger (who was admired by Alfred Jarry and André Breton), such as a study of a child kneeling at prayer—Lasker's basic repertory includes comparably "bent" forms—marked vertically from thigh up, horizontally below. True, Lasker's Symbolism never quite keeps a straight face, but that doesn't mean it's only a joke: wit does require that at least two terms be entertained in the mind at once, even if that is too much to expect of most citizens of the artworld now. At the same time, "people" are already "talking about" our own fin-de-siècle, where Lasker has *been* for some years. Because Lasker's art assumes a kind of engineered disengagement, I notice under its sway that Filiger's devoted critic Charles Chassé found in that artist's work "beaucoup de mécanisme."[4]

In a wider cultural history, Lasker's characteristically detached, feeling-at-a-distance approach to painting—half "Look, no hands," half "Don't blame me"—also recalls 1900 as a moment of newly extreme technological detachment, what with the first atomizing, Seuratesque "data processing"

---

transparency which sounded the death-knell of rhetorical eloquence in painting," *à la* the famous playing-card trope. There is a critical duplicity in his text, however, because by this point the reader has already been coaxed repeatedly to concede that *all* rhetoric or eloquence goes by the boards with Manet: e.g., "Every strain of eloquence, feigned or genuine, is done away with" (48). So in some sense any remark beginning "His eloquence, needless to say, had nothing in common with the turgid . . ." (72) must be bankrupt before the thought is complete.

3. As quoted in Sterling, *Still Life Painting,* 123; cf. Bataille, *Manet,* 42.

4. Charles Chassé, *Le Mouvement symboliste dans l'art du XIXe siècle* (Paris, 1947), 114.

not only of the telegraph but, especially, of the player piano, the latter especially fascinating today as paleodigital. Scott Joplin (1868–1917) saw his original piano rags pirated in his own day, with nervous breakdowns to show for it; Joshua Rifkin's deft revival of the rags as art music only gave White America occasion for another massive effacement: Joplin is now the anonymous soundtrack composer of *The Sting* (1973). As to the piano rolls themselves, those punch-cardlike records of note sequences disencumbered of Joplin's, Rifkin's, or anybody else's heart and soul: it would be interesting to speculate, in light of Lasker's specially detached abstraction, on whether "pianola" music constitutes an Aristotelian representation in the sense of a rendering or *rendition* (which is to say, a *mimesis*) at all. With Lasker, it is as if we got to hear Joplin live and it turned out he had worked extra hard to sound just like a pianola.

As to heavy, turnpike modernism before and after 1900: how about Manet's own *The Ham,* with its dashlike patterned wallpaper(?) background; or even, for the sangfroid of the mint-green diagonal bands of its copper balustrade, not to mention the stripe effect of its shutter slats, the famous *Balcony,* of 1868? Curiously, not even in postmodernism is it easy to shake off Manet as the great progenitor (for a surprising adumbration of David Salle, check out Manet's 1874 *Monet Painting in His Studio*). But the rather videoesque striated grilles of many Lasker paintings also recall a kind of horizontal hatching used in Synthetic Cubist paintings of Picasso, either as borrowed from the structural givens of a pair of shutters (*Window,* 1921) or as an imposed structural differentiation (*Table with a Cup,* 1922)—though I must contain myself here because nobody now wants to bother about such things.

In light of Lasker I also notice, in earlier American modernism, a telling likeness, overriding the two painters' discrete preoccupations, between a characteristic "leathern" facture in the art of Marsden Hartley and the almost outrageously untransmuted materiality of Lasker's paint-job, with its reverse naturalism—like some decorative sycamore bark made in rubbery plastic in Taiwan, or pigment as margarine rather than "buttery." I am thinking, for instance, of Hartley's *West Brookville, Maine* (1939), where a heavy, solid, patchwork of painterly stucco quartered in zones of rough strips renders spruce logs as felled parallel and evenly stacked, plus regularly spaced trees still standing and about to be cut. Artist for artist, one might even find pertinent to Lasker's way of painting Hartley's personalist tender-toughness, except that Lasker's equivalent is critically *an*esthetic.

Looking so switched-off, Lasker's work shows unexpected structural affinities with that aspect of Abstract Expressionism that was knowingly Euro-Surreal. For instance, as a kind of basso supporting a melodic "figuration," his striated patches recall images by Baziotes, such as the milky *Jungle,* of 1951. What a difference of attitude, however: it is as if Lasker laid down a thin ground of, as it were, nonfat milk, and then went and put the heavy cream back on top of that. Significantly, vis-à-vis French-style modernism, the two-step process makes not for intensification or rarefaction but for the opposite, an almost chemical materialism, synthetic in the common sense even if also, differently, of Synthetism. Equally synthetic in the popular sense are his arch or lurid colors—which a student of mine, to Lasker's delight, once contemptuously characterized as deriving "from the K-Mart School of Color Painting."

One afternoon in the spring of 1985, I think, when Peter Nagy was in Boston and I invited him to make a double-time sweep through the Fogg, Peter pointed out the remarkably Lasker-like fusing and flat overlay of motifs in Motherwell's *Wall Painting* (1950), in which it is as if Motherwell had sought to de-apply the graphicism of Matisse's *Jazz* collages—those forms in bikinis—in paint. Motherwell's work is obviously more homogenized and sedate than Lasker's. Yet in a more Beat, saxophonic way Lasker makes pink look "cool." Tellingly, even his graphic sense evokes the sophisticated postwar style of the designer Paul Rand, including "intellectual" book jackets, in the 1950s. Lasker's paintings are altogether abstract— more purely, in fact, than they seem if you are still looking for signs of Renaissance picture structure—only they do not parade their abstraction. His is as it were a special kind of third-stream, post–Modern Jazz Quartet sensibility.

A limply flat painting by Lasker from 1978, *5 of Spades,* evokes early Lichtenstein or Warhol even more than a famous trope of early modernist critique. Actually, James Laver, discussing playing cards in a precocious 1948 article "Good Bad Painting," observed that it was in fact only in the nineteenth century that playing-card designs underwent their to us conventional doubling, with two reversible tops, which suggests that we should be careful not to assume that before a certain point in the 1800s a reference to cards implies the antipictorialism of a reversible design.[5] Now the playing-card trope for Postimpressionist flatness, including Courbet's rather

---

5. James Laver, "Good Bad Art," *The Studio,* CXXXVI/667 (October 1948). Laver was also fascinated, it happens, by a Victorian propensity to "cement fragments of broken porcelain" all over objets d'art.

redneck insult to the *Olympia,* is by now too boring to rehearse, except that, via Cézanne and Cubism, and in analogy with chess as a cerebral theme, its abstract connotation of gaming may lead into that different cliché, of art as play.

Let me interject a point from an insightful early modern aesthetician who nowadays never even has the honor of being hit-listed in antimodernist purges, Vernon Lee. Reviewing then new German "empathy" theory at the turn of the century, she reached the point of suggesting that decoration itself "might be explained as a parasitic excrescence of play upon work." This was a challenge not only to the Romantic poet Schiller's idea of play as creative freedom but also to Herbert Spencer's notion of art as surplus energy discharged in free play. But "freedom," according to Lee, "is not the aim of the artistic process, but its necessary condition, since we do not act freely in order to take pleasure in freedom, but please ourselves because we happen to be free to do so."[6] Considering Lee's reversal helps me to understand something I before only sensed, how some of the wit in Lasker's paintings depends on their looking stubbornly belabored even as they look so well-groomed. How ruthlessly, come to think of it, Lasker handles the decorative banging-out, again and again, of the almost-the-same, hardly spontaneous cadenzas and "ornamentation."

One painting by Lasker from 1987, *Fashionable Obscurity,* has a purple, "high-key" field, like a color in a yuppie sportswear catalogue for "jocks" of no team. Onto this is applied, or rather, into it is more or less inlaid, an array of broad, strugglingly hand-drawn vertical stripes of mudlike ocher. Stripes and field alike are overlaid interruptively by twin amorphous white patches striped vertically with black, each of which is further overlaid by a linear, signlike motif in red—a pointless hieroglyph something like a fusion of the "heart" and "spade" of playing cards. (Giving two instances of the same red motif on differently shaped but similarly striped white patches, side by side, recalls Rauschenberg's anti-Expressionist self-simulation in closely doubling painterly quirks from *Factum I* over into *Factum II,* both of 1957.) Here, too, as elsewhere, Lasker juxtaposes two different *kinds* of color, as different as attitudes, one tending toward the gorgeous and the at least caricaturally feminine and the other toward a dumb *profondo* look that by rights should be caricaturally masculine, the latter playing as if den pieces to the boudoir air of the former, or, by a stretch, Baroque to their Rococo.

---

6. Vernon Lee (pseud. of Violet Paget), "Recent Aesthetics," *The Quarterly Review,* CXCIX/398 (April 1904).

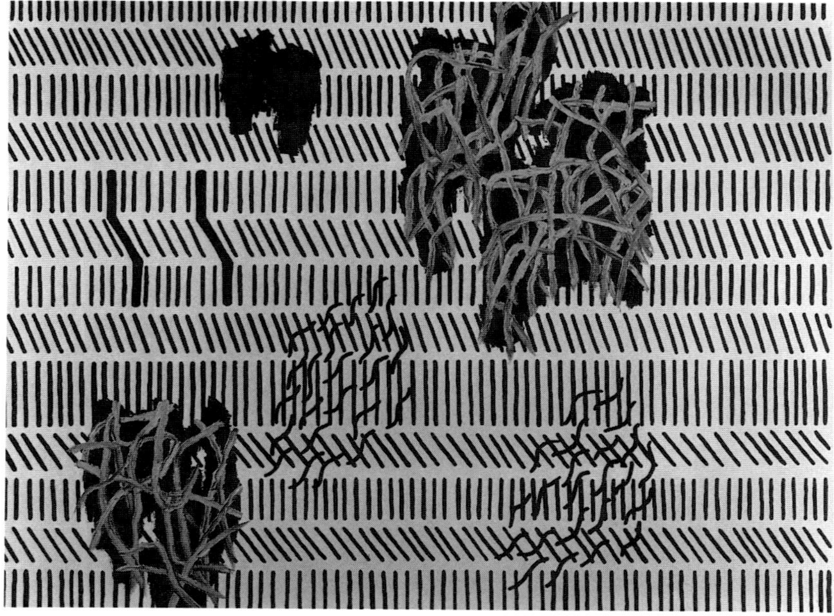

Fig. 34   Jonathan Lasker, *Spiritual Entertainment*, 1987, oil on linen, 80 x 100 inches.

By belabored I mean also to imply *driven,* in the sense of Artaud's *The Theater and Its Double* (1938)—this in spite of Jean Baudrillard's attempt to swallow up Artaud, Pac-Man–like, assuming him to a mere "referential" of what he wrote. Take the idea of *"matter as revelation,* suddenly dispersed in signs to teach us the metaphysical identity of concrete and abstract and to teach us this *in gestures made to last."*[7] Thanks probably to the cult of Baudrillard, the pop-intellectual Marshall McLuhan of the 1980s, there is a current, wrongheaded sense of a "double" as some kind of deracinated simulacrum, as if, in Lasker's case, the works were nothing more than stand-ins for abstract paintings. This is simply not what Artaud termed "the double," which is anything but inert. A snatch or two from Artaud in gear shows how unsuitable to any ironically distanced posture his "double" ought to be (his definitive example being the Balinese theater): "As if waves of matter were tumbling over each other, dashing their crests into the deep

7. Antonin Artaud, *The Theater and Its Double,* trans. Mary Caroline Richards (New York, 1958), 59; emphases in original.

and flying from all sides of the horizon to be enclosed in one minute portion of tremor and trance—to cover the void of fear."[8] Copying the words down, I began to think of the following in respect to a threat of anxious immobility in Lasker's, in one sense switched-off, in another quite brazen, icings of paint: "A chaotic boiling, full of recognizable particles and at moments strangely orderly, crackles in this effervescence of painted rhythms in which the many fermatas unceasingly make their entrance like a well-calculated silence."[9] It's the fermatas that really do it, by analogy with the blatant gaps in Lasker's structures; but the nearly swooningly farfetched overall conviction counts too.

It cannot have escaped Lasker that his own work, however *smart,* is much less simplistic and shows rather less "attitude" than fashion dictates. He seems to paint out of suave disgust with the way things are, perhaps with disgust for the pseudoradical philistines' antipathy toward painting. Thus I see his work not as an empty, ill-defined "double" for painting, that is, as part of current bourgeois anti-art voodoo, but as a true "treble" to that false "double," or better—as the German translator of the original version of this essay gave it, in 1987 (though who, here, could be expected to know about church music)—as a kind of "descant," gliding up an octave above its given basis.

Lasker's barky, stuccolike facture, *an*esthetized as it is, does manage to affirm painting. Baudrillard generalizes with dumbfounding crudity in his remarks on "The Stucco Angel" (welcome to the eighties), but his slapdash insult to historical truth takes on interest before Jonathan Lasker's heavy, stuccoish impastos. "Stucco exorcises the unlikely confusion of matter into a single new substance, and is prestigious theatrically because [it] is itself a representative [i.e., representational?] substance, a mirror of all the others":[10] here is at least the flavor, let's say, of Lasker's kind of significance. But while Baudrillard's cynicism as to the possibility of sublimating (negligible) matter into (appreciable) immaterial effect conveniently sweeps a great deal of worthy art, old and new, out of the way, in today's circumstances—including by now even debasements of Baudrillard!—even blasphemous anti-painting has sufficiently to entail *painting per se* to count.

I keep speaking of Baudrillard, against my will. If only he conveyed a

---

8. Ibid., 65.

9. Ibid., 61.

10. Jean Baudrillard, *Simulations,* trans. P. Foss, P. Patton, and P. Beitchman (New York, 1983), 88.

sense that his brutalization of Artaud, whose thought was no delicate bloom, had been *sportif,* we could thank him for cleverly driving us back to the original "double" that got marginalized before "margins" themselves became so *hot.* Certainly the Artaudian double is no coy postmodern tap-dance. When, under the heading "An Affective Athleticism," Artaud calls on the actor (read artist) "to make use of his emotions as a wrestler makes use of his muscles," seeing "the human being as a Double, like the Ka of the Egyptian mummies, like a perpetual specter from which the affective powers radiate," he calls for unnervingly vivid affect (not *none*), for "virtues which are not those of an image but carry a material sense."[11] Far from implying business as usual, this seems to indicate a toughened, materialized version of dramatic "image." I now find myself dwelling on Artaud, in turn; but he heads me into the special "double," or double-negation of the simple, mistaken double, in Lasker's art.

An actor, or artist, should be like a wrestler? What can this mean right now, with even *that* debased? You don't have to be Barthes to see that there is an artworld as blaspheming of its own classic equivalent, not only as profiteering, as the world of "pro" wrestling, as I have written elsewhere. If Lasker's appliqués of disjunct forms are at all like the shadow puppets or the body-ornamented dancers of Artaud's East Indies (already admired by Derain among the Fauves), haven't the similar ballet tights with wild arabesque designs of Nijinsky lately resurfaced with Artaudian underclass outrageousness in the figured tights of Ravishing Rick Rude, of the "World Wrestling Federation" (an operation so *purely* commercial that, like Jeff Koons, it simply self-advertises)? Some would see Lasker that way, and enthusiastically; but then, for his double-negation of painting, I see him instead as more like an Arthur Craven, the boxer who rates as a Dadaist, but only because he *really did box.* While I'd hate in effect to hand over Lasker to the French, the Artaudian aspect of his work isn't unrelated to the Artauderie of that great anti-painter whose art is very much *real painting,* Jean Dubuffet, either.

Contemporaneous with *The Theater and Its Double,* with its wittily defensive imputation to a painting by Lucas van Leyden of "metaphysical" ideas ("I am sorry to use this word, but it is their name"[12]), was the famous lecture by Heidegger, "The Establishment by Metaphysics of the Modern World Picture" (1938), published as "The Age of the World Picture" (and

---

11. Artaud, *Theater,* 134–35, for these passages.
12. Ibid., 36.

supplemented in *Holzwege, 1952*). Here the philosopher maintains not that a new, Cartesian world-picture replaced a premodern one, but rather that the Cartesian method uniquely effected the very representability of the world as such. This "modern" world-picture being (or having been?) *the* world-picture, the very condition of appearing altogether new "is peculiar to the world that has become picture." The picturability, as such, of the world, Heidegger sees as essentially modern; and the very word "picture" *(Bild)* "now means the structured image *(Gebild)* that is the creature of man's producing."[13] The very understanding of its coming into being is tinged by a sense that almost from its first comprehensibility the world-picture would have to dissipate.

Is it rash to find here, half a century later, some inevitable "postmodernity" implicit in modernity itself, or is that a thought only an amateur could get away with? Clearly, Jonathan Lasker dallies with mechanisms of *de*piction already subverted in a century of modern painting: a now almost pointlessly imagic drawing-in-paint; stripes dopily adrift from their mates in a more air-headed than atmospheric field; loose parts from the old Erector Set of perspective. Some of us have been quite happy that the preposterous old picturability has been defunct since about 1910, so why should we feel any disappointment on that score? And if we never wanted to "buy into" the puritan postmodernists' interminable funeral for painting, well, we can admire how Lasker manages to concoct representations of our present, not altogether unfortunately unpicturable, condition. "No age lets itself be done away with by a negating decree," says Heidegger, adding—as with so much art today—"Negation only throws the negator off the path."[14] Heidegger also says that "What belongs properly to the essence of the picture is . . . system"; and "Where the world becomes picture, the system . . . comes to dominance," though "where the system is in the ascendancy, the possibility always exists also of its degenerating into the superficiality of a system that has merely been fabricated and pieced together."[15] This integral doubt in the artifice of picturing *at all* seems to me rather like what Lasker negotiates in his art. Lasker's painting is no mere postmodernist documentation of the disenfranchised means and mechanics of representation; neither is it antimodernist by simple "negating decree."

---

13. Martin Heidegger, "The Age of the World Picture," in his *The Question Concerning Technology and Other Essays,* ed. and trans. William Lovitt (New York, 1977), 115–54, here 134, with n. 18 (ed.) on Heidegger's word *Gebild.*

14. Ibid., 138.

15. Ibid., 141.

Here, in the 1952 appendices Heidegger added to his "World-Picture" essay, it seems that "the melting down of the self-consummating essence of the modern age," which in context is practically to say of picturability itself, "into the self-evident, is being accomplished." To my eyes, Lasker reflects this condition with a practically Nietzschean hilarity. Nietzschean in its own right is the way, for Heidegger, the collapse has to occur in order for there to be "fertile soil for Being to be in question in an original way"; hence, "Only there where the consummation of the modern age attains the heedlessness [or better, recklessness *(Rücksichtlosigkeit)*] that is its peculiar greatness is future history being prepared."[16]

To be sensitive to the tremors in the foundations beneath us is perhaps almost to be condemned to a dandyish exclusivity. If only the crumbling of the world-picture meant simply the final downfall of academicized representation in painting, we could simply cheer. By now, more has been crumbling than representational, or even modernist abstract, art. Lasker's reckless, *rücksichtlosige* images might be said to consist of shards of the modern world-picture, yet he still manages to paint them with a saving delight in painting. Of course, to the new Calvinist radicals, beyond the pale even of so-called Neo-Geo, so naughty an intimacy with paint almost calls for the pillory and stocks. But in his own way Lasker is as critical as any. In a published statement he noticeably refrains from prevailing nihilism in explaining that it is painting's very "capacity to present the viewer with both a fictive experience and an actual experience simultaneously" that allows it to "examine the very mechanism of fiction" and the way we invest meaning in its "random graphic marks."[17] Even in its dandyism, Lasker's art is strong on *de*fense: it is as if unwilling to "play ball" without putting up a fight.

Despite the risk of a dandyism of *appreciation,* my thoughts on Lasker seem to be spiraling outward. Collins's and Milazzo's piquantly crafty suggestion that Lasker's "strife" between figure and ground might be likened to "the social phenomenon of 'class struggle' " calls the attention of irony to art's shared frontier with social life.[18] Somewhere between the large world of the class struggle and the little world of a single painting is the artworld, where, as the sociologist Levin Schücking could write more

16. Ibid., 153; in the original, Heidegger, *Holzwege,* 4th ed. (Frankfurt am Main, 1963), 103.

17. Jonathan Lasker, " 'Nature Study,' 'Idiot Savant,' 'Ascension,' " *Effects: Magazine for New Art Theory,* no. 3 (Winter 1986).

18. Tricia Collins and Richard Milazzo, "Tropical Codes," *Kunstforum International,* no. 83 (March–May 1986), 308–37, here 326.

than four decades ago, "one can become a success only if, following the American device, one 'gets talked about.'" And Schücking seems quite relevant to Lasker where he explores the sociology of traditional high-class taste as anti-individualistic and accustomed to think in types: "The complete exposure of the life of the emotions, like all that is ruthless in expression, is . . . bound to be unattractive. . . . It is always revealing things that must at all costs be suppressed."[19] Lasker, I think, deals with such deep-seated detachment just enough for his willful *an*estheticism to be manifest as an "isometric" strength. It is the bad-taste part, then, that begins to seem more than dandyish or indulgent, given that upper-class types, conditioned by concern with inheritance, consign art to a decorative place in their scheme of life and tend to be repelled by eccentricity; then again, "Repulsion wears off. Unconscious compromises are made between earlier ideals and that which is constantly seen or heard." In other words, as Schücking quotes Max Lieberman as saying, "Take the picture away, or I shall begin to like it."[20]

It is hardly as a mere child of his age that I admire Lasker in his art— certainly not in the sense that "the children of this world are in their generation wiser than the children of light" (Luke 16:8). Yes, Lasker's art is this-worldly instead of "transcendental," but its very wit must be good for the spirit too. "You have as much laughter as you have faith," it has been said. Oscar Wilde? No, Luther.[21]

---

19. Levin L. Schücking, *The Sociology of Literary Taste*, International Library of Sociology and Social Reconstruction (New York, 1945), 63.

20. Ibid., 61.

21. Martin Luther, from a Latin commentary on Psalm 126.

28

ANTIC GRAVITY:
JEREMY GILBERT-ROLFE

It is nearly two decades since Jeremy Gilbert-Rolfe opened his essay on Brice Marden with an epigraph from "Against Georg Lukács," an essay by Bertolt Brecht: "Anyone who saw me at work would think I was only interested in questions of form."[1] Some might just as superficially think that of his own work in painting, if not his critical writing. But Gilbert-Rolfe really is a *dialectical* materialist, unlike the puritanical Millionaire-Marxists of the 1980s, whose disdain for manual work is evident in all they say about painting. Once, half-kidding, I asked him just what "praxis" was supposed to mean. "Don't you know," he replied, "praxis is what intellectuals do."

An exhibition of Gilbert-Rolfe's paintings, in New York, the winter of 1989–90, went, I want to say, almost loudly unremarked. If it was already too demanding to see a theoretician's practical work, here, on top of that, was one whose office it supposedly is to be tryingly brainy, daring to *amuse.*

---

1. Jeremy Gilbert-Rolfe, "Brice Marden's Painting," *Artforum,* October 1974, 30–38, reprinted under the original title "A Mystery Story" in his *Immanence and Contradiction: Recent Essays on the Artistic Device* (New York, 1985).

You see, unlike Brecht, or for that matter, Charlie Chaplin, our well-off Cromwellian Roundheads don't know from *docere-delectare;* and no more in the artworld than in America at large can most people handle the *play* of intelligence. Well, here was praxis in paint, in very solid painting, yet also with an element of installational, if not institutional, mounting. More threatening still, the high seriousness of the former did not preclude wit in the latter. Artists talked about the exhibition, guardedly. It wasn't so simply obvious what you were *supposed* to say—as if this artist didn't know—as there we stood, staring at the paintings in the last five minutes of the 1980s.

True, Gilbert-Rolfe's paintings are as a rule self-sufficient formal propositions that don't mind being beautiful; but it was hardly out-of-bounds for Gilbert-Rolfe, who concerns himself in theory and practice alike with the painting as a semiotic and ideological totality, to produce something counting understatedly as an "installation." For if semiotics and ideology cannot encompass context, one wonders what good they are. On the other hand, no one has to tell Gilbert-Rolfe that to address context only, without ever taking responsibility for concrete-specific form, might be to hide behind a kind of ecological naturalism the fact that one had small experience of what Barnett Newman called the "genetic moment."

Two odd items were strategically "installed" at opposite ends of the Anne Plumb Gallery, bracketing everything else—except for one painting hanging neutrally downstairs—and establishing between them, as if between goalposts, an open field for the essentially aesthetic spectacle of the actual artworks. Fore and aft, as aesthetic extremeties irreconcilable in every way except as conceptual opposites, these were like mountaineers' cairns or like the boundary markers of a prospector's claim, highlighting between them Gilbert-Rolfe's postformalist obsession with the left- and righthand margins of his individual paintings. Meanwhile, a lateral polarity—full/empty—left the entire righthand wall of the gallery completely unhung, blank.

The unique piece at the far end was *Brown Limit*, a humble homage to Ryman (even in that like Ryman's own humility) consisting of a small irregular quadrilateral of torn brown paper bearing a squarish load of white paint and push-pinned all around onto a wall painted *pink*. Inevitably more troubling, by itself but even more as "installing" a polar opposition between caricaturally West Coast versus East Coast art, was that piece's opposite number: like the challenging goalpost of the entry end-zone, on a wall rubbed with dry "Ultramarine Yellow" (!) pigment, hung *Blasphemy,* this with a faint handwritten pink text, Darboven-repetitive, and, running down its lefthand edge in big letters: "B-E-A-U-T-I-F-U-L" (reversed, left-right) and, alongside, "B-R-I-L-L-I-A-N-T." If in this piece the sense of artworld blasphemy in conjoining mirroring flatteries of the "beautiful" and the "brilliant" is readily available—less obvious in time will have been the fact of its appearance at a moment when literal, legal blasphemy was under dispute, thanks to a Mr. Rushdie, in 1989, when this and the other paintings were painted—this semi-outrageous painting-cum-wall was nevertheless not unsubtle in its partying, beachball way.

The lettering of *Blasphemy* is in flat, standard sans-serif capitals, but with homemade details: extra-loopy initial *B*'s for both words and lowercase hooks on the *U*'s in "beautiful." You might almost need sunglasses to realize, but this trait does recall the bulgy signature lettering in paintings by, yes, Ryman. All the more, then, with *Brown Limit* down at the other end of the gallery, an "asymmetric dualism" was composed.[2] Now one should not only be allowed to see but also to say when a painting is a joke, all the more when the joke is intelligent. Here the up-to-down sans-serif lettering references the (sideways) R-E-D, Y-E-L-L-O-W, and B-L-U-E letters, some of "real" wood (boy, oh boy!), running, top to bottom, down Jasper Johns's famous 1963–64 *Field Painting*. Yet as also resembling, almost like it or not, the book-spinelike B-A-U-H-A-U-S down the corner of Gropius's famous 1924–25 building, it recalls a phase of Central European cultural history important to Gilbert-Rolfe not only for modernism in art but also for developments in linguistic theory and, to be sure, politics.

Come to think of it, for several years Gilbert-Rolfe's work may have been similarly pointing back to an even earlier, foundational modernity. Much as an honestly middle-class, Biedermeier beauty of rectitude appears as an element of Viennese *Sezession* design, Gilbert-Rolfe's rigorously simple punctuational banding of the lateral extremeties of the smooth canvas, now seriously qualified by a bold plasticity of facture, can be seen in analogy with the Secession moment as itself marked by a predilection for banded ornamental edges. Nothing, after all, more profoundly disqualifies the last generation's simplistic "formalist" critique of painting than its desperate attempt to hold to an essentially Postimpressionist, as if once radically

---

2. Technically, this concerns a word's being at once pulled between homonymy with any other words it sounds like and synomymy with any differently sounding words of similar meaning—a visual parity despite apparent stylistic incompatibility; see Sergej Karcevskij, "The Asymmetric Dualism of the Linguistic Sign" (1929), trans. Wendy Steiner in Peter Steiner, ed., *The Prague School: Selected Writings, 1929–1946,* University of Texas Press Slavic Series, no. 6 (Austin, University of Texas, 1982), 47–54.

Secessionist, sense of *design*. Germanic or French, the great art of the years immediately preceding the First World War was a challenge to an aesthetic left that had become a "new right" not unlike that of latter-day American, design-obsessed formalists.

Let me point out that in the theory of the great Viennese modernist architect of the Secession moment, Otto Wagner—who seems to have ignored important British (socialist) theoretical currents in order to engender a modernism with chance of effect in the (capitalist) real world[3]— subtle but telling differences may be detected just before and after 1900. From earlier to later editions of Wagner's *Modern Architecture* I detect a shift from simple (or simplistic?) affirmation of flatness to a more penetratingly structural complexity that entails color.[4] Neither, in Gilbert-Rolfe's recent paintings, need a sheer pigmentation of even blatantly pleasurable color elaborating previously sparer, though not necessarily "purer," planar grid structures, indicate aesthetic or political retreat.

Political economy is inevitably evoked by the title of Gilbert-Rolfe's *Exchange,* at 40 by 40 inches considerably smaller and more compact than his other recent, mostly 58-inch paintings. Yet exchange and even "exchange value" carry wider connotations too, as when the sociologist Simmel says, "Every interaction has to be regarded as an exchange: every conversation, every affection (even if it is rejected), every game, every glance at another person."[5] So, too, the field of the modernist painting has concerned Gilbert-Rolfe far less as a "figured," gestalt "ground" than as an interactive field of operations in which tactical moves or game-plays are developed. Here, at the left of *Exchange,* is a vertical band of stretched-out *T*'s, linked

---

3. See Harry Francis Palgrave's introduction to his translation and variorum edition of Wagner's *Modern Architecture: A Guidebook for His Students to This Field of Art* (Santa Monica, Calif., 1988), esp. 29–30.

4. In answer to the question "how should we build?" Wagner, first, in 1896 and 1898, recommends not only a "panel-like" surface treatment and "the greatest simplicity," but "horizontal lines in the style of classical antiquity"; then, in 1904 and 1914, he alters this last phrase in the same text to "lines of load and support." And where before 1900 he propounds a "simple, . . . practical, . . .—one might almost say—military approach," afterward Wagner adds to his sense of bare, monumental simplicity the subliminal ornamental value of "distribution of color patches." Ibid., 124 with 136 n. 156; 85, with 130 n. 71; 88, with 131 n. 78, respectively.

5. Continuing: "When we exchange love for love, we have no other use for its inner energy and, leaving aside any later consequences, we do not sacrifice any good. When we share our intellectual resources in a discussion, they are not thereby reduced; when we display the image of our personality, and take in those of other people, our possession of ourselves is not at all reduced by this exchange." Georg Simmel, *The Philosophy of Money* (1900; 2d ed., 1907), trans. Tom Bottomore and David Frisby (London, 1978), 82.

in alternating yellow and black, punctuated with blue, while a large expanse of sweepingly horizontal pink brushwork is deckled at the righthand edge against a thin margin of black. The very *paint job* of this and other new works shows thickness of brushwork as *making* (something), not presuming it to be, *material,* like the thickening or thickness *(Verdickung, Dichtheit)* of linguistic material itself in poetic *(dichterisch)* consciousness—and how many times, over the years, must Gilbert-Rolfe and I have discussed Brecht's *Verfremdungseffekt* or its Russian modernist equivalent, *ostranenie?* The differently worked parts stand in mutual yet nonrelational conjunction, the artist himself having said that one of his driving concerns as an abstract painter is "the possibility of articulating relationships of nonrelationship."[6]

Gilbert-Rolfe and I have talked over such matters for a long time, and not without certain by-now-ritual disagreements, either, over *(drumroll, please)* "French thought."[7] I can at least acknowledge the significance to the artist of a critical sense of the edge not as locus of formal fetishizing but as ideologically emblematic of withdrawal from dependence on the ordering authority of the *center.* Fine! Of course, it is what Gilbert-Rolfe does with his notion of marginality that matters. Already before that he had come to limit himself to a square canvas along whose left- and righthand edges an impacted colorism is effected in narrow vertical bands that *border,* without sealing off, the bracketed field. In the new paintings the field has more to say in terms of color and paint handling even as it *spaces* the left and right edges apart; but the lateral margins are themselves more structurally articulated than ever, now with rather digitally subdivided bands, like some new form of harmonic notation or solid-state electronic circuitry. However "figuratively" one wants to read this affirmatively *marginal* activity, it shows the paintings as forthrightly and rigorously contrived, wised-up.

It was not with irony that Gilbert-Rolfe himself explained his own critical sense of marginality to David Shapiro: "I'm reluctant to grant the

---

6. The other, "space as an invisibility made visible"; David Shapiro, "Jeremy Gilbert-Rolfe: Painting, Integrity, Multiplicity" (interview), *Bomb,* no. 21 (Fall 1987), 42–45, here 43.

7. In particular the writings, let's say (I resist reciting cult names), of Jacques Sélavy. I, for one, see no obligation to entertain a theory of painting that embraces so willingly the trivial work of Adami, the French intellectuals' Peter Max; also, I find worthless almost any remark about painting that still takes so for granted the unreformed notion of a *picture* that it can barely be made to pertain to the condition of abstract *painting.* Also, the supposed untranslatability of *passe-partout,* in a thirteen-page fan-dance at the beginning of the self-styled *Truth in Painting,* is ridiculous: *passe-partout* simply and precisely means "mat"; yes, one has to see how the term is *used* (in English as in French), but to do so may be to come up against the condition of *graphics* rather than of "painting" anyway.

authority required by the concept of the marginal." The trouble, for one thing, is that the philistines, including the pseudoradicals of the eighties, are only too happy when fine art willingly assumes a marginal standing: "For those who need to eliminate Painting and Poetry, and as far as I can see, Prose, Sculpture, Cinema as a literary form, and also argument itself, from cultural life, all these things belong at the margins. All the easier to do just a bit of cropping and have done with them altogether." Otherwise, however: "I think cultural forms might be most subversive when most irrelevant. What could be more threatening to the megalomania of power than that which couldn't be fitted in, the irrelevant? One should struggle to be irrelevant, which is to say to be irresponsible where the power apparatus is concerned."[8]

Knowingly, with pretty, stereotypically feminine colors, "French thought" and all, in this particular exhibition Gilbert-Rolfe put himself on the defensive in New York. Born and bred in England—where, empirically enough, the very word "colours" still connotes concrete pigments before disembodied hues—by an interesting location/dislocation that makes me think of Orwell's essay "Wordsworth in the Tropics," he has for years been working in Los Angeles, where even a Rococo palette has never been "uncool." It also happens that he is interested in Goethe's color theory within the wider poetics of German Romanticism, not just as color. *Just color?* Just whose certification should such-and-such a palette, or for that matter, any other range of choices, in painting or film or any other art, require, to present itself as ungratuitous?

In the Marden essay Gilbert-Rolfe wrote on Manet in light of French cinematography, and he has also written on Matisse and woman and the feminine (entertaining even the beauty of fashion). Of the recent paintings, *Baltic Meaning,* with gray patches punctuating the lefthand border of a sky-blue field, has something of the left-edge segmentation of Matisse's own *The French Window* (1914), but its edge handling also, differently, suggests the sprocket holes of actual cinematographic film.

Face it, to us in New York a large part of the problem with "L.A." is the way *they* go on and on about the *movies,* that great new popular art of the (first) Secession period.[9] Something, however, that has interested Gilbert-

---

8. Shapiro, "Gilbert-Rolfe," 42.

9. Allow *me* to marginalize for a moment. Curiously, although in their *Dialectic of Enlightenment,* written in 1944, Max Horkheimer and Theodor W. Adorno often sound like two uppity Euros beached in California, for whom nothing can ever be good enough stateside, they did like "Betty Boop," this despite a critical slight against her by Erwin Panofsky. In 1934 Panofsky had found

Rolfe and me alike is the evocatively cinematographic example of *good* "aura" experienced while on one's back, gazing up from under a tree on a sunny day in Walter Benjamin's famous 1936 "Mechanical Reproducability" essay, a feature of that canonized text that simplistic academic critique still prefers to ignore. Besides, Arthur Danto may be onto something where he argues, as part of his end-of-art theory, that the free heightening of Fauve color was painting's vivifying response to a newly winning perceptual conviction of literal movement in the film.[10] The point, then, would be not so much one palette against another as getting the painter's color to do something besides just sit there, as if on a beach, bouncing back the light.

I know it seems almost punning to liken to actual film sprockets the fairly regular punctuations of *Baltic Meaning* or comparable punctuations along both left and right edges of *Asiatic,* a "big-sky" field that becomes as almost gorgeously painterly as its cloudy-colored white-on-white will permit. Then again, *Forget,* its main area very painted-out white, can as well evoke a flaring of white on the film screen as a coloristic overload of Newton's physicist's (rather than Goethe's painter's) white light.[11]

It is significant that in the Marden essay, in analyzing a film still from Godard's *Alphaville* (1965) that had been cropped on the announcement card of a Marden exhibition of 1972, Gilbert-Rolfe punctiliously defends and restores the correct frame proportions. If the uniformly square format of his own new, and many prior, works might not in itself seem cinematographic, it happens that in Hollywood in 1930 Eisenstein himself had argued against further widening the film screen and in favor of a square format

---

the "mild pornography" of turn-of-the-century films "much less objectionable than the now extinct Betty Boop films"; "Style and Medium in the Motion Pictures," as revised in *Critique,* I/3 (January–February 1947), 5–28, here 7. But according to the two Frankfurt critics, "The misplaced love of the common people for the wrong which is done them . . . calls for Mickey Rooney instead of the tragic Garbo, for Donald Duck instead of Betty Boop"; *Dialectic of Enlightenment* (1947), trans. John Cumming (New York, 1982), 134. Having Panofsky *against* Boop and Horkheimer and Adorno *for* seems odd in light of the claim that the Boop films, which were by the Austrian-born Max Fleischer, who made military instructional films for Pershing during World War I, gained from a "publicity" approach: Marie-Thérèse Poncet, *L'Esthétique du dessin animé* (Paris, 1952), 34–35.

   10. Arthur C. Danto, "The End of Art," in Berel Lang, ed., *The Death of Art* (New York, 1984), 3–35, here 22; also in Danto's *The Philosophical Disenfranchisement of Art* (New York, 1986), 81–115, here 101.

   11. Not dissimilarly, Francis Steegmuller wonders whether, when Flaubert noticed that on the desert a black rock seen from a distance can look bright white, he might have been stimulated by examining his friend Maxime Du Camp's photographic negatives: *Flaubert in Egypt: A Sensibility on Tour: A Narrative Drawn from Gustave Flaubert's Travel Notes and Letters,* trans. and ed. Francis Steegmuller (1972; repr. Chicago, 1979), 134n.

Fig. 35   Jeremy Gilbert-Rolfe, *Asiatic*, 1989, oil on
canvas, 68 x 68 x 1 inches.

that could be masked left and right edges to produce vertical shots for
contrast with the normal horizontal. To Eisenstein, the unvaryingly horizontal film image was charged to a sentimental "nostalgia of infinite horizons,
of fields, of plains and deserts," for a "peasant and farmer yesterday."[12]
And that *painting* has tended to retain a horizontal format, the great
filmmaker held, concerns "an undue weight placed upon compositional

______

12. Sergei Eisenstein, "The Dynamic Square" (1930/31), in his *Film Essays and a Lecture,* ed. Jay
Leyda (Princeton, 1982), 48–65, here 51–52. Rather Suprematistically, Eisenstein recommends
"the one and only form equally fit by alternate suppression of right and left, or of up and down,
to embrace all the multitude of expressive rectangles of the world. Or used as a whole to
engrave itself by the 'cosmic' imperturbability of its *squareness* in the psychology of the audience."

proportions of the nineteenth century pre-impressionistic period—the worst period of painting—the 'narrative' type of picture."[13]

Already by virtue of their banded or otherwise rather telegraphic-notational left and right (soundtrack?) margins, the paintings stretch slightly against a self-evident squareness, as undisguised as their literal squareness remains. This effect is all the more complex because Gilbert-Rolfe's painted edges wrap around the sides of the canvas, with horizontal increments thus accruing as if in compensation for the consignment of the material square's left and right margins to bands and to almost inlaid, intarsialike, banded inflections. The artist thinks of this bringing of the sides into the game as a taking of responsibility, in denial of whatever arty fuss has tended to burgeon on the sides of canvases since the late modernist discard of the frame. In any case, it isn't about certifying the thing as a dumbly inert object.

Taking these effects together with Sergei Eisenstein's express antinarrativity as regards what Panofsky, before Benjamin, would soon consider a new and specifically materialist art,[14] we may move on to the now too-often stylistically trivialized question of Minimalism. Gilbert-Rolfe's *Air Force,* notably, has a Fritz Glarner–like vertical split or rift, like a geologic fault, between a large area of light blue to the left and a smaller of darker blue to the right. To the extent that this amounts to a contrariwise rotation of conventional landscape blues (upper-sky darker, lower-sky lighter), their now antipictorial abutment becomes unconventionally intensified, and the slightness of tonal shift, almost severe.

Must any such forceful negation of pictorialism be taken as evidence of

---

13. Ibid., 55, pointing, further, to the images of medieval manuscript painting for their prescenographic "freedom" from rigid bounds (and denying the mystique of the golden section). Meyer Schapiro on marginal "drôlerie" in medieval manuscript painting pertains: such features "are a convincing evidence of the artist's liberty, his unconstrained possession of the space, which confounds the view of mediaeval art as a model of systematic order and piety"; thanks to such liberty, "we are not limited to the alternatives: symbolic or decorative," for "there are other kinds of meaning (as in metaphor, parody and humor) which need not be symbolic in the coded manner . . ."; "Marginal Images and Drôlerie" (1970), in his *Late Antique, Early Christian and Mediaeval Art,* Selected Papers, III (New York, 1979), 196–98.

14. Panofsky, "Style and Medium," 27: "The processes of all the earlier representational arts conform . . . to an idealistic conception of the world. These arts . . . start with an idea to be projected into shapeless matter. . . . The painter works on a blank wall or canvas which he organizes into a likeness of things and persons according to his idea (however much this idea may have been nourished by reality). . . . It is the movies, and only the movies, that do justice to that materialistic interpretation of the universe which, whether we like it or not, pervades contemporary civilization."

Minimalism, whether or not one would consider Barnett Newman—whose work first inspired Gilbert-Rolfe to come to the United States—a Minimalist (as neither he nor I do)? The very format of these paintings matters in view of the blatant nonproportionality, or redundantly self-evident proportionality, of the square, the cube, and other regular geometric figures in so much Minimal art. Obviously, all objects "have" proportions, but if a square painting manages to override its one-to-one squareness it has in one sense managed to be more than an "object." As a matter of fact, I can find no single painting, or even print, by Newman that is exactly square. Yet here is the opposite situation: all these Gilbert-Rolfe paintings *are* square, but they don't necessarily *look* exactly so, especially when seen frontally (not that *that* is an illusion, either). Each is a square with markedly asymmetric color bands, like Newman's "zips" either ragged or crisp— alternatives whose binary potential both painters' work exploits. Newmanesque indeed is the painting that hung by itself in the basement of the gallery, titled, in direct allusion, *Who's Intimidated by Yellow, Blue and Red* (1989), where a big black middle area is cut through by bright, percussive color zips. (And are not Newman's "zips," too, like filmic verticals, if not scratches, even reminiscent of early, perhaps especially German, abstract film?) Its sassy title notwithstanding, *Who's Intimidated* pretends neither to "mug" the Newmanesque sublime nor, as it were, to "tail" in its slipstream.

In an interview with Marjorie Welish, Gilbert-Rolfe has said, "Artists brought up in the 1960s lack ideas; in the 1970s, they lack skill."[15] Well, if those brought up in the 1980s often lack a sense of art as anything but ironic, shifty, we stand to gain something in the 1990s by Gilbert-Rolfe's disarmingly tricky, sometimes even wittily Cavalier (versus Roundhead), way of being dead-serious. All along, his painterly rigor has been driven by that least puritanical of spiritual engines: the sentient intelligence.

---

15. Marjorie Welish, "The Studio Revisited," *Arts Magazine,* September 1989, 55–60, here 56.

29

DAVID ROW, C. S. PEIRCE, AND THE TEXTURE OF THOUGHT IN PAINTING

Resemblances to Al Held, early or late, to the Frank Stella of broad-banded geometries, or to Sean Scully's paired panels, one striped this way, the other that, probably seem more vivid to someone just now tuning in and seeking to locate David Row than to anyone who has seen it all unfold. Given the way things are, how can one expect to lay out Reinhardt, Held, Stella, and so on; then perhaps to reconsider, say, Valerie Jaudon's banded decorative matrices, and ever expect to get to ask how Row's work relates to and differs from all theirs? For that matter, what about (1) the fundamentally linguistic stylizations of nature on the Shang and Chou bronzes, (2) Roger Fry on that, and (3) the eventual crisis of formalism? (Meanwhile, [4] do they even spell it "Shang" or "Chou" anymore?) At least one can state that Row is not alone, and not because his painting is derivative but because it *makes sense.*

Language, when it is on, live, entails some kind of spill back and forth between likeness and differentiation. A simple, admittedly calculated, example: if I say that Row's images show the complexity of ships' rigging, yet also the trackable "logic" thereof, the first term runs a risk of appeal

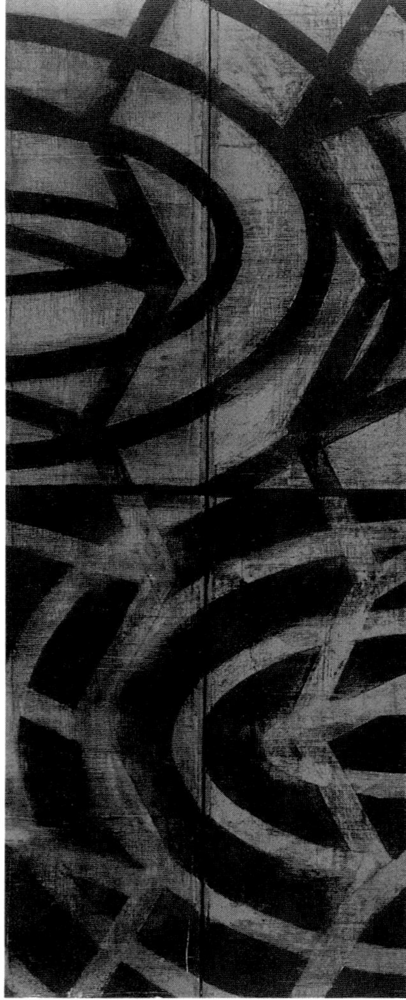

Fig. 36   David Row, *Vert de Grèce*, 1987, oil and wax on canvas, 80 x 32 inches.

by sentimental association until tempered and clarified by arrival of the second, as if with one grid of meaning overlaying another. This, I mean to suggest, is quite like the compounding seriality of symmetric and asymmetric reversal and skewed overlay by which Row builds up his image with stencils of banded matrices. Note in the sentence—and by extension, see in the paintings—how the relation of initial assertion to subsequent, specifying qualification, with a resultant complexity, is itself "asymmetrical." The priority of sequence is not a priority of meaning; if anything, meaning spills back onto the first thought from the second, as significance (not mere complication) builds up in the paintings.

One large painting of 1989 is a sort of triptych-plus, entirely black-on-black but for a margin of underpainting in other colors showing through along the bottom edge. Hung with a wide gap of wall between the third and fourth panels, all the same height, its sequence is one of varying width: narrow-wide-narrow-(gap)-intermediate. A pair of overlapping, wide vertical oval rings at the left overrides the first abutment of panels, while at the right a broader, "more circular" pair (again, similarity in difference) breaks across the gap of wall. Across an implied horizontal division running the length of the painting there swells up and down a symmetrical system of broad bands whose fannings-out and gatherings-in, like cables of a suspension bridge, do not coincide with splits between canvases but generate a separate scheme of slow, percussive optical beats. Alternations between gloss and matte bands and interstices (the glossy bands thicker, on top of the matte) themselves alternate, above and below, so that while here or there gloss or matte may be said to play figure to the other's field as ground, all elements are suspended in a charged mutuality. The whole large zigzagging image is checked from collapsing into perspectival illusion by a strong forward thrust. In fact, there isn't any "air space" to speak of, only an embeddedly crystalline, solid-state inflection that even the stretch of exposed wall does not fracture.

Vital to what I mean by Row's sheer linguistic is a mutuality of symmetry and asymmetry that implies and calls forth yet larger symmetry embracing further differentiation. Significantly, Row tends to produce not only single paintings on paired abutting canvases but also "braces" of paintings that are structurally alternative to, not simply mirrorings of, one another. Taking on a mutuality of its own, such a brace is more than a proto-"series" of two (the aesthetically astute metallurgist Cyril Stanley Smith has called "the nineteenth-century ideal molecule of a compound" one that would consist only of one atom of one element and one of another). Two black-and-white, almost vyingly positive-and-negative, paintings: each offers a stacked, two-canvas vertical image, split left and right in black/white reversal, with a pair of overlapping vertical ellipses and a system of zigzagging angles. One, dominated by the rhomboidal segment of a hip-slung Brancusian zigzag—half, whole and then again half a unit, vertically—has, if one insists, a black field in its left half and white at the right; in the other, where the rings or ellipses are more prominent as centered, symmetrically angled zigzags "belt" in and then out again, torsolike. That these works can look so completely different only magnifies the sense of articulated duality already active in any one painting by Row.

Row's "painter's" linguistic shows up, I think, a problem in the thought of C. S. Peirce, the founder of American "pragmatism" and a philosopher of interest to critics and artists for his linguistic distinctions among "icon" (which entails "likeness"), "index," and "symbol." Peirce—who happens to have found the Geodetic Survey a much more congenial outfit to work for than had Whistler—proves hasty, however, with visually embodied thought; in respect to its discussion of a pair of diagrams, his essay "How to Make Our Ideas Clear" (1878) could almost be titled "How to Pretend Our Ideas Are Clearer than They Are." Despite having at some stage surely *drawn* the originals himself, hence presumably taking some pains to establish their initial distinctions, Peirce sets these up to illustrate "imaginary distinctions . . . often drawn between beliefs which differ [N.B.] only in their mode of expression"—not that "the wrangling which ensues" isn't "real enough," and no wonder. He takes it as obvious that believing "any" objects are arranged as in Figure 37a (97 equidistant dots in an orthogonal grid forming an octagon with 5 dots top, bottom, left, and right) and then as (re-?)arranged in Figure 37b (97 equidistant dots in a diagonal grid forming an octagon with 4 dots top, bottom, left, and right) are "one and the same belief."

Well, yes and no, much as the squared-away 48-star flag of the early Johns paintings sort of is, but also is certainly not, the zigzag-fielded 49-

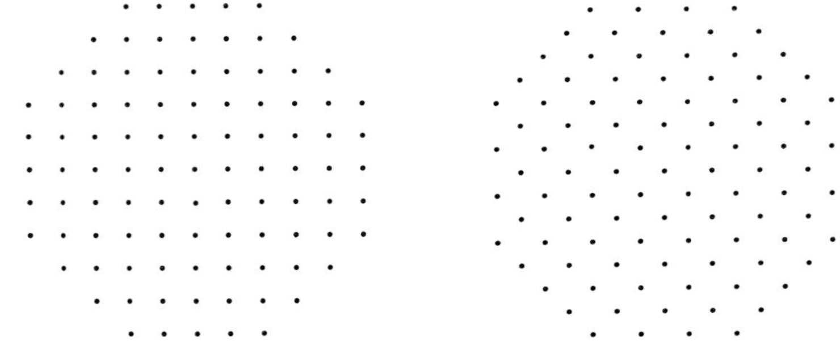

Fig. 37a, b. Diagrams in C. S. Peirce, "How to Make Our Ideas Clear" (1878), after *The Philosophical Writings of Peirce*, ed. Justus Buchler (New York, 1955).

star U.S. flag of Alaska's admission to the Union or the 50-star "Hawaiian" flag of today. Notwithstanding the short-haul efficiency of the dash to a practical "bottom line," Peirce will eventually brush up against the material texture of one mimesis *(rendering)* or another: if beliefs only matter in their consequences, "no mere differences in the manner of consciousness of them can make them different beliefs, any more than playing the same tune in different keys is playing different tunes." But if so, why do composers specify one particular key for the rendition or realization of their abstract structure? Without wanting to sweep pragmatism itself crudely aside, Dewey and all, I cannot overlook that here may be one deep root of the cheery, all-American philistinism of "What you see is what you get." Just imagine telling Aristotle that two renditions or renderings differ *only,* merely, in their mode of expression!

Remember the routine where someone picks up a piece of sheet music and says, reading aloud without any sense of the necessary intonation, "I don't understand these lyrics: 'You say "tomato," I say "tomato"; you say "potato," I say "potato" ' "? That is quite like the position Peirce is in when he refuses to acknowledge the mimetic differences between his diagrams, one plainly orthogonal, the other just as plainly diagonal in design. And that is very different from the live and essential asymmetries of David Row's paintings, where inflections that are neither arbitrary nor, exactly, "contrived" are generated within the essentially cognitive process of his painting. As penetrating as he otherwise can be, what Peirce misses with his very different diagrams is just what David Row's painting insists upon, redoubling itself in a way that realizes and heightens subtle difference. Row's very faithfulness to the materiality of oil-in-wax must be what makes it possible for him to extend that materiality to his thinking process and so also to anchor his pure abstractions in the world.

SOURCES AND ACKNOWLEDGMENTS

1. *Art Journal,* L/1 (Spring 1991), 34–41, as expanded from "Alberti's 'Window': Art-Historiographic Note on an Anti-Modernist Misprision," *Source: Notes in the History of Art,* VIII/4 (Summer 1989).

2. "On Neolithic Ultramodernity," in *Idols: The Beginning of Abstract Form,* exhibition catalogue, Ariadne Galleries, New York, 30 November 1989–31 January 1990, 11–14.

3. "Some Little (Modern) Marvels of High Finesse," *Upstart,* 1984, 32–33.

4. "Utopian Pen Pals: Bruno Taut and His Circle," *Art in America,* LXXIV/5 (May 1986), 19, 21.

5. *Art in America,* LXXV/1 (January 1987), 13–14.

6. "Living Modern," *Art in America,* LXXIV/2 (February 1986), 27–31.

7. Adapted from "Chance Is zee Fool's Name for Fait," introduction to Joseph Mascheck, ed., *Marcel Duchamp in Perspective,* Artists in Perspective (Englewood Cliffs, N.J.: Prentice-Hall, 1975), 10–16.

8. Adapted from "Propulsion," in *Atlantic Sculpture,* exhibition catalogue, Art Center College of Design, Pasadena, 8 June–11 July 1987, unpaginated (where discussion extends to St. C. Cemin, A. D. Christian, J. Fisher, W. Knowlton, J. Otterson, W. Saunders, N. Vital, and A. Wilding).

9. *Maureen Connor: New York,* exhibition catalogue, Alfred Kren Gallery, New York, December 1986, 6–10.

10. Expanded from "Poetic Objects by Robert Gober, Michael Venezia on View in SoHo," *The New York Observer,* 9 November 1987, 16.

11. *Art in America,* LXXII/3 (March 1984), 108–13.

12. *Art in America,* LXXV/3 (March 1987), 104–13.

13. *Doug and Mike Starn,* exhibition catalogue, Stux Gallery, New York, 25 April–26 May 1990, unpaginated.

14. Unpublished.

15. *Res: Anthropology and Aesthetics,* no. 4 (Autumn 1982), 93–117.

16. Expanded from "Art: Polke on Display," *The New York Times,* 14 November 1986, sec. C, 30.

17. "Street-Wisdom: Painting from Nowsville," from *Judy Rifka,* exhibition catalogue, Knight Gallery, Spirit Square Arts Center, Charlotte, N.C., 13 April–10 June 1984, and the Anderson Gallery, School of the Arts, Virginia Commonwealth University, Richmond, 6 September–7 October 1984, unpaginated.

18. *Arts Magazine,* LIX/7 (March 1985), 131–34.

19. Excerpted from "Autorevisions: 'Influence' in Text and Architext," *Upstart,* 1985, 22–23, 46, with supplementation.

20. "Snake Oil for Sprained Hearts: Julio Schnitzel Speaks to Joe Masheck," *New Observations,* no. 24 (1984), 7–10.

21. "The Artist as Cynic," *The New Leader,* LXX/9 (29 June 1987), 22–23.

22. "Bidlo's Pablo," *Art in America,* LXXVI/5 (May 1988), 172, 174–75.

23. Condensed from "Piecing Things Together," *Sean Scully: Paintings, 1985–86,* exhibition catalogue, David McKee Gallery, New York, unpaginated.

24. Adapted from "David Reed," in Joseph Masheck, *Smart Art* (Point, 1) (New York, 1984), 116, and "Abstract Ironies," *The New Leader,* LXIX/5 (20 October 1986), 21–22.

25. Adapted from *LAICA: Journal of the Los Angeles Institute of Contemporary Art,* V/42 (Summer 1985), 42–44.

26. *Re-Presenting the '80s,* exhibition catalogue, Simon Watson Gallery, New York, 1989, unpaginated.

27. *Arts Magazine,* LXIV/5 (January 1990), 38–43; expanded from "Painting and Its Treble: Reflections on Lasker," in *Jonathan Lasker: Acht Bilder,* exhibition catalogue, Galerie Michael Werner, Cologne, 1987, unpaginated.

28. Unpublished.

29. *David Row,* exhibition catalogue, John Good Gallery, New York, 11 March–8 April 1989, unpaginated.